# THE COMPLETE
# Do-It-Yourself
# Personnel
# Department

*Second Edition*

## MARY F. COOK

**PRENTICE HALL**
Paramus, New Jersey 07652

**Library of Congress Cataloging-in-Publication Data**

Cook, Mary F.
    The Complete do-it-yourself personnel department / Mary F. Cook—2nd ed.
       p.   cm.
    Includes index.
    ISBN 0-527490-7 (cloth)
    1. Personnel management.   2. Personnel management—Forms.   I. Title.
  HF5549.C7239   1997                            97-6352
  658.3—dc21                                CIP

Printed in the United States of America

10  9  8  7  6  5  4  3         10  9  8  7  5  4  3  2

This publication is designed to provide accurate and authoritative information in regard to the subject matter covered. It is sold with the understanding that the publisher is not engaged in rendering legal, accounting, or other professional service. If legal advice or other expert assistance is required, the services of a competent professional person should be sought.
—From the Declaration of Principles jointly adopted by a Committee of the American Bar Association and a Committee of Publishers and Associations

ISBN 0-13-083422-X (cd-rom)    ISBN 0-13-527490-7

9 780130 834225    90000

---

**ATTENTION: CORPORATIONS AND SCHOOLS**

Prentice Hall books are available at quantity discounts with bulk purchase for educational, business, or sales promotional use. For information, please write to: Prentice Hall Special Sales, 240 Frisch Court, Paramus, New Jersey 07652. Please supply: title of book, ISBN number, quantity, how the book will be used, date needed.

---

**PRENTICE HALL**
**Paramus, NJ 07652**

On the World Wide Web at http://www.phdirect.com

# ABOUT THE AUTHOR

MARY F. COOK is President of Mary Cook & Associates, a Denver-based human resources consulting firm established in 1983. Ms. Cook has many years experience as a corporate human resources generalist and as a human resources consultant. She has written articles for business magazines, newspapers, and trade journals. She is an award-winning author of more than a dozen books. Ms. Cook's HR trends forecasting has been quoted in *Success Magazine* and appears in the *Human Resources Yearbook* published annually.

Ms. Cook is a recipient of the top national research award from the Society for Human Resource Management and awards from the Colorado Society for Human Resource Management. She is a member of the Denver Women's Press Club, the Colorado Author's League, and the Author's Guild.

Ms. Cook can be reached at 1-800-606-9716.

### CURRENT BOOKS BY THE AUTHOR

*The Human Resources Yearbook, 1991 through 1997 Editions,* Prentice Hall

*The AMA Handbook on Recruitment and Retention,* AMACOM Books

*Consulting on the Side,* John Wiley & Sons

# CONTENTS

## CHAPTER 3
## REGULATORY COMPLIANCE—117

## CHAPTER 4
## EMPLOYEE COMMUNICATIONS—191

# CHAPTER 5
## PERSONNEL POLICIES—219

# CHAPTER 6
## COMPENSATION AND BENEFITS—283

# CHAPTER 7
## HANDLING DISCIPLINE AND DISCHARGE—349

# CHAPTER 8
## SAFETY, ACCIDENT REPORTING, AND OSHA REGULATIONS—369

# CHAPTER 9
## LABOR RELATIONS—393

# CHAPTER 10
## PERSONNEL LETTERS AND MEMOS—407

## CHAPTER 11
## PERSONNEL CHECKLISTS—471

## CHAPTER 12
## SAMPLE PERSONNEL FORMS—501

# PREFACE

The response from users to the first edition of *The Complete Do-It-Yourself Personnel Department* was gratifying. Since that edition was published, there have been many changes in federal regulations relating to the Human Resources function. In addition, tremendous changes in the workplace have affected personnel policies, procedures, and employee relations issues in companies of all sizes.

More changes are anticipated. When the first edition was published in 1991, over 80 percent of all new jobs were being created by small business owners. In the 2000s, it is expected that even more jobs will be created by small and mid-size companies. As corporations have downsized, outsourcing in all areas—including HR—has grown. As a result, whether you are an HR manager working inside a corporation, a consultant, or a CEO or manager of a smaller company, your need for fast access to essential information and the tools to implement the personnel function is more critical than ever.

The second edition of *The Complete Do-It-Yourself Personnel Department* will help you make sense of the different issues, myriad rules and regulations, policies and procedures you need to run the HR side of your business. It covers regulations and provides updated information as well as common sense, easily understood guidelines for resolving everyday HR problems. Its handy forms, policies, sample letters, and checklists will make your HR function run smoothly. This book is such a handy resource, you may wonder what you ever did without it.

# WHAT THIS BOOK WILL DO FOR YOU

The second edition of *The Complete Do-It-Yourself Personnel Department* provides the information you will need to establish or manage a human resource function in your company. If you are a CEO or HR manager of a small or mid-sized business, or an HR consultant, the information, policies, procedures, guidelines, sample letters, and checklists will save a great deal of your valuable time in addressing the hundreds of HR issues and problems that arise every workday.

Here is just a sampling of what you will find in this valuable resource:

- 50 ways to save money in the personnel area
- Job descriptions
- Interview checklists
- Performance evaluation forms
- Matrix of Federal Regulations and posters
- Layoff checklist and sample notices
- Discipline procedures and sample memos and forms
- Termination forms

- Employment forms and record keeping requirements
- A comprehensive legal review of the Fair Labor Standards Act
- Tested personnel letters and memos
- Sample Employee Handbook
- Sample Personnel Policy Manual
- Compensation and benefit plans
- Family and Medical Leave Policy and Form

The book also includes tips, glossaries, and most-used tables and formulas for quick reference.

## HOW TO USE THIS BOOK

Each chapter of the book provides short, practical, easy-to-use policies, procedures, and tools in a key area of the HR function. If you need a sample employment advertisement, or some interview questions quickly before a last minute interview, turn to Chapter 1. This chapter also includes an *Interviewing and Selection Handbook* that will get you up-to-speed quickly on the latest information about this topic. If you want to be sure that you are keeping appropriate personnel records, turn to Chapter 2 on Personnel Recordkeeping and you will find exactly what you should and should not be keeping in an employee personnel file. This chapter also includes the federal record retention requirements that will tell you how long you need to keep personnel records.

Large corporations and small businesses alike find it difficult to keep up with federal regulations that relate to organizations and know which ones actually apply to them. Chapter 3 provides an easy-to-read matrix of key federal regulations. This matrix also provides information on what posters a business must display and where anyone can quickly order the state or federal posters they need. This chapter also provides a list of termination pay requirements by state. There is also an American with Disabilities (ADA) compliance checklist and a sample letter to change and use to fit your needs in case you are asked to provide an accommodation under the ADA.

Chapter 4 provides a sample employee handbook which you can tailor to your own needs and have your attorney review, saving hours of costly time. Chapter 4 also includes valuable information on starting an employee newsletter and offers other ideas for effective employee communications.

Chapter 5 includes a checklist for writing a personnel policy manual and lists the key issues in the successful implementation of personnel policies. There is also a sample personnel policy manual that you can adapt to fit your company's needs. Chapter 6 provides easy-to-implement ideas for designing a salary program including model wage grades and salary rates and ranges adaptable to any company. This chapter also includes information on employee benefits and examples of what other companies offer in the way of benefits. The difficult subjects of discipline and discharge are covered at length in Chapter 7. There is a sample disciplinary policy, and sample forms and letters to assist in this hard-to-manage area.

Chapter 8 addresses concerns about safety, accident reporting, and OSHA issues. It includes a list of the top OSHA violations. You will also find a sample Guide to Accident and Injury Reporting which you can adapt to your needs. There is also a glossary of Occupational Safety and Health Terminology. Chapter 9 discusses key issues in labor relations and what you need to know about plant closings and layoffs.

Any CEO, manager, or HR consultant can save hours of effort by using the many sample HR letters that are included in Chapter 10. This chapter is a real time-saver for anyone who has to write a letter or memorandum about a personnel issue.

Chapter 11 contains checklists that will quickly assist in any personnel area when you are rushed and need to know the key issues you face in managing that element of the HR function. Then to make your life even easier, Chapter 12 provides sample forms that you can copy and adapt to fit your specific needs. Again, this chapter will save you hours of valuable time hunting for a form when you are in a hurry and need to get a specific personnel issue covered quickly.

Take a few minutes to read the Table of Contents and leaf through the book to get an understanding of what is included in each area of the HR function. Then you'll have a good idea of how and when the book can save you valuable time.

# 1

# RECRUITING, INTERVIEWING, AND SELECTION

## Procedures and Forms

- Recruiting Ads
- Using a Recruitment Advertising Agency
- Identifying and Recruiting the Best Workers
- Recruiting and Employment Routine
- Checklist of Recruiting and Employment Forms
- Ad Checklist
- Sample Forms and Letters
- Seven Steps to Successful Selection
- Pros and Cons of Employment Testing Including Drug Testing
- Sample Interviewing and Selection Handbook
- An Internal Job-Posting System
- Recruiting Persons with Disabilities—an Important and Underutilized Resource
- How to Save Money by Using Temporary Help
- Illegal Employment Practices
- Making a Job Offer
- New Employee Orientation
- Handling Relocation

# Recruiting, Interviewing, and Selection
## Procedures and Forms

Attracting and hiring the best employees are two of the most important elements for success in any business. If you don't have the right people in your jobs when you need them, your bottom line will be adversely affected. Your management and supervisory people have a tremendous responsibility to recruit and hire the people who will be effective and who will stay with your organization in order to achieve a positive return on your investment in recruiting and training. We need to continuously look for new and better ways to recruit competent workers, including use of the internet.

The old methods of recruiting and employment won't attract the people we want to attract today. What can you do to turn your recruiting activity into a "with it," savvy business operation that hits the right market?

## RECRUITING ADS

Design recruiting ads that attract today's worker. People today are concerned with the quality of work life and self-fulfillment. The style of ads and other recruiting literature is a barometer of a company's philosophy and commitment to employee concerns.

**Advertising**   Only certain jobs today are filled through help-wanted ads. They are basically technical, service and clerical, white- and blue-collar jobs. Exceptions to this are professional jobs advertised in your local paper or the *Wall Street Journal,* or high-level positions that warrant an expensive box ad on the financial page of your local paper. These ads are usually "blind" ads that list a box number for replies and don't show the company name. Remember, however, that some people will not reply to blind ads.

**Television Advertising**   TV ads are popular. They are often used by large companies as demand for skilled employees has increased. The main consideration here, naturally, is the cost. Local commercial spots can cost as little as $ 100, depending on the market, while national 60-second spots can cost hundreds of thousands of dollars. The key here is to identify accurately the audience you wish to reach before you spend the money.

**Recruiting Sources**   Keep track of sources when you hire people in order to identify the best recruiting sources for each job. Eliminate those activities that are not providing the best candidates and gear up the ones that are. Trim the recruiting efforts that are not paying off and spend the money where it brings the best return. Use association contacts, networking sources, and your current employees as recruiters.

## How to Implement These Ideas

One of the quickest ways to get up-to-speed on current advertising techniques is to read the classified ads in the newspapers in which you wish to run your ads. Find the style and wording that appeals to you and fits your jobs. Read through the ads a second time as though you were an applicant looking for that job. What attracts you? What turns you off? Do the ads reflect an open, interested attitude on the part of the employer? Do you get a feel for their management style? Is it participatory or autocratic? Will people of all ages and ethnic backgrounds respond? Will both men and women apply and feel welcome? Will disabled applicants feel you want them to respond? The ad form provided in this chapter will assist you in writing and placing your ads.

## Placing an Ad

Call the classified ad department of the newspaper of your choice. If you haven't received a classified ad packet and know exactly what size type and the size of the ad you need ask the ad taker to help you. Tell the person how you want it to look and provide an idea citing an ad in one of their recent papers as an example. They can look it up and quickly see what you want.

If you are placing TV ads it's best to go to the TV station the first time or ask an account executive to come to your office and help you design your spot. You can get a better idea of what it will cost you. Following are a few sample ads:

### Sample Help-Wanted Ad

**CHIEF EXECUTIVE OFFICER**

We're an exciting new company that could become one of the great international growth stories of the century. We design, manufacture, and market an advanced new communication system based on a major electronic breakthrough. This exciting new technology enables us to produce a system that is smaller, more effective, and less expensive than any other product of its kind on the market today.

We are looking for a dynamic, effective leader who can guide this new company to a successful future in the world marketplace. We have already secured our financing and now seek an extraordinary manager/CEO with impeccable credentials, an entrepreneurial spirit, and a hands-on approach to the top position in the company.

We need a person with consumer-oriented product experience. The ideal candidate will have no illusions about the prodigious amount of talent, effort, and commitment required to reap the substantial rewards that are possible. This CEO will assume full authority for the worldwide operations of this company. An exceptional compensation package including a significant equity position will be negotiated. This is a once-in-a-lifetime opportunity for the right person.

Send your résumé in strictest confidence.
Box CO222, New York, NY I0110

### Note

This ad is designed to appeal to a top-level executive with impeccable credentials. It communicates that this is a fantastic opportunity with the best package of compensation and benefits available today, that only the most highly qualified persons should bother to apply. It conveys the idea that it's a wonderful opportunity for the right person and there will be pressure to succeed. The successful applicant must be prepared to expend whatever effort and personal time is necessary to get the job done.

### *Sample Help Wanted Ad*

#### NATIONAL SALES MANAGER

At XXX Company our people have taken us farther, faster than any company in history. What makes us so different? We've created a unique corporate environment—an environment that fosters creativity and personal satisfaction. We give our employees the opportunity to stretch and explore their talents.

Our distinctive approach to business translates into much more than producing a great product. It means personal achievement and satisfaction in a job well done.

As the Regional Sales Manager for our company you'll provide leadership in the New York office. Our sales staff will look to you for guidance in setting and achieving mutually agreed upon goals and objectives.

To qualify you should have sales experience in our field, be technically qualified, and be a dynamic, goal-oriented professional. You'll need a BS degree or equivalent experience. You must have leadership qualities as evidenced by previous experience. You'll need excellent presentation skills, and you must be willing to travel.

We offer you excellent compensation and benefits in an unequaled work environment. If you're interested in this position, please submit your resume to XXX Company, Dept. SM322, P.O. Box 43271, New York, NY 10110.

We are an Affirmative Action employer M/F/V/D

### Note

The ad appeals to today's worker. It tells prospective applicants the company has a forward-thinking, creative, and participatory management environment that gives employees an opportunity for personal satisfaction in their work. The ad makes the reader feel that this company is truly interested in its employees.

### *Sample Help Wanted Ad*

#### NURSING PROFESSIONALS

**DIVERSIFICATION**                                                      **CHALLENGE**

Whatever your area of expertise, we have a great place for you to work. Our healthcare facility offers the opportunity to work in several areas ranging from acute care to community health. We serve a multicultural patient population. If diversification and challenge are not currently part of your current job description, come and check out the opportunities available at ABC Health Care Systems.

We are proud of our current staff and are pleased to announce the recipient of our third quarter Excellence in Nursing Award. She's Jane Brown, RN, BSN, MSN. Jane is coordinator of the children's program and another fine example of our high standards of nursing excellence. Jane says, "Our healthcare system offers a unique advantage in the industry, the opportunity to diversify and use all of your skills. We are large enough that we can provide many unusual opportunities."

PICTURE

We offer excellent pay and benefits and the opportunity for personal and professional growth. To find out more about the positions available now, send your résumé to:

ABC Healthcare Systems
Equal Opportunity Employer M/F/V/D

---

**Note**

This ad immediately addresses two of the biggest complaints nurses have about their jobs: the inability to do the type of nursing they like to do and the lack of opportunity for diversification. Because nurses reading the ad might not believe it, the picture and statement of a currently-employed and highly qualified nurse is included.

---

*Sample Help-Wanted Ad*

---

### RETAIL SALES PROFESSIONALS

$80,000 per year
COMMISSION . . .

THAT'S WHAT HAPPENS
WHEN YOU SELL QUALITY

XYZ Company-you've heard our name and you know our quality. We want your class and your entrepreneurial spirit.

If you have a warm demeanor, a great deal of confidence, and a track record of selling top quality merchandise to elegant customers in an opulent environment, you're someone we'd like to talk to.

$80,000 is an average annual figure for a full-time sales professional in our store. It can be much greater if you are a capable energetic salesperson.

We offer excellent benefits and a 30% store discount. Please apply in person.
Equal Opportunity Employer M/F/V/D

---

**Note**

This ad appeals to an experienced person who has a track record of selling expensive merchandise in a classy store. It says: "We want a go-getter who can sell, and we will pay the right person well." It appeals to a narrow group of people who are probably doing the same job now in another store. This ad gets the job done. It will probably attract qualified people from a more down-scale store wanting to move up in the retail industry.

---

*Sample Help-Wanted Ad*

---

### SECRETARY/ADMINISTRATIVE ASSISTANT

Our company, one of the leading computer organizations in this area, has an exciting opportunity for a Secretary/Administrative Assistant to one of our executives.

The person in this job will have a lot of variety in an entrepreneurial setting with a great deal of autonomy and opportunity for creative problem solving. There is occasional travel to plan and set up group meetings around the country.

We are looking for a person who is flexible and has good interpersonal skills. You will need Microsoft Word and a good working knowledge of business systems. You must be organized and a self-starter.

We offer an exciting participatory business environment, excellent compensation and benefits including tuition refund, and other personal growth opportunities.

Send résumé and salary requirements to:

Equal Opportunity Employer M/F/V/D

## Note

The ad conveys the sense that this company is forward-thinking and uses a participatory management approach to its people. Many companies are trying to attract young professionals, and this company is trying to do it by offering a tuition refund program. It also says that this company is interested in "growing" its people and promoting from within.

## Manager's Tip

Notice that the organizations running these ads are appealing to applicants by stating that they want the best people and in order to get them they are providing a good place to work, a place to be proud of. Not only that, they are providing competitive benefits and pay and an atmosphere of excellence with growth opportunities. Read other ads in the paper and compare. Many of them only tell the applicant what the company wants and expects. They are one-dimensional. They convey an attitude of autocratic management and show little interest in what the applicant is looking for.

Many classified ads in newspapers and magazines include a picture of the company's current employees to show their apparent satisfaction with the organization.

### EFFECTIVE METHODS OF FILLING OPEN POSITIONS

| Most Effective Ways to Fill Jobs | Managers and Executives | Professionals | Technical, Including Data Processing | Administrative, Accounting, etc. | Clerical | Laborers and Service Workers |
|---|---|---|---|---|---|---|
| Ads in local newspapers | | x | x | x | x | x |
| Ads on TV and radio | | x | x | x | x | x |
| Employment agencies | x | x | x | x | x | |
| Executive search firms | x | | | | | |
| College campus recruiting | | x | | x | | |
| Employee referrals | | x | x | x | x | x |
| State Job Service | | | | | x | x |
| Walk-in applicants, unsolicited résumés | | | | | x | x |

Note: There are times when one of the above methods of filling a job would work better than another, but over a long period the ones checked should prove most effective.

## Manager's Tip

When recruiting hard-to-fill jobs: Flexibility is the answer. Be open-minded regarding working hours, job-sharing, working at home, temporary help and other alternative working situations. Gear company procedures to workers needs.

# USING A RECRUITMENT ADVERTISING AGENCY

Recruit advertising agencies provide a valuable service to companies when it comes to notifying the public of employment opportunities available in their company. A specialized recruitment agency deals with recruitment communications and nothing else. It is expert at handling the whole business of recruitment advertising and employee communications, from in-column ad placement to technologies like the Internet and the World Wide Web.

Specifically, a recruitment advertising agency develops, prepares, and places advertising to help a company communicate its recruitment message. This message may appear in print media (newspapers, trade publications, directories, direct mail), in broadcast media (radio, television), and other media (billboards, transit signs, point-of-purchase displays). It may also appear in brochures or on specialty items, display booths, and the Internet.

In choosing the right recruitment advertising agency, you should consider an agency that is familiar with your company's employment marketplace, has experience handling a similar budget, has a history of success using a variety of media, and has a proactive approach to total quality.

The basic service areas of a recruitment advertising agency include:

- Account Management—Account executives, and account coordinators can provide ad placement, ad tracking, strategic media planning, creative services coordination, Internet services, project management, and proof of publication. Other specialty services include a confidential reply service and answering, prescreening, and interviewing services.

- Creative copy, design, and production—Copywriters provide headlines, body copy, and conceptual art suggestions. Art directors can provide original design, illustration, and photography. Also, production artists can work with your staff using an integrated computer network to generate fast, error-free camera ready art.

- Research—Advanced research systems offer recruiters round-the-clock access to extensive databases. They also compile facts, figures, and recommendations for a variety of business needs.

- Accounting—Provide custom invoicing and tear sheets of your ads.

One company that provides these services is Nationwide Advertising Services at (800) 627-4723.


# IDENTIFYING AND RECRUITING THE BEST WORKERS

If you are going to have all the workers you need to fill your jobs you must be flexible in the way you deal with a more diverse workforce. Today's worker may:

- work shorter hours and a shorter work week
- work at home

- work part time
- share a job with another person
- ask to work early evenings to share child care with a working spouse
- request help with child care because he or she is a single parent and works the night shift
- get an extension of company benefits for a domestic partner
- be retired from one job and seeking a second career
- be over fifty
- be a person with a disability
- meet his/her future spouse on the job or participate in at least one work romance
- work together with a spouse in the same company and possibly in the same department
- bring a child to work if the job can be done effectively with a child present-or bring the child to an on-site day-care center
- have to change careers and be retrained at least twice in a lifetime
- lose at least one job either through merger, or to a computer or robot
- be healthier because of health and fitness programs offered on the job
- use a personal computer on the job
- own company stock through a profit-sharing program
- own a share in the company through a leveraged buyout
- be more outspoken on personal rights issues like privacy and termination-at-will
- want more say in the way his/her job is done
- refuse to take lie-detector or other controversial types of tests
- be more likely to have tried or used drugs in the past
- be bilingual—probably Spanish speaking
- have legally or illegally immigrated to the United States
- be a member of a minority group—Asian, Hispanic, or African-American
- be a two-income family member or be a single-parent head of household
- want comparable pay for work of comparable worth, an issue that won't go away as more women enter the workforce. An estimated 75 percent of all women over the age of sixteen will be in the workforce in the 1990s.
- insist on flexible benefits so that, in a two-income household, the benefits won't overlap
- hold several jobs off and on through a lifetime in order to attain a desired life style

Get your management group together over gourmet snacks some early evening and brainstorm ways to identify and recruit the types of employees you need to fill your open positions. Tap the brainpower you have on staff to help in the recruiting function.

# RECRUITING AND EMPLOYMENT ROUTINE

Two of the key personnel functions are recruiting and employment. Certain forms should be completed and procedures followed in order to comply with government regulations.

1. When a job opens that you cannot fill from within the company, have the manager complete an employment requisition form. This form describes the job and assists the person who has to place the ad, to understand the job. In case of a civil rights suit it also helps you to remember what jobs have been open and who filled them. Maintain requisitions in a looseleaf binder. The requisition also helps you keep track of the number of open jobs you have. Review job descriptions before you place ads and interview to ensure you know the job.

2. If you are going to place an ad, type it up ahead of time and make a copy. Keep that copy with the employment requisition or in a separate file. Insist that all ads be placed through the personnel administrator and that they carry the EEO/AAP designation.

3. Have all applicants fill out the employment application. Even if they have a resume, they must complete and sign the application. The application is the legal document. Be sure the application conforms to state and federal regulations and gives you permission to investigate a prospective employee.

4. Set up files on applicants. You can file them by job category and then alphabetically. You must maintain applicant files for one year. Don't accept applications unless you have jobs available, because you will build a tremendous backlog of applications.

5. You may wish to keep a computerized applicant log. It saves a great deal of time when applicants call in to see if their resume or application is still on file. The log can be maintained by year and month. The log is a great help if you are a federal contractor and have a desk audit by the Office of Federal Contract Compliance and need to furnish applicant data.

6. Screening applicants is an important step in the hiring process. You will save hours of your time and the managers' time in interviewing if you learn to screen applicants using your application form. Train your receptionist or personnel clerk to look for:
   • Breaks in employment
   • Omissions on the application
   • Overall professionalism in completing the application

7. Interviewing process and skills are important; The interview should be planned. You should know the job to be filled and plan the questions to be asked. Avoid overlap by using a list of questions to be asked in personnel and a separate list of more technical questions to be asked by the department manager. There are some questions you may not ask. Get together after the interview and compare notes. Post-interview forms can be used to record interview information.

8. Reference checking is an important element of the hiring process. No one should be hired without a reference check. There has been a tremendous rise in negligent hiring lawsuits in the past few years. Use reference check forms and guidelines.

9. After the person has been hired to fill the open position, you can pull the employment requisition out of the pending looseleaf binder and file it in a "filled requisition file," noting the name of the person who filled the job and the hire date.

10. Federal contractors should use a "filled position summary sheet." It greatly simplifies your job in case of a desk audit.

11. When a person is hired, send a "new employee confirmation letter." This letter confirms the details under which the person was hired so there is no misunderstanding later. Always quote salary as a monthly figure. Courts have ruled that when a yearly salary was quoted in an employment letter it implied the person was guaranteed the job for a year.

12. Be sure the new employee receives an employee handbook and signs the acknowledgment form and that the employee is given an orientation to the company and a review of company benefits.

13. Set up an employee personnel file. The type of file you use is up to you. Some people like to clip down every piece of paper in a heavy file. Others like to put everything into an envelope-type file. If you use a regular file, put clips on both sides. File everything to do with status changes on the right hand side and everything to do with hiring, promotion, and termination on the left. Set up a separate file for benefits.

   Maintain a personnel data sheet on the top of the right side of the file folder, and log all personnel changes on the sheet as you file them. Then, when you have to pull out a file and look to see when the employee's last raise or last promotion occurred, you have information quickly available. Also, maintain emergency contact and phone numbers on this sheet for quick reference. Retain these files for five years after termination.

14. Send the payroll information sheet with all the employee information on it to the payroll department to be processed.

15. Use a PC to purchase a software package that will maintain your entire employee base on the computer. When you get calls about employees all you have to do is call up the data on the screen. You don't have to pull the individual personnel files.

16. Have all necessary employment forms completed as soon as the employee is hired.

---

**Manager's Tips**

- Always have classified ads run by your personnel person to control costs and content.

- Review the requisitions form and be sure you know the job before you run an ad and conduct interviews. This saves a lot of time and effort.

- If you take applications all the time—even when you don't have jobs open—you must file the applications and you then have a obligation to call those old applicants when a new job opens. You can build a tremendous backlog of paper in your files. You could also be building statistics that could have an adverse impact on your affirmative action program. It's a good idea to accept applications only when you have a job to fill.

# CHECKLIST OF RECRUITING AND EMPLOYMENT FORMS

❑ Job Description

❑ Employment Requisition

❑ Ad Checklist

❑ Classified ad form

❑ Application

❑ Applicant EEO/Affirmative Action Information

❑ Telephone Reference Check Guide

❑ Education Reference Verification

❑ Employment Confirmation Letter

❑ Letter Requesting Employment Verification

❑ Applicant Rejection Letter

❑ Post-Employment Form

❑ Immigration Form I-9, Employment Eligibility Verification

❑ Employee Agreement and Handbook Acknowledgment Form

❑ Confidentiality Agreement (if applicable)

❑ Personnel Data Sheet

❑ New Employee Orientation Checklist

❑ Personnel Action or Status Form

# JOB DESCRIPTION OUTLINE

| | |
|---|---|
| JOB TITLE: | STATUS |
| JOB CODE: | DATE: |
| DIVISION: | REVISION NO.: |
| REPORTS TO: | REVISION DATE: |

## POSITION SUMMARY:

*Please provide a brief summary of the position. This information will be used for position announcements and advertisements.*

## PRINCIPAL ACCOUNTABILITIES:

*Please make a list of job tasks stating what is done and how it is done. Begin each sentence with a verb using present tense singular. For example: <u>Analyze</u> financial data using spreadsheet software. <u>Prepare</u> reports using Wordperfect 5.1 software.*

JOB TITLE:

DATE:

PAGE_____ OF_____

## JOB REQUIREMENTS:

### EDUCATION:

*List minimum acceptable educational requirements to do this job.*

### EXPERIENCE:

*List number of years of experience in the job and specific knowledge requirements.*

### SKILLS:

*List analytical, organizational, interpersonal, technical, managerial skills, and so on.*

## SUPERVISORY RESPONSIBILITIES:

*Please list the number of people supervised and their job titles. If you do not supervise, put "none."*

## EQUIPMENT TO BE USED:

*Please list computers, fax machines, telephones, calculators, floor waxers, power tools, fork lifts, and so on.*

## TYPICAL PHYSICAL DEMANDS:

*Please list job requirements such as lifting standing, sitting, and so on. Try to be specific. Example: "Must be able to lift 50 pounds," "must sit 7 hours a day," "must be able to drive a car."*

## TYPICAL MENTAL DEMANDS:

*List the mental requirements of the job. Example: "must be able to do simple math calculations" or "must be able to analyze complex information."*

## WORKING CONDITIONS:

*Please list examples such as "must work evenings and/or weekends," "job requires driving _____% of the time," "works in a typical office setting," "works outside 90% of the time," and so on.*

THIS JOB DESCRIPTION DOES NOT CONSTITUTE A CONTRACT FOR EMPLOYMENT

## PERSONNEL REQUISITION FORM (Please type)

| Job Title | Salary Range | Hourly Rate | Requisition Number | Department/Location | Current Date |
|---|---|---|---|---|---|
| | | | | | Date Needed |

☐ Replacement

☐ *New Position   Approved _____ Yes _____ No

☐ Exempt   ☐ Non-exempt

Name of Vacating Employee

Regular Full-time _____   Regular Part-time _____

Temporary _____ (3 mo. max) Agency _____

Reason for Vacancy or New Position

Skills Required

Education or Equivalent Experience

Essential Job Functions

1. _____
2. _____
3. _____
4. _____
5. _____
6. _____
7. _____
8. _____

Additional Job Information Including Physical/Mental Demands

*Board Approval/Signature (if $40,000 annual salary)

Schedule Interviews Through (Name/Extension) _____

Supervisor

Manager's Signature

Director or Vice President's Signature

President's Signature

### HUMAN RESOURCE DEPARTMENT USE ONLY

| Position Filled By | Start Date | Starting Salary | HR Approval |
|---|---|---|---|
| | | | |

## Ad Checklist

A high percentage of jobs will be filled by help-wanted ads and recruiting literature, but many ads are sterile and boring. There is no way to know exactly how effective advertising is, even if you keep records of applicants who respond to your ads. Here are some ideas to keep in mind when running ads:

- ❏ People are attracted by class. If you can afford it, use display ads. Be sure the ads reflect the company personality.
- ❏ Use a clean-cut type style and graphics.
- ❏ The first few words need pizzazz to hook the reader and appeal to the people you want to attract. They should be printed in large type.
- ❏ Make sure your ad is placed under the appropriate job classification.
- ❏ Use your company logo.

What you're looking for:

- ❏ List specific skills.
- ❏ List work experience required.
- ❏ State whether relocation is necessary.
- ❏ State educational requirements.
- ❏ Indicate whether the job requires regular travel.
- ❏ State whether you will train.
- ❏ Use the EEO/AAP designation.

Benefits:

- ❏ Provide a good review of your overall benefit program and any other items (such as "mountain location" or "mild year-round climate") that you consider a benefit.

What *not* to include:

- ❏ References to age or sex or any other discriminatory language.

# HELP WANTED ADVERTISING FORM

Position _____ Reg. # _____

Department/Division _____

Charge To _____Cost Center

Person Requesting Ad _____

    Phone Ext. _____

Ads must be sent to the Human Resources Department by:

    Monday 5:00 P.M. for Wednesday placement

    Thursday 5:00 P.M. for Sunday placement

_____

Newspaper _____

Run Ad _____Day(s) _____Date(s)

Under Heading(s) _____

Please insert the following ad for the above position:

E9E/M/F/D/V

_____

**FOR HUMAN RESOURCES DEPARTMENT USE ONLY**

Ad Ordered_____(Date) _____(Newspaper)

Price $ _____

Re-run: Run Ad _____Day(s) _____Date(s)

Re-run Ordered _____(Date) _____(Newspaper)

Re-run Price $ _____

# APPLICATION FOR EMPLOYMENT
## An Equal Opportunity Employer

We do not discriminate on the basis of race, color, religion, national origin, sex,
age, or disability. It is our intention that all qualified applicants be given equal
opportunity and that selection decisions be based on job-related factors.

Each question should be fully and accurately answered. No action can be taken on this application until all questions have been answered. Use blank paper if you do not have enough room on this application. PLEASE PRINT, except for signature on back of application. In reading and answering the following questions, be aware that none of the questions are intended to imply illegal preferences or discrimination based upon non-job-related information.

Job Applied For _____ Today's Date _____

Are you seeking:  Full-time ☐  Part-time ☐  Temporary ☐  employment?   When could you start work? _____

| Last Name | First Name | Middle Name | Telephone Number |
| --- | --- | --- | --- |

| Present Street Address | City | State | Zip Code |
| --- | --- | --- | --- |

Are you 18 years of age or older? .................................................................... Yes ☐   No ☐
(If you are hired you may be required to submit proof of age.)

Social Security Number _____ If hired, can you furnish proof you are eligible to work in the U.S.?   Yes ☐   No ☐

---

Have you ever applied here before? ...................... Yes ☐   No ☐   If yes, when? _____

Were you ever employed here? ........................... Yes ☐   No ☐   If yes, when? _____

Have you ever been convicted of any law violation (except a minor traffic violation)? ............................................... Yes ☐   No ☐

If yes, give details _____
(A "Yes" answer does not automatically disqualify you from employment, since the nature of the offense, date, and the job for which you are applying will also be considered.)

Are you now or do you expect to be engaged in any other business or employment? ........................................... Yes ☐   No ☐

If yes, please explain _____

For Driving Jobs Only:   Do you have a valid driver's license? ................................................................ Yes ☐   No ☐

Driver's License Number _____ Class of License _____
Have you had your driver's license suspended or revoked in the last 3 years? ............................................... Yes ☐   No ☐

If yes, give details: _____

List professional, trade, business or civic activities and offices held. (Exclude labor organizations and memberships which reveal race, color, religion, national origin, sex, age, disability or other protected status.) _____

---

| LIST NAME AND ADDRESS OF SCHOOLS | Number of Years Completed | Diploma/ Degree/ Certificate | Subjects Studied |
| --- | --- | --- | --- |

High School or GED: _____

College or University: _____

Vocational or Technical: _____

What skills or additional training do you have that are related to the job for which you are applying? _____

What machines or equipment can you operate that are related to the job for which you are applying? _____

List names of employers in consecutive order with present or last employer listed first. Account for all periods of time including military service and any periods of unemployment. If self-employed, give firm name and supply business references.

**PLEASE GIVE MONTH AND YEAR.**

| NAME OF EMPLOYER | | JOB TITLE AND DUTIES |
|---|---|---|
| ADDRESS | | |
| CITY, STATE, ZIP CODE | | DATE OF EMPLOYMENT: FROM — TO |
| | | PAY: START $ — FINAL $ |
| SUPERVISOR | TELEPHONE | REASON FOR LEAVING |

| NAME OF EMPLOYER | | JOB TITLE AND DUTIES |
|---|---|---|
| ADDRESS | | |
| CITY, STATE, ZIP CODE | | DATE OF EMPLOYMENT: FROM — TO |
| | | PAY: START $ — FINAL $ |
| SUPERVISOR | TELEPHONE | REASON FOR LEAVING |

| NAME OF EMPLOYER | | JOB TITLE AND DUTIES |
|---|---|---|
| ADDRESS | | |
| CITY, STATE, ZIP CODE | | DATE OF EMPLOYMENT: FROM — TO |
| | | PAY: START $ — FINAL $ |
| SUPERVISOR | TELEPHONE | REASON FOR LEAVING |

| NAME OF EMPLOYER | | JOB TITLE AND DUTIES |
|---|---|---|
| ADDRESS | | |
| CITY, STATE, ZIP CODE | | DATE OF EMPLOYMENT: FROM — TO |
| | | PAY: START $ — FINAL $ |
| SUPERVISOR | TELEPHONE | REASON FOR LEAVING |

Have you worked under any other name? ................................................................................ Yes ☐ No ☐

If yes, give names: _____

Are you presently employed? ................................................................................ Yes ☐ No ☐

If yes, may we contact your present employer? ................................................................ Yes ☐ No ☐

Have you ever been fired from a job or asked to resign? ................................................ Yes ☐ No ☐

If yes, please explain: _____

Give three references, not relatives or former employers.

| Name | Address | Phone |
|---|---|---|
| | | |
| | | |
| | | |

### PLEASE READ EACH STATEMENT CAREFULLY BEFORE SIGNING

I certify that all information provided in this employment application is true and complete. I understand that any false information or omission may disqualify me from further consideration for employment and may result in my dismissal if discovered at a later date.

I authorize and agree to cooperate in a thorough investigation of all statements made herein and other matters relating to my background and qualifications. I understand that any investigation conducted may include a request for employment and educational history, credit reports, consumer reports, investigative consumer reports, driving record, and criminal history. I authorize any person, school, current and former employer, consumer reporting agency, and any other organization or agency to provide information relevant to such investigation and I hereby release all persons and corporations requesting or supplying information pursuant to such investigation from all liability or responsibility to me for doing so. I understand that I have the right to make a written request within a reasonable period of time for complete disclosure of the nature and scope of any investigation. I further authorize any physician or hospital to release any information which may be necessary to determine my ability to perform the job for which I am being considered or any future job in the event that I am hired.

I understand that compliance with the Company's Corporate Code of Conduct is a condition of my employment.

I understand I may be required to successfully pass a drug-screening examination. I hereby consent to a pre- and/or post-employment drug screen as a condition of my employment, if required.

**I UNDERSTAND THAT THIS APPLICATION OR SUBSEQUENT EMPLOYMENT DOES NOT CREATE A CONTRACT OF EMPLOYMENT NOR GUARANTEE EMPLOYMENT FOR ANY DEFINITE PERIOD OF TIME. IF EMPLOYED, I UNDERSTAND THAT I HAVE BEEN HIRED AT THE WILL OF THE EMPLOYER AND MY EMPLOYMENT MAY BE TERMINATED AT ANY TIME, WITH OR WITHOUT CAUSE AND WITH OR WITHOUT NOTICE.**

I have read, understand, and by my signature consent to these statements.

Signature: _____ Date: _____

This application for employment will remain active for a limited time. Ask the organization representative for details.

## APPLICANT EEO OR AFFIRMATIVE ACTION INFORMATION

It is the policy of this organization to provide equal employment opportunity to all qualified applicants for employment without regard to race, color, religion, national origin, sex, age, veteran status or disability. Various agencies of the government require employers to invite applicants to identify themselves as indicated below.

**COMPLETION OF THIS FORM IS VOLUNTARY AND IN NO WAY AFFECTS THE DECISION REGARDING YOUR APPLICATION FOR EMPLOYMENT. THIS FORM IS CONFIDENTIAL AND WILL BE MAINTAINED SEPARATELY FROM YOUR APPLICATION FORM.**

---

### PLEASE PRINT

Name: _____ Date: _____
      Last            First         Middle

Position Applied for: (list only one) _____

**What is your race/ethnic origin?**          **What is your sex?**
  ❏ White                                        ❏ Male
  ❏ Hispanic                                     ❏ Female
  ❏ American Indian/Alaskan Native
  ❏ Black
  ❏ Asian/Pacific Islander

---

**Are you a Vietnam Era Veteran?** . . . . . . . . . . . . . . . . . . . . . . . . ❏ Yes    ❏ No

A person who served on active duty for a period of more than 180 days any part of which occurred between 8/5/64 and 5/7/75, and was discharged or released therefrom with other than a dishonorable discharge or for a service connected disability.

**Are you a disabled veteran?** . . . . . . . . . . . . . . . . . . . . . . . . . . . ❏ Yes    ❏ No

A person entitled to disability compensation under laws administered by the Veterans Administration for disability rated at 30% or more, or a person whose discharge or release from active duty was for a disability incurred or aggravated in the line of duty.

**Do you have a mental or physical disability?** . . . . . . . . . . . . . . . . ❏ Yes    ❏ No

A person who has a mental or physical impairment that substantially limits one or more major life activities, who has a record of such impairment, or who is regarded as having such an impairment.

# APPLICANT APPRAISAL FORM

Name of Applicant _____ Position _____

Department/Company _____ Interview Date_____

This rating form will become a part of the applicant's personnel record which may be made available to governmental compliance agencies upon request.

| DO NOT FILL OUT IN THE PRESENCE OF APPLICANT<br>Review the current job description and your interview notes and rate the candidate in all categories below. Comment in each section. | Outstanding | Above Average | Average | Below Average |
|---|---|---|---|---|
| ESSENTIAL JOB FUNCTIONS—Comment on ability to perform the essential functions of this job. | | | | |
| EXPERIENCE—How does previous experience relate to current job opening? | | | | |
| MENTAL/PHYSICAL CAPABILITIES—Verbal ability, judgment, analytical skills, logic, decisiveness, and so on. Can the applicant perform the physical requirements of the job? | | | | |
| EDUCATION/SKILLS—Degree(s), professional licenses, registration, certifications, languages, equipment, computer skills, and so on. | | | | |

ADDITIONAL COMMENTS:

Reason applicant was/was not hired (use applicant disposition codes and comments as needed—see other side for codes).
_____
_____

For additional comments use back of form.

Overall Appraisal:
    Outstanding _____ Above Average _____ Average _____ Below Average _____
    Recommend employment for current opening: Yes _____ No _____ Applicant Disposition Code _____
    Future consideration: Yes _____ No _____ If yes, for _____ position
    Recommendation based upon: Application Review _____ Interview _____ References _____

Signature of Interviewer:              Date Completed:

## APPLICANT APPRAISAL FORM

Name of Applicant _____ Date _____

Position _____

Interviewer _____ Division _____

| **Please comment on the following items** | **Rate from 1 to 6** |
|---|---|

*Knowledge and Experience*—How does previous knowledge and experience relate to current open position?

_____    _____

_____

_____

_____

_____

_____

*Mental and Physical Capabilities as They Relate to This Job*—Verbal ability, judgment, analytical, logical, decisive, resourceful, imaginative, can/cannot meet specific physical requirements of this job. Explain.

_____    _____

_____

_____

_____

_____

_____

*Interpersonal Skills*—Does applicant communicate with credibility and confidence?

_____    _____

_____

_____

_____

_____

_____

*Goals, Maturity, Adaptability, Self Confidence*—Does applicant show initiative, persistence, drive, defined goals, a mature outlook, seem adaptable, flexible and confidant in abilities? Explain.

_____    _____

_____

_____

_____

_____

_____

**Applicant Appraisal Form
Page 2**

**Rate from
1 to 6**

*Supervision and management experience* Discuss in depth management training and experience, including managing a diverse workforce.

_____   _____

_____

_____

_____

_____

_____

_____

_____

*Knowledge of budgeting, financial analysis, business and human services planning.*

_____   _____

_____

_____

_____

_____

_____

_____

_____

*Rate applicant on other factors relevant to this job.*

_____   _____

_____

_____

_____

_____

_____

_____

_____

Total Points   _____

References checked:    Yes _____   No _____

Background checked:    Yes _____   No _____

# CHECKING REFERENCES

Employers have an obligation to check references on anyone they intend to hire. If you hire someone who later becomes violent and harms other employees, you could be held liable if you did not properly check the employee's background before you put the person on your payroll. There have been several court cases where employers were held liable for the acts of employees who became violent and hurt (and in some cases killed) fellow workers. Be sure your employment application has a section that gives you the right to run credit and background checks, and that the applicant signs the employment application form.

## TELEPHONE REFERENCE CHECK

Applicant's Name _____

Company Contacted _____ Phone No. _____

1. When did the applicant work for your company? From_____ To_____

2. What was the applicant's position/title? _____

3. What information can you give concerning:
   Quality of work?

   _____

   _____

   _____

   Quantity of work?

   _____

   _____

   _____

   Attendance?

   _____

   _____

4. Did this person get along well with others?   Yes_____   No_____

5. Why did he/she leave your company?

   _____

   _____

   _____

6. Is he/she eligible for rehire with your company?   Yes_____   No_____
   If not, why? _____

   _____

   _____

Additional Comments: _____

_____

_____

Information From _____ Title _____

Reference Check Made By _____ Date _____

# EDUCATION VERIFICATION REFERENCE

### Employer's Request for Information

The EMPLOYER will fill in the appropriate areas and send this form to the college, together with a stamped, self-addressed return envelope.

Date_____

| NAME AND ADDRESS OF SCHOOL | TO BE RETURNED BY THE SCHOOL TO |
|---|---|
| | EMPLOYER _____ |
| | EMPLOYER REPRESENTATIVE _____ |
| | ADDRESS _____ |
| **ATTN: OFFICE OF THE DEAN** | _____ |

REQUEST TO SCHOOL: The individual named below is being considered for employment as_____

(Type of position)

Applicant indicates attendance at above school. Your cooperation in furnishing the following information will expedite consideration of the applicant.

| APPLICANT'S NAME AND ADDRESS | | | ON REGISTER OF THIS SCHOOL | | | |
|---|---|---|---|---|---|---|
| | | Class | MONTH | YEAR | MONTH | YEAR |
| LAST *(fill in)* | FIRST *(fill in)* | Number (1) | FROM | | TO | |
| APPLICANT INDICATES ATTENDANCE AT THIS COLLEGE | | | DATE OF BIRTH AS GIVEN BY APPLICANT (FOR SCHOOL RECORD IDENTIFICATION AND VERIFICATION) | | | |
| FROM | | TO | MONTH | DAY | | YEAR |
| GRADUATION DATE | TYPE OF DIPLOMA | | GRADE POINT AVERAGE | | | |
| HAS APPLICATION BEEN MADE FOR ADMISSION TO GRADUATE SCHOOL OR OTHER SPECIAL SCHOOL? NO ❑    YES ❑ | | | | | | |

This information supplied below will be treated as confidential by the employer.

REMARKS: (AWARDS, HONORS, CLASS OFFICES HELD, ACTIVITIES)

_____

_____

_____

_____

_____

SIGNED _____    TITLE _____    DATE _____

# SAMPLE EMPLOYMENT CONFIRMATION LETTER

Date _____

Name
Address

Dear _____:

We want to welcome you to the _____ Company as ____*(job title)*___ of the _____ Division located in _____. This position is an important one to our organization and we look forward to having you join our company and contribute your excellent experience and technical expertise.

Your first day of employment is _____, and your monthly salary will be $_____. In addition, after completing our 90-day evaluation period you will be eligible to participate in the medical, dental and life insurance benefits. Long term disability and family medical coverage under our medical plan is also available at your cost.

We want to start out on a positive note, but it is also important for both of us to understand our employment arrangements. Our company is an "At Will" employer and we think it is important to understand that either of us can terminate our employment arrangement at any time.

We are very pleased to be working with you and look forward to your participation on our management team. Best wishes for success in your new position. If you accept these employment terms, please sign below and return one copy of this letter to me.

Sincerely,

Vice President
Human Resources

Accepted:

_____          _____
Name                                        Date

## LETTER REQUESTING EMPLOYMENT VERIFICATION

Mr. John Smith
Personnel Director
Financial Services Corporation
815 16th Street NW
Washington, D.C. 20006

Ref:  Employment Verification
Carol L. Mills

Dear Mr. Smith:

The person identified above is being considered for employment and has signed our
employment application form authorizing this inquiry. We would appreciate a statement
of your experiences with this person when she was employed by your company. Please
provide the information requested on the bottom of this letter and return the letter to us
in the enclosed self-addressed stamped envelope at your earliest convenience. Your
reply will be held in strict confidence. We sincerely appreciate your cooperation and will
reciprocate with employment information on your applicants should the need arise.

Sincerely,

John Watson
Velcare Corporation

------------------------------------------------------------------------

### CONFIDENTIAL

Applicant Name _____
and Address: _____

Name and Location of _____
Former Company: _____

Dates Employed:_____
General Work Record: _____

## APPLICANT REJECTION LETTER

Date _____

Dear _____:

Thank you for your response to our recent advertisement for the position of _____
_____.

We appreciated the opportunity to review your credentials and were pleased that you are interested in employment with the _____ Company.

We have narrowed our search to those few applicants who have the specific qualifications and experience we need for this position. Although your credentials do not specifically meet our current needs, we will retain your resume for six months in the event that an appropriate career opportunity becomes available.

Thanks again for your interest. We wish you the best of luck in your job search.

Sincerely,


Vice President
Human Resources

# POST EMPLOYMENT FORM

This questionnaire can be completed after a person is hired. Please complete the following:

EMPLOYEE'S NAME: _____

     Date of Birth: _____

     Social Security Number: _____

     Marital Status: _____ Date of Marriage: _____

     Maiden Name: _____

     Previous Married Name: _____

     Dates of Military Service: _____ to _____

*EMERGENCY INFORMATION:*

*Name of Person to Notify in Emergency:* _____

*Telephone: (Home)* _____ *(Business)* _____

*Any medical condition the agency should be aware of:* _____

_____

NAME OF EMPLOYEE'S SPOUSE: _____

     Date of Birth: _____

     Social Security Number: _____

     Maiden Name: _____

     Address if different: _____

     Employed by: _____

     Phone: (Home)_____ (Business) _____

     Occupation: _____

DEPENDENTS CLAIMED/RELATIONSHIP:

     _____

     _____

     _____

     _____

**Our Affirmative Action Program and Governmental Reporting Requirements require the following information:**

Sex: _____Male _____Female

Ethnic Group: _____Caucasian _____Black _____Asian _____Hispanic _____American Indian

Handicapped Status: _____Yes _____No If yes, what is handicap?_____

Disabled Veteran: _____Yes _____No If yes, do you receive disability pay? _____Yes _____No

Vietnam Veteran? _____Yes _____No U.S. Citizen? _____Yes _____No

**Manager's Tip**

This information can be requested after the person is hired, and is needed for company records and EEO reporting.

## U.S. Department of Justice
Immigration and Naturalization Service

OMB No. 1115-0136

**Employment Eligibility Verification**

Please read instructions carefully before completing this form. The instructions must be available during completion of this form. **ANTI-DISCRIMINATION NOTICE. It is illegal to discriminate against work eligible individuals. Employers CANNOT specify which document(s) they will accept from an employee. The refusal to hire an individual because of a future expiration date may also constitute illegal discrimination.**

**Section 1. Employee Information and Verification.** To be completed and signed by employee at the time employment begins

| Print Name: Last | First | Middle Initial | Maiden Name |
|---|---|---|---|
| Address (Street Name and Number) | | Apt. # | Date of Birth (month/day/year) |
| City | State | Zip Code | Social Security # |

I am aware that federal law provides for imprisonment and/or fines for false statements or use of false documents in connection with the completion of this form.

I attest, under penalty of perjury, that I am (check one of the following):
☐ A citizen or national of the United States
☐ A Lawful Permanent Resident (Alien # A_____)
☐ An alien authorized to work until____/____/____
    (Alien # or Admission #_____)

Employee's Signature

Date (month/day/year)

**Preparer and/or Translator Certification.** (To be completed and signed if Section 1 is prepared by a person other than the employee.) I attest, under penalty of perjury, that I have assisted in the completion of this form and that to the best of my knowledge the information is true and correct.

| Preparer's/Translator's Signature | Print Name |
|---|---|
| Address (Street Name and Number, City, State, Zip Code) | Date (month/day/year) |

**Section 2. Employer Review and Verification.** To be completed and signed by employer. Examine one document from List A OR examine one document from List B **and** one from List C as listed on the reverse of this form and record the title, number and expiration date, if any, of the document(s)

| List A | OR | List B | AND | List C |
|---|---|---|---|---|
| Document title: _____ | | _____ | | _____ |
| Issuing authority: _____ | | _____ | | _____ |
| Document #: _____ | | _____ | | _____ |
| Expiration Date (if any): ___/___/___ | | ___/___/___ | | ___/___/___ |
| Document #: _____ | | | | |
| Expiration Date (if any): ___/___/___ | | | | |

**CERTIFICATION - I attest, under penalty of perjury, that I have examined the document(s) presented by the above-named employee, that the above-listed document(s) appear to be genuine and to relate to the employee named, that the employee began employment on** (month/day/year) ___/___/___ **and that to the best of my knowledge the employee is eligible to work in the United States. (State employment agencies may omit the date the employee began employment).**

| Signature of Employer or Authorized Representative | Print Name | Title |
|---|---|---|
| Business or Organization Name | Address (Street Name and Number, City, State, Zip Code) | Date (month/day/year) |

**Section 3. Updating and Reverification.** To be completed and signed by employer

| A. New Name (if applicable) | B. Date of rehire (month/day/year) (if applicable) |
|---|---|

C. If employee's previous grant of work authorization has expired, provide the information below for the document that establishes current employment eligibility.

Document Title:_____ Document #:_____ Expiration Date (if any):___/___/___

I attest, under penalty of perjury, that to the best of my knowledge, this employee is eligible to work in the United States, and if the employee presented document(s), the document(s) I have examined appear to be genuine and to relate to the individual.

| Signature of Employer or Authorized Representative | Date (month/day/year) |
|---|---|

Form I-9 (Rev. 11-21-91) N

## LISTS OF ACCEPTABLE DOCUMENTS

| LIST A | | LIST B | | LIST C |
|---|---|---|---|---|
| **Documents that Establish Both Identity and Employment Eligibility** | **OR** | **Documents that Establish Identity** | **AND** | **Documents that Establish Employment Eligibility** |

**LIST A — Documents that Establish Both Identity and Employment Eligibility**

1. U.S. Passport (unexpired or expired)

2. Certificate of U.S. Citizenship *(INS Form N-560 or N-561)*

3. Certificate of Naturalization *(INS Form N-550 or N-570)*

4. Unexpired foreign passport, with *I-551 stamp or* attached *INS Form I-94* indicating unexpired employment authorization

5. Alien Registration Receipt Card with photograph *(INS Form I-151 or I-551)*

6. Unexpired Temporary Resident Card *(INS Form I-688)*

7. Unexpired Employment Authorization Card *(INS Form I-688A)*

8. Unexpired Reentry Permit *(INS Form I-327)*

9. Unexpired Refugee Travel Document *(INS Form I-571)*

10. Unexpired Employment Authorization Document issued by the INS which contains a photograph *(INS Form I-688B)*

**OR**

**LIST B — Documents that Establish Identity**

1. Driver's license or ID card issued by a state or outlying possession of the United States provided it contains a photograph or information such as name, date of birth, sex, height, eye color, and address

2. ID card issued by federal, state, or local government agencies or entities provided it contains a photograph or information such as name, date of birth, sex, height, eye color, and address

3. School ID card with a photograph

4. Voter's registration card

5. U.S. Military card or draft record

6. Military dependent's ID card

7. U.S. Coast Guard Merchant Mariner Card

8. Native American tribal document

9. Driver's license issued by a Canadian government authority

**For persons under age 18 who are unable to present a document listed above:**

10. School record or report card

11. Clinic, doctor, or hospital record

12. Day-care or nursery school record

**AND**

**LIST C — Documents that Establish Employment Eligibility**

1. U.S. social security card issued by the Social Security Administration *(other than a card stating it is not valid for employment)*

2. Certification of Birth Abroad issued by the Department of State *(Form FS-545 or Form DS-1350)*

3. Original or certified copy of a birth certificate issued by a state, county, municipal authority or outlying possession of the United States bearing an official seal

4. Native American tribal document

5. U.S. Citizen ID Card *(INS Form I-197)*

6. ID Card for use of Resident Citizen in the United States *(INS Form I-179)*

7. Unexpired employment authorization document issued by the INS *(other than those listed under List A)*

**Illustrations of many of these documents appear in Part 8 of the Handbook for Employers (M-274)**

Form I-9 (Rev. 11-21-91) N

## EMPLOYEE AGREEMENT AND HANDBOOK ACKNOWLEDGMENT FORM

This employee handbook describes the highlights of the company policies, procedures, and benefits. In all instances the official benefit plan tests, trust agreements, and master contracts as appropriate are the governing documents. Your employee handbook is not to be interpreted as a legal document or an employment contract. Employment with the Company is at the sole discretion of the Company and may be terminated with or without notice at any time for any reason. Nothing in this handbook constitutes an express or implied contract or assurance of continued employment or implies that just cause is required for termination.

Understood and agreed:


_____

(Employee's signature)


_____

Date


**Manager's Tip**

It is important that every employee sign such an employee agreement and that it be retained in the personnel file. This will help protect the Company if there is legal action by the employee charging that he or she did not know the company policies and procedures. A thorough employee orientation and review of the handbook followed by receipt of this signed acknowledgment form could help the company.

## CONFIDENTIALITY AGREEMENT

The nature of services provided by the (organization's name here) requires that information be handled in a private, confidential manner.

Information about our business or our employees or clients will not be released to people or agencies outside the company without our written consent; the only exceptions to this policy will be to follow legal or regulatory guidelines. All memoranda, notes, reports, or other documents will remain part of the company's confidential records.

Personal or identifying information about our employees (such as names, addresses, phone numbers or salaries) will not be released to people not authorized by the nature of their duties to receive such information, without the consent of management and the employee.

I agree to abide by this Confidentiality Agreement.

_____

Name

_____

Witness

_____

Date

**Manager's Tip**

This form can be used for organizations that have goods or services of a proprietary nature, but it doesn't fit all situations. Adjust accordingly, or have it reviewed by legal counsel.

# PERSONAL DATA SHEET

Name _____     Change of Address _____

Address _____     _____

_____     _____

Hire Date _____     Emergency Contact and Phone:

Telephone No. _____     _____

SS Number _____     _____

Marital Status _____     Spouse Name _____

Spouse Work Phone _____

| Type of Personnel Change | Date | Pay Increase | Merit/Promotion/Other |
|---|---|---|---|
|  |  |  |  |
|  |  |  |  |
|  |  |  |  |
|  |  |  |  |
|  |  |  |  |
|  |  |  |  |
|  |  |  |  |
|  |  |  |  |
|  |  |  |  |
|  |  |  |  |
|  |  |  |  |
|  |  |  |  |
|  |  |  |  |
|  |  |  |  |
|  |  |  |  |
|  |  |  |  |

**Note** _____

Place this form in the front of the personnel file and update as each personnel change occurs. This saves you a great deal of time when you need to check the employee's current status and past history. You may prefer to maintain this information in the computer.

# NEW EMPLOYEE ORIENTATION

*NOTE:*  All employees must attend an orientation session.

---

Employee's Name: _____  SSN: _____

Job Title: _____ Dept. _____ Date: _____

---

HUMAN RESOURCES DEPARTMENT: The information checked below has been given or explained to the employee.

---

*Compensation and Benefits*

- Time sheet/card ( )
- Payroll procedures ( )
- Insurance Program Booklet ( )
- Voice Booklet ( )
- Educational Assistance ( )
- Credit Union ( )
- Stock Purchase Plan ( )
- Savings Bond Plan ( )
- Sick Benefits—A&S—Limitations, and so on ( )

*Leaves, Promotions, and Transfers*

- Performance Evaluations ( )
- Promotions ( )
- Transfers ( )
- Vacations ( )
- Holidays ( )
- Absences—Tardiness ( )
- Jury Duty ( )
- Leaves of Absence— Maternity—Medical & Family, and so on ( )

*General*

- Code of Conduct ( )
- Employee Handbook ( )
- Complaints and Grievance Procedures ( )
- I.D. or Entrance Card ( )
- Introduction to the Department ( )
- Parking Facilities ( )
- Safety Guidelines ( )
- First Aid and Requirements for Reporting Injury ( )
- Bulletin Boards/Company Events ( )
- Voluntary Resignation Notice ( )
- Termination Procedures ( )

**SUPERVISOR:** The following is a checklist of information necessary to orient the new employee to the job in your department. Please check off each point as you discuss it with the employee and return to the Human Resources Department to be placed in the employee's personnel file.

---

*Welcome the New Employee*

- Review copy of employee's application. Be familiar with employee's ( )
  experience, training, and education.
- Review job description with employee, including the duties, responsibilities, ( )
  and working relationships.
- Discuss with the employee the unit organization and the department division ( )
  organization. Explain the function of your department/division as related to
  the total organization and how the employee fits in.
- Confirm that employee has a copy of employee handbook, and has read and ( )
  understands it.

*Introduce Employee to Co-Workers*

- Indicate to each co-worker the new employee's position. ( )
- Explain the functions of each person as you introduce the new employee. ( )

*Show New Employee Around the Facility*

- Tour the department, plant, or company. ( )
- Explain where lavatories, coffee areas, and parking facilities are located. ( )
- Explain the various departments within the organization. ( )

*Introduce the New Employee to Job*

- Insure that new employee's working area, equipment, tools and supplies are ( )
  prepared and available.
- Explain the levels of supervision within the department. ( )
- Provide new employee with necessary or required training. ( )
- Explain use of:   Telephone (personal/company calls) ( )
  Copy machines ( )
  Company vehicles ( )
  Mail procedures ( )
  Supply procedures ( )
  Personal expense reimbursement ( )

- Explain hours of work/overtime/call-in procedures.                     (  )
- Give new employee department telephone number.                         (  )
- Review location of department's first aid equipment.                   (  )
- Explain housekeeping responsibilities.                                 (  )

*Future Follow-Up*

- Set date and time within one week to cover any questions or concerns   (  )
  of the new Employee.

_____

_____          _____
Supervisor's Signature                    Employee's Signature

_____          _____
Supervisor's Title                        Date

_____
Department

_____
Date

*Note:*   Return this form to the Human Resources Department.

## PERSONNEL STATUS FORM

| Name | Effective Date |
|---|---|
| Address | Social Security Number |

| Department | Salary Grade | ☐ Full Time ☐ Exempt |
| Job Title | Salary | ☐ Part Time ☐ Nonexempt<br>☐ Temporary ☐ Other _____<br>Hours per week _____<br>Schedule _____ |

**Employment**

☐ New Hire ☐ Reinstatement

☐ Rehire ☐ Other

_____

**Termination**

☐ Resignation ☐ Layoff

☐ Quit Without Notice ☐ Other

☐ Discharged

_____

| **Status Change** | **From** | **To** |
|---|---|---|
| ☐ Exempt/Nonexempt | _____ | _____ |
| ☐ Schedule | _____ | _____ |
| ☐ Department | _____ | _____ |
| ☐ Salary Grade | _____ | _____ |
| ☐ Salary | _____ | _____ |
| ☐ Title | _____ | _____ |
| ☐ Leave of Absence | _____ | _____ |
| ☐ Other | _____ | _____ |

Comments _____
_____
_____
_____

Requested by _____ Date _____

Approved by _____ Date _____

Approved by _____ Date _____

# SEVEN STEPS TO SUCCESSFUL SELECTION

The recruiting and selection process takes a great deal of time. Most of us spend too much time interviewing applicants who are not qualified. We need to work smart to attract the right people. Consider adding the following seven steps to your selection process:

1. Much time is spent interviewing applicants for jobs when the position's specifications and requirements are not clear. Many times even hiring managers haven't defined the job clearly in their own minds. Job responsibilities are frequently blown out of proportion, resulting in too high an expectation of the job on the part of the person hired. To avoid a lengthy, costly recruiting process and a poor selection decision, it is important to know the precise job specifications, including daily interfaces, ability to commit to the company, interpersonal skills, and levels of sophistication and experience.

2. A brief discussion with the hiring manager could save hours of interviewing time later. It's important to understand what the manager wants in the person to be hired. What are the person's obvious objectives and "hidden agendas"?

3. Identify the best recruiting source for the open position. The interviewing process will be successful only if you are able to attract the most qualified candidates for the job. You frequently have to try several sources until you're successful at attracting the best candidates for a job.

4. Use an assessment approach to reviewing applicants and choosing the top candidates. Assess the following qualities:
   - Technical skills
   - Academic credentials
   - Credentials for the position
   - Experience in the field
   - Past successes
   - "Can do" qualities
   - "Will do" qualities
   - Past promotions
   - Attitudes
   - Interpersonal skills
   - Knowledge of your business

5. Check the applicant's credentials, employment references, academic history, and so on.

6. Conduct a thorough selection interview. Cover such items as education, work experience, the "can do" qualities of the applicant; watch for good listening, speaking, and interpersonal skills. Determine the applicant's technical expertise by asking open-ended questions about job assignments. Encourage open discussion by putting the applicant at ease at the beginning of the interview.

7. After you have put together a complete file of information on your top three candidates, the hiring manager must make a decision based on the data collected. Use a form to evaluate the top candidates initially. A form tends to make you more objective about the data gathered. Ask yourself which candidate best fits the job specifications and the internal environment of the department and the company.

An effective employee selection program should be tailored to the needs of the organization and should be simple to carry out on a day-to-day basis. Eliminate unnecessary and redundant paperwork.

# PROS AND CONS OF EMPLOYMENT TESTING INCLUDING DRUG TESTING

Employers can hardly be blamed for wanting to test applicants and employees for drug use and for honesty. According to experts, drug and alcohol abuse account for business losses of over $33 billion annually. Some estimates have gone as high as $60 billion. Another $40 billion is attributed annually to employee theft. On the other hand, applicants, employees, and civil libertarians feel that all testing is frustrating, nerve-wracking, and an invasion of privacy. What direction will the issue of testing take in the next few years?

Testing is now more prevalent than ever in the United States. The use of tests to measure the qualifications of employees and job applicants has been recognized as a valid employment practice under Title VII of the Civil Rights Act. Any professionally developed ability test that is not designed intended or used to discriminate against persons in one of the protected groups, that is, women, minorities, older workers, and the handicapped, is specifically authorized for use. The professionally developed test must also be professionally validated as a true predictor of job performance.

The Equal Employment Opportunity Commission and the Office of Federal Contract Compliance still look at adverse impact when they review an employer. Adverse impact in testing is considered to be demonstrated where there is a three-point score spread on a hundred-point scale between the average score of whites on an employment test and the average score of minority group persons. The disparity is regarded as statistically significant.

When an organization is concerned about honesty—for example, a bank employee who handles a great deal of money—the bank may use some type of honesty test on the employee. During the past few years the most popular honesty test has been the polygraph. Hundreds of thousands of businesses across the country began using polygraph exams in the 1980s, until more and more evidence surfaced showing the polygraph was not always 100 percent accurate as a predictor of honesty. The Polygraph Protection Act passed by Congress in 1988 prohibits private employers from giving lie-detector tests to current or prospective employees.

Today organizations have turned to a paper and pencil honesty test. John E. Reid & Associates of Chicago pioneered the paper and pencil honesty test. The Stanton Corporation based in Charlotte, N.C. is probably the largest publisher of honesty tests in the U.S. Stanton sells millions of tests each year to hotels, restaurants, retailers, convenience stores, manufacturers, and so on. A sample question on the Stanton tests states: "The amount I stole from my employer was (a) 0, (b) $5, (c) $25, (d) $100, or (3) $500." There is a space for an explanation. Many job applicants actually circle one of the last four items and provide an explanation. You wouldn't think you could identify a thief by simply asking, but sometimes you can. Over 2 million people have taken the Stanton test. Some states are moving to outlaw the paper- and-pencil honesty test. Massachusetts is one state that has passed a law that refers to them as the paper and pencil polygraph.

Another controversial area is drug testing. Drug testing for new hires is becoming more common. The number of companies testing current employees and applicants has risen from 5 percent in 1982, to over 60 percent today. A positive drug test will almost always result in being rejected for a job or perhaps being fired from a current job. Many companies have turned to employee assistance programs (EAPs) for help in getting current employees off drugs or alcohol. Some legal questions remain unanswered about who can test whom for what, but more employers are administering drug tests, especially for new hires.

The Drug-Free Workplace Act requires federal contractors and federal grantees to maintain drug-free workplaces through anti-drug policies and drug-awareness programs for employees. A number of federal agencies, including the Department of Transportation and the Department of Defense, have issued regulations requiring employers to have drug-free workplace policies that include drug testing of employees under certain circumstances and specific sanctions against violators. Mandatory drug testing policies under these and other provisions have come under legal scrutiny. Employers currently administering a drug and alcohol testing policy or considering the adoption of such a policy should thoroughly review federal and state laws and agency regulations to ensure that they are in compliance and, where deficient, take the necessary corrective steps prior to implementation.

Here are some additional facts:

- False positives are rare, despite widespread reports to the contrary. The American Association for Clinical Chemistry, conducted a test of 47 labs. It showed a 99.2 percent accuracy rate. Most false positives result from mishandling at the lab, although a false positive can result if a person has taken ibuprofen, a common nonprescription drug found in some pain relievers. Pre-test questioning can avoid most false positives.

- Tests are harder to beat than people realize. Diluting a urine sample with water or substituting a drug-free sample isn't as easy as it sounds. Water taps are not available in rooms where tests are taken, and most "clean" samples purchased through the mail require that water be added.

New, more sophisticated tests are being examined. Testing human hair may be a far more reliable way to test for drugs and is already being used by the Navy in California.

Personality tests, once very popular, seemed to take a nose-dive in the late 1970s but they have come back strong in some mid-size and large organizations today. The tests run the gamut from the standard psychological test such as the 46-year-old Minnesota Multiphase Personality Inventory (MMPI) to the Myers Briggs Type Indictor and the personality assessment test sold by Praendix, Inc. of Wellesley Hills, Massachusetts. The MMPI consists of up to 566 statements and requires a true, false or "cannot say" answer to questions such as "I avoid getting together with people," or "I have a great deal of self-confidence." The Praendix test produces a personality assessment that consists of a list of phrases and adjectives including "life of the party," "sympathetic," and "aggressive," and two questions: "Which of these adjectives describes how you think you are expected to act by others?" and "which of these adjectives describes who you *really are*?". In this test, if you select the word *patient,* for example, as an apt description of yourself, it might mean you are good at detail and work best when reporting to others of higher authority. Those who select *impatient* might be good managers, focusing on the big picture. These kinds of tests are frequently challenged in court when hiring decisions are made based on the results of the tests.

The Equal Employment Opportunity Commission has issued Guidelines on Employment Testing Procedures. These guidelines lay down the ground rules for employers to use in the administration and use of employment tests. Prior to this time, there were no rules concerning the use of tests by employers other than the somewhat educationally oriented *Standards for Educational and Psychological Tests and Manuals* published by the American Psychological Association.

The Equal Employment Opportunity Commission Guidelines were largely ignored by most employers until court decisions began to give great deference to the Equal Employment Opportunity Commission Guidelines and upheld them as proper administrative rules. The use of tests continued unabated until court decisions such as *Griggs v. Duke Power Company* and *United States v. Georgia Power Company* startled employers and who then began to limit their use of tests.

In the *Agreement Between United States Steel Corporation and the United Steelworkers of America* (September 1, 1965) the parties agreed to conduct a survey of written tests, to examine the relationship of the test to qualifications required for work and to study the administrative procedures used in conjunction with testing programs. In the next labor agreement in the steel industry, the parties agreed that any test used in determining the qualifications of an employee must be a job-related test. This is the first occurrence of the term *job-related* as applied to testing and which later appeared in a court decision. The agreement further required that:

- Tests shall be fair in their makeup and in their administration.
- Tests shall be free of cultural, racial, or ethnic bias.
- Testing procedures shall include procedures for notifying an employee of his/her deficiencies and offering counseling as to how they may be overcome.

The Equal Employment Opportunity Commission has revised its guidelines which were issued in 1966. The 1966 Guidelines had been called "Guidelines on Employment Testing Procedures." The revision of these guidelines was called "Guidelines on Employee Selection Procedures." The Office of Federal Contract Compliance has also issued guidelines on testing.

The key issue in all the regulations and guidelines is that tests used for employment or promotions must be job-related, fair, and uniformly administered.

The following is a testing "Bill of Rights." Employees should have the:

- Right to know the title, nature, and use of a test
- Right to a second chance (retesting)
- Right to minimal age-sex-race-culture bias

- Right to knowledge of score with interpretation
- Right to counseling or feedback on performance and means of improvement
- Right to fair and accurate administration and scoring
- Right to use of a valid test
- Right to examination or evaluation of test by a neutral third party
- Right to know method of scoring
- Right to appeal or challenge the procedure

# SAMPLE INTERVIEWING AND SELECTION HANDBOOK

## *Key Instructions*

The following interviewing and selection handbook is provided here to give you step-by-step guidelines for interviewing applicants and selecting new employees. These guidelines include sample questions, questions you may not ask until after the applicant is hired, ways to interview, preparing for the interview, and how to interview difficult applicants. It also provides information on how to select the best employees and specific guidelines for rating applicants.

This interview and selection handbook can be invaluable not only to you but to all of your supervisors and managers who have hiring responsibility. Copy it and furnish it to your outlying offices and field personnel. It can also be the basis for a supervisor's workshop on the topic of interviewing and selection.

# Interviewing and Selection Handbook

## CONTENTS

# INTRODUCTION

This handbook will assist managers with interviewing skills, provide appropriate systematic selection tools, and reduce overlap between personnel and departmental interviews. The information is based on sound personnel selection techniques.

Regardless of its size or type of organization, the key to successful operation of any business depends on the recruiting, selection, and placement of individual employees in timely fashion.

There are no shortcuts to the selection process. Proper systematic selection consists of matching the individual to the job. The best way to achieve effective selection is with a structured interview program in which the interviewer maintains control-ensuring that the applicant's education and experience are reviewed from the broadest standpoint, keeping questions from overlapping, cutting the amount of time spent on the interview, helping to objectively evaluate the applicant, and evaluating the applicant immediately after the interview.

Interviewing and selection don't have to be difficult. Make it simple by organizing yourself. Get the necessary information and tools you need to do the job and then set aside the time you need to do it well.

Turnover is expensive. A business can save a great deal of money by having effective screening, interviewing, and selection processes.

# BASIC CONCEPTS

This is a how-to manual. The basic principles are stated in the following concepts:

1. The effectiveness of any organization depends largely on its human resources. While many factors are important in developing a good team, selection is critical because the basic capacity of an individual places a ceiling on his or her ultimate performance.

2. Selection is based upon the concept that no applicant is good or bad *per se,* but qualified/qualifiable or unqualified for a given job. In the final analysis, selection is an individual prediction of whether *this* person fits the requirements of *this* job.

3. The evaluation of job applicants assumes that the reasons which cause a person to succeed or fail on the job can be predicted in advance. While the prediction of human behavior is not an exact science, giant strides have been made which can greatly improve your "batting average" in selecting good employees.

4. Proper selection is as much in the interests of the applicant as the employer. A poor choice of jobs can retard an individual's career progress, impairing self-confidence and even placing the person in the position of failing. Appropriate selection, on the other hand, helps an individual grow and develop at a healthy pace in a career which provides personal fulfillment as well as job satisfaction and financial rewards.

5. The selection process is an expensive one. The *direct* costs of recruiting, screening, testing, and interviewing applicants are high enough, to say nothing of the expense involved in training and supervising new employees. But the *indirect* costs of poor selection are much higher. Lost productivity, poor service, high turnover, and low morale all result from poor selection decisions.

6. The best predictor of future behavior is past behavior. Long-standing habits, attitudes, and needs seldom change; they are formed early and remain relatively constant throughout life. Of course, significant changes in human behavior do occur. Just as good athletes tend to repeat their successes year after year, problem employees likewise tend to remain problems year after year. A sound selection system examines past performance through the interview (in addition to review of current skills) to predict future behavior.

7. Efficient and economic selection must be a systematic process, following a logical, step-by-step procedure. Each step in the selection process should be designed to help you make good choices. Initial techniques, such as the review of a resume or application form, are gross screening devices intended to eliminate the obviously unqualified. The more expensive and time-consuming procedures, like the comprehensive interview, are reserved for qualified applicants who warrant a full evaluation.

8. While the system helps you gather data in an orderly fashion, the final interpretation requires judgment. After the job has been analyzed and the person evaluated, someone must match the job as a whole to the individual as a whole. A systematic selection program can help provide as much information as possible and thereby minimize the chances of a poor decision.

9. Many factors are required for success on the job, but the lack of any one characteristic may cause a person to fail. It is relatively easy to identify the limitations of an applicant. What is more difficult—and far more important—is identifying the attributes of success. Successful selection does not occur until the "right" person has been placed in the "right" job.

10. Supportive interviewing is a relatively new factor in the interviewing process. The purpose of a supportive interview is to screen applicants "in" instead of screening them "out." Basically, this means not taking the information received in an interview at face value. Whether it is negative or positive, probing allows you to look at the applicant more objectively.

# APPLICANTS

While the basic principles of efficient selection remain the same for all kinds of people, procedures necessarily vary depending upon the professional level of the applicant. There is a distinction between technical, clerical, and professional or managerial applicants. The interviews are handled in a slightly different manner.

To elicit the necessary responses, good questioning techniques must be established. This is accomplished by various methods: (1) the unstructured question and structured question; (2) the use of silence; (3) reflecting feelings; (4) active listening; (5) assertions of understanding and the like. All of the above methods will provide the required information to make an objective selection.

The technical or clerical applicant interview is inclined to deal more with the applicable skills. The questioning technique applies directly to previous education and on-the-job experience—that is, primarily job-related questions.

On the other hand, the clinical/professional/managerial interview takes longer to conduct, and the questioning techniques include verbal communication abilities, management philosophies, as well as job-related questions dealing with education and previous on-the-job experience.

It is important in all interview situations to initially establish a climate of rapport, mutual interest, and respect.

## Screening the Applicant

Your human resources person will screen applications to determine whether they meet the minimum requirements for the job. If they do, the applications should be forwarded to the department manager.

## Interviewing Applicants

After the decision is made that the applicant is qualified for the position, a thorough interview should be conducted.

## Accepting the Applicant

When an applicant is interviewed and hired, references should be checked.

## Rejecting the Applicant

Applicants who do not get a job should receive a letter thanking them for applying for the position.

# APPLICANT FORMS

A position requisition form should be completed to assist managers in communicating their needs. The requisition form should be retained, it provides information needed to complete annual EEO reports. This form should be completed in full, specifying information on education, skills, and duties to be performed. To accomplish this, refer to the job description which will provide a basic understanding of the job and state the job requirements.

Once the essential and desired requirements have been established, each manager should state needs clearly and simply on the requisition form. If, for example, the individual must be able to function with virtually no supervision, this should be listed; if a college degree or equivalent experience is desired, this should be entered. The job accountabilities should be stated as simply as possible.

List as much information as possible including job duties, starting salary, travel requirements, and necessary skills.

# APPLICATION

## Preliminary Screening

Initial information on an applicant may be obtained by screening applications and resumes. This information is used to screen out applicants who fail to meet the basic specifications for the job. If, for example, a college degree is required, but one of the applicants did not complete high school, he or she can be screened out on the basis of that information alone, thereby saving time to evaluate more completely those candidates who meet the initial requirements. *Note:* There must be a bona fide, job-related need to insist on a college degree or a high school diploma. In most jobs you must consider applicants who have equivalent job experience.

## Résumés

While résumés do provide some data, their value is limited because it is the applicant who decides which facts to include and which to omit. Obviously, the individual is more interested in marketing himself/herself than providing information needed for effective screening. You can't always rely on the information contained in resumes.

## Application Form

Your application form should be designed to obtain maximum data without imposing on the applicant, either by asking the individual to complete a unnecessarily lengthy form or by requesting information of a private nature. The form must comply with civil rights and affirmative action program guidelines. By analyzing the data on the application form, the employer can determine whether the applicant meets the minimum requirements for the position, especially in terms of such evident characteristics as experience and skills. The application form also provides the information necessary for conducting reference checks after the interview. Finally, by examining the application form carefully, the employer can be altered to special areas which require a thorough investigation in the interview. It is necessary that every candidate complete the application form as one of the basic steps in the selection system. The application form is the formal document.

EEO and affirmative action guidelines indicate certain questions are inappropriate to ask applicants. It is appropriate to ask these questions after the person has been hired, however, and a post-hiring form may be completed.

# INTERVIEWS

A *comprehensive* interview follows a definite plan, and the interviewer may pursue important points in detail. A sample form has been included in this manual for use as a guide for comprehensive interviews.

## Interview Checklist

As interviewers gain experience, they develop their own style. The following items may prove useful in the development stage:

***Preparing for the Interview*** The interviewer should study the application form and any other information about the applicant *before* beginning the interview. In this way, the interviewer can plan to explore those areas which require special attention and skip over questions already answered.

***Setting the Stage*** It is essential that the interview be conducted in quiet surroundings with a minimum of distractions. If at all possible, a private office should be used and interruptions avoided.

***Establishing Rapport*** The interviewer must ease the tension and make the applicant feel welcome and comfortable. Techniques such as offering coffee and getting on a first-name basis are still valid. But a word of caution is in order. Some interviewers go beyond the bounds of rapport and become friendly to the point that their objectivity is biased by personal consideration. While it is all very well to discuss skiing with the applicant, for example, this can be disastrous if it prejudices one's thinking about the individual's job qualifications.

***Conducting the Interview*** A good interview progresses from nonthreatening, job related questions to more personal and potentially sensitive areas. It begins with a discussion of work history, career interests, and education—all matters which the applicant expects.

***Encouraging the Candidate to Talk*** In the fact-finding stages of the interview, it is the applicant who has the facts and the interviewer who wants the information. Hence, the candidate should be encouraged to talk and the interviewer to listen (try for at least 75 percent of the time). On occasion, an interviewer may have to use "silence" to stimulate an otherwise reluctant applicant, but most candidates will be happy to talk given the chance. The danger is that the interviewer will seize on the applicant, propounding personal ideas and opinions to this "captive audience," and generally dominate the conversation.

***Taking Adequate Time*** It takes time to conduct a thorough interview. As much as one to two hours may be needed to review the background of a mature, professional or managerial prospect. An inexperienced clerical applicant, truck driver, or geologist, on the other hand, might be interviewed in twenty minutes. The cardinal rule in all cases is to take whatever time is needed to get all the facts required for making a good decision.

*Using the Conversational Approach*   While the interview should follow a plan, specific questions should be phrased in a natural, conversational way. Sometimes, there are good reasons for varying the sequence of the interview. The interviewer should remain in control at all times. It is dangerous to let an applicant "run away with the interview and as in the résumé, present his or her story as he or she sees fit. Direct questions may be needed to pinpoint the specific reasons underlying such common generalities as "no opportunity for advancement," which is often given as the reason for leaving a previous place of employment.

*Avoid Leading Questions*   A leading question is one which gives the respondent a cue to what the audience expects to hear. Questions should be asked in such a way that the applicant must provide a narrative answer—not just a "yes" or "no." Ask open-ended or unstructured questions.

*Emphasizing the Important*   The employment interview should focus on work history in particular (and what the applicant has done in general) in order to predict successfully what the applicant is likely to do in the future. Past behavior is the best predictor of future performance. Most of the interview time should be devoted to experience and education.

*Avoiding Moral Judgments*   You should suppress personal feelings about the behavior, morals, and standards of an applicant. Nor should you assume that you are a counselor whose role in life is "helping" applicants or criticizing their pattern of life. Instead, it is your purpose to find out what the applicant has done-and then, later, to decide whether the applicant meets the requirements of the position under consideration.

*Taking Notes*   It may be necessary to take notes of the information collected in the interview. It helps the interviewer to analyze the data after the applicant has gone. It also helps the individual be thorough and systematic in covering all important aspects of the applicant's background. Few candidates will be disturbed by the note taking process. This note taking, however, should be limited, with the interviewer maintaining as much eye contact with the applicant as possible while writing.

*Obtaining Precise information*   It is human nature for candidates to fill out the application in such a way as to make themselves look "good." Likewise, the applicant will not call attention to periods of unemployment, involuntary terminations and so forth. For this reason, it is important that the interviewer find out what the applicant has done by accounting for all time in his or her life since the individual has left school. Reasons for leaving jobs must be probed carefully. Then, if contradictions between the application form and the interview are obtained, it is necessary to examine the reason for the inconsistency. It is unfortunate, but true, that a significant number of applicants will provide false information—much of which can be uncovered in a careful interview.

***Listening with the Third Ear***   The skillful interviewer listens to what is really being communicated, not just what is being said. It is estimated that a person can think seven times as fast as normal speech; an alert interviewer will use that time to analyze in depth what the interviewee is saying. Good listening is an active, not a passive, process. One can become very perceptive in the interview by listening hard to the undertones of the conversation.

***Selling the Job***   The interview is a two-way street. After the interviewer has the necessary information from the applicant, it is only fair to discuss the job and the organization. It is best to hold this discussion at the end of the employment interview, to avoid the applicant's slanting answers to meet the qualifications of the job. There is another reason as well: if the interviewer is convinced that an applicant is highly desirable, the interviewer should make every effort to interest the individual in joining the organization. If, on the other hand, the interviewer believes the applicant is not qualified or qualifiable for employment, then he or she should not try to "sell" the candidate. Never "oversell" applicants. After they get into the job they might be disappointed and leave.

***Concluding the Interview***   After sufficient information has been exchanged between the interviewer and the applicant, and both are satisfied they have the information needed, the interviewer should then discuss the next step in the selection process. This step may well be a meeting between the applicant and the prospective supervisor to ascertain the personal chemistry between them and to discuss the technical requirements of the job. If the applicant is not to receive further consideration for employment, he or she should be notified graciously and tactfully-so that time may be spent more profitably in seeking work elsewhere.

# QUESTIONING TECHNIQUES

To obtain the necessary answers from an applicant, use good questioning techniques. These include the following:

**Unstructured Question** Cannot be answered by a "yes" or "no"—will enable the applicant to speak openly. This helps the interviewer to better ascertain and understand the applicant's views. Questions beginning with *who, what, when, where, why,* and *how* will elicit unstructured answers.

**Structured Question** Places the applicant in a position to answer either "yes" or "no." The answer need not be elaborated on. For example:

Q. Did you like your last job?
A. Yes.

**Unstructured Question Combined with Structured Question** A structured question may be followed by an unstructured question to help clarify the applicant's feelings, pinpoint a fact, or obtain additional information. For example:

Q. Did you like your last job?
A. Yes.
Q. What in particular did you like?
A. Well, . . .

**Use of Silence** A brief pause between questions allows the applicant time to elaborate on an answer if he or she desires.

**Reflective Feelings** The interviewer paraphrases the applicant's statement as to content and feelings. Phrases beginning with: "it seems that . . ." or "it sounds like . . ." reflect feelings.

**Active Listening** The interviewer repeats or restates what the applicant has said, usually in the form of a question. Applicant is then aware of the interviewer's interest. For example:

Q. What did you think of your previous supervisor?
A. He was all right, but a bit overbearing.
Q. Overbearing? Would you explain?
A. Well, he . . .

**Assertions of Understanding** Neutral phrases that will place the applicant in a position so as to elaborate on his or her answer. These phrases include: "I understand," "Uh-huh," "Yes, I see," and the like.

# UNSTRUCTURED QUESTIONS

## Open-Ended Questions

- Tell me about . . .
- Would you tell me about . . .
- I'd be interested in knowing . . .
- How did you feel about . . .
- Would you explain . . .
- I'm not certain I understand . . .
- Would you explain in more detail?
- What do you mean by that?
- Tell me more about . . .
- Perhaps you could clarify . . .
- What was there about . . . that appealed to you?
- Has there been any opportunity to . . .

# SAMPLE QUESTIONS

- One of the things we want to talk about today is your experience. Would you tell me about your present job?
- What do you feel were your major responsibilities in your last job?
- In your last job, what duties did you spend most of your time on?
- What were some of the things about your job that you found difficult to do? Why do you feel this way about them?
- How do you feel about the progress you have made with your present company?
- In what ways do you feel your latest job has developed you to take on even greater responsibilities?
- What are some of the reasons you had for leaving your last job?
- What were some of the things you particularly liked about your last job?
- Most jobs have "pluses" and "minuses." What were some of the "minuses" in your last job?
- Do you consider your progress on the job representative of your ability? Why?
- What do you feel is a satisfactory attendance record?
- In what areas do you feel your supervisor in your past job could have done a better job?
- What are some of the things your boss did that you particularly liked or disliked?
- How do you feel your supervisor rated your job performance?
- What did your supervisor feel you did particularly well? What were major criticisms of your work? How do you feel about these criticisms?
- What are some of the things in a job that are important to you? Why?
- What are some of the things you would like to avoid in a job? Why?
- How do you feel your last company treated its employees?

# INAPPROPRIATE QUESTIONS

## Questions That Are Inappropriate to Ask Candidates for Employment

Questions seeking the following information may not be asked of an applicant before he or she is hired:

- Date of birth
- Maiden name
- Previous married name
- Marital status
- Name of spouse
- Spouse's occupation and length of time on the job
- Spouse's place of employment
- Number of children and their ages
- Arrest record
- Convictions may be asked about, but you may not refuse employment before conviction unless it is a bona fide job qualification
- Whether child care has been arranged for the children
- Reasons which would prevent an applicant from maintaining employment
- Ancestry
- National origin/race
- Age
- Sex
- Religion
- Whether or not the person has a disability
- Affiliations with a union
- Garnishment of wages

Keep in mind that much of the above is the type of information necessary for personnel records and employee benefit programs once the individual is employed. However, the point that must be understood is that the information is obtained after employment and, therefore, can have no bearing on the employment decisions.

## Questions That Are Inappropriate to Ask Candidates for Promotion

Again, the same type of information listed above is illegal to seek from any candidate being considered for promotion or transfer within the company. Since the employee has a work history with the company, discussions with the current supervisor and review of the personnel records as to work performance and potential are far more valuable in evaluating an employee's qualifications than any of the above information. The interviewer should concentrate on the employee's qualifications, past performance, and potential ability to meet the job needs. It is not appropriate to ask an applicant or an employee being considered for promotion about disabilities.

# COMMON INTERVIEWING ERRORS

- Asking leading questions
- Making decisions too early in the interview
- Following a set pattern of investigation, not recognizing individual differences
- Lacking knowledge of precise job requirements
- Letting pressure of duties shorten interview time
- Doing more talking than the candidate
- Failing to direct the interview, thereby wasting time
- Becoming overly enthusiastic about a person during the initial interview
- Not knowing what to look for
- Tending to be overly influenced by individual factors, rather than considering the applicant as a whole
- Lacking skill in asking questions, in motivating the applicant, in probing, and in recording interview data

Other criticisms made of interviews and the mistakes that are frequently made in an interview include:

- Allowing one undesirable factor to influence judgment
- Lack of preparation for the interview
- Under the pressure to fill a job, making a decision before the facts are in, and then setting up the interview so that the candidate is selected
- Tending to become too routine, instead of adapting each interview to the individual
- Being interviewed by the candidate instead of doing the interviewing

# CHECKLIST FOR EVALUATING INTERVIEW DATA

Items preceded by a minus sign represent examples of unfavorable findings with respect to a given trait; those preceded by a plus sign represent examples of favorable or positive findings:

## Maturity

- − Tends to rationalize failures
- + Has learned to accept limitations
- − Displays chronic dissatisfaction with jobs, working conditions, peers, and superiors
- + Has career goals and is optimistic about them
- + Has mature outlook on life and work in general

## Emotional Adjustment

- + Has shown an ability to maintain composure in face of adversity or frustration
- + Has been able to maintain emotional balance in face of trying personal circumstances
- − Has had problems with bosses or teachers on more than one occasion
- − Is unable to deal with others' shortcomings
- − Evidence that person allows emotions to rule business decisions

## Team Player

- + Seems to have operated successfully as a member of a team
- − Is strongly motivated to be the "star"
- + Seems to place the accomplishments of the group ahead of personal ego
- + Has a degree of empathy and social sensitivity
- − Displays poor interpersonal skills and shows tendency toward intolerance

## Tact

- + The manner in which person phrased remarks during interview reflects tact and consideration
- − In discussing relationships with subordinates, the person seems to reflect a lack of consideration and sensitivity
- + The person is a good listener

## Adaptability

- + Has shown an ability to handle a number of job assignments simultaneously
- − Applicant's approach reflects a tendency to be structured . . . maybe a perfectionist

+ Seems to like jobs involving contact with many types of people and diverse job situations

## Tough-Mindedness

+ Seems willing to take a stand for what is right
− Might not be sufficiently demanding of subordinates when the situation calls for it
− Seems overly concerned with the feeling of others
− Ability to delegate might be questionable based on what seems to be an unreasonable attention to detail
+ Has a positive assertive nature

## Initiative

+ Has demonstrated ability to operate successfully without close supervision
+ Seems to have reached out for increasing responsibility
+ Evidence indicates the person is a self-starter
− Seems to dislike unstructured situations

## Follow-Through

− Changes jobs too often
+ Once the person starts a job, seems to hang in there
− Seems to start more things than can be completed
+ Has achieved one or more career goals

## Self-Confidence

+ Reflects a realistic appraisal of abilities
+ General manner and style reflect poise
− Does not have sufficient confidence to discuss shortcomings
− Appears over-confident and boastful
− Lacks a sense of self-confidence in the interview process

## Personality

+ Personality has considerable impact
− Tends to be introverted
+ Has an outgoing, personable style
− Is ego-oriented
+ Displays empathy and sensitivity

## Honesty and Sincerity

+ Is willing to give credit when credit is due.
− Tends to exaggerate own accomplishments
− Stories seem to be inconsistent in terms of other statements or findings
− Bragged about "pulling a fast one"
+ Willing to discuss unfavorable aspects of work experience in interview

These items are just a few elements that can be used effectively to assist in evaluating an applicant. Not all of them pertain to every applicant, but they will trigger ideas that will get you thinking about specific qualities you need for a particular job. You will come up with other questions and be able to make evaluations as you become more proficient at the interviewing process.

*Remember:*   Half of interviewing is *listening.* When you listen to an applicant, you glean far more information than when you are talking to an applicant

It is helpful to write a summary of assets and shortcomings immediately after the interview has taken place. Concern yourself with the most important findings in terms of the applicant's overall qualifications. Summarize your findings.

Interviewing is an art. As you progress and get better at it, you can relax and enjoy the interaction and the personal give and take that makes the effort worthwhile. It is worthwhile when you find yourself hiring the best people for your jobs, and when your "batting average" improves over time.

# DECISION AND IMPLEMENTATION

The final decision must match the "whole person with the "whole job." This requires a thorough analysis of both the person and the job; only then can an intelligent decision be made as to how well they will "fit" together. To evaluate the person, it is necessary to analyze all the data collected on the individual: résumé, application form, reference checks, interview materials. To understand the job, it is necessary not only to review the formal job description, but also to identify some feeling for the supervisor and work group to which the prospective employee will be assigned.

Then you must weigh all the facts intelligently and come to a sound conclusion. *This element of judgment is of critical importance.* Up to this point the selection system will have helped gather data together in a systematic fashion—but how this data is evaluated depends upon the judgment of the evaluator. A summary form has been provided to help you make a decision on the critical strengths and limitations of the applicant. The ultimate decision—whether to hire the person—depends not only upon the individual and the organization, but also upon the labor market and other factors. Other factors include such items as government regulations, your affirmative action program, and company needs, and should be taken into account when making employment decisions.

Final decisions are generally made with two factors in mind: the applicant's qualifications for a given job opening and potential for future promotion. These two should be kept separate. The best decisions are generally those which match an applicant to a specific position. Looking into the future and trying to determine what a person's potential may be five or ten years from now is difficult. Nevertheless, this may have an important bearing on the employment decision and must be taken into account.

## "Can Do" vs. "Will Do" Characteristics

*Can do* qualities denote a person's intelligence, education, training, experience, skills, aptitudes, and so forth. But, it is the *will do* characteristics—drive, determination, stability, and maturity—that determine whether the person will put these basic abilities to good use.

The unskilled evaluator will often pay more attention to *can do* factors than *will do* qualities—the former are easier to evaluate. But it is equally true that more failures may be attributed to a lack of the necessary *will do* characteristics.

In essence, *an employer is interested in hiring an achiever,* a person who performs on the job and gets the work done, or gets work done through others. What the person will do in the future is best determined by what has been done in the past. Hence, the emphasis in this manual has been placed on work history in particular and achievement in general.

This emphasis on *will do* characteristics is based upon several well-established principles:

- Actual behavior is largely determined by a person's habits or character traits, such as initiative and perseverance.
- These traits develop early in life and seldom change.

- These habits can be determined from a detailed analysis of past behavior.
- Future behavior can be accurately predicted by looking at past behavior.

The interview and reference checks provide the basic data on *will do* characteristics. The interview largely measures the *can do* qualities. Taken together, they provide a good picture of the whole person.

# WHEN NOT TO ACCEPT APPLICATIONS

If you do not have an open position, don't keep accepting applications. You are required to retain applications for five years and to call those people *before* you interview current applicants. Also, by taking applications when you do not have a job open, you are *building* your applicant statistics. You could open yourself to a charge of "adverse impact," that is, not hiring a significant number of women and minorities based on their representations in your applicant base.

You don't have to accept applications if you don't have a job opening. Applicants constantly walking in your office can disrupt your business. Have a sign made to put in your reception area that says:

"We are not accepting applications today, but thanks for coming in."

When you do have openings and are accepting applications, you can save a great deal of your manager's time by establishing interview hours. Have a sign made such as:

"We are accepting applications from 9:00 to 11:00 and 2:00 to 4:00."

# AN INTERNAL JOB-POSTING SYSTEM

Before you go outside the company to recruit new employees it's a good idea to consider people you already have on the payroll. A frequent complaint of employees is that their company goes outside to fill open positions rather than give promotional opportunities to current employees who might be qualified for the job.

A few years ago, it was unthinkable to post open positions in a nonunion salaried environment. But over the past few years, with Equal Employment Opportunity, the need for companies to maximize their human resources and increasing concern for individual career progression, job posting has become common.

## *How One Company's Job-Posting System Works*

### ELIGIBILITY

- All regular employees who have completed their evaluation period and are not under a performance improvement or disciplinary warning plan are eligible to use the open position listing policy in order to request consideration for a position that would constitute a growth opportunity.
- Employees who have been promoted or transferred, or who have changed jobs for any reason, must wait six months before applying for a different position.

### POLICY

- A list of open positions will be communicated to all employees in all facilities. Notices will include information on job title, salary grade, department, supervisor's name and title, location, brief description of the job content, qualifications, and instructions concerning whether candidates will be expected to demonstrate their skills during the interview process.
- Basic job qualifications and experience needed to fill the job will be listed on the sheet. Employees should consult with the human resource department if there are questions concerning the promotional opportunities associated with the job.
- Open position lists will remain on bulletin boards for five working days.
- Forms for use in requesting consideration for an open position may be obtained from the human resource department.
- The human resource department will review requests to substantiate the employee's qualifications for the position.
- The hiring manager will review requests for employees inside the company before going outside the company to fill the position.
- It is the responsibility of the employees to notify their managers of their intent to interview for an open position.
- The hiring manager makes the final decision when filling the position; however, the guidelines for filling any open position are based on the employees' ability, qualifications, experience, background, and the skills they possess that will allow them to carry out the job successfully. It is the responsibility of the hiring manager to notify the previous manager of the intent to hire the employee.

- Employees who are aware of a pending opening, and who will be on vacation when the opening occurs, may leave a request with the human resource department for consideration.

- It is the manager's responsibility to ensure that the human resource department has notified all internal applicants that they did or did not get the job before general announcement by the manager of the person who did get the job.

- "Blanket" applications will not be accepted. Employees should apply each time a position they are interested in becomes available.

- Since preselection often occurs, employees should be planning for their career growth by scheduling time with potential managers before posting, to become acquainted with them, and to secure developmental information to be used in acquiring appropriate skills for future consideration.

- There are occasions when jobs will not be listed. Two such examples might be (1) when a job can be filled best by natural progression or is a logical career path for an employee, and (2) when a job is created to provide a development opportunity for a current high-performance employee.

- In keeping with this policy, managers are encouraged to work with employees in career development in order to assist them in pursuing upward movement in a particular career path or job ladder.

## What the Human Resource Department Does

- Reviews applications for open positions, and checks to see if applicants meet minimum time-on-the-job requirements.
- Reviews background material of applicants with hiring manager. Hiring manager selects the employees qualified for interviews.
- Notifies all applicants who will not be interviewed, and gives them the reasons why.
- Provides counseling to applicants who will not be interviewed.
- Answers questions from interviewed candidates concerning selection, if the interviewing extends beyond the normal three-week period.

## What the Manager Does

- Selects employees to be interviewed for the position.
- Screens interviewed applicants (may contact previous manager for reference).
- Decides who is the best-qualified candidate.
- Informs the human resource department of the selection and provides reasons for rejecting unsuccessful applicants.
- Notifies the successful applicant and his or her current manager. Arranges release dates with the current manager (normally two weeks).
- Completes application forms in full, at the bottom of the form, and answers all appropriate question blocks as necessary.

- Notifies the unsuccessful candidates, advising them of reasons for rejection.
- Makes sure that the interview process does not extend more than three weeks beyond the date the notice comes off the bulletin board.

## *Some Pros and Cons of Posting Open Positions*

### PROS

- Fewer employees look for new jobs or transfers because they find suitable jobs through the posting system.
- The program makes upward mobility easier.
- It creates better morale by making employees aware of open positions.
- Employees have more control over career progression.
- It assists with affirmative action programs.
- It affords better use of the human resources.

### CONS

- The program lengthens the process of filling jobs.
- It creates a chain reaction, and more jobs have to be filled. Employees who don't get jobs require counseling and may become disgruntled.

# RECRUITING PERSONS WITH DISABILITIES—AN IMPORTANT AND UNDERUTILIZED RESOURCE

The Americans with Disabilities Act (ADA) was signed into law by President Bush on July 26, 1990. Unlike most other federal legislation prohibiting discrimination against persons with disabilities, it broadly covers private industry and does not require that entities covered receive federal funding or be a government contractor. The definition of disability means with respect to an individual:

1. A physical or mental impairment that substantially limits one or more major life activities of such individual;
2. a record of such impairment; or
3. being regarded as having such impairment.

Who needs to comply:

- All employers with 25 or more employees must comply effective July 26, 1992.
- All employers with 15–24 employees must comply effective July 26, 1994.

# JOB BID FORM

Name _____ Date _____

Current Department _____

Current Supervisor_____

Job Applying for _____ Dept._____

Your qualifications for the job: _____

_____

_____

_____

_____

_____

_____

Other qualifications such as degrees, licenses: _____

_____

_____

_____

_____

_____

_____

_____

_____
Employee Signature

- - - - - - - - - - - - - - - - - - - - - - - - - - - - - - - - - - - - - - - - - - - - - -

## TO BE COMPLETED BY THE HUMAN RESOURCES DEPARTMENT

Date employee was interviewed _____

Did this employee get the job? _____yes _____no

Why didn't employee get the job? _____

_____

_____

Has employee's supervisor been notified? _____

Has employee been notified? _____

_____
Human Resource Representative

Employment criteria:

- Employers may not discriminate against an individual with a disability in hiring or promotion if the person is otherwise qualified for the job.
- Employers can ask about one's ability to perform a job, but cannot inquire if someone has a disability or subject a person to tests that tend to screen out people with disabilities.
- Employers will need to provide "reasonable accommodation" to individuals with disabilities. This includes steps such as job restructuring and modification of equipment.
- Employers do not need to provide accommodations that impose an "undue hardship" on business operations.

In addition to complying with the Americans with Disabilities Act, any employer with a federal contract must include an affirmative action clause in all contracts or subcontracts. The clause must include the following:

- The contractor agrees not to discriminate against any handicapped person who is qualified to perform the job and also agrees to take affirmative action to hire, advance, and treat handicapped people without discrimination.
- The contractor agrees to abide by all Department of Labor rules and regulations.
- In the event of noncompliance, the contractor will be declared in default.
- The contractor agrees to post notices of affirmative action in conspicuous places around the plant.
- The contractor agrees to notify all union or worker representatives that they are covered by the affirmative action law.
- The contractor includes the affirmative action clause in all subcontracts or purchase orders of more than $2,500.

Each contractor holding a contract or subcontract of $50,000 or more and having at least fifty employees is required to develop and maintain an affirmative action program that sets forth policies and practices regarding handicapped employees. A sample program is provided in this kit.

This program may be kept separate from other affirmative action programs, or it may be integrated into the other programs; if this is done, it must be identifiable and retrievable.

The program must be reviewed and updated each year. Explanations of major changes must be readily available to employees and to applicants for jobs. There have been proposals to increase the dollar amounts and the number of employees covered.

Handicapped job applicants and employees who want to be covered by affirmative action may be asked to identify themselves. They are told that:

- The information is to be given voluntarily and will be kept confidential.
- Refusal to give it will not subject the person to any kind of adverse treatment.

We've talked about the letter of the law, but how do you go about creating an environment where persons with disabilities are welcomed into the organization? Here are some ideas and some actions to be taken:

- Build acceptance of persons with disabilities by managers, supervisors, and all employees through internal communications.
- Use personnel audits to ensure that affirmative action programs are followed.
- Use all recruiting sources, such as state employment services, vocational rehabilitation, sheltered workshops, college placement officers, state education agencies, labor organizations, and organizations of and for handicapped people.
- Recruit candidates at schools for handicapped students—blind, deaf, mentally handicapped, physically handicapped.
- Get advice on placement, recruitment, training, and accommodations from vocational rehabilitation, voluntary health organizations, handicapped groups, and others.
- Review employment records of persons with disabilities to find out whether their full abilities are being used.
- Try to attract qualified persons with disabilities from outside the labor force, through organizations to which they belong.

**SPREADING THE WORD**  To gain full support of affirmative action within the company, it should be publicized in the policy manual; in company publications; by special meetings for executives, managers, and supervisors; in employee orientation programs; in meetings with unions; in nondiscrimination clauses in union contracts; and on company bulletin boards.

**EXECUTIVE RESPONSIBILITY**  An executive of the company should be appointed director of affirmative action activities and should have top-management support. The director's duties should include developing policy statements, affirmative action programs, and communications activities; identifying problem areas and developing solutions; arranging for audit and reporting systems; serving as liaison between the contractor and enforcement agencies and organizations of and for handicapped people; keeping management informed of developments in affirmative action; and arranging for career counseling of handicapped employees.

**CARRYING OUT THE PROGRAM**  To make certain that the greatest possible number of people benefit from affirmative action, the contractor should do things such as:

1. Look over the employee selection process to be sure handicapped people aren't being considered only for certain stereotyped kinds of jobs.
2. Hold briefing sessions for recruiting sources, letting them know about company policies, future job openings, and the like.
3. Carefully select personnel people to ensure that they will implement affirmative action.

4. Include handicapped people in the personnel department.

5. Take part in career days, work-study programs, and other efforts that reach out into the community, as well as other activities that include handicapped people.

# HOW TO SAVE MONEY BY USING TEMPORARY HELP

One of the fastest growing industries in the country today is the temporary help industry. Industry figures show that more than 90 percent of American businesses and practically all of the Fortune 500 companies currently use temporary help on a regular basis. An estimated 5 percent of the entire work force works on a temporary basis, and that number is expected to triple.

Temporary help fills two key needs:

- The need of most organizations for a readily available work force for short periods.
- The need of many experienced skilled people to work, but not on a permanent, full-time basis.

Organizations all over the country have been merging, downsizing and eliminating entire levels of management. Where they once were quick to hire full-time personnel, they now are more likely to fill jobs on a temporary basis. By keeping permanent staff lean and supplementing with temporary help, companies are eliminating significant payroll costs.

## *Eight Creative Uses for Temporary Help That Can Lower Payroll Costs*

1. Placing employees on the payroll of a temporary help service during their evaluation period can minimize a company's unemployment compensation rates.

2. Temporary help teams are a new service offered by some agencies. Teams of word processors, data processors, sales people, and so on, can staff a whole department until permanent staffing is arranged.

3. Retirements cause an organization to lose valuable employees at a time when a particular project is crucial to the business plan. A temporary help service can assist by transferring the person to their payroll, thus easing the pressures on both the company and the employee.

4. Before a company recruits a regular, full-time employee for a new position, a temporary worker can be used to determine if a valid position really exists.

5. Use temporary help for one-time demands involving special projects such as product sampling, assembling an annual report, taking or doing the extensions on inventory, and a data processing conversion program. A temp can go in for a short term and complete the project.

6. Smoother transitions can be delivered when temporary workers are used during office or plant relocation as job vacancies occur.

7. Temporaries can fill crucial spots until a hiring freeze is lifted.

8. Sometimes exactly the right applicant comes along, but it takes a week or more to process the paperwork for authorization to hire the person. During this delay, the prospect may consider another attractive offer. If a manager can place the applicant on the job, but on a temporary service firm's payroll immediately, the problem of losing the applicant may be averted.

If you are in the process of choosing a temporary help service, here are six questions you should ask in order to make a good decision:

1. How long has the temporary help service been in business? (It takes a fair amount of time to develop a backlog of well-trained, experienced personnel.)
2. What recruiting methods and screening procedures are used in hiring temporary employees?
3. What kinds of training programs are there for temporaries, particularly in the more specialized areas such as word processing? (Dig for detailed information.)
4. What sort of insurance or bonding coverage is carried for the protection of the company in case of loss?
5. What are the billing rates for various job classifications?
6. What is the policy on transferring a temporary employee to the client company's payroll?

Some advance planning before the temporary arrives will save time and get the work flowing as quickly as possible. Here's a checklist of seven items to help you get organized before the temporary arrives:

1. A list of the basic duties and responsibilities of the position, including a list of work priorities.
2. A summary of company procedures, work hours, lunch periods, parking areas, and so on.
3. A calendar of important events that will affect the temporary person.
4. A current list or file of frequently used names, titles, telephone numbers, and addresses.
5. Directions on how mail is to be handled and how additional supplies may be secured.
6. An index to office files, indicating any that are to be locked at the close of the day.
7. A set of samples of regularly prepared reports and forms that will be used.

## ILLEGAL EMPLOYMENT PRACTICES

Under current legislation it is unlawful to:

1. Refuse to consider for employment, or otherwise discriminate against any person because of race, color, national origin, sex, religion, physical disability, or age.

2. Show a bias in help-wanted advertising for or against applicants based on race, color, national origin, sex, religion, or age unless you can prove your requirements are bona fide occupational qualifications.

3. Use any screening techniques for employment or promotion, such as paper and pencil tests or questionnaires that cannot be proved to be directly job related.

4. Categorize job candidates on the basis of race, color, national origin, sex, religion, or age.

5. Condone or permit sexual harassment of employees.

6. Segregate employees by race, religion, or national origin with respect to working areas, toilets, lockers, and recreational facilities.

7. Cause or attempt to cause an employer to discriminate against any person because of race, age, religion, national origin, sex, or veteran status through actions initiated by a union.

8. Refuse to hire a woman because separate facilities would have to be provided. Nor can an employer refuse to hire a woman because he/she would have to pay her special benefits such as premium overtime or rest periods required by state law. (Note: An employer would have to give men the same benefits as women.)

9. Perpetuate past discriminatory practices that have led to statistical imbalances in the workforce.

10. Discharge, lay off, or otherwise terminate an employee on the basis of race, religion, sex, national origin, or age.

**Manager's Tip**

These practices reflect the thrust of current legislation and the dangers inherent in careless personnel practices and techniques. Most of you are aware of these issues, but you may want to provide your staff with this extra emphasis on employment practices.

## MAKING A JOB OFFER

There are pros and cons on the subject of whether or not you should confirm an employment agreement in writing. Some attorneys prefer their clients not put employment statements in a letter to a prospective employee, fearing a court might later say the letter is an employment contract. The problem with not putting your employment offer in writing, however, is that an employee might later say you offered more at the time you hired the person than you actually did. For example: You offer an applicant a salary of $6,000 per month plus an incentive bonus which is discretionary. Later, when the bonus is awarded, it is $10,000 and the employee feels it is not enough and says that you promised an incentive bonus of $25,000. You state again that the bonus is discretionary, and he says in your initial hiring discussions, you told him the bonus would be at least $25,000. Setting out the specifics of a compensation package eliminates the possibility of a misunderstanding. If you do make a compensation offer in writing, be sure to state clearly more than once that you are an "At-Will" employer, and that the letter should not be construed in any way as an employment contract. Put a line at the bottom of the letter and the words "Accepted and Agreed" and ask the applicant to sign and return the letter for the personnel file. Be sure to state the salary as a monthly rather than an annual amount. Courts have ruled that because the salary stated in an offer letter was stated as an annual amount the employee who was terminated before the end of the year, should have received the full annual amount of compensation.

# NEW EMPLOYEE ORIENTATION

It is important to get the new employee up to speed quickly. It saves you money in lost work time and helps maintain the quality of your work product.

Design a new employee orientation that covers all the company policies and procedures, the employee's compensation and benefits package, the departmental procedures, and any other items of general interest. Be sure the employee is introduced to everyone in the department. Also, the employee should know everyone in the company with whom he or she will be working or interacting in any way.

Use the New Employee Orientation Form furnished in this chapter and revise it to fit your specific needs.

## Handling Relocation

Relocation can be expensive. Most mid-size and small companies try not to hire someone they have to relocate. If you do decide to relocate an applicant, however, use a relocation form such as the one that follows and ensure costs are approved in advance.

# APPROVAL OF ESTIMATED RELOCATION EXPENSES AND ALLOWANCES

Name _____     Social Security Number _____

Account to be Charged _____     Position Title _____

Old Location _____     New Location _____

Effective Date of Hire _____     Present Residence:  Own_____  Rent ____

Married_____  Single_____  Head of Household_____  Number of Dependents _____

|  | *Estimated Cost* | *Actual Cost* |
|---|---|---|
| Cost of moving household goods | _____ | _____ |
| Employee travel and lodging to new location | _____ | _____ |
| Family travel and lodging to new location | _____ | _____ |
| Househunting travel and lodging for employee and/or spouse | _____ | _____ |
| Federal income tax allowance | _____ | _____ |
| Any other special items to be allowed | _____ | _____ |

Employee's signature _____     Date _____

APPROVALS:

Department Manager _____     Date _____

Vice President _____     Date _____

Chief Financial Officer _____     Date _____

President _____     Date _____

Board (if required) _____     Date _____

# 2

# PERSONNEL RECORDKEEPING

- Mandatory New Hire Reporting
- Employee Information and Recordkeeping Requirements
- Information to Include in the Personnel File
- Payroll Procedures and Relative Statutes
- Pay Terminology and Definitions
- Record Retention Requirements
- Maintaining Control of Staffing Levels
- Monthly Payroll Fund
- How to Figure Recruiting and Selection Costs
- Frequently Used Personnel Calculations, Formulas, and Tables
- Sample Human Resources Calculations and Reports

# Personnel Recordkeeping

Recordkeeping is important, and employee personnel records should be maintained in the personnel department. Managers and supervisors should not maintain separate files in their desks. Let employees see their personnel files by contacting the personnel department and viewing the file in the department with the personnel manager present.

When changes occur in any of the following categories, the personnel manager should be notified so the changes can be reflected promptly in the employee's pay and benefits:

- Name
- Address
- Telephone number
- Marital status
- Number of dependents
- Beneficiaries

Following is a clause regarding personnel files that you should consider putting in your personnel policy:

> The company: (1) collects, uses, and retains only that personnel information which is required for business or legal reasons; (2) provides each employee with a chance to make sure that what is in his/her personnel record is correct; (3) restricts the internal availability of personnel information to those with a valid business need to know; (4) releases personnel information outside only with employee approval, except to verify employment or to satisfy legitimate investigatory or legal needs. All records concerning your employment with the company are company property and will be maintained by the company. You may review those records or files which are maintained on you, including your personnel file, at any time. Requests to review your records should be made to the personnel manager.

Much of personnel recordkeeping is done because it is required by federal or state regulations. We keep records of people who are hired, promoted, and terminated for EEO purposes. OSHA files are required, and we have to fill out OSHA Form 200 when an employee is hurt on the job. Most of the personnel records are retained in the employee's personnel file. These files should be maintained in a special room in locked file cabinets. There is a privacy issue surrounding employee files, and only the personnel manager and the immediate supervisor should have access to the files. There are times when another supervisor or executive may have a "need-to-know" reason for seeing an employee file, but generally the files should be treated in a confidential manner with restricted access.

*Responding to Telephone Requests for Information on an Employee*

Information on employees including addresses, telephone numbers, salaries, and so on should not be given out over the telephone. If a bank needs to verify salary for a home loan, for example, the form should come to the personnel department in writing and there should be a statement on the form signed by the employee giving the employer permission to provide that information.

## MANDATORY NEW HIRE REPORTING

The Personal Liability and Work Opportunity Reconciliation Act of 1996 (welfare reform bill) required in part that all states have a mandatory new hire reporting program in place by October 1, 1997. States which already had such a program had until October 1, 1988 to meet minimum federal requirements. The report must include, at minimum, the employee's name, address and Social Security number, and the employer's name, address and federal employer identification number. The states may add additional fields, such as date of hire or birth. Employers may report by W-4 an equivalent form, by paper, magnetic media, or electronic transmission. Employers must also make the information available to employment security agencies for use in reducing unemployment compensation fraud.

## EMPLOYEE INFORMATION AND RECORDKEEPING REQUIREMENTS

The chart on the next page provides general recordkeeping requirements in seven major personnel functional areas.

## INFORMATION TO INCLUDE IN THE PERSONNEL FILE

- Application
- Résumé
- Post-employment form
- Letter of confirmation
- Personnel data sheet
- Employee handbook acknowledgment form
- Performance appraisals
- Computer printouts showing all activity on the employee
- Forms on leave of absence
- Any correspondence regarding pay, leaves, and performance
- Separation notice and termination information

**Manager's Tip**

There should be no medical information retained in the personnel file. A separate benefits file should be created for privacy reasons. The benefits file should be available only to the immediate supervisor or an executive with a valid need to know the information.

## EMPLOYEE INFORMATION AND RECORDKEEPING REQUIREMENTS

| Recruiting | Employment | Changes in Employment | Compensation & Benefits | Health & Safety | Discipline | Termination |
|---|---|---|---|---|---|---|
| 1. Advertising Records application | 1. Completed form completed | 1. Personnel action operation showing changes | 1. Established hours of reports | 1. Accident & injury | 1. What is your policy? documentation | 1. Need to file all |
| 2. Records of jobs listed with an outside recruiting firm | 2. Reference check form | 2. Update computer records | 2. How flextime works (if applicable) | 2. OSHA Form 200s | 2. What forms must be used, procedures followed? | 2. Review copies of warning notices |
| 3. EEO records (where you recruit minorities) | 3. Immigration I-9 form properly completed | 3. Benefits or compensation changes | 3. Wages to be paid—how time cards are handled | 3. Worker's compensation forms | 3. Are there progressive steps in carrying out discipline? | 3. Completed supervisor's checklist for termination |
| 4. Applicant log | 4. Bond forms (if required) | 4. If a job was opened internally file job bid forms | 4. Exempt or non-exempt is overtime paid? | | 4. Does the employee have the opportunity to respond to disciplinary notices? | 4. Has employee returned all company property? |
| 5. Applicant files (by job category then date) | 5. W-4 form | 5. Payroll notifications | 5. Provide information on pay periods | | 5. Records retained where and for how long? These records should be maintained in a separate file. | 5. If it is a voluntary termination? Be sure employee signs voluntary separation form. |
| 6. Record of internal job bids received for any open position | 6. Set up personnel file | | 6. Review payroll deductions | | 6. Has supervisor treated employee fairly? | 6. Will employee be eligible to collect unemployment compensation? |
| | 7. Enter on computer via personnel status form | | 7. How are garnishments handled? | | | |
| | | | 8. When and how do pay raises occur? | | | |
| | | | 9. Maintain benefits records in a separate file | | | |

# PAYROLL PROCEDURES AND RELEVANT STATUTES

Salaries represent a major element in the cost structure of most businesses. The largest single expense incurred by some service businesses may be the compensation paid to employees. Many different regulations relate to your company's payroll expense.

Payroll accounting procedures are influenced significantly by state and federal statutes. These laws levy taxes based on payroll amounts, establish remittance and reporting requirements for employers, and establish minimum standards for wages paid and hours worked.

## *Federal Insurance Contributions Act*

In the mid-1930s, the federal government enacted a national Social Security program to provide a continuing source of income during retirement. The program has been expanded several times since then, one example being the enactment of the Medicare program providing hospital and medical insurance for persons 65 years of age and older. Today, in addition to health insurance benefits for eligible people, Social Security provides monthly payments to workers and their dependents when a worker retires, is disabled, or dies.

Monthly benefit payments and hospital insurance protection under Medicare are financed by taxes on employees, their employers, and self-employed people. Approximately nine out of ten employed persons in the United States currently have Social Security protection through this process. Medical insurance under Medicare is financed by premiums and from the general revenue of the federal government. The Federal Insurance Contributions Act (FICA) establishes taxes levied on both employee and employer. The schedule of tax rates and the amount of earnings subject to the tax are amended from time to time.

FICA tax applies to wages paid to employees during a calendar year, up to a certain amount per employee. The amount of earnings subject to the FICA tax is adjusted yearly for changes in the Consumer Price Index. Near the end of each year, the Social Security Administration announces the earnings base for the following year. The employee's tax is deducted from each paycheck by the employer. The employer and the employee are taxed at the same rate.

## *Federal Unemployment Tax Act*

The Federal Unemployment Tax Act (FUTA) is also part of the federal Social Security program. The states and the national Social Security Administration work together in a joint unemployment insurance program. FUTA raises funds to help finance administration of the unemployment compensation programs operated by the states. Generally, funds collected under this act are not paid out as unemployment compensation benefits, but are used to pay administrative costs at the federal and state levels. In times of high unemployment, however, the federal government may appropriate funds from its general revenue to provide extended unemployment benefits.

FUTA generates funds through a payroll tax levied on employers. however, employers are entitled to a credit against this tax for unemployment taxes paid to the state.

The amount due on federal unemployment insurance taxes must be reviewed quarterly. If undeposited taxes exceed $100 at the end of any of the first three quarters of a year, a deposit must be made in a Federal Reserve bank or authorized commercial bank during the first month of each quarter. If the amount due is $100 or less, no deposit is necessary. By January 31, each employer must file Form 940, Employer's Annual Federal Unemployment Tax Return, for the preceding year. If the annual tax reported on Form 940, less deposits made, exceeds $100, the entire amount due must be deposited by January 31. If this amount is $100 or less, it may either be deposited or remitted with Form 940.

## State Unemployment Compensation Taxes

Benefit payments to compensate individuals for wages lost during unemployment are handled through unemployment compensation programs administered by each state. Generally, a worker who becomes unemployed through no fault of his or her own, who is able to work, and who is available for work is eligible for unemployment benefits. The duration and amount of benefits typically depend on the worker's length of employment and average wage during a previous base period.

The funds for unemployment benefits are generated in most states by a payroll tax levied on employers. In a few states, the employee must also contribute. Because of the credit allowed against the FUTA tax, states often establish their unemployment tax rate for new employers at 5.4 percent of the first $10,000 of wages paid each employee. However, the rate may vary over time according to an employer's experience rating. Employers with records of stable employment may pay less than the basic rate. An employer with a favorable experience rating who pays less than the basic rate is still entitled to the maximum 5.4 percent credit against the federal unemployment tax.

FICA, FUTA, and state unemployment taxes are levied on certain maximum amounts of payroll. Throughout the calendar year, employers must be aware of the fact that a greater amount of each period's wages may no longer be subject to one or more of these taxes.

The filing and payment requirements for unemployment compensation taxes vary among the states. Often, however, employers must pay the taxes when they file quarterly reports. Some states require payments more frequently, sometimes monthly, if the taxes owed by an employer exceeds a set level.

## Federal Income Tax Withholding

As an employer you are required to withhold federal income taxes from wages and salaries paid to employees. The amount of income tax withheld from each employee is based on the amount of the employee's wages, the employee's marital status, and the number of withholding allowances to which the employee is entitled. When first employed, each employee reports marital status, Social Security number, and number of withholding allowances to the employer on Form W-4. Employees file new W-4s if withholding allowances or marital status change. Employees are entitled to each of the withholding allowances for which they qualify, including one for the employee, one for his or her spouse, and one for each dependent. Additional allowances may be claimed if the employee or spouse is age 65 or older. Blind employees may also claim one or more additional allowances based on expected excessive itemized deductions on their annual income tax return.

Employers usually use the government's wage-bracket tables to determine the amount of federal income taxes to withhold from each employee. These tables indicate the amounts to withhold at different wage levels for different numbers of withholding allowances.

Alternatively, employers may use the percentage method, which is especially useful when no wage-bracket tables pertain to the length of the payroll period in question. Both the wage-bracket tables and the percentage method incorporate a graduated system of withholding. That is, the withholding rates increase as the earnings subject to withholding increase.

## State Income Tax Withholding

Most states now have an income tax that is withheld by employers. Payroll procedures for withholding state income taxes are similar to those for withholding federal income taxes. Taxes related to payroll amounts may be levied on the employee, the employer, or both.

## Employee or Independent Contractor?

Salaries and wages paid to employees provide the basis for withholding taxes and levying payroll taxes on the employer. Independent contractors are not subject to the supervision and control of another party (the employer). The following elements establish the existence of an employer-employee relationship: (1) the employer has the power to discharge the worker; (2) the employer sets the work hours for the worker; and (3) the employer furnishes a place to work. An independent contractor, on the other hand, may also perform services for a business firm, but that firm does not have the legal right to direct and control the methods used by the person. Independent contractors are in business for themselves; examples include some accountants, lawyers, and physicians.

## Remittance and Reporting Requirements

The legislation levying taxes on payroll amounts also specifies the procedures for remitting those taxes to the government and establishes the reports an employer must file. A good system of payroll accounting ensures that these payments are made and reports are filed on time.

## FICA Taxes and Federal Income Taxes

Employer remittance and reporting requirements are the same for both employer's and employee's FICA taxes and federal income taxes withheld, because these taxes are combined for payment and reporting purposes. Generally, remittances are deposited in a

Federal Reserve bank or authorized commercial bank. The specific remittance requirements vary depending on the combined dollar amount of the taxes. An employer has three banking days to make a deposit if the unpaid taxes are at least $3,000 by the 3rd, 7th, 11th, 15th, 19th, 22nd, 25th, or last day of the month. At the end of any month, undeposited taxes of $500–$3,000 must be deposited within 15 days. If the undeposited taxes are less than $500 at the end of a calendar quarter, the amount must be deposited within one month (or paid with the employer's quarterly tax return).

Each quarter, employers file an Employer's Quarterly Federal Tax Return, Form 941, with the Internal Revenue Service. On this form, the employer schedules a record of its liability for FICA taxes and withheld income taxes throughout the quarter and reports its deposits of these taxes.

By January 31, an employer must give each employee two copies of Form W-2, Wage and Tax Statement, which specifies the employee's total wages paid, the federal income taxes withheld, the wages subject to FICA tax, and the FICA tax withheld for the preceding calendar year.

## Fair Labor Standards Act

The Fair Labor Standards Act establishes minimum wage, overtime pay, and equal pay standards for employees covered by the act and sets recordkeeping requirements for their employers. The act's coverage has been amended several times since its passage in 1938. Its provisions now extend, with certain exemptions, to employees directly or indirectly engaged in interstate commerce and to domestic service workers. Executive, administrative, and professional employees are exempt from the act's minimum wage and overtime provisions. A covered employee must be paid an amount equal to at least $1^{1}/_{2}$ times the employee's regular pay rate for every hour over 40 worked in a week. Some states such as the state of California require payment of overtime for over 8 hours worked in a day. Check the laws in your state.

## Equal Pay Act of 1963

Under the Equal Pay Act of 1963, employers may not discriminate on the basis of sex in the rates paid to men and women employees performing equal work on jobs demanding equal skill, effort, and responsibility and having similar working conditions. The equal pay provisions also provide that employers must eliminate illegal pay differentials by a means other than reducing employee pay rates. The law does permit wage differentials between men and women when due to a job-related factor other than sex, such as a difference based on a bona fide merit system, or a point factor job evaluation system.

Employers are required under the law to maintain a detailed record of each employee's wage and hours, including the hour and day the employee's work week begins, the regular hourly rate of pay, the total overtime pay for any week in which more than 40 hours are worked, the deductions from and additions to wages, and the employee's total wages paid each period. The law does not prescribe any particular form for these records. The payroll records maintained in a typical payroll accounting system contain much of this information, which is also needed to comply with other laws and regulations.

## Other Payroll Deductions

In addition to FICA taxes, federal income taxes, and state and local income taxes, other items may be deducted from an employee's gross earnings in arriving at the net take-home pay for the period. Each additional deduction must be authorized by the employee. Often this is done individually, although in some instances the union contract provides the authorization needed by the employer. Examples of these items are payments for:

- Union dues
- Premiums on life, accident, hospital, surgical care, major medical insurance, 401(K) plan
- Loan from employee's credit union
- U.S. savings bonds
- Contributions to charitable organizations

## Payroll Records

The nature of a company's payroll records and procedures depends on the size of the work force and the degree to which the recordkeeping is automated. In some form, however, two records are basic to most payroll systems—the payroll register and individual employee earnings records.

## The Payroll Register

The payroll register, prepared each pay period, lists the company's complete payroll in detail. Each employee's earnings and deductions for the period are contained in the payroll register.

An employee receives an amount equal to gross earnings less total deductions for the pay period. These net earnings are shown in the payment section of the payroll register, along with the number of the check issued by the company in payment of the wages.

## Individual Employee Earnings Record

Employers maintain an individual earnings record for each employee. This record contains much of the information needed for the employer to comply with the various taxation and reporting requirements established by law.

The individual earnings record contains the details on earnings and deductions shown on the payroll register. in addition, the cumulative gross earnings alerts the employer when an employee's yearly earnings have exceeded the maximum amounts to which the FICA and unemployment taxes apply.

Employers prepare Form W-2, the wage and tax statement sent to every employee each year, from the individual employee earnings records. Although Form W-2 is sent only once and covers an entire year, employers typically provide employees with an earnings statement each pay period, detailing the earnings and deductions for that period. These earnings statements may be a detachable portion of the employee's paycheck or may be enclosed as a separate document with the paycheck.

In order to ensure your company is complying with all federal, state, and local pay regulations, you should hire a qualified personnel/payroll person to maintain records and manage the payroll function. These regulations change from year to year and it is a good idea to have your accountant regularly review changes in state and federal regulations and tax laws.

# PAY TERMINOLOGY AND DEFINITIONS

AUTOMATIC PAY INCREASES/GENERAL ADJUSTMENTS. Some organizations have automatic pay increases at specified intervals. These organizations have a fixed-rate type of pay structure. This results in employees in certain job classifications with the same number of years of service to the organization earning the same salary. This is typical of the civil service.

BASE-RATE STRUCTURE. An organization that has no type of compensation other than pay shows only a base pay structure. If there are additional forms of compensation, they may be reflected in total compensation. Many companies pay bonuses at certain levels, and it's important when making external comparisons through surveys to be sure you compare base pay to base pay, and that the bonuses and other perks are listed separately.

BENCHMARK JOBS. When using a point method of measuring jobs, evaluations of a selected group of representative jobs help to clarify various factors and establish a framework for evaluating and comparing jobs throughout the organization. If you are installing a job evaluation system from scratch, establishing benchmark jobs saves time, effort, and cost by providing points of comparison throughout the organization. Benchmark jobs should be easy to define, non controversial, and representative of the organization in general.

BONUS. A bonus can be almost anything other than base pay or perks. Most bonuses are cash, usually determined at the end of the fiscal year after profit and loss statements are completed. Other bonus payments might be in the form of company stock, stock options, and so on.

CALL-BACK PAY. This is hourly pay guaranteed for a certain minimum number of hours when an hourly worker is called to work at a time other than the ordinary shift.

CALL-IN PAY. This is hourly pay guaranteed for a specified number of hours if the worker is called to work on a day that is not an ordinary workday.

CAREER LADDERS. These are successive promotional steps in an occupational or professional area that allow movement up through the organization. There is normally at least a 15 percent increase in pay between each step.

**Career planning.**   Job descriptions and performance appraisals form the basis for planned career development in most organizations and include identifying needed skills and abilities for higher level jobs and scheduling the training needed to prepare for those jobs.

**Centralized/decentralized compensation program.**   A centralized salary program is designed, implemented, and administered at the corporate level. A centralized compensation program is less complex, easier, and less costly to administer in one location. The main characteristic is its uniformity throughout the organization—it can address the diverse needs of separate groups, but it has the same overall guidelines. A centralized compensation effort provides more control over internal equity and uniform administration. A company that has union contracts may decentralize hourly pay. Hourly pay administration will follow union contract provisions and can follow administrative guidelines without regard for the type of company organization.

**Compa-ratio.**   The compa-ratio is a person's current salary as a percentage of the midpoint of their salary range.

**Compensation survey.**   Companies that wish to compare their salary ranges and actual pay practices participate in compensation surveys. The surveys include companies in their industry and their location. It is important to compare actual benchmark jobs when using the data of any survey. When participating in a compensation survey, it's a good idea to have a third party collect the data and produce the survey so that raw data are not exchanged. There might be antitrust implications.

**Compression.**   Compression is the narrowing of pay differentials between employees who should be paid at varying levels. Three of the most common situations where compression can occur are:

- Subordinate vs. supervisor
- New hire vs. senior employee
- Superior performer vs. average performer

The obvious problems associated with inequities caused by salary compression are poor morale and performance, unwillingness to accept promotions, and higher turnover.

**COLA.**   An increase based on measure of cost of living (nationally) used in union contracts.

**Cost-of-living allowances or geographic differentials.**   Some corporations pay cost-of-living allowances to employs they ask to relocate to areas of this country or overseas where the cost of living is significantly higher than the cost of living at their current location.

**Deferred compensation plan.**   This is compensation awarded to an employee where payment is deferred. Deferred compensation is usually in the form of cash or stock. Some plans require purchase by the employee and might be (1) employee savings plans, (2) stock purchase plans, or (3) stock options. Some plans that do not require purchase by the employee are (1) stock bonuses, (2) profit-sharing plans, and (3) deferred cash compensation. Deferred compensation plans are desirable because of their tax advantages.

**EQUITY.** There are two main kinds of equity, internal and external. The perceptions that employees have of equity are so varied that they are difficult to define. Equity seems to exist as an individual perception that is influenced by a variety of factors, a perceived sense of rewards. Equity is seen by most people as the balance between output and the pay received for the job done. It is also a perception that persons are paid fairly within their work group, their total organization, and externally compared to other companies in the same industry.

**EXEMPT EMPLOYEES.** Exempt employees are salaried and hold managerial, supervisory, administrative, professional, or sales positions. They are exempt from the overtime provisions of the Fair Labor Standards Act.

**INCENTIVES.** Incentives are frequently part of an executive's total compensation package. Incentives may include such items as added compensation, commissions, bonus plans, prizes, awards, stock options, and profit sharing.

**MATURITY CURVE DATA.** Maturity curve data are a comparison of pay levels with years of experience. We traditionally look at technical people like scientists and engineers in relation to the number of years since receiving their degrees. This kind of analysis is a normal characteristic of most engineering salary surveys. Maturity curve data are not normally found in other salary surveys, but are available from professional organizations.

**MERIT INCREASES.** A merit increase system rewards employees for job performance and ties job performance to the percentage increase in pay.

**NONEXEMPT EMPLOYEES.** Nonexempt employees are hourly paid employees who are paid overtime for working more than 40 hours in a week. The tests that determine whether a job is exempt or nonexempt are set out in the Fair Labor Standards Act.

**REPORT-IN PAY.** This is hourly pay guaranteed when work is called off because of something like bad weather or machine breakdown.

**SALARY BUDGET.** The human resource manager normally prepares a budget for the organization's pay increases. Personnel and payroll policies and the company's total financial philosophy are taken into account. The formal budget is normally established after a survey of the external competitive situation and a review of the company's resources and financial condition.

# RECORD RETENTION REQUIREMENTS

Personnel recordkeeping is an important function in any company. It is regulated by the federal government, and when not carried on adequately it's an area where a company is vulnerable to litigation. It's a good idea to review federal recordkeeping requirements every year or so to ensure your compliance. The following table lists most federal record retention requirements.

| Record | Period of Retention | Statutes |
|---|---|---|
| **Advertisements Regarding Job Openings, Promotions, Training Programs or Overtime Work** | One Year | Age Discrimination in Employment Act 29 CFR 1627.3 and 29 CFR 1627.4 |
| **Affirmative Action Compliance Programs** (Federal contractors, sub-contractors) Written affirmative action programs, including required workforce analysis and utilization evaluation. Records and documents on nature and use of tests, validations of tests, and test results as required. | Not specified. When the Labor Department's Office of Federal Contract Compliance Programs audits organizations, they may request records from current year and the previous year. | Executive Order 11246 41 CFR 60 |
| **Age Records** Date of Birth, if under 19 | Three Years | Fair Labor Standards Act 29 CFR 516 Walsh-Healey Act 41 CFR 50.201 Age Discrimination in Employment Act, 29 CFR 1627.3 |
| Date of Birth | Three Years | |
| **Americans with Disabilities Act—Employer Records** Same employer record retention requirements as the Civil Rights Act of 1964 as Amended, Title VII. Following the Title VII requirements (along with the requirements of other acts which afford protection from employment discrimination such as the Age Discrimination Act, Immigration Reform & Control Act, Vietnam Veterans Readjustment Assistance Act, Vocational Rehabilitation Act) is considered a helpful defense against an ADA discrimination charge. | | |
| **Applicant identification / Flow Logs** According to the Office of Federal Contract Compliance Programs (OFCCP), an internal audit and reporting system designed to monitor the progress of an affirmative action program should include applicant flow records. Such a record should contain the name of the applicant, date of application, race, sex, referral source, job applied for, interview information, and disposition of the application (hired, rejected and on what basis, no openings, and so forth). The highest year of school completed and pre-employment test results might also be of interest to the OFCCP. Such records must be kept separate from the files or records used by the employer in making hiring decisions. | Not specified. When the Labor Department's Office of Federal Contract Compliance Programs audits organizations, they may request records from current year and the previous year. | Title VII 29 CFR 1607.4 Executive Order 11246 41 CFR 60 |

| Record | Period of Retention | Statutes |
|---|---|---|
| **Application, Résumés or Other Replies to Job Advertisements, including Temporary Positions** | One Year<br><br>One year from date record was made or human resource action was taken, whichever is later. | Age Discrimination in Employment Act<br>29 CFR 1627.4<br>Title VII<br>29 CFR 1602.14 |
| **Apprenticeship Selection and Programs**<br>For apprenticeship programs:<br>• chronological list of names and addresses of all applicants, dates of application, sex and minority-group identification, or file of written applications containing same information; other records pertaining to apprenticeship applicants, for example, test papers, interview records, and<br>• any other records made solely for completing report EEO-2 or similar reports. | Two years from date application was received or period of successful applicant's apprenticeship, whichever is later.<br><br>One year from the due date of the report. | Title VII<br>29 CFR 1602.20<br><br><br><br>Title VII<br>29 CFR 1602.20 |
| **Bloodborne Pathogens/Infectious Material Standard**<br>Protects employees who may be occupationally exposed to blood or other infectious materials.<br>• Written exposure control plan.<br><br>• Medical records.<br>• Training records. | Not specified. Must be available to workers and kept current.<br>Duration of employment + thirty years<br>Three Years | Occupational Safety and Health Act<br>29 CFR 1910.1030 |
| **Child Labor Provisions—Age Certificates** | Employers may protect themselves from unintentional violation of the child labor provisions by keeping on file an employment or age certificate for each minor to show that the minor is the minimum age for the job. Certificates issued under most State laws are acceptable for purposes of the Act. | Fair Labor Standards Act<br>29 CFR 570.5 |
| **Citizenship or Authorization to Work**<br>Immigration and Naturalization Services Form I-9 (Employment Eligibility Verification form) for **all** employees hired after November 6, 1986. | Three years from date of hire or one year after separation, whichever is later. (Minimum of three years.) | Immigration Reform Control Act<br>8 CFR 274A.2 |

| Record | Period of Retention | Statutes |
|---|---|---|
| **Demotion Records** | One Year | Age Discrimination in Employment Act<br>29CFR1627.3<br>Title VII<br>29CFR 16902.14 |
| **Discrimination or Enforcement Charges**<br>• Personnel records relevant to charge of discrimination or enforcement against employer, including records relating to charging party and to all other employees holding positions similar or sought after, such as application forms, test papers or performance documentation. | Until final disposition of charge or action. | Age Discrimination in Employment Act<br>29 CFR 1602.20<br>Title VII, 29 CFR 1602.14<br>Americans with Disabilities Act<br>29 CFR 1602.14<br>Executive Order 11246<br>41 CFR 60 |
| • Minimum Wage and Overtime Charges | Two Year Minimum. However, Department of Labor may request records back three years. | Fair Labor Standards Act<br>29 CFR 516 |
| • Also see:<br>— Citizenship or Authorization to Work<br>— Handicapped Applicant & Employee Complaints<br><br>— Insurance / Welfare and Pension / Retirement Plans<br>— Labor Organizations & Employer Records<br>— Occupational Injuries & Illnesses<br>— Payroll—Basis on which Wages are Paid<br>— Physical / Medical<br>— Polygraph Test<br>— Veterans—Hiring Records<br><br>— Veterans—Military Leave | | Immigration Reform and Control Act<br>ADA & Vocational Rehabilitation Act of 1973<br>Empl. Retirement Income Security Act<br>Landrum-Griffin Act<br>Occupational Safety and Health Act<br>Equal Pay Act<br>OSHA, ADEA, ADA and FMLA<br>Employee Polygraph Protection Act<br>Vietnam Veterans Readjustment Assistance Act<br>Vietnam Veterans Readjustment Assistance Act |
| **Drug Testing Records (Required by Dept. of Transportation)**<br>• Breath alcohol test with results of .02 or higher<br>• Positive controlled substances tests<br>• Documentation of refusals to test<br>• Calibration documentation<br>• Evaluation and referrals<br>• Copy of calendar year summary | 5 years | Omnibus Transportation Employee Testing Act of 1991<br>Federal Aviation Administration (FAA)<br>14 CFR Part 121 (Appendix to Subpart J)<br>Federal Highway Administration (FHWA)<br>49 CFR 382.401<br>Federal Railroad Administration (FRA)<br>49 CFR Part 219 (Appendix to Subpart J) |

| Record | Period of Retention | Statutes |
| --- | --- | --- |
| **Drug Testing Records, Continued**<br>• Information on the alcohol and controlled substances collection process<br>• Information on training | Two Years | Federal Transit Administration (FTA)<br>49 CFR Part 653.71<br>Research and Special Programs Administration (RSPA) |
| • Negative and canceled controlled substances test results<br>• Alcohol test results of less than .02 alcohol concentration | One Year | 49 CFR 199.27 |
| **Earnings Per Week** | Three Years | Age Discrimination in Employment Act<br>29 CFR 1627.3<br>Fair Labor Standards Act<br>29 CFR 516 |
| **Employer Information Report**<br>For employers with 100 or more employees, a copy of the EEO-1 Form (Employer Information Report) must be kept. | A copy of the most current report filed for each reporting unit must always be kept at each unit or at company or divisional headquarters. | Title VII<br>29 CFR 1602.7 |
| **Employment Contracts**<br>Individual Employment Contracts (where contracts or agreements are not in writing, a written memorandum summarizing the terms) include collective bargaining agreements, plans and trusts. | Three Years | Fair Labor Standards Act<br>29 CFR 516 |
| **Employment Tax Records** | Four Years | Internal Revenue Code<br>26 CFR 31.6001-1 |
| **Family And Medical Leave Act (FMLA) Employer Records Leave Under FMLA—Exempt Employees**<br>If employees are not subject to FLSA's recordkeeping regulations for purposes of minimum wage or overtime compliance, an employer need not keep a record of actual hours worked provided that:<br>• Eligibility for FMLA leave is presumed for any employee who has been employed for at least 12 months.<br>• A written record is maintained as to the agreement between the employer and employee regarding reduced or intermittent leave and the employee's normal schedule or average hours. | Three Years<br>No particular order or form of records is required. | Family and Medical Leave Act<br>29 CFR 825.110<br>29 CFR 825.206<br>29 CFR 825.500 |

| Record | Period of Retention | Statutes |
|---|---|---|
| **Leave Under FMLA—Non-exempt Employees**<br>Employers shall keep records pertaining to their obligations under the Act in accordance with the recordkeeping requirement of the Fair Labor Standard Act (FLSA). Records kept must disclose the following:<br>• Basic payroll identifying employee data (name, address, and occupation), rate or basis of pay and terms of compensation, daily and weekly hours worked per pay period, additions to or deductions from wages, total compensation paid.<br>• Dates FMLA leave is taken.<br>• Hours of the leave if FMLA is taken in increments.<br>• Copies of employee notices of leave furnished to the employer and copies of all general and specific notices given to employees.<br>• Documents describing employee benefits or employer policies and practices regarding the taking of paid and unpaid leaves.<br>• Premium payments of employee benefits.<br>• Records of any dispute between the employer and an employee regarding designation of leave as FMLA leave. | Three Years<br>No particular order or form of records is required. | Family and Medical Leave Act<br>29 CFR 825.500<br>29 CFR 825.110<br>29 CFR 516 |
| **Garnishment Documents**<br>NOTE: The terms of some state garnishment laws are more protective of the employee than the provisions of the Federal law. | Federal garnishment laws are enforced under the Fair Labor Standards Act. Refer to Payroll Records—Additions or Deductions from Wages Paid. | Fair Labor Standards Act<br>29 CFR 516 |
| **Group Health Insurance Coverage After Certain Qualifying Events**<br>Employers need records showing covered employees and their spouses and dependents:<br>• have received written notice of continuing group health insurance and COBRA rights,<br>• whether the employee and his or her spouse and dependents elected or rejected coverage. | Not specified by regulations | Internal Revenue Code<br>Sec. 4980 B (f)(6)<br>ERISA Sections 606 (1) and 502 (c)(1) |

| Record | Period of Retention | Statutes |
| --- | --- | --- |
| **Hazardous Materials Exposure** Records of any personal or environmental monitoring of exposure to hazardous materials. | Thirty years | Occupational Safety and Health Act 29 CFR 1910.1200 |
| Records of "significant adverse reactions" to health or the environment that may indicate "long-lasting or irreversible damage," "partial or complete impairment of bodily functions," "impairment of normal activities which is experienced by all or most of the persons exposed at one time," and "impairment of normal activities which is experienced each time an individual is exposed." Records must contain original allegation: abstract of allegation, including name and address of plant site that received allegation, date allegation received, implicated substance, description of alleger, description of alleged health effects, results of any self-initiated investigation of allegation, and copies of any other required reports or records relating to allegation. | Thirty years for records of significant adverse reactions to employees' health; five years for all other allegations, including environmental or consumer charges; thirty years for employee health-related allegations arising from any employment related exposure. | Toxic Substances Control Act from Environmental Protection Agency—applies primarily to chemical manufacturers. 40 CFR 717 |
| **Hiring Records** | One year from date record made or personnel action taken, whichever is later. | Title VII 9 CFR 1602.14 |
| **Homeworker Programs** Payroll or other record specifying date on which work given out to or begun by each industrial homeworker and amount of such work; date on which work turned in by worker, and amount of work; kind of articles worked on and operations performed; piece rates paid; hours worked on each lot of work turned in. | Not specified. (Upon request, all records must be made available for inspection and transcription by Wage-Hour Division administrators.) | Fair Labor Standards Act—Homeworker Regulations 29 CFR 516.31 |
| Name and address of each agent, distributor, or contractor through whom homework is distributed or collected, and name and address of each homeworker to whom homework is distributed or from whom homework is collected by the agent, distributor, or contractor. | Not specified. (Upon request, all records must be made available for inspection and transcription by Wage-Hour Division administrators.) | Homeworker Regulations 29 CFR 516.31 |

| Record | Period of Retention | Statutes |
|---|---|---|
| **Homeworker Programs, Continued**<br>Homeworker handbook in which each homeworker records daily and weekly hours worked, piece work information, and business-related expenses. | At least two years after the handbook is filled completely or the homeworker is terminated. Employers must "keep and preserve" handbook as submitted by each homeworker and, upon request, make the handbook available for inspection by the Wage-Hour Division of the Labor Department. The handbook must include a statement signed by the employer attesting to the accuracy of the entries. | Homeworker Regulations<br>29 CFR 516.31 |
| **Insurance / Welfare and Pension / Retirement Plans**<br>• Benefit plan descriptions.<br>• Records providing the basis for all required plan descriptions and reports necessary to certify the information including vouchers, worksheets, receipts, and applicable resolutions. | Full period that plan or system is in effect, plus one year after termination of the plan.<br><br>Not less than six years after filing date of documents. | Age Discrimination in Employment Act<br>29 CFR 1627.3<br><br>Employee Retirement Income Security Act<br>29 CFR 2520.101-1 thru 2520.104b-30 |
| **Job Orders Submitted to Employment Agency or Union** | One Year | Age Discrimination in Employment Act<br>29 CFR 1627.3 |
| **Labor Organization and Employer Records**<br>Employers are subject to certain annual reporting requirements which include filed reports showing: any loans to a union/union official or representative; agreements with or payments to any labor relations consultant, worker or other individual for the purpose of persuading employees about their union sentiments; and any expenditures to obtain information about the activities of employees or a union in connection with a labor dispute. | Documents to support the accuracy of required reports must be retained for at least five years from filing the report. | Labor Management Reporting and Disclosure Act of 1959<br>29 CFR 405.9 |
| **Layoff Selection** | One Year<br><br>One year from date record made or personnel action taken, whichever is later. | Age Discrimination in Employment Act<br>29 CFR 1627.3<br>Title VII<br>29 CFR 1602.14 |

| Record | Period of Retention | Statutes |
|---|---|---|
| **Material Safety Data Sheets (MSDS)**<br>• Employers must have a MSDS on file for each hazardous chemical they use and ensure copies are readily accessible to employees in their work area. | No specific time—must be maintained in a current fashion. | Occupational Safety and Health Act<br>29 CFR 1910.1200 |
| • Employer must keep records of chemicals used, where they were used and for how long. | Thirty Years | Occupational Safety and Health Act<br>29 CFR 1910.1200 |
| **Occupational Injuries and Illnesses**<br>"Log and Summary of Occupational Injuries and Illnesses"—OSHA Form 200. Job-related injuries and illnesses must be recorded within six days of their occurrence. | Five years following the end of the year to which records relate. | Occupational Safety and Health Act<br>29 CFR 1904.2 |
| "Supplementary Record of Occupational Injuries and Illnesses"—OSHA Form 101. Provides details on each recordable injury and illness. | Five years following the end of the year to which records relate. | Occupational Safety and Health Act<br>29 CFR 1904.4 |
| **Older Workers Benefit Protection Act—Employer Records**<br>Same employer record retention requirements as Age Discrimination in Employment Act (ADEA). | No specific requirement. Keeping waivers forever is considered a helpful defense against an ADEA waiver of rights discrimination charge. | Older Workers Benefit Protection Act<br>29 CFR 1627.3 and 1627.4<br>29 CFR 1602.20 |
| Waiver of Age Discrimination in Employment Act rights. | | |
| **Order, Shipping, and Billing Records**<br>From the last date of entry, the originals or true copies of all customer orders or invoices received, incoming or outgoing shipping or delivery records, as well as all bills of lading and all billings to customers (not including individual sales slips, cash register tapes or the like) which the employer retains or makes in the usual course of business operations. | Two Years | Fair Labor Standards Act<br>29 CFR 516 |
| **Payroll Records-Additions or Deductions from Wages Paid**<br>All records used by the employer in determining additions to or deductions from wages paid. | Three Years | Fair Labor Standards Act<br>29 CFR 516 |

| Record | Period of Retention | Statutes |
|---|---|---|
| **Payroll Records for Age Discrimination in Employment Act** <br> Payroll or other records containing each employee's name, address, date of birth, occupation, rate of pay, and compensation earned per week. | Three Years | Age Discrimination in Employment Act <br> 29 CFR 1627.3 |
| **Payroll Records—Basis on which Wages Are Paid** <br> • The basis on which wages are paid must be documented in sufficient detail to permit calculation for each pay period. The records may include payment of wages, wage rates, job evaluations, merit and incentive programs and seniority systems. <br> • The basic reason for these records is to give the Wage-Hour Division an indication on whether or not sex discrimination exists. <br> • Although there is no specific form furnished by the Wage-Hour Division for calculation of the benefit costs, the data necessary to calculate these costs should be readily available to Wage-Hour audit personnel. | Two Years | Equal Pay Act <br> 29 CFR 516 |
| **Payroll Records for Davis-Bacon Act & Service Contract Act** <br> (Federal contractors, sub-contractors) Payroll records listing name, address, social security number, job classification, rate of pay, daily and weekly number of hours worked, deductions made, and actual wages paid. | Three Years after completion of contract | Davis-Bacon Act <br> 29 CFR 5.1 and 5.5 <br> Service Contract Act <br> 29 CFR 4.6 |
| **Payroll Records for FLSA—Exempt Employees** <br> (*Bona fide* executive, administrative, professional and outside sales employees.) <br> • Name in full of employee (as used for social security record purposes) and identifying number or symbol, if such is used on payroll records. <br> • Home address, including zip code. <br> • Date of birth, if under 19 years of age. <br> • Sex and Occupation <br> • Time of day and day of week on which employee's work week begins, if this varies between employees; otherwise a single notation for the entire establishment will suffice. <br> • Total wages paid each pay period. <br> • Dates of payment and pay period covered. | Three Years <br> Records of hours worked is recommended for Department of Labor Wage and Hour audits. | Fair Labor Standards Act <br> 29 CFR 516 |

| Record | Period of Retention | Statutes |
|---|---|---|
| **Payroll Records for FLSA—Non-Exempt Employees**<br>All required for Exempt Employees plus:<br>• Regular hourly rate of pay for any week when overtime is worked and overtime compensation is due. (May be in the form of vouchers or other payment data.)<br>• Daily hours worked and total hours worked each workweek. (Workday may be any consecutive 24-hour period and workweek is any fixed and regularly recurring period of seven consecutive days.)<br>• Total daily or weekly straight-time earnings or wages due for hours worked during the workday or workweek.<br>• Total premium pay for overtime hours. This amount excludes the straight-time earnings for overtime hours recorded under the above item.<br>• Total additions to or deductions from wages paid each pay period including employee purchase orders or wage assignments. Also, in individual employee records, the dates, amounts, and nature of the items which make up the total additions and deductions. | Three Years | Fair Labor Standards Act<br>29 CFR 516 |
| **Payroll Records for Title VII**<br>Rates of pay or other terms of compensation. | One year from date record made or personnel action taken, whichever is later. | Title VII<br>29 CFR 1602.14 |
| **Payroll Records for Walsh-Healey Act**<br>(Federal contractors, sub-contractors) Basic employment and earning records, wage-rate tables, and work-time schedules. Employment records, including name, address, sex, occupation. date of birth of each employee under 19 years of age, and wage-hour records, complete with identifying number of contract on which each employee is working. | Two years from date of last entry or last effective date, whichever is later.<br>Three years from date of last entry. | Walsh-Healey Act<br>41 CFR 50.201<br>Walsh-Healey Act<br>41 CFR 50.201 |
| **Physical/Medical Records Under ADEA and ADA**<br>Results of physical examinations considered in connection *with personnel action.* | One Year | Age Discrimination in Employment Act<br>29 CFR 1627.3<br>Americans with Disabilities Act<br>29 CFR 1630.14 |

| Record | Period of Retention | Statutes |
| --- | --- | --- |
| **Physical / Medical Records Under FMLA**<br>Records and documents including an FMLA leave request relating to medical certifications, recertification or medical histories of employees or employees' family members, shall be maintained in separate files/records and be treated as confidential medical records, except that:<br>• Supervisors and managers may be informed regarding necessary restrictions and accommodations, not the nature of the condition.<br>• First aid and safety personnel may be informed (when appropriate) if the employee may/might require emergency treatment.<br>• Government officials investigating compliance with FMLA shall be provided relevant information. | Three Years<br>No particular order or form of records is required. | Family Medical Leave Act<br>29 CFR 825.500 |
| **Physical / Medical Records Under OSHA**<br>Complete and accurate records of all medical examinations *required by OSHA law.* | Duration of employment, plus 30 years unless a specific OSHA standard provides a different time period. | Occupational Safety and Health Act<br>29 CFR 1910.2 |
| **Plant Closing or Mass Layoff Notice**<br>A 60-day advance notice before a plant closing or mass layoff. | Not specified by regulation.<br>Enforcement action is through the courts. | Worker Adjustment and Retraining Notification Act<br>20 CFR 639.3(a) |
| **Polygraph Test**<br>Polygraph investigation of a workplace theft or other incident or activity resulting in economic loss to the employer. A copy of statement provided to employees setting forth specific incident or activity under investigation and basis for testing. | Three years from date polygraph test is conducted or from date examination is requested, whichever is later. | Employee Polygraph Protection Act<br>29 CFR 801.30 |
| Polygraph investigation of criminal or other misconduct involving, or potentially involving, loss or injury to the manufacture, distribution or dispensing of controlled substances. Records specifically identifying the loss or injury in question and the nature of the employee's access to person or property being investigated. | Three years from date polygraph test is conducted or from date examination is requested, whichever is later. | Employee Polygraph Protection Act<br>29 CFR 801.30 |

| Record | Period of Retention | Statutes |
| --- | --- | --- |
| **Polygraph Test Continued** Copy of notice provided to polygraph examiner identifying persons to be examined. | Three years from dale polygraph test is conducted or from date examination is requested, whichever is later. | Employee Polygraph Protection Act 29 CFR 801.30 |
| Copies of all opinions, reports, charts, written questions, lists, and other records relating to employee polygraph tests (for example, records of number of examinations conducted each day, records specifying duration of each test period) that have been furnished to the employer by the polygraph examiner. | Three years from date polygraph test is conducted or from date examination is requested, whichever is later. | Employee Polygraph Protection Act 29 CFR 801.30 |
| **Promotion Records or Notices** | One year from date record made or personnel action taken, whichever is later. | Title VII 29 CFR 1602.14 |
| | One Year | Age Discrimination in Employment Act 29 CFR 1627.3 |
| **Recall Selection** | One Year | Age Discrimination in Employment Act 29 CFR 1627.3 |
| **Sales and Purchase Records** A record of: (1) total dollar volume of sales or business, and (2) total volume of goods purchased or received during such periods (weekly, monthly, quarterly, and so on) and in such forms as the employer maintains in the ordinary course of business. | Three Years | Fair Labor Standards Act 29 CFR 516.5 |
| **Seniority or Merit Rating Systems** | For the full period the plan or system is in effect, plus one year. | Age Discrimination in Employment Act 29 CFR 1627.3 |
| **Termination Records** | One year from date record made or personnel action taken, whichever is later. One Year | Title VII 29 CFR 1602.14 Age Discrimination in Employment Act 29 CFR 1627.3 |

| Record | Period of Retention | Statutes |
| --- | --- | --- |
| **Test Records** <br> • Tests used in connection with employer administered aptitude or other employment test. <br> • Tests—Federal Contractors & Sub-contractors. Records and documents on nature and use of tests, validations of tests, and test results as required. | One Year <br><br> Not specified. When the Labor Dept.'s Office of Federal Contract Compliance Programs audits organizations, they request records from current and previous year. | Age Discrimination in Employment Act <br> 29 CFR 1627.3 <br> Title VII <br> 29 CFR 1607.4 <br> Executive Order 11246 <br> 41 CFR 60 |
| **Time Worked Records** <br> All basic time and earnings cards or sheets and work production sheets of individuals where all or part of the employee's earnings are determined. | At least two years. | Fair Labor Standards Act <br> 29 CFR 516 |
| **Training Selection** | One Year <br> 29 CFR 1627.3 <br> One year from date record made or personnel action taken, whichever is later. | Age Discrimination in Employment Act <br><br> Title VII <br> 29 CFR 1602.14 |
| **Transfer Records** | One Year <br> 29 CFR 1627.3 <br> One year from date record made or personnel action taken, whichever is later. | Age Discrimination in Employment Act <br><br> Title VII <br> 29 CFR 1602.14 |
| **Veterans—Hiring Records** <br> Organizations with federal contracts or subcontracts of $10,000 or more must file an annual report—Form VETS-100—that lists, by job category and hiring location, the number of Vietnam-era and disabled veterans hired during a 12-month period. The data are used to determine whether employers are fulfilling their affirmative action obligations, as well as the legal requirement to list job vacancies with the Job Service. | One Year | Veterans Readjustment Assistance Act <br> 61 CFR 250 |
| **Veterans—Military Leave** <br> Organizations must grant leaves of absence to perform military obligations. Service limits are set on the amount of lime an employee may spend in active duty and still be eligible for re-employment. Employees are re-employed to their former position or a position of like status and pay with seniority and vacation as if they had not taken a military leave. | Not specified by regulations. The service limit on the time an employee may spend in active duty and still be eligible for re-employment can be up to five years. | Uniformed Services Employment and Reemployment Rights Act <br> Sec. 4311 and 4312 |

| Record | Period of Retention | Statutes |
|---|---|---|
| **Vocational Rehabilitation Act—Handicapped Applicant & Employee Records** | | |
| • (Federal contractors, subcontractors) For handicapped applicants and employees, complete and accurate employment records are required. The Department of Labor suggests that this requirement may be met by annotating the application or personnel form for the handicapped employee or applicant to indicate each vacancy, promotion, and training program for which he or she was considered, including a statement of reasons for any rejection that compares the handicapped individual's qualifications to those of the person selected. Also, any accommodations actually undertaken should be attached. | One Year | Vocational Rehabilitation Act 41 CFR 60.741.52 |
| • Complaints under the Vocational Rehabilitation Act | One Year | Vocational Rehabilitation Act 41 CFR 60.741.52 |
| **Wage-Rate Tables** | | |
| All tables or schedules (from their last effective date) of the employer which provide the piece rates or other rates used In computing straight-time earnings, wages, or salary, or overtime pay computation. | Two years. However, Department of Labor may request records back three years. | Fair Labor Standard Act 29 CFR 516 |

*NOTE: This list is not all-inclusive and is subject to change when new regulations are passed.*

# MAINTAINING CONTROL OF STAFFING LEVELS

It is difficult to maintain control over the numbers of people hired in any organization. There are a couple of simple ways to do it on a monthly basis:

1.  Draw-up an organization chart for each of your current departments. Put everyone on the chart with their salaries and titles. Add up the total salaries by department and put that figure at the top of the form. A sample form appears on the next page. Adapt the form to your particular needs. The first chart you complete for each of your departments can be the starting point for the approved budget.

Prepare a cover page to accompany all the charts. It should provide data on the entire organization showing number of positions and total salaries.

Update the charts as people are hired and terminated.

To control staffing, state that when anyone is added to the charts after a certain date (when staffing has been approved), managers must complete an employment requisition form (see sample).

Maintain employment requisitions that have been approved and the updated organization charts as your control system.

2.  You can control staffing levels and hiring by approving an overall budget each year for every department. Use the form, Monthly Staff Level Report, that follows. Adapt the form to your specific needs. Require anything over the approved budget to be approved by the president.

# MONTHLY PAYROLL TREND

Using a Lotus 123 or Excel spreadsheet, produce a monthly payroll trend report for all your business locations. See sample report which follows.

# ORGANIZATIONAL CHART - EMPLOYEE STAFFING

BRANCH/COST CENTER _____ Admin - 9993 _____

DATE _____

Approved Salary Budget $14,500/mo.    $13,300/Actual _____
Approved Filled Positions _____ 5 _____

   Positions Added YTD _____ 1 _____
   Terminations     YTD _____ 1 _____

Over/Under Budget     $1200/mo   under
Over/Under Positions     --- _____

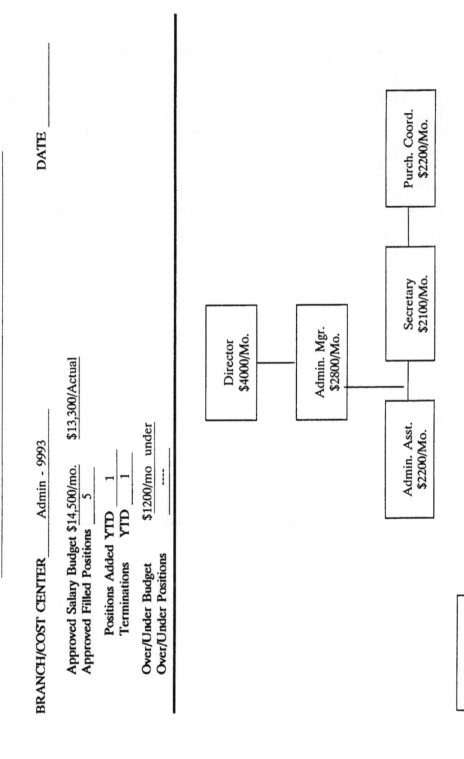

## MONTHLY STAFF LEVEL REPORT

Department _____     Month of _____     Year _____

| Department | Staff Level | | | Total Staff Level* Prior Month | Total Staff Level* Current Month | Total Staff Level* (last year) Current Month | Current Budgeted Levels | Variance (Current Month Budget Minus Current Month Actual) |
|---|---|---|---|---|---|---|---|---|
| | Exempt | Nonexempt | Vacancies | | | | | |
| Administration | 2 | 3 | — | 5 | 5 | 4 | 13.3 | +1200 |
| Marketing | 4 | 5 | — | 9 | 9 | 7 | 30.0 | +4000 |
| Production | 3 | 90 | 2 | 93 | 94 | 92 | 150.0 | +30.0 |
| Data Processing | 2 | 4 | — | 6 | 6 | 5 | 90.0 | +15.0 |
| Totals | 11 | 102 | 2 | 118 | 118 | 117 | 283.3 | +50.0 |

*Including Vacancies

## MONTHLY PAYROLL TREND
## XYZ COMPANY

| | 12/31/95 Head Count | | | | 03/31/96 Head Count | | | | 04/30/96 Head Count | | | |
|---|---|---|---|---|---|---|---|---|---|---|---|---|
| | Overhead | Capitalized | Sales | Total | Overhead | Capitalized | Sales | Total | Overhead | Capitalized | Sales | Total |
| New York | 120 | 83 | 60 | 363 | 136 | 75 | 64 | 275 | 143 | 76 | 65 | 284 |
| Mid-Atlantic Division | | | | | | | | | | | | |
| Maryland | 14 | 38 | 48 | 100 | 14 | 43 | 46 | 103 | 13 | 40 | 50 | 103 |
| Virginia | 57 | 56 | 56 | 169 | 56 | 54 | 57 | 167 | 56 | 54 | 56 | 166 |
| Total Mid-Atlantic Division | 71 | 94 | 104 | 269 | 70 | 97 | 103 | 270 | 69 | 94 | 106 | 269 |
| California Division | | | | | | | | | | | | |
| Northern California | 19 | 16 | 19 | 54 | 17 | 16 | 18 | 51 | 17 | 15 | 18 | 50 |
| Southern California | 30 | 22 | 26 | 78 | 30 | 23 | 25 | 78 | 33 | 22 | 26 | 81 |
| Total California Division | 49 | 38 | 45 | 132 | 47 | 39 | 43 | 129 | 50 | 37 | 44 | 131 |
| Arizona Division | | | | | | | | | | | | |
| Phoenix | 28 | 31 | 36 | 95 | 29 | 30 | 36 | 95 | 27 | 32 | 33 | 92 |
| Tucson | 12 | 8 | 20 | 40 | 13 | 8 | 14 | 35 | 13 | 8 | 14 | 35 |
| Total Arizona Division | 40 | 39 | 56 | 135 | 42 | 38 | 50 | 130 | 40 | 40 | 47 | 127 |
| Nevada | 4 | 4 | 3 | 11 | 26 | 9 | 12 | 47 | 25 | 9 | 12 | 46 |
| XYZ Corporate | 80 | 0 | 0 | 80 | 84 | 0 | 0 | 84 | 82 | 0 | 0 | 82 |
| American Mortgage, Inc. | 132 | 0 | 0 | 132 | 134 | 0 | 0 | 134 | 140 | 0 | 0 | 140 |
| Financial Companies, Inc. | 21 | 0 | 0 | 21 | 20 | 0 | 0 | 20 | 20 | 0 | 0 | 20 |
| Total All Divisions | 517 | 258 | 268 | 1043 | 559 | 258 | 272 | 1089 | 569 | 256 | 274 | 1099 |

| 12/31/95 | 03/31/96 | 04/30/96 |
|---|---|---|
| Active Division Difference YTD     20 | Active Divisions Difference YTD     46 | Active Divisions Difference YTD     56 |
| Inactive Divisions Difference YTD     (101) | | |
| All Divisions Difference YTD     (81) | All Divisions Difference YTD     46 | All Divisions Difference YTD     56 |
| (All) Difference Current Month     (7) | (All) Difference Current Month     1 | (All) Difference Current Month     10 |

# HOW TO FIGURE RECRUITING AND SELECTION COSTS

The cost to hire is probably one of the most difficult indices to develop because there are both tangible and intangible cost factors. There are two categories to be concerned with: those that can be measured (tangible), and those that cannot be measured (intangible). Intangible factors can create as significant an impact upon the efficiency and organization of the corporation as the measurable costs.

TANGIBLE COSTS INCLUDE:
- Advertising
- Employment agency fees
- Publications used in recruiting
- Medical examinations for selection
- Security, credit, and reference checks
- Personnel department overhead (office space, personnel staff compensation, and so on)
- Telephone calls
- Stationery and other office supplies
- Interviewing costs
- Relocation costs
- Data processing costs
- Related clerical costs
- Other recruitment costs
- Testing equipment and material costs

INTANGIBLE COSTS INCLUDE:
- Disorientation of the department
- Disruption of morale
- Increase in employee complaints
- Reduced management efficiency
- Reduced morale
- Generally lower productivity
- The stimulation of additional turnover
- Overhiring in order to maintain an average work force

Some items we might include as intangible on closer examination might be determined to be tangible costs. Depending on the industry, they might include more on-the-job accidents, higher scrap rates, additional overtime, larger human resource staff in order to handle replacement needs, and so on.

Following is a sample cost-to-hire computation:

# XYZ COMPANY
# SAMPLE COST-TO-HIRE COMPUTATION

*Search and Selection*

| | |
|---|---|
| Advertising | $ 1,884.00 |
| Employee handbooks | 248.60 |
| Medical examinations | 525.00 |
| Security, credit, reference checks | 1,350.00 |
| Personnel department overhead | 27,393.11 |
| Interviewing costs | 1,847.80 |
| Relocation | 40,000.00 |
| Telephone | 436.00 |
| Subtotal | $73,684.51 |

*Assignment and Placement*

| | |
|---|---|
| Personnel department overhead | $12,898.85 |
| Administrative expenses | 706.00 |
| Follow-up telephone calls | 172.00 |
| Stationery and other supplies (incl. data processing forms) | 1,263.00 |
| New employee orientation costs | 1,505.00 |
| Subtotal | $16,544.85 |

*Training*

| | |
|---|---|
| Training department overhead | $27,129.00 |
| Follow-up telephone calls | 272.00 |
| Makeup pay during training period | 20,400.00 |
| Subtotal | $47,801.00 |

*Retention*

| | |
|---|---|
| Publications (holiday/birthday cards, employee newsletters) | $ 2,830.00 |
| Professional expenses | 4,500.00 |
| Increased benefits | 14,856.00 |
| Personnel department overhead | 12,898.85 |
| Miscellaneous costs | 3,165.50 |
| Subtotal | $38,250.35 |

*Terminations*

| | |
|---|---|
| Outplacement fees | $ 4,000.00 |
| Follow-up telephone calls | 72.00 |
| Stationery and other supplies | 1,126.00 |
| Lost production | 23,828.00 |
| Subtotal | $29,026.00 |

**Summary Analysis—Cost to Hire**

It cost XYZ Company:

$73,684.51 to find and relocate people

16,544.85 to assign and place them

47,801.00 to train them

38,250.35 to retain them

29,026.00 to terminate them

# FREQUENTLY USED PERSONNEL CALCULATIONS, FORMULAS, AND TABLES

## *Figuring a Salaried Employee's Hourly Pay*

Figure 40 hours worked in a week × 52 weeks in a year = 2080 hours. 24 pay periods divided into 2080 hours = a factor of .011538.

Multiply the employee's semi-monthly salary by a factor of .011538 to get the hourly rate.

Example:  The semi-monthly salary is $2500.00.

$2500.00 × .011538 = $28.85 hourly rate.

## *Figuring Absenteeism*

$$\frac{\text{Number of person days lost through job absence during period}}{\text{Average number of employees} \times \text{number of work days}} \times 100$$

The rate can be computed based on the number of hours instead of days. In a study of 143 organizations the absentee rate ranged from 1.8% to 11.4%, with the average being 4%.

## *Figuring Turnover*

$$\frac{\text{Number of employee separations during the month}}{\text{Total number of employees at midmonth}} \times 100$$

# SAMPLE HUMAN RESOURCES CALCULATIONS AND REPORTS

Using the following formula, turnover is calculated quarterly on a calendar year basis. To derive a quarterly figure, the firm needs, first of all, to keep track of the number of employees and the number of terminations for each month during the quarter.

## Job Functions to Be Measured

In this sample calculation, the formula is kept simple and workable by limiting the number of individual departments/job functions for which turnover will be calculated. The number of employees and terminations will be reported for the following departments:

SINGLE-FAMILY RESIDENTIAL PRODUCTION:    Includes loan officers, both salaried and commissioned, loan processors, branch managers, underwriters, closers, and other functions.

SINGLE-FAMILY RESIDENTIAL SERVICING/LOAN ADMINISTRATION:    Includes employees who perform functions in cashiering, remitting, hazard insurance, property taxes, customer service, payoffs, assumptions, collections, foreclosures, and REOs. Excludes employees who perform functions in servicing acquisitions, loan setup, or personal insurance.

ALL OTHER DEPARTMENTS:    Includes marketing and administration departments. Both exempt and non-exempt positions are included in the employee count. Full-time employees are counted as one employee, part-time employees as one-half person. We included part-time employees because they often constitute a significant element of the real estate company's work force. Employees on leaves of absence, such as maternity leave, are counted.

## Measuring Terminations

Both voluntary and involuntary terminations are included in counting terminations. For example, voluntary terminations such as resignations and retirements are included. Involuntary terminations include workers who are fired but not laid off. Layoffs can constitute a significant percentage of involuntary terminations; however, they should not be included in the calculation because they may artificially inflate the amount of turnover in the firm for a given year. Unlike involuntary terminations which represent an expense to the company because the position must be refilled, layoffs represent a reduction in cost, since these positions are presumably not to be refilled. However, because of their overall impact on the industry, the firm may want to do a separate calculation on the percentage of layoffs. For purposes of this example, terminations are not broken down into voluntary/involuntary categories.

## Turnover Report

The following formula has been developed to be used in conjunction with a turnover report. The numbered examples below correspond to the numbers on the report.

EXAMPLE 1: TURNOVER BY QUARTER    Divide the number of terminations for the quarter by the average number of employees. Average number of employees is derived by adding the number of employees for the quarter and dividing by 3 to determine the percentage of turnover for that quarter.

**Example:** 24 terminations in Residential Production divided by 291 average employees for that department = 3.4% turnover in Residential Production for the first quarter.

**EXAMPLE 2: TURNOVER ANNUALIZED BY QUARTER**  Divide the percentage of turnover for the quarter (according to Example 1 above) by 3 (the number of months in the quarter) to determine the average per month percentage of turnover.

**Example:**  The total percentage of turnover for the second quarter for all departments was 5.2%. This figure divided by 3 equals 1.7%.

Multiply the average per month percent of turnover by 12 to derive the annualized percentage of turnover for the quarter.

**Example:** 1.7% × 12 = 20.8%

**EXAMPLE 3: YEAR-TO-DATE TURNOVER**  Add the average number of employees for each quarter and divide by the number of quarters to derive the year-to-date number of employees.

**Example:**  579 (first quarter) + 598 (second quarter) = 1,177 employees for the first two quarters. 1,177 divided by 2 equals 588.

Add the number of terminations for each quarter to derive the year-to-date number of terminations.

**Example:**  24 (first quarter) + 31 (second quarter) = 55 terminations for the first two quarters.

Divide the year-to-date number of terminations by the year-to-date average number of employees to derive the year-to-date percentage of turnover.

**Example:**  55 (terminations for the first two quarters) divided by 588 (year-to-date average number of employees) = 9.35% (year-to-date percentage of turnover).

Divide year-to-date percentage of turnover by six (number of months in first two quarters).

**Example:**  9.35% divided by 6 = 1.56% (annualized quarterly turnover).

Multiply annualized quarterly turnover by 12 to derive annualized yearly turnover.

**Example:**  1.56% × 12 = 18.7%

**EXAMPLE 4: ANNUALIZED YEAR-TO-DATE TURNOVER**  Divide the year-to-date percentage of turnover by the number of months included to derive the year-to-date average monthly turnover.

**Example:** 16.1% (year-to-date percentage of turnover for the first three quarters) divided by 9 (number of months for first three quarters) = 1.8% (year-to-date average monthly turnover).

Multiply the year-to-date average monthly turnover by 12 to derive the annualized year-to- date percentage of turnover.

**Example:** 1.8% (year-to-date average monthly turnover) by 12 = 21.6% (annualized year-to-date percentage of turnover).

EXAMPLE 5: YEAR-END TURNOVER    Divide the total average number of employees for each quarter by 4 (number of quarters in the year) to derive the average number of employees for the year.

**Example:** 2,373 (total average number of employees for 4 quarters) divided by 4 = 593 (average number of employees for year).

Divide the total number of terminations for the year by the average number of employees for the year to derive the percentage of year-end turnover.

**Example:** 114 (total number of terminations for the year) divided by 593 (average number of employees for the year) = 19.2% (percentage of turnover for the year).

Note

The Department of Labor table that follows will save you time in computing hours worked and overtime.

## COEFFICIENT TABLE FOR COMPUTING EXTRA HALF-TIME FOR OVERTIME

This table may be used for computing overtime on piecework, bonuses, commissions or fixed salaries for varying hours. Refer to Part 778 of Title 29 of the CFR for guidance regarding when the coefficient method is applicable.

This form has been prepared for use by employers who may find the coefficient table to be a time saver when computing the extra half time for hours worked over 40 in a workweek.

| Hours | Even | 1/4 | 1/2 | 3/4 | 1/10 | 2/10 | 3/10 | 4/10 | 6/10 | 7/10 | 8/10 | 9/10 |
|---|---|---|---|---|---|---|---|---|---|---|---|---|
| **40** | | 0.003 | 0.006 | 0.009 | 0.0012 | 0.0025 | 0.0037 | 0.0049 | 0.0074 | 0.0086 | 0.0098 | 0.0110 |
| 41 | 0.012 | .015 | .018 | .021 | .0134 | .0146 | .0157 | .0169 | .0192 | .0204 | .0215 | .0227 |
| 42 | .024 | .027 | .029 | .032 | .0249 | .0261 | .0272 | .0283 | .0305 | .0316 | .0327 | .0338 |
| 43 | .035 | .038 | .040 | .043 | .0360 | .0370 | .0381 | .0392 | .0413 | .0423 | .0434 | .0444 |
| 44 | .045 | .048 | .051 | .053 | .0465 | .0475 | .0485 | .0495 | .0516 | .0526 | .0536 | .0546 |
| 45 | .056 | .058 | .060 | .063 | .0565 | .0575 | .0585 | .0595 | .0614 | .0624 | .0633 | .0643 |
| 46 | .065 | .068 | .070 | .072 | .0662 | .0671 | .0680 | .0690 | .0708 | .0717 | .0726 | .0736 |
| 47 | .074 | .077 | .079 | .081 | .0754 | .0763 | .0772 | .0781 | .0798 | .0807 | .0816 | .0825 |
| 48 | .083 | .085 | .088 | .090 | .0842 | .0851 | .0859 | .0868 | .0885 | .0893 | .0902 | .0910 |
| 49 | .092 | .094 | .096 | .098 | .0927 | .0935 | .0943 | .0951 | .0968 | .0976 | .0984 | .0992 |
| 50 | .100 | .102 | .104 | .106 | .1008 | .1016 | .1024 | .1032 | .1047 | .1055 | .1063 | .1071 |
| 51 | .108 | .110 | .112 | .114 | .1086 | .1094 | .1101 | .1109 | .1124 | .1132 | .1139 | .1146 |
| 52 | .115 | .117 | .119 | .121 | .1161 | .1169 | .1176 | .1183 | .1198 | .1205 | .1212 | .1219 |
| 53 | .123 | .124 | .126 | .128 | .1234 | .1241 | .1248 | .1255 | .1269 | .1276 | .1283 | .1289 |
| 54 | .130 | .131 | .133 | .135 | .1303 | .1310 | .1317 | .1324 | .1337 | .1344 | .1350 | .1357 |
| 55 | .136 | .138 | .140 | .141 | .1370 | .1377 | .1383 | .1390 | .1403 | .1409 | .1416 | .1422 |
| 56 | .143 | .144 | .146 | .148 | .1435 | .1441 | .1448 | .1454 | .1466 | .1473 | .1479 | .1485 |
| 57 | .149 | .151 | .152 | .154 | .1497 | .1503 | .1510 | .1516 | .1528 | .1534 | .1540 | .1546 |
| 58 | .155 | .157 | .158 | .160 | .1558 | .1564 | .1569 | .1575 | .1587 | .1593 | .1599 | .1604 |
| 59 | .161 | .162 | .164 | .165 | .1616 | .1622 | .1627 | .1633 | .1644 | .1650 | .1656 | .1661 |
| 60 | .167 | .168 | .169 | .171 | .1672 | .1678 | .1683 | .1689 | .1700 | .1705 | .1711 | .1716 |
| 61 | .172 | .173 | .175 | .176 | .1727 | .1732 | .1737 | .1743 | .1753 | .1759 | .1764 | .1769 |
| 62 | .177 | .179 | .180 | .181 | .1779 | .1785 | .1790 | .1795 | .1805 | .1810 | .1815 | .1820 |
| 63 | .183 | .184 | .185 | .186 | .1830 | .1835 | .1840 | .1845 | .1855 | .1860 | .1865 | .1870 |
| 64 | .188 | .189 | .190 | .191 | .1880 | .1885 | .1890 | .1894 | .1904 | .1909 | .1914 | .1918 |
| 65 | .192 | .193 | .195 | .196 | .1928 | .1933 | .1937 | .1942 | .1951 | .1956 | .1960 | .1965 |
| 66 | .197 | .198 | .199 | .200 | .1974 | .1979 | .1983 | .1988 | .1997 | .2001 | .2006 | .2010 |
| 67 | .201 | .203 | .204 | .205 | .2019 | .2024 | .2028 | .2033 | .2041 | .2046 | .2050 | .2054 |
| 68 | .206 | .207 | .208 | .209 | .2063 | .2067 | .2072 | .2076 | .2085 | .2089 | .2093 | .2097 |
| 69 | .210 | .211 | .212 | .213 | .2106 | .2110 | .2114 | .2118 | .2126 | .2131 | .2135 | .2139 |
| 70 | .214 | .215 | .216 | .217 | .2147 | .2151 | .2155 | .2159 | .2167 | .2171 | .2175 | .2179 |
| 71 | .218 | .219 | .220 | .221 | .2187 | .2191 | .2195 | .2199 | .2207 | .2211 | .2214 | .2218 |
| 72 | .222 | .223 | .224 | .225 | .2226 | .2230 | .2234 | .2238 | .2245 | .2249 | .2253 | .2257 |
| 73 | .226 | .227 | .228 | .229 | .2264 | .2268 | .2271 | .2275 | .2283 | .2286 | .2290 | .2294 |
| 74 | .230 | .231 | .232 | .232 | .2301 | .2305 | .2308 | .2312 | .2319 | .2323 | .2326 | .2330 |
| 75 | .233 | .234 | .235 | .236 | .2337 | .2340 | .2344 | .2347 | .2354 | .2358 | .2361 | .2365 |
| 76 | .237 | .238 | .239 | .239 | .2372 | .2375 | .2379 | .2382 | .2389 | .2392 | .2396 | .2399 |
| 77 | .240 | .241 | .242 | .243 | .2406 | .2409 | .2413 | .2416 | .2423 | .2426 | .2429 | .2433 |
| 78 | .244 | .244 | .245 | .246 | .2439 | .2442 | .2446 | .2449 | .2455 | .2459 | .2462 | .2465 |
| 79 | .247 | .248 | .249 | .249 | .2472 | .2475 | .2478 | .2481 | .2487 | .2491 | .2494 | .2497 |
| 80 | .250 | .251 | .252 | .252 | .2503 | .2506 | .2509 | .2512 | .2519 | .2522 | .2525 | .2528 |
| 81 | .253 | .254 | .255 | .255 | .2534 | .2537 | .2540 | .2543 | .2549 | .2552 | .2555 | .2558 |
| 82 | .256 | .257 | .258 | .258 | .2564 | .2567 | .2570 | .2573 | .2579 | .2582 | .2585 | .2587 |
| 83 | .259 | .260 | .261 | .261 | .2593 | .2596 | .2599 | .2602 | .2608 | .2611 | .2613 | .2616 |
| 84 | .262 | .263 | .263 | .264 | .2622 | .2625 | .2628 | .2630 | .2636 | .2639 | .2642 | .2644 |
| 85 | .265 | .265 | .266 | .267 | .2650 | .2653 | .2655 | .2658 | .2664 | .2666 | .2669 | .2672 |

**TO CONVERT INTO WEEKLY EQUIVALENT:** Multiply SEMIMONTHLY salary by 0.4615; MONTHLY salary by 0.2308; ANNUAL salary by 0.01923.

**TO CONVERT INTO STRAIGHT-TIME HOURLY EQUIVALENT FOR 40 HOURS:** Multiply WEEKLY salary by 0.025; SEMIMONTHLY by 0.01154; MONTHLY salary by 0.00577; ANNUAL by 0.00048.

**TO CONVERT INTO TIME AND ONE-HALF HOURLY RATE BASED ON 40 HOUR WEEK:** Multiply WEEKLY salary by 0.0375; SEMIMONTHLY by 0.0173; MONTHLY salary by 0.00866; ANNUAL by 0.000721.

**CAUTION:** Be sure straight-time earnings are not below legal minimum.

**INSTRUCTIONS**

**General.** In determining the extra half-time that is due for overtime pay after 40 hours, the method of calculation commonly used is to divide the straight-time earnings by the total number of hours worked and multiply the result by the number of overtime hours divided by two. For instance, the

Computation for 48 hours would be $\dfrac{\text{Earnings}}{48} \times \dfrac{8}{2}$; for 50 hours, $\dfrac{\text{Earnings}}{50} \times \dfrac{10}{2}$; for 47 ¾ hours,

$\dfrac{\text{Earnings}}{47\,¾} \times \dfrac{7\,¾}{2}$. The table on the reverse side contains the decimal equivalents of the fraction,

$\dfrac{\text{O.T. Hours}}{\text{Total Hr. X 2.}}$

For example, the decimal for 48 hours is $\dfrac{8}{48 X2} = \dfrac{1}{12} = .083$; for 50 hours it is $\dfrac{10}{50 X2} = \dfrac{1}{10} = .1$;

and for 47 ¾ hours $\dfrac{7\,¾}{47\,¾\,X\,2} = \dfrac{7.75}{95.5} = .081$.

**How to use:** (a) Multiply the straight-time earnings for an overtime week by the applicable decimal and the result will be the extra half-time due. Thus, by using the decimals in the table (on the reverse side) the computations performed are, in effect, exactly the same as if the equivalent fractions were used, with the advantage of having eliminated the long division necessitated by the fractions. For example:

(1). A pieceworker earns varying wages each week. In a 43 9/10 hour week he earned $153.65 straight-time. The coefficient for 43 9/10 hours is .0444. .0444 X $153.65 = $6.82, additional half-time due. $153.65 + $6.82 = $160.47, the pieceworker's total pay for the week.

(2). Jones is paid a weekly salary of $180.25. He worked 51½ hours. The coefficient for 51½ hours is .112. .112 X $180.25 = $20.19. $180.25 + $20.19 = $200.44, Jones total pay for the week.

(b) The decimal table can also be used effectively when back wages are due because of additions to wages (such as a weekly bonus) that were not included in the regular rate in computing overtime. For example:

(1). An employee worked 48 hours and received a production bonus of $9.60 which was not included in the regular rate. Thus, $9.60 X .083 = $0.80, the additional half-time due on the bonus.

(2). Jones in the same week (example (a), (2) above) received a production bonus of $25.00. .112 X $25.00 = $2.80, the additional half-time due on the bonus. $180.25 + $20.19 + $25.00 + $2.80 = $228.24, Jones' total earnings. A further short-cut (combining (a), (2), and (b), (2)) would be: $180.25 + $25.00 = $205.25 X .112 = $22.99 + $205.25 = $228.24, Jones' total earnings.

(c) **Short-cuts For Computing Back Wages.** When both the overtime hours and the earnings vary, individual weekly computations must be made. However, if an employee is paid at a constant hourly rate, time can be saved by adding the unpaid overtime hours during the period and multiplying the total by one-half the hourly rate. When the weekly hours vary and the straight-time earnings are constant, add the decimals for the overtime weeks and multiply the total by the earnings for 1 week. When the weekly hours are constant but the earnings vary, add the earnings for the overtime weeks and multiply the total by the decimal for 1 week. For example:

| VARYING HOURS—CONSTANT EARNINGS | | | CONSTANT HOURS—VARYING EARNINGS | |
|---|---|---|---|---|
| Hours | Decimal | Earnings | Hours | Earnings |
| 42 | 0.024 | $180.25 | 47 | $164.50 |
| 43 | .035 | 180.25 | 47 | 159.80 |
| 46 | .065 | 180.25 | 47 | 162.15 |
| | .124 x $180.25 = $22.35 | | | $486.45 x .074 = $36.00 |

**WAGE AND SALARY CONVERSION TABLE**

| Hour | Week | Month | Year | Hour | Week | Month | Year | Hour | Week | Month | Year |
|---|---|---|---|---|---|---|---|---|---|---|---|
| 3.35 | 134.00 | 580.67 | 6968.00 | 4.35 | 174.00 | 754.00 | 9048.00 | 7.067 | 282.69 | 1225.00 | 14700.00 |
| 3.365 | 134.62 | 583.33 | 7000.00 | 4.40 | 176.00 | 762.67 | 9152.00 | 7.212 | 288.46 | 1250.00 | 15000.00 |
| 3.40 | 136.00 | 589.33 | 7072.00 | 4.45 | 178.00 | 771.33 | 9256.00 | 7.50 | 300.00 | 1300.00 | 15600.00 |
| 3.45 | 138.00 | 598.00 | 7176.00 | 4.50 | 180.00 | 780.00 | 9360.00 | 7.692 | 307.69 | 1333.33 | 16000.00 |
| 3.50 | 140.00 | 606.67 | 7280.00 | 4.55 | 182.00 | 788.67 | 9464.00 | 8.077 | 323.08 | 1400.00 | 16800.00 |
| 3.55 | 142.00 | 615.33 | 7384.00 | 4.60 | 184.00 | 797.33 | 9568.00 | 8.173 | 326.92 | 1416.67 | 17000.00 |
| 3.60 | 144.00 | 624.00 | 7488.00 | 4.65 | 186.00 | 806.00 | 9672.00 | 8.51 | 340.38 | 1475.00 | 17700.00 |
| 3.65 | 146.00 | 632.67 | 7592.00 | 4.70 | 188.00 | 814.67 | 9776.00 | 8.654 | 346.15 | 1500.00 | 18000.00 |
| 3.70 | 148.00 | 641.33 | 7696.00 | 4.75 | 190.00 | 823.33 | 9880.00 | 8.75 | 350.00 | 1516.67 | 18200.00 |
| 3.75 | 150.00 | 650.00 | 7800.00 | 4.80 | 192.00 | 832.00 | 9984.00 | 8.894 | 355.77 | 1541.67 | 18500.00 |
| 3.80 | 152.00 | 658.67 | 7904.00 | 4.808 | 192.31 | 833.33 | 10000.00 | 9.134 | 365.38 | 1583.33 | 19000.00 |
| 3.85 | 154.00 | 667.33 | 8008.00 | 4.85 | 194.00 | 840.67 | 10088.00 | 9.615 | 384.62 | 1666.67 | 20000.00 |
| 3.90 | 156.00 | 676.00 | 8112.00 | 4.90 | 196.00 | 849.33 | 10192.00 | 10.096 | 403.84 | 1750.00 | 21000.00 |
| 3.95 | 158.00 | 684.67 | 8216.00 | 4.95 | 198.00 | 858.00 | 10296.00 | 10.577 | 423.08 | 1833.33 | 22000.00 |
| 4.00 | 160.00 | 693.33 | 8320.00 | 5.00 | 200.00 | 866.67 | 10400.00 | 11.058 | 442.31 | 1916.67 | 23000.00 |
| 4.05 | 162.00 | 702.00 | 8424.00 | 5.288 | 211.54 | 916.67 | 11000.00 | 11.539 | 461.54 | 2000.00 | 24000.00 |
| 4.10 | 164.00 | 710.67 | 8528.00 | 5.625 | 225.00 | 975.00 | 11700.00 | 12.02 | 480.77 | 2083.33 | 25000.00 |
| 4.15 | 166.00 | 719.33 | 8632.00 | 6.058 | 242.31 | 1050.00 | 12600.00 | 12.50 | 500.00 | 2166.67 | 26000.00 |
| 4.20 | 168.00 | 728.00 | 8736.00 | 6.202 | 248.08 | 1075.00 | 12900.00 | 12.98 | 519.23 | 2250.00 | 27000.00 |
| 4.25 | 170.00 | 736.67 | 8840.00 | 6.25 | 250.00 | 1083.33 | 13000.00 | 13.46 | 538.46 | 2333.33 | 28000.00 |
| 4.30 | 172.00 | 745.33 | 8944.00 | 6.49 | 259.62 | 1125.00 | 13500.00 | 13.94 | 557.69 | 2416.67 | 29000.00 |
| 4.327 | 173.08 | 750.00 | 9000.00 | 6.731 | 269.23 | 1166.67 | 14000.00 | 14.42 | 576.92 | 2500.00 | 30000.00 |

Note

This table is handy when you're quickly trying to figure for example, the hourly rate for a person making $1,750 per month. The hourly rate is $10.096.

# 3

# REGULATORY COMPLIANCE

- Key Federal Statutes Affecting Employment, Termination, EEO, Compensation, and Benefits
- Fair Labor Standards Act (FLSA)
- Federal Guidelines on Affirmative Action
- Drug-Free Workplace Act of 1988
- Employee Polygraph Protection Act
- What to Do When a Wage-Hour Investigator Calls to Announce a Visit
- What You Need to Know About the Consolidated Omnibus Budget Reconciliation Act (COBRA)
- Employers Who Have Medical Plans Must Provide Notice of COBRA Amendments
- Posters Required by Federal Statute
- Complying with the Immigration Reform and Control Act of 1986
- The Objective of Workers' Compensation
- Unemployment Compensation
- Personal Privacy and Employee Rights
- ADA Compliance Checklist and Sample Accommodation Letter
- Family and Medical Leave Act and Certification Form

# REGULATORY COMPLIANCE

Today every organization has to be concerned with federal and state regulatory compliance in the area of personnel administration and human resource management. Since the 1980s the federal administrations have been strongly pro-business, but there have also been more new laws affecting business than at any other time in our history.

All this legislation regulates how we do business, how we and our employees are taxed, how we manage employees, what benefits we must provide, and how long we must provide them. Federal legislation is sometimes difficult to find out about and to understand. Many small business owners don't even know exactly what laws pertain to them, or where to go to get valid information.

The list that follows provides an easy-to-read non-"legalese" list of key federal regulations that pertain to the hiring, managing, and termination of employees. It is not a complete list because nearly every month new legislation is passed that impacts how we do business.

Complying with federal regulations is not easy. Furthermore, it can be expensive and time-consuming. Most business people need help at one time or another from attorneys or consultants who have background and experience in human resource management.

## KEY FEDERAL STATUTES AFFECTING EMPLOYMENT, TERMINATION, EEO, COMPENSATION, AND BENEFITS

Following is a brief overview of key regulations that relate to the human resource management function.

### Title VII of the Civil Rights Act of 1964, Including Equal Employment Opportunity Act of 1972

Prohibits job discrimination based on race, color, religion, sex, national origin, age, and handicap pertaining to hiring, promotion, demotion, transfer, layoff, termination, compensation and benefits, and selection for training for those individuals in protected classes. Protected classes are defined as individuals over age 40, females, Black, Hispanic (Latin American, Mexican, Puerto Rican), Asian, Pacific Islander, Oriental, American Indian, Native American, and Alaskan Native.

## 1980 Sexual Harassment Guidelines Were Added to Title VII of the Civil Rights Act

Prohibits harassment and provides that an employer is responsible for the acts of its agents and supervisory employees with respect to sexual harassment.

## Executive Orders 11246, 11375, 11141, and 12067; Title 41 of Code of Federal Registry; Section 503 of the Rehabilitation Act of 1973

Pertains to federal government employees, federal contractors and subcontractors. Provides equal opportunity to all qualified persons; prohibits discrimination based on race, creed, color, national origin, handicap, sex and age; and other equal employment opportunity guidelines.

## Age Discrimination in Employment Act of 1967, Amended in 1978 and 1986 (ADEA)

Prohibits job discrimination based on age for individuals over age 40, regarding hiring, promotion, demotion, transfer, layoff, termination, compensation, and benefits, and selection for training. Disallows mandatory retirement.

## Section 402 of the Vietnam Era Veterans Readjustment Assistance Act of 1974

Section 402 relates to the Vietnam veteran's equal employment opportunity. It requires affirmative action in hiring qualified Vietnam Era vets for government contractors with contracts of $10,000 or more.

## Immigration Reform and Control Act of 1986

Prohibits hiring of individuals who are not legal residents of the U.S. or who do not have legal certification to be employed in the U.S. Requires proof of citizenship.

## Freedom of Information and Privacy Act of 1974

Applies to most federal government agencies as well as private businesses and state and local governments which contract with federal agencies. Provides certain safeguards for an individual against an invasion of privacy. Pertains to required record keeping, and access to and disclosure of records.

## Fair Labor Standards Act of 1938, Amended in 1966 (FLSA)

Wage and hour law. Establishes minimum wage, maximum hours, overtime pay, equal pay, and child labor standards, unless an exemption applies (for example, for executives, administrative staff, salespersons, and others).

## Equal Pay Act of 1963 (Amendment to Fair Labor Standards Act)

Provides for equal pay for females and males for work of an equal skill, effort, and responsibility, and performed under similar working conditions (excludes differences based upon longevity, merit, production, or any basis other than sex).

## Rehabilitation Act of 1973

Designed to promote the employment of people with handicaps by banning discrimination.

## Pregnancy Discrimination Act of 1978

Establishes the eligibility for pregnancy-related benefits, including health insurance, disability income plans, and leaves of absence, on equal terms with other disabilities.

## Employee Retirement Income Security Act of 1974 (ERISA)

Provides standards for employers' funding and vesting of employee benefits and pension plans.

## Health Maintenance Organization Act of 1973 (HMO)

Provides for health maintenance organizations (HMOs) in the U.S. There are now 120 qualified HMOs in the U.S.

## HMO Act Amendments

In 1988, the HMO Act had its first significant amendments affecting employer-HMO relationships since initial passage. These amendments affect only federally qualified HMOs. The amendments include: nondiscriminatory employer contributions, a new rate setting method, disclosure of calculations, a self-referral option, and repeal of dual choice in 1995.

## Omnibus Budget Reconciliation Act of 1986

Pertains to pension participation and taxation.

## Consolidated Omnibus Budget Reconciliation Act of 1986 (COBRA)

Covers continuation of health and dental insurance benefits to employees and their dependents at group rates upon the employees' termination from an employer, if employee pays premiums.

## Occupational Safety and Health Act of 1970 (OSHA)

Pertains to providing a safe and healthy workplace, and provides guidelines to follow and forms that must be completed when an accident occurs. In addition, under new Hazard Communication Standards, OSHA requires every workplace in the country to identify and list hazardous substances on the premises and train employees how to use them.

## Tax Reform Act of 1986

Revision of the U.S. tax law. Changes the way benefits are taxed and the levels at which workers and employers are taxed. The Act contains changes to compensation and benefit provisions of the Internal Revenue Code.

## Technical and Miscellaneous Revenue Act

Provides corrections and changes to the Tax Reform Act of 1986. Contains numerous changes to compensation and benefit provisions of the Internal Revenue Code. Reduced the penalty for violation of COBRA among other things. There are revisions in the area of healthcare, cafeteria plans, dependent care, and educational assistance.

## Worker Adjustment and Retraining Notification Act

Requires employers of 100 or more full-time workers to give 60 days' advance notice of closings or major layoffs. Became effective February 4, 1989. Impacts employers who are closing a facility or an operating unit with 50 or more workers, or who will lay off from 50 to 499 employees.

## Polygraph Protection Act

In 1988, Congress passed the Employee Polygraph Protection Act which prohibits most private employers from using lie detector examinations either for pre-employment screening or for screening during the course of a worker's employment.

## The Americans with Disabilities Act of 1990

The legislation prohibits employment discrimination of the disabled by businesses with fifteen or more employees (although the limit is actually twenty-five employees for two years). The Bill guarantees 43 million disabled Americans, including AIDS victims, rights to employment, transportation, and the use of restaurants and other businesses.

## Drug-Free Workplace Act of 1988

Relates to federal contractors with contracts of $25,000 or more, mandating they provide a drug-free workplace. Contractor must post notices and establish an awareness program.

## Resource Conservation and Recovery Act (RCRA)

Provides regulations and guidelines for all businesses in the U.S. regarding the handling of hazardous waste. Oversight of this Act is conducted by the Environmental Protection Agency (EPA). The EPA now requires organizations generating even small quantities of hazardous waste to train all workers to be thoroughly familiar with waste handling and emergency procedures.

## Trade and Competitiveness Act of 1988

Provides programs to companies and their workers to help industries hurt by foreign competition to retrain their workers through the Job Training Partnership Act.

## Family and Medical Leave Act of 1993

The Family and Medical Leave Act of 1993 (FMLA) provides up to 12 weeks of leave for the care of a newborn or newly adopted child, or for personal or family illness, with the guarantee of their regular or an equivalent job upon return to work. To be eligible, employees must be employed for at least 12 months, and have provided 1,250 hours of service during the 12 months before the leave is requested. An employee must first use any accumulated sick leave and vacation time when taking FMLA. The balance of the time after the employee uses all sick leave and vacation time will be unpaid. The total amount of this leave can be only 12 weeks. A FMLA Leave of Absence Form must be completed and approved. The Company should pay their portion of the employee's medical benefits while an employee is on an approved FMLA.

## Small Business Job Protection Act of 1996

The Small Business Job Protection Act (SBJPA) became law on August 20, 1996. This law increased the minimum wage to $4.75 per hour October 1, 1996 and to $5.15 per hour September 1, 1997. The Act also contains a number of provisions that affect the administration and design of benefit plans. Major changes:

- Allow tax-exempt non governmental employers to offer 401(k) plans.
- Reinstate the tax exclusion for employer-provided educational assistance.
- Make available a $5,000 tax credit for qualified adoption expenses, or a $5,000 income exclusion for employer-reimbursed adoption expenses.
- Modify the rules for determining whether a worker is an employee or independent contractor for employment tax purposes.

## Health Insurance Portability and Accountability Act of 1996

The changes made by the Health Insurance Portability and Accountability Act (HIPAA) are generally effective for plan years beginning after June 30, 1997. The new law applies equally to insured and self-insured employer group health plans, as well as to HMOs offered by employers. State and local government plans may elect to have certain provisions of the Act not apply to them.

The following provisions of the Act have the greatest impact on employers:

- Restrictions on basing eligibility or premiums on health-related factors.
- Restrictions on the duration of preexisting condition exclusions.
- Requirement that employers and insurance companies provide certification of coverage periods.
- Guaranteed availability and renewability of health coverage.
- Expansion of COBRA health care continuation coverage.
- Favorable tax treatment of long-term care insurance and accelerated death benefits.
- Phase out of the loan interest deduction for corporate-owned life insurance.

## The Personal Liability and Work Opportunity Act of 1996 (Welfare Reform)

This Act includes a number of changes that tighten the Earned Income Tax Credit. Employers who take a tax credit for hiring a person off welfare must comply with the tax provisions of this regulation. In addition, the Act requires a mandatory new hire reporting program effective October 1, 1997.

## The Newborns' and Mothers' Health Protection Act of 1996

This Act is effective January 1, 1998, and covers any employer that has a group health plan either insured or self-insured. The Act prohibits group health plans from restricting hospital stays for childbirth to less than a 48-hour minimum stay for a normal delivery and a 96-hour stay for a caesarean delivery. In addition, the plan may not require prior authorization to qualify for the 48- or 96-hour minimum stay.

## The Mental Health Parity Act of 1996

This Act is effective January 1, 1998, and covers employers with 50 or more employees. The new parity requirement applies to benefits furnished on or after September 30, 2001. The Act provides that group health plans that offer mental health coverage may not set annual or lifetime limits for mental health coverage that are more restrictive than those for medical and surgical coverage.

## State Laws

State laws cover virtually all of the above areas, plus:

**WORKERS' COMPENSATION ACTS** Provide workers' compensation benefits for job-related injuries, death, and disease, regardless of whether the employer or employee was at fault. Benefits provided through insurance paid for and provided by the employer. Employee gives up the right to sue the employer in turn for compensation through the employer-provided insurance.

**EMPLOYMENT SECURITY ACTS**    Provide for payment of unemployment compensation to individuals who have been separated from their jobs due to no fault of their own.

## Labor Relations Laws

*COMMON LAW AFFECTING EMPLOYMENT*
*Employment-at- Will*
*Wrongful Discharge*
*Constructive Discharge*

---

**Important**

---

If you have more questions about these laws or you are contacted by a federal agency regarding an investigation you should retain an attorney versed in the specific law under which you are being investigated.

# FAIR LABOR STANDARDS ACT (FLSA)

The Fair Labor Standards Act (FLSA) was originally enacted by Congress in 1938. Its basic intent was to ensure that the number of jobs paying a minimum wage made maximum use of the available labor force. The minimum wage on October 1, 1996 was $4.75 per hour; on September 1, 1997 it increases to $5.15 per hour. The Act sets forth legal standards concerning minimum wages, hours of work, overtime pay, equal pay, use of child labor, and record keeping that must be complied with by those employers covered by the Act. To create the needed incentive for employers to hire a maximum number of employees, Congress established an employer penalty for working employees more than the established 40 hour work week by adding the requirement that an overtime premium rate must be paid above the 40 hours worked in any week. We should note that there is overlapping jurisdiction between the federal and various state wage and hour laws. In order to comply with both laws an employer needs to comply with whichever law is most burdensome to it. For example, if the state minimum wage is $3.50 per hour and the federal minimum wage is $5.15 per hour, an employer covered by both laws must pay $5.15 per hour in order to comply with both laws. Likewise, if the state law requires payment of time and one-half after 8 hours in a day (which is the case in California), while the federal law requires time and one-half after 40 hours in a work week, the employer must pay time and one-half after 8 hours, assuming the employer was covered by both laws. Again, whichever law is the most burdensome to an employer is the law that must be adhered to. Check your State's overtime regulations.

The FLSA is administered and enforced by the Department of Labor, Wage and Hour Division of the Employment Standards Administration through its 10 regions. Each region has area offices in most metropolitan locations where claims are received, investigated, hearings conducted, and determinations made. Regional offices coordinate regulatory matters with the division concerning rules, regulations, and interpretations of the Act. Typically, it is the area office that conducts periodic audits of employer payroll records to determine compliance with the Act, and such audits can be either scheduled activities of a routine nature or in response to an industry or employer pattern of complaints by employees.

Complaints can be registered, and claims filed, by employees within two years from the date an event covered by the Act occurred. This statute of limitation can be extended to three years in cases where it can be demonstrated that the employer's action was a willful violation of the Act, meaning that the employer knew about the law but chose to ignore it for the purpose of imposing a detrimental effect on the employee (e.g., refusal to pay overtime wages due the employee). Where the employer is found to have unwittingly violated or otherwise not complied with the provisions of the Act, a hearing or investigative officer will normally only require that the employer pay what- ever is due the employee, and may additionally impose a small fine on the employer for the violation. However, wage claims that are lost by employers in court often carry the costs of back pay, liquidated damages (equal to the amount of back pay), and attorney fees.

## Who Is Covered Under FLSA?

The original Act was made to apply to private and nonprofit sector employers and their employees. However, amendments brought employees of hospitals, nursing homes, public schools, and local transit operations within the minimum wage and overtime provisions of the FLSA, and in 1985 the U.S. Supreme Court decision brought all public employees under coverage of the Act. While some of these various employees have special conditions in their application to the FLSA, it has now become easier to designate who is *not* covered than those who are. Those who are *not* covered by the FLSA are:

- Boards of Directors
- Legal Advisors
- Independent contractors
- Bona Fide Volunteers
- Elected Officials
- Official's Staff Members
- Political Appointees
- Prison Laborers

Every other employed person is covered by the Act as either exempt or nonexempt, meaning they are ineligible for overtime pay if classified as exempt or eligible if nonexempt. A third category is those employees who have special conditions associated with their employment wages and hours. Fundamentally then, every covered employee should fall into one of these three categories:

| EXEMPT EMPLOYEES | NONEXEMPT EMPLOYEES | SPECIAL CONDITION EMPLOYEES |
|---|---|---|
| • Executive | • Hourly | • Law Enforcement |
| • Administrative | • Piecework | • Fire Fighters |
| • Professional | | • School Personnel |
| • Outside Sales (Commissioned) | | • Hospital and Nursing Home Staff |
| • Seasonal Recreation Employees | | |

## Which Jobs Are Exempt or Nonexempt?

The easiest way to determine which jobs are either exempt or nonexempt is to first establish which jobs in your organization are exempt in accordance with *both* federal and state definitions. Why? Because there are going to be fewer exempt jobs in any organization compared to the number of nonexempt jobs. Such was the intent of Congress based on their original goal of enticing employers to hire as many workers as their payrolls could absorb. To achieve that end, the criteria for employees considered exempt from the overtime provisions had to be limited. That defined limitation came in the form of two independent tests, one or the other of which must be used by employers to determine whether or not a specific job is exempt or nonexempt.

These tests are referred to as the "long and short tests." The long test provides detail on the job's duties, responsibilities, authorities, obligations, and minimum *salary*. The long test also measures the employee's duties on a weekly basis; therefore the determination of exempt or nonexempt status can likewise be seen as a weekly event. Conversely, the short test requires fewer conditions associated with the employee's duties and responsibilities, but requires a higher minimum salary for the employee to be considered exempt. Moreover, under the short test employees do not lose their exemption if they perform nonexempt work in some weeks as long as their work overall is exempt. The following excerpt from the exempt definitions contained in 29 C.F.R. Part 541 should help you make determinations of which of your jobs, and therefore employees, are exempt. All other employees will thereby be nonexempt unless they meet other exempt or special conditions, which may require more than cursory research on your part. In any case, you should bear in mind that it is the job contents and conditions that determine its exempt or nonexempt status, not the employee, the job title, or mere preferences of management.

## Executive Employees

An employee who meets *either* the "long test" or the "short test" as specified below is considered exempt.

LONG TEST FOR EXECUTIVE EMPLOYEES   An executive employee must meet *all* of the following requirements in order to he exempt from the FLSA minimum wage and overtime provisions:

1. *Duties:* Primarily management of the agency, department, or subdivision.
2. *Supervision:* Customarily and regularly directs two or more other employees.
3. *Authority:* Possesses the power to hire or fire employees, or whose suggestions are given substantial weight in such decisions, including promotions.
4. *Discretion:* Customarily and regularly exercises discretionary power.
5. *Work Responsibility:* Does not devote more than 20 percent of his or her hours in a workweek to the performance of activities not closely related to items (1) through (4).
6. *Compensation:* Is paid not less than $155 per week exclusive of board, lodging, or other facilities.

**SHORT TEST FOR EXECUTIVE EMPLOYEES** An executive must meet *all* of the following requirements to he exempt:

1. *Compensation:* Is paid not less than $250 per week exclusive of board, lodging, or other facilities.
2. *Duties:* Primarily management of the agency, department, or subdivision.
3. *Supervision:* Customarily and regularly directs 2 or more other employees.

**DEFINING AN EXECUTIVE EMPLOYEE** The regulations provide some guidance as to the application of the executive exemption test. For example, managerial and supervisory functions are described in the following manner:

Interviewing, selecting, and training of employees; setting and adjusting their rates of pay and hours of work; directing their work; maintaining their production or sales records for use in supervision or control; appraising their productivity and efficiency for the purpose of recommending promotions or other changes in their status; handling their complaints and grievances and disciplining them when necessary; planning the work; determining the techniques to be used; apportioning the work among the workers; determining the type of materials, supplies, machinery or tools to he used or merchandise to he bought, stocked, and sold; controlling the flow and distribution of materials or merchandise and supplies; providing for the safety of the men and the property.

The "primary duty" requirement for management is generally, though not always, a 50 percent test. In some cases, the employee can therefore spend less than 50 percent of his or her time on management and still qualify for the executive exemption.

The words "customarily and regularly" regarding the exercise of discretion signify a greater frequency than occasional, but less than constant.

## Administrative Employees

An employee who meets *either* the "long test" or the "short test" for administrators is exempt.

**LONG TEST FOR ADMINISTRATIVE EMPLOYEES** An administrative employee must meet *all* of the following requirements in order to be exempt from the FLSA minimum wage and overtime provisions:

1. *Duties:* Primarily consist of either—
   a. non-manual or office work directly related to management policies or general business operations; or
   b. performance of administrative functions in an educational establishment in work related to academic instruction or training.
2. *Discretion:* Customarily and regularly exercises discretion and independent judgment.
3. *Supervision:*
   a. regularly and directly assists a person employed in an executive or administrative capacity; or

b. performs under only general supervision work requiring special training, experience, or knowledge, or

c. executes special assignments and tasks under only general supervision.

4. *Work Responsibility:* Does not devote more than 20 percent of work time to activities not directly or closely related to performance of administrative work.

5. *Compensation:* Is paid not less than $155 per week exclusive of board, lodging, or other facilities.

**SHORT TEST FOR ADMINISTRATIVE EMPLOYEES**  An administrative employee must meet *all* of the following requirements to be exempt:

1. *Compensation:* Is paid at least $250 per week exclusive of board, lodging, or other facilities.

2. *Duties:* Primary performance of office or non-manual work directly related to management policies or general business operations, or the performance of functions in the administration of an educational establishment, or a department or subdivision thereof, in work directly related to the academic instruction or training.

3. *Responsibilities:* Primary duty *includes* work requiring the exercise of discretion and independent judgment.

**DEFINING AN ADMINISTRATIVE EMPLOYEE**  The regulations provide some guidance as to the application of the administrative exemption test. For example, the phrase "directly related to management policies or general business operations" can include: advising management, planning, negotiation, representing the organization, consulting, safety direction, wage rate analysis, and systems analysis in computers.

Similar to the executive exemption, the "primary duty" requirement is not necessarily a 50 percent test.

## Professional Employees

An employee who meets *either* the "long test" or the "short test" for professionals under the FLSA is exempt.

**LONG TEST FOR PROFESSIONAL EMPLOYEES**  A professional employee must meet *all* of the following requirements to be exempt from the FLSA minimum wage and overtime provisions:

1. *Duties:* Primarily work requiring—

a. advanced learning acquired by a prolonged course of specialized intellectual instruction as distinguished from general academic education, apprenticeships, or routine training; or

b. original or creative work depending primarily on invention, imagination, or talent; or

c. teaching, tutoring, instructing, or lecturing for a school system or educational institution.

2. *Discretion:* Work requiring the consistent exercise of discretion and judgment.

3. *Work Product:* Predominantly intellectual and varied in character and which cannot be standardized in relation to a given period of time.

4. *Work Responsibility:* Must devote not more than 20 percent of his or her hours to activities not essential, part of, or necessarily incident to the work.

5. *Compensation:* Is paid not less than $170 per week exclusive of board, lodging, or other facilities.

SHORT TEST FOR PROFESSIONAL EMPLOYEES    A professional employee must meet *all* of the following requirements to be exempt:

1. *Compensation:* Is paid not less than $250 per week exclusive of board, lodging, or other facilities.

2. *Duties:* Primarily consist of performing work requiring advanced learning or work as a teacher.

3. *Discretion:* Must include work that requires the consistent exercise of discretion and judgment or work requiring invention, imagination, or talent in a recognized field of artistic endeavor.

DEFINING A PROFESSIONAL EMPLOYEE    The regulations provide some guidance as to the application of the professional exemption test.

The "primary duty" requirement is, by reference, the same as for executives and administrators. Professional work is not purely mechanical or routine, since it involves discretion. "Predominantly intellectual" means that the job is varied and not routine mental, mechanical, manual, or physical work. In order for routine work to be exempt, it should be an essential part of and necessarily incident to the professional work.

## Other General Exemptions

There are numerous other general exemptions from the minimum wage and overtime provisions of the FLSA. Employers interested in exploring the prospect of whether or not specific positions in their employ are exempt under these definitions should consult with authoritative legal counsel based on the regulations noted.

- Amusement or recreational establishment employees
- Agricultural employees
- Retail and service establishment
- Certain retail or service establishment employees
- Certain domestic service workers, baby-sitters, and companions
- Outside sales representatives
- Fishing and offshore seafood processing
- Small newspapers and weeklies
- Seamen on foreign vessels

Partial exemptions from only the FLSA overtime provisions—not the minimum wage requirements—have been granted for other occupations, including:

- Employees of interstate motor carriers, railroads, and air carriers
- On-shore seafood processing
- Seamen
- Taxi drivers
- Certain employees of auto dealers
- Movie theater employees
- Certain forestry employees

# FEDERAL GUIDELINES ON AFFIRMATIVE ACTION

The following guidelines on Affirmative Action for federal contractors were established by Executive Order 11246.

**EXEMPTION:** Companies that do less than $10,000 in business with the federal government per year. Covered employers must:

- refrain from discriminating against any employee or job applicant because of race, color, religion, sex, or national origin;
- take affirmative action to ensure that applicants are employed and employees are treated during their employment without regard to race, color, religion, sex, or national origin (the obligation extends to working conditions and facilities such as restrooms, as well as hiring, firing, promotions, and compensations);
- state in all solicitations or advertisements that all qualified applicants will receive consideration without regard to race, color, religion, sex, or national origin;
- advise each labor union with which they deal of their commitments under the order;
- include the obligations under the order in every subcontract or purchase order, unless specifically exempted;
- comply with all provisions of the order and the rules and regulations issued; furnish all information and reports required; permit access to books, records and accounts for the purpose of investigation to ascertain compliance; and
- file regular compliance reports describing hiring and employment practices.

The mandatory starting point for affirmative action programs is analysis of areas in which the employer may be under utilizing "protected" persons. The employer must consider at least the following factors:

- minority population of the labor area surrounding the facility;
- size of the minority unemployment force in the labor area;
- percentage of minority workforce as compared with the total workforce in the immediate area;

- general availability of minorities having requisite skills in the immediate labor area;
- availability of minorities having requisite skills in an area in which the employer can reasonably recruit;
- availability of promotable minority employees within the employer's organization;
- anticipated expansion, contraction, and turnover in the labor force;
- existence of training institutions capable of training minorities in the requisite skills; and
- degree of training the employer is reasonably able to undertake to make all job classes available to minorities.

Sex-Biased Guidelines:   In addition to its affirmative action guidelines, the OFCCP issued a special set of guidelines on sex discrimination. These guidelines prohibit employers from:

- making any distinction based on sex in employment opportunities, wages, hours, and other conditions;
- advertising for workers in newspaper columns headed "male" and "female" unless sex is a bona fide occupational qualification for the job;
- relying on state protective laws to justify denying a female employee the right to any job that she is qualified to perform; and
- denying employment to women with young children or making a distinction between married and unmarried persons, unless the distinctions are applied to both sexes.

The guidelines also specify that covered employers take affirmative action to recruit women to apply for jobs from which they have been previously excluded.

# DRUG-FREE WORKPLACE ACT OF 1988

The Drug-Free Workplace Act presented here is a guideline for federal contracts. However, most companies today must consider setting up policies that relate to control of drugs on the job. Referring to the federal regulations will help you write and implement drug control policies for your company.

### SEC. 5151. SHORT TITLE.

This subtitle may be cited as the "Drug-Free Workplace Act of 1988."

(41 USC 701)

### SEC. 5152. DRUG-FREE WORKPLACE REQUIREMENTS FOR FEDERAL CONTRACTORS.

(a) Drug-Free Workplace Requirement.—

(1) Requirement for persons other than individuals.—No person, other than an individual, shall be considered a responsible source, under the meaning of such

term as defined in section 4(8) of the Office of Federal Procurement Policy Act (41 U.S.C. 403(8)), for the purposes of being awarded a contract for the procurement of any property or services of a value of $25,000 or more from any Federal agency unless such person has certified to the contracting agency that it will provide a drug-free workplace by—

(A) publishing a statement notifying employees that the unlawful manufacture, distribution, dispensation, possession, or use of a controlled substance is prohibited in the person's workplace and specifying the actions that will be taken against employees for violations of such prohibition;

(B) establishing a drug-free awareness program to inform employees about—

(i) the dangers of drug abuse in the workplace;

(ii) the person's policy of maintaining a drug free workplace;

(iii) any available drug counseling, rehabilitation, and employee assistance programs; and

(iv) the penalties that may be imposed upon employees for drug abuse violations;

(C) making it a requirement that each employee to be engaged in the performance of such contract be given a copy of the statement required by subparagraph (A);

(D) notifying the employee in the statement required by sub- paragraph (A), that as a condition of employment on such contract, the employee will—

(i) abide by the terms of the statement; and

(ii) notify the employer of any criminal drug statute conviction for a violation occurring in the workplace no later than 5 days after such conviction;

(E) notifying the contracting agency within 10 days after receiving notice under subparagraph (D)(ii) from an employee or otherwise receiving actual notice of such conviction;

(F) imposing a sanction on, or requiring the satisfactory participation in a drug abuse assistance or rehabilitation program by, any employee who is so convicted, as required by section 5154; and

(G) making a good faith effort to continue to maintain a drug- free workplace through implementation of subparagraphs (A), (B), (C), (D), (E), and (F).

(2) REQUIREMENT FOR INDIVIDUALS.—No Federal agency shall enter into a contract with an individual unless such contract includes a certification by the individual that the individual will not engage in the unlawful manufacture, distribution, dispensation, possession, or use of a controlled substance in the performance of the contract.

(b) SUSPENSION, TERMINATION, OR DEBARMENT OF THE CONTRACTOR—

(1) GROUNDS FOR SUSPENSION, TERMINATION, OR DEBARMENT.—Each contract awarded by a Federal agency shall be subject to suspension of payments under the contract or termination of the contract, or both, and the contractor thereunder or the individual who entered the contract with the Federal agency, as applicable, shall be

subject to suspension or debarment in accordance with the requirements of this section if the head of the agency determines that—

(A) the contractor or individual has made a false certification under subsection (a);

(B) the contractor violates such certification by failing to carry out the requirements of subparagraph (A), (B), (C), (D), (E), or (F)of subsection (a)(1); or

(C) such a number of employees of such contractor have been convicted of violations of criminal drug statutes for violations occurring in the workplace as to indicate that the contractor has failed to make a good faith effort to provide a drug-free work place as required by subsection (a).

(2) CONDUCT OF SUSPENSION, TERMINATION, AND DEBARMENT PROCEEDINGS.—(A) If a contracting officer determines, in writing, that cause for suspension of payments, termination, or suspension or debarment exists, an appropriate action shall be initiated by a contracting officer of the agency, to be conducted by the agency concerned in accordance with the Federal Acquisition Regulation and applicable agency procedures.

(B) The Federal Acquisition Regulation shall be revised to include rules for conducting suspension and debarment proceedings under this subsection, including rules providing notice, opportunity to respond in writing or in person, and such other procedures as may be necessary to provide a full and fair proceeding to a contractor or individual in such proceeding.

(3) EFFECT OF DEBARMENT.—Upon issuance of any final decision under this subsection requiring debarment of a contractor or individual, such contractor or individual shall be ineligible for award of any contract by any Federal agency, and for participation in any future procurement by any Federal agency, for a period specified in the decision, not to exceed 5 years.

## EMPLOYEE POLYGRAPH PROTECTION ACT

You are required by law to post a notice about the Employee Polygraph Protection Act on your premises where applicants and employees can see it. Following is a sample of the poster. You can order it from the U. S. Department of Labor, Employment Standards Administration, Wage and Hour Division, Washington, DC 20210.

# NOTICE
# EMPLOYEE POLYGRAPHY
# PROTECTION ACT

The employee Polygraph Protection Act prohibits most private employers from using lie detector tests either for pre-employment screening or during the course of employment.

## PROHIBITIONS

Employers are generally prohibited from requiring or requesting any employee or job applicant to take a lie detector test, and form discharging, discipline, or discriminating against an employee or prospective employee for refusing to take a test or for exercising other rights under the ACL.

## EXEMPTIONS*

Federal, State and local governments are not affected by the law. Also, the law does not apply to tests-given by the Federal Government to certain private individuals engaged in national security related activities.

The Act permits polygraph (a kind of lie detector) tests to be administered in the private sector, subject to restrictions, to certain prospective employees of security service firms (armored car, alarm, and guard), and of pharmaceutical manufacturers, distributors and dispensers.

The Act also permits polygraph testing, subject to restrictions, of certain employees of private firms who are reasonably suspected of involvement in a workplace incident (theft, embezzlement, etc.) that resulted in economic loss to the employer.

## EXAMINEE RIGHTS

Where polygraph tests are permitted, they are subject to numerous strict standards concerning the conduct and length of the test. Examinees have a number of specific rights, including the right to a written notice before testing, the right to refuse or discontinue a test, and the right not to have test results disclosed to unauthorized persons.

## ENFORCEMENT

The Secretary of Labor may bring court actions to restrain violations and assess civil penalties up to $10,000 against violators. Employers or job applicants may also bring their own court actions.

## ADDITIONAL INFORMATION

Additional information may be obtained, and complaints of violations may be filed, at local offices of the Wage and Hour Division, which are listed in the telephone directory under U.S. Government, Department of Labor, Employment Standards Administration.

**THE LAW REQUIRES EMPLOYERS TO DISPLAY THIS POSTER
WHERE EMPLOYEES AND JOB APPLICANTS CAN READILY SEE IT.**

*The law does not preempt any provision of any State or local law or any collective bargaining agreement which is more restrictive with respect to lie detector tests.

U.S. Department of Labor
Employment Standards Administration
Wage and Hour Division
Washington, DC 20210

# WHAT TO DO WHEN A WAGE-HOUR INVESTIGATOR CALLS TO ANNOUNCE A VISIT

It doesn't happen very often, and when it does it is usually because an ex-employee has filed a complaint with the Wage-Hour Division of the U.S. Department of Labor. The most frequent complaints are about a company's procedures for payment of overtime.

Most people in companies today understand that the Fair Labor Standards Act requires business to pay overtime to all hourly non-exempt employees at the rate of time-and-one-half for all hours worked in excess of 40 in a week. If you are not doing that you are in violation of the law. There is also a lot of misunderstanding about what constitutes an exempt or non-exempt position. The Fair Labor Standards Act thoroughly covers this issue. There are specific criteria for executive, administrative, professional and outside sales people that you should become familiar with.

When the investigator calls, it is normal procedure to give a few days' notice of the visit and at that time there is usually an indication of what the investigator wants to see. It is usually the time cards for a specific department and for a certain period of time.

It is common for a company to be in violation of the Fair Labor Standards Act at one time or another. The violation is usually unintentional, and occurs because the employer is unfamiliar with the duties or the working hours of a specific employee somewhere in the organization. Another common violation occurs when you don't know the actual hours being worked by all of the employees.

An employee could work a half hour overtime everyday and not record that time on the time card. Everything is fine until the employee gets upset about something, quits, and goes to the Labor Department to complain about not being paid the overtime.

Also, when an investigator from the Labor Department comes to your place of business to investigate a wage claim, he/she will ask to review your Immigration I-9 forms to see if you have a form on every employee and that it is completed correctly. Do not file I-9 forms in the personnel files. File them in a separate file. You can then hand that file to an investigator without providing the full personnel file. Fines can be significant for not having I-9's or not having them properly completed.

Most Wage and Hour Investigators are pleasant people who are just doing their job, but you should assume that they are there for investigative purposes and that normally they do not have your company's welfare foremost in their minds. Investigators are paid to find violations.

Treat the investigator with courtesy and honor all reasonable requests. Indicate you have nothing to hide and it is your desire to comply with the Act. Do not, however, volunteer any documents or information that is not specifically requested. It's not in your best interest to help the investigator support conclusions that may be detrimental to your business. The authority of the Wage and Hour Division is very broad however, and no useful purpose can be served by objecting to the investigator viewing or copying any data which is relevant to the payment of wages including overtime or the proper completion of Immigration I-9 forms. Once again, only provide data the investigator asks for, do not provide entire payroll computer printouts or any information that is not requested. The investigator has no right to remove data from your premises, but can copy the information at your site.

Find an empty room or office and put the investigator there to look at the requested information. Hopefully the investigator will find "no cause" for the complaint and in that event, may just call you and say no violation was found and therefore the investigation is closed. If there is a problem, however, the investigator may ask for a meeting to discuss the violation.

If there are violations, you should seek competent advice. Don't just accept a determination without fully considering all facts. Have your legal counsel review your rights. Without competent advice the company could incur a liability for unpaid wages.

Page 138 contains a sample letter to the Wage Hour Division of the Department of Labor regarding a claim. If you need to write such a letter, revise this one to fit your needs.

## WHAT YOU NEED TO KNOW ABOUT THE CONSOLIDATED OMNIBUS BUDGET RECONCILIATION ACT (COBRA)

COBRA significantly changed the way employers handle benefits when an employee terminates. Following is an overview of COBRA regulations with sample letters you should send employees.

The Consolidated Omnibus Budget Reconciliation Act of 1986 (COBRA) requires employers with twenty or more employees to give employees and dependents who are covered by an employer-sponsored healthcare plan the option to continue their health plan coverage at group rates for substantial periods of time after certain "qualifying events" that would otherwise result in an employee's or dependent's loss of coverage. An employee has a right to choose continuation coverage if he or she loses group health coverage because of a reduction of hours of employment or the termination of employment (for reasons other than gross misconduct).

Such continuation coverage is for an 18-month period. The spouse of an employee covered by a group health plan has the right to choose continuation coverage for three years, if the employee dies, if the employee's employment is terminated (for reasons other than gross misconduct) or the employee's hours of employment are reduced, if the spouse and the employee are divorced or legally separated, or if the employee becomes eligible for Medicare. Likewise, a dependent child of an employee covered by a group health plan has the right to continue coverage for a three-year period if the employee dies, if the employee's employment is terminated (for reasons other than gross misconduct) or the employee's hours of employment are reduced, if the parents are divorced or legally separated, if the employee becomes eligible for Medicare, or if the dependent ceases to be a "dependent child" under the terms of the group health plan.

The employee or dependent has sixty days from the date he or she would otherwise lose health plan coverage to exercise the continuation coverage option. If continuation coverage is selected, the employee or dependent must pay for the coverage (at group health plan rates). This law applies to group health plans for plan years beginning on or after July 1, 1986, except for plans maintained pursuant to collective bargaining agreements. In the case of collectively bargained plans, COBRA does not apply to plan years beginning before the later of (a) the date on which the last collective bargaining agreement relating to the plan terminates, or (b) January 1, 1987.

## SAMPLE LETTER TO REPRESENTATIVE OF WAGE AND HOUR DIVISION ON THE DEPARTMENT OF LABOR REGARDING CLAIM

Mr. Jonathan Wright                                          Date _____
Wage and Hour Division
Department of Labor
1800 Sherman Street
Denver, CO 80203

RE:     Claim No. 478265 Jennie Welsh

Dear Mr. Wright:

In response to your request for information on our hours of work, we provide the following work schedules:

> *Day Shift*
> 8:00 A.M. to 5:00 P.M.
> One hour paid for lunch
>
> *Night Shift*
> 5:00 P.M. to 2:00 A.M.
> One hour paid for dinner

We have investigated the claim by Mrs. Jennie Welsh. She feels that she should be paid for overtime because she reported to work 15 minutes early every day and took only one-half hour for lunch for a period of three months, commencing July 5 and ending October 7.

Our investigation shows that Mrs. Welsh did in fact work these hours. They were not her regularly scheduled hours, however, and she completed her time cards as having worked 8:00 A.M. to 5:00 P.M. each day with a one-hour lunch period.

Mrs. Welsh's supervisor substantiates her claim. It is not company policy to allow employees to change their work schedules. However, because her supervisor allowed the altered schedule, we feel an obligation to reimburse Mrs. Welsh for the overtime of three hours and forty-five minutes per week for the three-month period.

We have instituted an audit of our procedures and payroll records to ensure that other employees have not participated in similar practices. If you need further information or explanation of the claim, please give me a call at (303) 222-1111.

Sincerely,


Walter Reed
Director, Human Resources

COBRA does impose significant administrative and recordkeeping burdens on employers, because employers are required to notify employees and their spouses (if any) who are covered by healthcare plans that they will have the option to continue healthcare insurance coverage after a qualifying event occurs. COBRA also requires employers to notify each employee and his or her spouse as soon as they are covered by the employer- sponsored plan that the option to continue healthcare coverage will be available following a qualifying event. Employers also must notify their plan administrators that qualifying events have occurred within thirty days after such qualifying events occur. The employee or dependent is responsible for giving notice of a divorce, legal separation, or a dependent child's loss of coverage.

It is imperative that employers comply with the requirements of COBRA. Among other penalties, a covered employer who fails to provide a required healthcare continuation option will be denied a tax deduction for the expenses it incurs in maintaining all of its group health plans.

Also, employers with twenty or more employees must offer active employees and their spouses age 65 and over the same health insurance coverage that they offer younger workers. The employer plan must be the employee's or spouse's primary plan unless the employee or his or her spouse elects to be covered only by Medicare. Before the enactment of COBRA, this requirement did not apply to persons over age 70.

Following are several sample letters to employees which you can use to comply with COBRA regulations. (See pages 141–153.)

## EMPLOYERS WHO HAVE MEDICAL PLANS MUST PROVIDE NOTICE OF COBRA AMENDMENTS

Rules governing continuation of health care coverage, as initiated by the *Consolidated Omnibus Budget Reconciliation Act of 1986* (COBRA), have been amended. Employers must notify COBRA beneficiaries of some of the changes. The *Public Health Services Act* and ERISA also contain continuation coverage provisions that were similarly amended. This article refers to the continuation coverage laws collectively as COBRA.

Two recent laws amended COBRA: the *Small Business Job Protection Act* and the *Health Insurance Portability and Accountability Act* (HIPAA). The *Small Business Job Protection Act* clarified COBRA's multiple qualifying event rule regarding Medicare entitlement. Previously, it had appeared that if Medicare entitlement of a covered employee was a second qualifying event for a COBRA beneficiary, COBRA coverage would continue for another 36 months for any qualified beneficiary who was a spouse or dependent of the covered employee. The new law clarifies that the intention was to provide 36 months total coverage from the date of the initial qualifying event (i.e., termination of employment or reduction in hours) for the covered spouse and dependents—not an additional 36 months. This provision is effective retroactively for plan years beginning after December 31, 1989.

HIPAA amended several COBRA provisions, and the amendments become effective January 1, 1997, regardless of when the qualifying even occurred. The amendments

- Clarify that the 11-month extension of coverage for disabled qualified beneficiaries is not limited to former employees. The extension is available to any qualified beneficiary who is disabled.

- Change the law to allow the 11-month extension of coverage for qualified beneficiaries who are determined by the Social Security Administration to have been disabled on the date of the qualifying event (i.e., termination of employment or reduction in hours) or within the first 60 days of COBRA coverage. Currently, qualified beneficiaries must be disabled on the date of the qualifying event.

- Change the definition of qualified beneficiary to include a child born to, or placed for adoption with, the covered employee during the period of COBRA coverage. Currently, children born or placed for adoption during this period can be added to a qualified beneficiary's coverage, but are not considered qualified beneficiaries.

- Allow termination of COBRA coverage when the qualified beneficiary receives new group health coverage that does not contain any preexisting condition exclusions or limitations (other than those that do not apply or are satisfied due to HIPAA's preexisting condition provisions). This change is intended to coordinate with HIPAA's new limits on preexisting conditions.

*Note:* Because these regulations change frequently, you should check with your carrier once a year to make sure all COBRA communications are up-to-date and correct.

## SAMPLE COBRA LETTER TO EMPLOYEES
## SUMMARY OF RIGHTS AND OBLIGATIONS REGARDING
## CONTINUATION OF GROUP HEALTH PLAN COVERAGE

**TO:**　　　　　　Employees of XYZ Company

**FROM:**　　　　　Director Human Resources

**DATE:**

**SUBJECT:**　　　Continuation of coverage under the group health plan
　　　　　　　　　maintained by the Employer (the Plan)

---

**IT IS IMPORTANT THAT ALL COVERED INDIVIDUALS TAKE THE TIME TO READ THIS NOTICE CAREFULLY AND BE FAMILIAR WITH ITS CONTENTS.**

The Consolidated Omnibus Budget Reconciliation Act (COBRA) requires that the employer offer to employees, their spouses and dependents the opportunity for temporary extension of health (medical and dental) coverage called "continuation coverage" where coverage under the Plan would otherwise end due to certain specific events (listed below).

**To Whom Does This Continuation Apply?**

Continuation of coverage under a group health plan may be elected for the following Qualifying Events:

*Qualifying Events for Covered Employee*—If you are an employee of the XYZ Company and covered by the Company's medical and/or dental coverage, you may have the right to elect continuation coverage if you lose your group health coverage because of a termination of your employment or a reduction in your hours of employment.

*Qualifying Events for Covered Spouse*—If you are the spouse of an employee of XYZ Company and covered by the Company's medical and/or dental coverage, you may have the right to elect continuation coverage for yourself if you lose group health coverage under the Plan for any of the following reasons:

1. A termination of your spouse's employment or reduction in your spouse's hours of employment with XYZ Company;
2. The death of your spouse;
3. Divorce or legal separation from your spouse; or
4. Your spouse becomes entitled to Medicare.

*Qualifying Events for Covered Dependent Children*—If you are the covered dependent child of an employee covered by the Company's medical and/or dental coverage, you may have the right to elect continuation coverage for yourself if you lose group health coverage for any of the following reasons:

1. A termination of a parent's employment or reduction in the employee's hours of employment with XYZ Company;

2. The death of a parent employed by XYZ Company;

3. Parent's divorce or legal separation;

4. The parent employed by XYZ Company becomes entitled to Medicare;

5. You cease to be a "dependent child" under the XYZ Company Plan (i.e., you are between the ages of 19 and 25 and are no longer a full-time student, or you are over the age of 25 irrespective of whether or not you are a full-time student).

Rights similar to those described above may apply to retirees, spouses, and dependents if the employer commences a bankruptcy proceeding and these individuals lose coverage within one year of one or one year after the bankruptcy filing.

The taking of leave under the Family & Medical Leave Act does not constitute a qualifying event under COBRA.

**What Is the Election Period and Coverage?**

The employee or a family member has the responsibility to inform the Company/Plan administrator via enrollment/change form of a divorce, legal separation, or a child losing dependent status under the company's medical and/or dental coverage within 60 days of the date of the event or the date on which coverage would end under the Plan because of the event, whichever is later.

When the employer is notified that one of these events has happened, you will be notified that you have the right to choose continuation coverage. You have at least 60 days from the date you would lose coverage because of one of the events described above to inform the employer that you want continuation coverage.

If you do not choose continuation coverage within the 60-day election period, your opportunity to elect group health insurance coverage will end.

If a qualified beneficiary elects continuation coverage and pays the applicable premium, the employer will provide the qualified beneficiary with coverage that is identical to the coverage provided under the Plan to similarly situated employees and/or covered dependents.

**For What Period of Time May the Coverages Be Continued?**

1. **18 Months of Continued Coverage**

   If the event causing the loss of coverage is a termination of employment or a reduction in work hours, each qualified beneficiary will have the opportunity to continue coverage for 18 months from the date of the qualifying event.

2. **29 Months of Continued Coverage**

   Continuation of coverage can be extended to 29 months if a qualified beneficiary is disabled in accordance with the provisions of the Social Security Act at the time of the covered employee's termination of employment or reduction of hours. The extension to 29 months is available only if the qualified beneficiary provides notice of the determination of his or her disability under the Social Security Act within the 18-month period after the qualified event. The notice must be given within 60 days after the date of the disability determination to the employer. The employer must also be notified of any final determination that the qualified beneficiary is no longer disabled.

3. **36 Months of Continued Coverage**

   If the event causing the loss of coverage was the death of the employee, divorce, legal separation, or a dependent child ceasing to be a dependent child under the XYZ Company's medical and/or dental plan, each qualified beneficiary will have the opportunity to continue coverage *up to 36 months* from the date of the qualifying event.

**Secondary Events**—An extension of the 18-month continuation period can occur, if *during the 18 months* of continuation coverage, a secondary event takes place (divorce, legal separation, death, Medicare entitlement, or a dependent child ceasing to be a dependent). If a secondary event does take place, then the 18 months of continuation coverage can be extended to 36 months from the original qualifying event.

If a secondary event occurs, it is the responsibility of the qualified beneficiary to notify the employer. In no event, however, will continuation coverage last beyond 36 months from the date of the event that originally made the qualified beneficiary eligible for continuation coverage.

**Medicare Entitlement**—There is a special rule for Medicare entitlement. If a covered employee has an 18-month qualifying event and becomes entitled to Medicare during that period, the continuation coverage period for qualified beneficiaries (i.e., spouse less than 65 years old) other than the covered employee will be terminated 36 months from the date the covered employee becomes entitled to Medicare.

**Under What Circumstances May Coverage Under this Continuation Be Terminated?**

The law provides that *if elected and paid for,* continuation coverage may end prior to the maximum continuation period for any of the following reasons:

1. XYZ Company ceases to provide any group health plan to any of its employees;
2. Any required premium for continuation coverage is not paid in a timely manner;
3. An employee is covered under another group health plan that does not contain any exclusion or limitation with respect to any preexisting condition of such beneficiary;
4. A qualified beneficiary becomes entitled to Medicare (Medicare eligibility terminates coverage only for the Medicare-eligible individual)
5. A qualified beneficiary extended continuation coverage to 29 months due to a Social Security disability and a final determination has been made that the qualified beneficiary is no longer disabled;
6. A qualified beneficiary notifies the employer that they wish to cancel continuation coverage.

**When Must a Decision to Continue Be Made?**

A covered employee, spouse, or dependent has 60 days from the date coverage would otherwise terminate or the date the election notice is sent to you, whichever date is later.

**How and to Whom Are Premium Payments Made?**

For the first premium payment, you have 45 days from the date you elect to continue coverage to pay the retroactive premium. Thereafter, your premiums are payable on the first of each month. There is a grace period of 30 days for the regularly scheduled monthly premiums. If your payment is not received within this time basis, your insurance will be canceled. No statements will be sent.

**Important Notifications Required by an Employee, Spouse, and Dependent**

The employee, spouse, or other family member has the responsibility to inform the employer of a divorce, legal separation, or a child losing dependent status under the XYZ Company's medical and/or dental coverage. This notification must be made within 60 days from whichever date is later, the date of the event or the date on which coverage would be lost because of the event. Please check with the human resource department for procedures to follow in making this notification. *If this notification is not completed in a timely manner. then rights to continuation coverage may be forfeited.*

**Notification of Address Change**

To ensure that all covered individuals receive information properly and efficiently, it is important that you notify the employer of any address change as soon as possible. Failure on your part to do so may result in delayed notifications or a loss of continuation coverage options.

**Eligibility, Premiums, and Potential Conversion Rights**

A qualified beneficiary does not have to show that they are insurable to elect continuation coverage. The XYZ Company however, reserves the right to verify eligibility status and terminate continuation coverage retroactively if you are determined to be ineligible or if there has been a material misrepresentation of the facts. A qualified beneficiary may have to pay all of the applicable premium plus a 2% administration charge for continuation coverage. These premiums may be adjusted in the future if the applicable premium amount changes. In addition, if continuation coverage is extended from 18 months to 29 months due to a Social Security disability, the XYZ Company can charge up to 150% of the applicable premium during the extended coverage period. There is a grace period of 30 days for the regularly scheduled monthly premiums.

**Any Questions?**

If any covered individual does not understand any part of this summary notice or has questions regarding the information
or your obligations, please contact the Director of Human Resources at (303) 919-9990.

## SAMPLE LETTER TO BE SENT TO THOSE FORMER EMPLOYEES CURRENTLY ON COBRA AND THOSE EMPLOYEES WHO WILL GO ON COBRA AFTER JANUARY 1, 1997

Date _____

Mr. John Doe
123 Street
City, State 00000

Subject:        Changes In Group Health Plan Continuation Coverage

Dear Mr. Doe:

As you may be aware, on August 21, 1996, President Clinton signed into law the Health Insurance Portability and Accountability Act of 1996. While there were many provisions that will relate to Acme Company's group health plan in the future, there are a few changes that have taken effect as of January 1, 1997. These changes are noted below;

- Under the current rules, Qualified Beneficiaries disabled (as determined by the Social Security Administration) *on the date of a Qualifying Event* resulting from a termination of employment or reduction in working hours may be entitled to a total of 29 months of continuation coverage, rather' than the normal 18 months. Under the new law, if the Qualified Beneficiary is determined to have been disabled *at any time during the first 60 days of* continuation coverage, they are entitled to a total of 29 months of coverage.

- Under the current rules, children acquired after the date of any Qualifying Event (newborn or adopted) may have been eligible for coverage, *but not as a Qualified Beneficiary.* Under the new rules all newborns and adopted children must be eligible to be added to continuation coverage within XX days, and are considered to be *a Qualified Beneficiary* if enrolled.

In addition, the Small Business Job Protection Act recently clarified COBRA's multiple qualifying event rules as follows:

- Under' the current law, if Medicare Entitlement was a second Qualifying Event, the actual language of the law permitted 36 months *additional coverage.* Under the new law, this has been clarified to permit a *total of 36 months* for both Qualifying Events. This change is retroactively effective to January 1, 1990.

To assist you in understanding the group health plan coverage continuation provision, we are enclosing a copy of the rules that apply to the group health plan's coverage continuation provision that has been updated to reflect the changes in the law. Please take the time to read it carefully. If you have questions, please contact the Human Resources Department.

Sincerely,

# GROUP HEALTH PLAN
## COVERAGE CONTINUATION NOTICE

On April 7, 1986, a federal law called COBRA was enacted requiring that most employers sponsoring group health plans offer covered employees and their covered spouses and dependent children the opportunity' for a temporary extension of health coverage (called "continuation coverage") at group rates. This coverage is available in certain instances (called "qualifying events"), where coverage under the plan would otherwise end. This notice is intended to inform you, in a summary, of your rights and obligations under the continuation coverage provisions of the law. *Both you and your spouse should take the time to read this notice carefully.*

If you are an employee of (*employer's name*) covered by (*group health plan name*) you have a right to choose this continuation coverage if you lose your group health coverage because of a reduction in your work hours or the termination of your employment (for reasons other than gross misconduct on your part).

If you are the spouse of an employee covered by (*group health plan name*), you have the right to choose continuation coverage for yourself if you lose group health plan coverage under (*group health plan name*) for any of the following reasons:

(1)     Death of your spouse;

(2)     A termination of your spouse's employment (for reasons other than gross misconduct) or reduction in your spouse's hours of employment;

(3)     Divorce or legal separation from your spouse;

(4)     Your spouse becomes entitled to Medicare;

In the case of a dependent child of an employee covered by (*group health care name*), he or she has the right to continuation coverage if group health plan coverage under (*group health plan name*) is lost for any of the reasons listed above for a spouse or if his/her coverage under the plan terminates because s/he no longer qualifies as a dependent under the terms of the plan.

Under COBRA, the employee or a covered spouse or dependent child have the responsibility to inform the (*group health plan name*) Administrator of a divorce, a legal separation or a child losing dependent status under (*group health plan name*) within 60 days of the event or the date on which coverage would end with the plan because of the event. (*Name of employer*) has the responsibility to notify the Plan Administrator of the employee's death, termination, reduction in hours of employment or Medicare entitlement. Similar rights may apply to certain retirees and their spouses and dependent children if your employer commences a bankruptcy proceeding and these individuals lose coverage.

When the Plan Administrator is notified that one of these events has happened, the Plan Administrator will in turn notify you that you have the right to choose continuous coverage. Under COBRA, you have at least 60 days from the later of the date you would lose coverage because of one of the events described above or the date you are sent notice about your right to continued coverage to inform the Plan Administrator that you want continuation coverage. There is one exception, however. If you waive continuation coverage, you may revoke your waiver at any time before your 60-day election period ends, but, in that case, your continuation coverage begins on the date your waiver is revoked (it will not include coverage for the period between the date your regular plan coverage ends and the date your waiver is revoked).

Each affected individual may make his or her own decision when choosing continuation coverage. Unless the covered employee's election of continuation coverage says otherwise, that election will also cover his or her' spouse and/or dependent children who would also be losing coverage. If a spouse elects coverage, the spouse election will (unless otherwise stated) also cover the employee and dependent children who would also be losing coverage.

*If you do not choose continuation coverage within the 60-day period, your group health plan coverage will end.*

If you choose continuation coverage, (*name of employer*) is required to give you coverage which, as of the time coverage is being provided, is identical to the coverage provided under the plan to similarly situated employees or spouse or dependent child who have not experienced a qualifying event. The law requires that you be afforded the opportunity to maintain continuation coverage for up to 36 months unless you lost group health plan coverage because of a termination of employment or reduction in hours. In that case, the maximum continuation coverage period is 18 months. This 18-month period is extended to 36 months if other events (such as death, divorce, legal separation, Medicare entitlement, or a child is no longer a dependent) occur during that 18-month period.

In the case of qualifying events that are termination of employment or reduction of hours, the 18 months of continued coverage may be extended to 29 months. To receive their extended coverage, an individual must be determined to have been disabled (for Social Security disability purposes) on the date of the original qualifying event, or during the first 60 days Of continuation coverage, and notify the Plan Administrator of that determination within 60 days of receipt and within the original 18-month period. The affected individual must also notify the Plan Administrator within 30 days of any final determination that the individual is no longer disabled. In no event will continuation coverage last beyond 36 months from the date of the first event that originally made a qualified beneficiary eligible to elect coverage.

However, the law also provides that continuation coverage may be discontinued before the end of the maximum period for any of the following five reasons:

(1)     (*Name of employer*) no longer provides group health plan coverage to any of its employees;

(2)     The premium for the continuation coverage is not paid on time;

(3)     The qualified beneficiary becomes covered under another group health plan that does not contain any exclusion or limitation with respect to any preexisting condition he/she may have or is prohibited from enforcing the exclusion or limitation;

(4)     The qualified beneficiary becomes entitled to Medicare;

(5)     The qualified beneficiary's coverage was extended to 29 months due to disability and there has been a final determination that he/she is no longer disabled. In that case' continuation coverage will end on the first day of the month that begins more than 30 days after the date of the final determination that the individual is no longer disabled.

You do not have to show that you are insurable to choose continuation coverage. To receive continuation coverage, you must pay the full cost of the monthly premium plus a two percent administrative charge. If you experience a qualifying event, you will be notified about the premium rates and the due dates for payments. If you or a covered spouse or dependent child qualifies for extended continuation coverage as a disabled individual, 150 percent of the all cost of the monthly premium must be paid for the 19th through 29 months of the coverage. There is a grace period of at least 30 days for payment of the regularly scheduled premium. You have 45 days from the date you initially elect coverage to make your first payment. The law also requires that if; at the end of the 18-month or 36-month coverage continuation period, you must be allowed to enroll in an individual conversion health plan if offered under (*group health plan name*) at that time.

If you have questions about COBRA, contact (*Plan Administrator's name, business address, and phone*). Also, if you have changed marital status, or you or your spouse have changed addresses, please notify (*Plan Administrator*) at the above address.

## SAMPLE COBRA NOTICE TO TERMINATING EMPLOYEE

Dear _____,

The Consolidated Omnibus Budget Reconciliation Act of 1986 required that employers offer certain categories of individuals the opportunity to continue in the employers group health insurance plan within sixty (60) days of becoming eligible. Coverage may continue for eighteen (18) or thirty-six (36) months depending upon category of eligibility.

| Who is covered | Situation | Duration of coverage |
| --- | --- | --- |
| 1. Employee | Termination other than for "gross misconduct"; reduction in hours | 18 months |
| 2. Family members | Death of employee | 36 months |
| 3. Spouse | Divorce or legal separation from employee | 36 months |
| 4. Dependent child | For a child who ceases to be a dependent under terms of the health plan | 36 months |
| 5. Spouse | Employee reaches age 65 and makes Medicare primary health insurer | 36 months |

The cost to you is $_____. It is your responsibility to remit each month's premium to the Human Resources Manager no later than the first of each month. Failure to do so will result in cancellation of coverage.

_____I decline coverage

_____I elect coverage        _____ Monthly premium: _____

_____Category applies to me

Please print name of individual(s) covered.

_____        _____

_____        _____

_____        _____

_____        _____
Date                               Signature

## Sample COBRA Letter to Terminating Employee or Dependent

Mr. Eldon Johns                                        Date _____
32981 Harbor Street
Boston, MA 02215

Dear Eldon:

You are eligible to receive healthcare coverage from Putman Power Products Corporation as a result of the Consolidated Omnibus Budget Reconciliation Act (COBRA).

The regulation affects former employees, including retirees and dependents of employees whose coverage under our healthcare program has stopped.

Under this law, you may purchase the same medical, dental, and prescription drug coverage provided to current employees for up to 18 months. The attached sheet summarizes the items covered by the medical plan.

Your monthly cost is $_____ for individual coverage and $_____ for family coverage. This is equal to the company s cost of providing the same coverage to each of our current employees. You are not required to furnish proof of insurability to receive this coverage.

If you accept the coverage, you must complete, sign, and mail the enclosed application form to our Human Resources Department within 60 days of receipt of this letter. The premium is due within 45 days of your application for coverage and may be paid monthly or in a single payment. Your payments should also be mailed to the Human Resources Department.

Healthcare benefits under this program will stop automatically at the end of the 18-month period, or sooner if you stop making the payments, become covered under another employer's healthcare plan, or become eligible for Medicare. It could also stop if for some reason our company discontinued the employee healthcare plan.

Your dependent children automatically receive the same medical coverage as you if you choose to participate. They will have an opportunity to apply for the individual coverage for themselves when they no longer qualify as your dependents. This happens when they reach age 19, when they are no longer full-time students, or sooner if they get married.

If you fail to apply for coverage within 60 days of receiving this letter, or fail to send your first premium payment within 45 days of enrolling, you will forfeit your right to coverage under the healthcare plan.

If you have any questions about the program or the provision of the law, please write or call me at (212) 555-8931.

Sincerely,



Fred J. Corbin
Human Resources Manager

## SAMPLE ALTERNATIVE COBRA LETTER TO EMPLOYEES

Date _____

Dear Employee:

You and your eligible dependents may continue participation in the firm's group medical and dental plans even though certain events occur which would otherwise cause loss of coverage. This continued coverage is provided by the Consolidated Omnibus Budget Reconciliation Act (COBRA), a federal law enacted on April 7, 1986. This notice is intended to inform you of your rights and obligations under the continuation coverage provisions of the new law.

*How the Law Will Apply:*

1. Your coverage can be extended up to 18 months if one of the following "qualifying events" occurs:
   - Your employment with the firm terminates for any reason (including voluntary resignation or retirement) other than gross misconduct.
   - Your working hours are reduced to a level at which you would no longer be eligible for coverage.

2. Coverage for your eligible dependents can be extended up to 36 months if one of the following "qualifying events" occurs:
   - They are covered under the plans and you die while still employed.
   - You or your spouse become legally separated or divorced.
   - A dependent child reaches maximum age for coverage.
   - Your spouse or dependents are under age 65 when you become eligible for Medicare and are no longer an active employee.

*The Full 18- or 36-Month Extension Will Not Apply If:*

- All employer-provided medical or dental plans are terminated.
- You do not pay your required premium in a timely manner.
- You or your dependents become (an employee) covered by any other group medical and/or dental plan.
- Your former spouse remarries and becomes covered under another group medical and/or dental plan.
- A dependent becomes eligible for Medicare (Medicare eligibility terminates coverage only for the Medicare-eligible individual).

*How to Obtain This Continuation Coverage*

You or a family member must notify the plan administrator in the event of a divorce or legal separation, or if a child loses dependent status under the Plan. You must notify the plan administrator of the employee's death, termination of employment, reduction of hours, or Medicare eligibility. The plan administrator will, within fourteen days of receiving notification, inform you or the dependent of the right to choose continuation coverage. You do not have to show that you are insurable to choose continuation coverage. Please note that prompt notification is extremely important. You will have at least sixty days from the date you would otherwise lose coverage to inform the plan administrator is you want continuation coverage. If you do not elect continuation coverage, your group health plan coverage will end.

### *Your Cost for Continuation Coverage*

You will be charged the full cost of coverage under the group plan in which you are enrolled. We will no longer pay a portion of it. You will also pay a 2 percent administrative charge. (Note: This may still be less expensive and provide better coverage than an individual health policy.)

You may pay for the continuation coverage on a monthly basis. You must make your first payment within forty-five days after the date you elect the continuation of this coverage. Subsequent payments must be made to the Human Resources Manager by _____.

### *This Does Not Affect Your Normal Conversion Privilege*

You will still have the option to convert your group coverage to individual coverage. If you first elect continuation coverage under our group plan(s), your election period to convert to an individual policy will be the last 180 days of your continuation coverage. If you *do not wish* to continue coverage under the group plan(s), you must make your conversion election for individual coverage within thirty days of the date your regular group health coverage ends. The new continuation coverage option under our plan *does not* apply to life insurance. If you wish to convert your group life insurance to individual life insurance, you must elect to do so within thirty days of the date your regular group life insurance coverage ends.

If you have any questions about either the conversion option or the continuation coverage option, please call or write:

### (*Insert name of your carrier*)

Also, if you have changed marital status, or you or your spouse have changed addresses, please notify the plan administrator at the above addresses.

Sincerely,


Scott Macon
Human Resources Director

## WAIVER LETTER

(Be sure an employee who elects *not* to take COBRA coverage signs
a Waiver Letter like this one)

Date

XYZ Company
Human Resources Department
Denver, Co. 80237

RE: Waiver of Right to Continue Benefits under COBRA Continuation

Dear Plan Administrator:

I have received the notification of the right to continue certain covered benefits for
myself and my covered dependents, if any, and the cost computation form.

At this time, the undersigned Principal Qualified Beneficiary waives the right to purchase the continuation coverage. Family coverage, if provided, is also waived by signature of my spouse, if any in the space provided below.

In waiving this coverage, I (we) hereby acknowledge that at the end of the election period which is _____, my (our) decision will be final and irrevocable.

Sincerely,


_____

Signature of Employee


_____

Signature of Spouse

# POSTERS REQUIRED BY FEDERAL STATUTE

There are several posters required by federal regulations. Those posters, the statute, the posting requirement, and the office listing where they can be ordered are all provided on the attached sheets. Also attached is a sample Equal Employment Opportunity Policy statement and poster that should be posted on the same bulletin board as the other required posters.

Some states also require the company to identify regular paydays. If your state requires that posting you can use a small card to list your paydays, and post on your bulletin boards. The simplest way to ensure you have all the posters required by your particular state, as well as all required federal posters, is to order them from the G. Neil Companies, P.O. Box 450939, Sunrise, FL 33345. (800) 999-9111. Otherwise, you have to call the various federal and state offices and order each set individually.

# TERMINATION PAY REQUIREMENTS BY STATE

### WHEN YOU MUST PAY A DEPARTING EMPLOYEE

| STATE | FIRED EMPLOYEE | QUITTING EMPLOYEE |
|---|---|---|
| Alaska | Within 3 working days | Within 3 working days |
| Arizona | Next payday or within 3 working days | Next regular payday |
| Arkansas | Date of discharge | Next regular payday |
| California | Within 72 hours | Within 72 hours |
| Colorado | At time of discharge | Next regular payday |
| Connecticut | Next business day | Next regular payday |
| Delaware | Next regular payday | Next regular payday |
| D.C. | Next working day | Next working day |
| Florida | — | — |
| Georgia | — | — |
| Hawaii | Next working day | Next regular payday |
| Idaho | Next regular payday | Next regular payday |
| Illinois | Next regular payday | Next regular payday |
| Indiana | Next regular payday | Next regular payday |
| Iowa | Next regular payday | Next regular payday |
| Kansas | Next regular payday | Next regular payday |
| Kentucky | Next regular payday | Next regular payday |
| Louisiana | Within 3 days of separation | Within 3 days of separation |
| Maine | Next regular payday | Next regular payday |
| Maryland | Next regular payday | Next regular payday |
| Massachusetts | Day of discharge | Next regular payday |

| STATE | FIRED EMPLOYEE | QUITTING EMPLOYEE |
| --- | --- | --- |
| Michigan | Day of discharge | Day leaving |
| Minnesota | Within 24 hours of demand | Within 5 days |
| Mississippi | — | — |
| Missouri | Day of discharge | Day leaving |
| Montana | Immediately | Within 3 days |
| Nebraska | Day of discharge | Next regular payday |
| Nevada | Immediately | Within 24 hours of demand |
| New Hampshire | Within 72 hours | Next regular payday |
| New Jersey | Next regular payday | Next regular payday |
| New Mexico | Within 5 days of discharge | Next regular payday |
| New York | Next regular payday | Next regular payday |
| North Carolina | Next regular payday | Next regular payday |
| North Dakota | Within 24 hours | Next regular payday |
| Ohio | — | — |
| Oklahoma | Next regular payday | — |
| Oregon | Immediately | Within 2 working days |
| Pennsylvania | Next regular payday | Next regular payday |
| Rhode Island | Within 24 hours | Next regular payday |
| South Carolina | Generally within 48 hours | Next regular payday |
| South Dakota | Within 5 days | Next regular payday |
| Tennessee | — | — |
| Texas | On 6 days demand | On 6 days demand |
| Utah | Within 24 hours | Within 72 hours |
| Vermont | Within 72 hours | Next regular payday |
| Virginia | Next regular payday | Next regular payday |
| Washington | Next regular payday | Next regular payday |
| West Virginia | Within 72 hours | Next regular payday |
| Wisconsin | Within 3 days | Within 15 days |
| Wyoming | Within 24 hours | Within 72 hours |

## Government Addresses and Phone Numbers

### REGIONAL INFORMATION OFFICES-DEPARTMENT OF LABOR

138W 424 Trapelo Rd., Boston, MA 02135
1515 Broadway, New York, NY 10036
3535 Market St., Philadelphia, PA 19104
1371 Peachtree St. NE, Atlanta, GA 30309
230 5. Dearborn St., Chicago, IL 60604

555 Griffin Sq. Bldg., Dallas, TX 75202

911 Walnut St., Kansas City, MO 64106

1961 Stout St., Denver, CO 80294

450 Golden Gate Ave., San Francisco, CA 94102

909 First Ave., Seattle, WA 98174

### REGIONAL OFFICES-OCCUPATIONAL SAFETY AND HEALTH ADMINISTRATION

16–18 North St., 1 Dock Sq., Boston, MA 02109

1515 Broadway, Rm. 3445, New York, NY 10036

3535 Market St., Philadelphia, PA 19104

1375 Peachtree St. NE, Atlanta, GA 30367

230 S. Dearborn St., Chicago, IL 60604

555 Griffin Sq. Bldg., Griffin & Young Sts., Dallas, TX 75202

911 Walnut St., Kansas City, MO 64106

Federal Bldg., 1961 Stout St., Denver, CO 80294

Federal Office Bldg., 450 Golden Gate Ave., San Francisco, CA 94102

Federal Office Bldg., 909 First Ave., Seattle, WA 98174

Equal Employment Opportunity Commission
2401 "E" Street N.W.
Washington, DC 20506

U. S. Department of Labor
Employment Standards Administration
Wage and Hour Division
Washington, DC 20210

U. S. Department of Justice
Immigration and Naturalization Service
425 "I" Street N.W.
Washington, DC 20536

## *Equal Employment Opportunity Commission Field Offices*

**Albuquerque,** 505 Marquette, NW, Suite 1515, Albuquerque, NM 87101

**Atlanta,** 75 Piedmont Ave., NE, 10th Flr., Atlanta, GA

**Baltimore,** 109 Market Pl., Suite 4000, Baltimore, MD 21202

**Birmingham,** 2121 Eighth Ave., North, Birmingham, AL 35203

**Boston,** 150 Causeway St., Suite 1000, Boston, MA 02114

**Buffalo,** 210 Franklin St., Rm. 503, Buffalo, NY 14202

**Charlotte,** 1301 East Morehead, Charlotte, NC 28204

**Chicago,** 536 So. Clark St., Rm. 240, Chicago, IL 60605

**Cincinnati,** 550 Main St., Rm. 7015, Cincinnati, OH 45202

**Cleveland,** 1375 Euclid Ave., 6th Flr., Cleveland, OH 44115

**Dallas,** 1900 Pacific, 13th Flr., Dallas, TX 75201

**Denver,** 1531 Stout St., 6th Flr., Denver, CO 80202

**Detroit,** 660 Woodward Ave., Suite 600, Detroit, MI 48226

**El Paso,** 109 No. Oregon St., Suite 1112, El Paso, TX 79901

**Fresno,** 1313 P St., Suite 103, Fresno, CA 93721

**Greensboro,** 324 West Market St., Rm. B 27, Greensboro, NC 27402

**Greenville,** 7 North Laurens St., Suite 1001, Greenville, SC 29601

**Houston,** 405 Main St., 6th Flr., Houston, TX 77002

**Indianapolis,** 46 East Ohio St., Rm. 456, Indianapolis, IN 46204

**Jackson,** 100 West Capitol St., Suite 721, Jackson, MS 39269

**Kansas City,** 911 Walnut, 10th Flr., Kansas City, MO 64106

**Little Rock,** 320 West Capitol, Little Rock, AR 72201

**Los Angeles,** 3255 Wilshire Blvd., 9th Flr., Los Angeles, CA 90010

**Louisville,** 601 W. Broadway, Rm. 104, Louisville, KY 40202

**Memphis,** 1407 Union Ave., Suite 502, Memphis, TN 38104

**Miami,** 300 Biscayne Blvd. Way, Suite 414, Miami, FL 33131

**Milwaukee,** 342 North Water St., Rm. 612, Milwaukee, WI 53202

**Minneapolis,** 12 South Sixth St., Suite 1110, Minneapolis, MN 55402

**Nashville,** 404 James Robertson Pky., Suite 1820, Nashville, TN 37219

**Newark,** 744 Broad St., Rm. 502, Newark, NJ 07102

**New Orleans,** 600 South Street, New Orleans, LA 70130

**New York,** 90 Church St., Rm. 1501, New York, NY 10007

**Norfolk,** 200 Granby Mall, Rm. 412, Norfolk, VA 23510

**Oakland,** 1515 Clay St., Rm. 640, Oakland, CA 94612

**Oklahoma City,** 50 Penn Pl., Suite 504, Oklahoma City, OK 73118

**Philadelphia,** 127 North Fourth St., Suite 300, Philadelphia, PA 19106

**Phoenix,** 135 No. Second Ave., 4th Flr., Phoenix, AZ 85003

**Pittsburgh,** 1000 Liberty Ave., Rm. 2038A, Pittsburgh, PA 15222

**Raleigh,** 414 Fayetteville St., 2nd Flr., Raleigh, NC 27601

**Richmond,** 400 North Eighth St., Rm. 6213, Richmond, VA 23240

**San Antonio,** 727 East Durango, Suite B-601, San Antonio, TX 78206

**San Diego,** 880 Front St., Rm. 4S21, San Diego, CA 92188

**San Francisco,** 10 United Nations Plaza, 4th Flr., San Francisco, CA 94102

**San Jose,** 84 West Santa Clara Ave., Rm. 300, San Jose, CA 95113

# Equal Employment Opportunity is...

## THE LAW

### Private Employment, State and Local Government, Educational Institutions

**Race, Color, Religion, Sex, National Origin**
Title VII of the Civil Rights Act of 1964, as amended, prohibits discrimination in hiring, promotion, discharge, pay, fringe benefits, and other aspects of employment, on the basis of race, color, religion, sex or national origin.

Applicants to and employees of most private employers, State and local governments and public or private educational institutions are protected. Employment agencies, labor unions and apprenticeship programs also are covered.

**Age**
The Age Discrimination in Employment Act of 1967, as amended, prohibits age discrimination and protects applicants and employees aged 40-70 from discrimination in hiring, promotion, discharge, pay, fringe benefits and other aspects of employment. The law covers most private employers, State and local governments, educational institutions, employment agencies and labor organizations.

**Sex (wages)**
In addition to the sex discrimination prohibited by Title VII of the Civil Rights Act (see above) The Equal Pay Act of 1963, as amended, prohibits sex discrimination in payment of wages to women and men performing substantially equal work in the same establishment. The law covers most private employers, State and local governments and educational institutions. Labor organizations cannot cause employers to violate the law. Many employers not covered by Title VII, because of size, are covered by the Equal Pay Act.

If you believe that you have been discriminated against under any of the above laws, you should immediately contact:

**The U.S. Equal Employment Opportunity Commission**
2401 "E" Street, N.W.
Washington, D.C. 20506
or an EEOC District Office,
listed in most telephone
directories under U.S. Government.

### Employers holding Federal contracts or subcontracts

**Race, Color, Religion, Sex, National Origin**
Executive Order 11246, as amended, prohibits job discrimination on the basis of race, color, religion, sex or national origin, and requires affirmative action to ensure equality of opportunity in all aspects of employment.

**Handicap**
Section 503 of the Rehabilitation Act of 1973, as amended, prohibits job discrimination because of handicap and requires affirmative action to employ and advance in employment qualified handicapped individuals who, with reasonable accommodation, can perform the functions of a job.

**Vietnam Era and Disabled Veterans**
Section 402 of the Vietnam Era Veterans Readjustment Assistance Act of 1974 prohibits job discrimination and requires affirmative action to employ and advance in employment qualified Vietnam era veterans and qualified disabled veterans.

Applicants to and employees of companies with a Federal government contract or subcontract are protected under the authorities above. Any person who believes a contractor has violated its nondiscrimination or affirmative action obligations under Executive Order 11246, as amended, Section 503 of the Rehabilitation Act or Section 402 of the Vietnam Era Veterans Readjustment Assistance Act should contact immediately

**The Office of Federal Contract Compliance Programs (OFCCP)**
Employment Standards
Administration
U.S. Department of Labor
200 Constitution Avenue, N.W.
Washington, D.C. 20210
or an OFCCP regional or area office,
listed in most telephone directories
under U.S. Government, Department of
Labor

### Programs or activities receiving Federal financial assistance

**Handicap**
Section 504 of the Rehabilitation Act of 1973, as amended, prohibits employment discrimination on the basis of handicap in any program or activity which receives Federal financial assistance. Discrimination is prohibited in all aspects of employment against handicapped persons who, with reasonable accommodation, can perform the essential functions of a job.

**Race, Color, National Origin**
In addition to the protection of Title VII of the Civil Rights Act of 1964, Title VI of the Civil Rights Act prohibits discrimination on the basis of race, color or national origin in programs or activities receiving Federal financial assistance. Employment discrimination is covered by Title VI if the primary objective of the financial assistance is provision of employment, or where employment discrimination causes or may cause discrimination in providing services under such programs.

If you believe you have been discriminated against in a program which receives Federal assistance, you should immediately contact the Federal agency providing such assistance.

## Don't Forget...
### Equal Employment Opportunity is the Law!

# EQUAL EMPLOYMENT OPPORTUNITY POLICY

## (*Company Name*)

It is the ongoing policy of _____ and all individual locations to afford equal employment opportunity to qualified individuals regardless of their race, color, religion, sex, national origin, age, physical or mental handicap, veteran status, or because he or she is a disabled veteran, and to conform to applicable laws and regulations. In keeping with the intent of this policy, the Company will adhere strictly to the following personnel practices:

Recruitment, hiring and promotion of individuals in all job classifications will be conducted without regard to race, color, religion, national origin, age, sex, physical or mental handicap, veteran status, or because he or she is a disabled veteran, except where a bona fide occupational qualification exists.

Employment decisions will be made in such a manner as to further the principle of equal employment Opportunity.

Promotional decisions will be made in accordance with the principles of equal employment opportunity through the use of valid job- related criteria.

All other personnel actions such as compensation, benefits, transfers, training and development, educational assistance, and social and recreational programs will be administered without regard to race, color, religion, national origin, age, sex, physical or mental handicap, veteran status, or because he or she is a disabled veteran, except where a bona fide occupational qualification exists.

Thorough and documented analyses of all personnel actions will be conducted to insure compliance with the concept of equal opportunity.

Overall responsibility for the development and execution of our Affirmative Action Program is delegated to _____ as EEO/AAP Coordinator. The EEO/AAP Coordinator will provide the president of _____ with quarterly and special activity and progress reports.

_____          _____
Date                                     President

## Key Federal Regulations
## Relating to the Human Resources Function

| STATUTE | COVERAGE | BASIC REQUIREMENTS | POSTING PROVISION | ORDER POSTERS FROM |
|---|---|---|---|---|
| Fair Labor Standards Act (FLSA) | Employers engaged in interstate commerce | Pay minimum hourly rate and 1 1/2 hourly rate after 40 hours per week. Contains child labor restrictions; equal pay coverage | Minimum wage postings in conspicuous places to permit employees to readily observe on way to or from work | U.S. Department of Labor - WH Publication 1088 * |
| Walsh-Healey Act | Establishments engaged on a government contract exceeding $10,000 | Pay minimum hourly rate at 1 1/2 hours after 40 hours per week; also contains health and safety requirements and a notation on fringe benefits | In sufficient number of places to permit employees to observe on way to or from work (WH 99:832) | U.S. Department of Labor - Publication WH 99:832 * |
| Davis-Bacon Act | Employers on public construction contracts exceeding $2,000 | Pay minimum wages found by Labor Secretary to be prevailing in the area | Minimum wage to be paid, posted in prominent and easily accessible place at work site | U.S. Department of Labor * |
| Civil Rights Act of 1964 (Title VII) | Employers of 15 or more employees and engaged in interstate commerce | No job discrimination based on race, color, creed, religion, sex or national origin | In conspicuous places where notices to employees and job applicants will be seen. Bilingual postings required | EEOC * |
| Executive Order 11246, as amended | Federal government contractors and subcontractors; contractors under federally-assisted construction contracts | No job discrimination based on race, color, creed, religion, national origin or sex | In conspicuous places available to employees, job applicants and union representatives | U.S. Department of Labor * |
| Age Discrimination in Employment Act (ADEA) | Employers of 20 or more employees and engaged in interstate commerce | No job discrimination based on age 40 to 70 | In prominent and accessible places where readily observable by employees, job applicants and union representatives | EEOC * |
| Pregnancy Discrimination Act of 1978 (PDA) | All employers | Requires that women employees "affected by pregnancy, childbirth, or related medical conditions" be treated the same as other employees with medical disabilities in terms of leave and pay | Cover in personnel policy manuals and employee handbooks | N/A * |
| Occupational Safety and Health Act (OSHA) | Employers engaged in interstate commerce; effective Jan. 1, 1983, the following industries are exempt: retail trade, finance, insurance and real estate, and services | Employers must furnish employees a place of employment free from recognized hazards that might cause serious injury or death. Employers must comply with the specific safety and health standards issued by the Dept. of Labor. Employees must comply with safety and health standards, rules, regulations and orders issued under the Act | OSHA Form 200 posted in a conspicuous place in each establishment. Includes injury and illness totals for previous year; must be posted for 30 days annually during the month of February | OSHA * |

| STATUTE | COVERAGE | BASIC REQUIREMENTS | POSTING PROVISION | ORDER POSTERS FROM |
|---|---|---|---|---|
| Rehabilitation Act of 1973 | Federal government contractors and subcontractors (with a contract of $2,500 or more) | Take affirmative action to employ and advance in employment qualified handicapped persons | Display ADA Poster effective July 26, 1992 | U.S. Department of Labor * |
| Vietnam Era Veterans' Readjustment Act of 1974 | Federal government contractors and subcontractors (with a contract of $10,000 or more) | Take affirmative action to employ and advance in employment qualified Vietnam era veterans | Display poster or notice in conspicuous places available to employees and job applicants | EEOC * |
| Employee Polygraph Protection Act | All employers. Act exempts federal, state and local government employees | Employers prohibited from requiring or requesting employees or job applicants to take a lie detector test | Display poster in conspicuous places available to employees and job applicants | U.S. Department of Labor * |
| Drug Free Workplace Law | Federal contractors with contracts of $25,000 or more and Federal grantees | Certify to the contracting or granting agencies that they maintain a drug-free workplace by publishing and administering specific drug-free workplace policies and drug-awareness programs | Post company drug-free workplace notice and cover in personnel policy manuals and employee handbooks | Company-generated notice * |
| Worker Adjustment and Retraining Notification (WARN) | Any employer that employs 100 or more employees excluding part-time workers | Notice of plant closings and mass layoffs required | Notice must be posted for 60 days in advance of the layoff or plant closing | Company-generated notice |
| Immigration Reform and Control Act of 1986 (IRCA) | Law says you should hire only American citizens and aliens who are authorized to work in the U.S. | Verify employment eligibility and complete and retain Form I-9 | Display poster obtained from INS | U.S. Department of Justice Immigration and Naturalization Service (INS) * |
| The Immigration Act of 1990 | Counterpart to the Immigration Reform and Control Act of 1986 - Can hire only those authorized to work in the U.S. Covers new areas including workers of "distinguished merit" and employer-sponsored visas | Verify employment eligibility and complete and retain Form I-9 | Display poster obtained from INS | U.S. Department of Justice Immigration and Naturalization Service (INS) * |
| Older Worker's Protection Act of 1990 | Changes the Age Discrimination Act (ADEA) | Centers on two important issues: severance and early retirement. Tightens the rules on waivers (giving up the right to sue in exchange for an enhanced retirement package). | Same as ADEA | EEOC * |

| STATUTE | COVERAGE | BASIC REQUIREMENTS | POSTING PROVISION | ORDER POSTERS FROM |
|---|---|---|---|---|
| Americans With Disabilities Act of 1990 (ADA) | Employers of 25 or more, effective July 26, 1992. Employers of 15 or more, effective July 26, 1994. For employment section only | Employers may not discriminate against an individual with a disability in hiring or promotion if the person is otherwise qualified for the job<br><br>The Act also covers public transportation and public accommodations and these sections have different effective dates | Display poster of ADA employment and promotion regulations effective July 26, 1992 | U.S. Department of Justice Civil Rights Division Coordination and Review Section (Implementation and Enforcement by EEOC)<br>* |
| The Civil Rights Act of 1991 (CRA) | Basically restores Title VII by overruling five major court cases and strengthens the "disparate impact" theory<br><br>Under the new Act, an employer must demonstrate that educational requirements, physical requirements, etc. are job related and consistent with business necessity<br><br>Expands the scope and amount of monetary relief available to employment discrimination plaintiffs | Same as Title VII | Same as Title VII | EEOC<br>* |
| The Family and Medical Leave Act of 1993 | The law applies to all employers with more than 50 employees. It defines eligible employees as those who have been employed for at least 12 months and who have provided at least 1250 hours of service during the 12 months before the leave was requested.<br><br>The law provides up to 12 weeks of unpaid leave during any 12-month period. The employee must be guaranteed the same or equivalent job on return to work, and the employers must continue to pay their portion of medical benefits during the leave. | A covered employer must provide 12 weeks of unpaid leave if the employee provides appropriate documentation substantiating the need for the leave. | Cover in Manuals and Handbooks and post notices as required. | * |
| The Illegal Immigration Reform and Immigrant Responsibility Act of 1996<br>Effective September 30, 1996 | The Act's changes are designed to streamline the verification process and reduce the 1-9 verification burden on employers. | New programs when finalized will provide for confirmation of employment status through telephone or electronic communication.<br><br>The Immigration and Naturalization Service and the Social Security Administration are required to establish reliable and secure methods to confirm inquiries from employers. | Cover in Manuals and Handbooks and post notices as required. | * |

| STATUTE | COVERAGE | BASIC REQUIREMENTS | POSTING PROVISION | ORDER POSTERS FROM |
|---|---|---|---|---|
| **Small Business Job Protection Act of 1996** | Increased minimum wage to $4.75 hour October 1, 1996 and to $5.15 hour September 1, 1997.<br><br>Extends tax-exempt status of employer-paid educational assistance.<br><br>Establishes new roles for handling tip income tax credits.<br><br>Establishes safe harbor non-discrimination rules for 401(k) plans.<br><br>Creates savings incentive match plans for employees of small businesses. | Employers must pay minimum wage and comply to all new provisions of the Act. | Cover in Manuals and Handbooks and post notices as required. | * |
| **The Health Insurance and Portability Act of 1996** | Creates test program for tax-favored medical savings accounts (MSAs).<br><br>Treats costs of long-term care services and some long-term care insurance as medical expenses for tax purposes.<br><br>Imposes portability requirements on group health care plans. Includes several other general provisions. | Employers must comply with the portability and other tax related requirements. | Cover in Medical Plan documents and post notices as required. | * |
| **The Personal Liability and Work Opportunity Act of 1996 (the Welfare Act)** | Includes a number of changes that tighten the Earned Income Tax Credit.<br><br>Mandatory new hire reporting program, effective October 1, 1997 | Employers who take a tax credit must comply with new tax provisions of the act.<br><br>All employees | None | * |
| **The Newborns' and Mothers' Health Protection Act of 1996 (Effective after January 1, 1998)** | Covers any employer that has a group health plan (insured or self-insured) | The act prohibits group health plans from restricting hospital stays for childbirth to less than a 48-hour minimum stay for a normal delivery and a 96-hour stay for a cesarean delivery. In addition, the plan may not require prior authorization to qualify for the 48-hour or 96-hour minimum stay. | Cover in medical plan documents | * |
| **The Mental Health Parity Act of 1996 (Effective January 1, 1998)** | Covers employers with 50 or more employees. The new parity requirement will not apply to benefits furnished on or after September 30, 2001. | The act provides that group health plans that offer mental health coverage may not set annual or lifetime limits for mental health coverage that are more restrictive than those for medical and surgical coverage. | Cover in medical plan documents. | * |

*All state and federal posters may be ordered from the G. Neil Companies 1-800-999-9111.

# COMPLYING WITH THE IMMIGRATION REFORM AND CONTROL ACT OF 1986

Most companies are required to verify the work authorization and identity of all employees and applicants for employment. The Form I-9 must be completed for every new employee, and the forms must be retained for at least three years.

Methods by which the personnel department can verify applicant eligibility are provided on the Form I-9.

Some business people don't think they will ever be audited and have not taken the time and effort to verify work authorization. Donald Russell, Director of the Denver INS Office for the three-state area encompassing Colorado, Wyoming, and Utah says that more than a dozen companies within that district were cited in one year and more than thirty companies have been audited and are awaiting review.

The fines are substantial. An Aspen company that owns two restaurants was fined $52,500 after knowingly hiring three illegal workers and having more than 100 paperwork violations.

Although INS does carry out spot inspections, most of their information about violators comes from tips from disgruntled employees or other informants.

*It makes good economic sense to comply with federal law in this area. Don't take a chance by violating the documentation laws.*

---

### Manager's Tip

Purchase a large expandable alphabetical file and keep your I-9 forms in it. If an inspector comes in and asks to review your I-9s you don't have to go through all the personnel files pulling them out. Also Department of Labor, Wage and Hour inspectors coming into your company to investigate a complaint on wage and hour violations may ask to review your I-9 files while there.

---

## *What You Need to Know About the Immigration Law and Completion of the Immigration Form I-9*

If you employ persons to perform labor or services in return for wages or other pay, you must complete Form I-9 for:

**PERSONS HIRED AFTER MAY 31, 1987**   For these employees, you must complete a Form I-9 within three business days of the date of the hire. If you employ the person for less than three days, you must complete the Form I-9 before the end of the employee's first working day.

**PERSONS HIRED BETWEEN NOVEMBER 7, 1986 AND MAY 31, 1987**   For these employees, you must complete Form I-9 before September 1, 1987.

---

### Note:

If you employ people for domestic work in your private home on a regular basis, these requirements also apply to you.

---

You *do not* need to complete Form I-9 for:

- Persons hired before November 7, 1986
- Persons hired after November 6, 1986, who left your employment before June l, 1987
- Persons you employ for domestic work in a private home on an intermittent or sporadic basis
- Persons who provide labor to you who are employed by a contractor providing contract services (employee leasing)
- Persons who are independent contractors.

Persons who are self-employed do not need to complete Form I-9.

**Note:**

---

Congress is still considering major Immigration Law reform. Changes in the law may take place after publication of this book. Contact the U. S. Department of Justice, Immigration and Naturalization Service for current regulations.

March 20, 1996 was the deadline for immigrants with "green cards" (Form I-151) issued before 1979 to apply for a new card.

The replacement cards, issued by the Immigration and Naturalization Service, are pink and must be renewed every 10 years. The applications take six to eight months to process, and new cards are mailed to applicants.

You should be aware of the following:

- For employees hired *before* March 20, 1996—Employers *do not* have to reverify employment eligibility for those employees who used a green card issued before 1979 to establish employment eligibility on the I-9 Form.
- For employees hired *after* March 20, 1996—The original green cards *may not* be used as documentation to establish employment eligibility on the I-9 Form.

**U.S. Department of Justice**
Immigration and Naturalization Service

OMB No. 1115-0136
**Employment Eligibility Verification**

Please read instructions carefully before completing this form. The instructions must be available during completion of this form. **ANTI-DISCRIMINATION NOTICE.** It is illegal to discriminate against work eligible individuals. Employers **CANNOT** specify which document(s) they will accept from an employee. The refusal to hire an individual because of a future expiration date may also constitute illegal discrimination.

**Section 1.  Employee Information and Verification.** To be completed and signed by employee at the time employment begins

| Print Name:  Last | First | Middle Initial | Maiden Name |
|---|---|---|---|

| Address *(Street Name and Number)* | | Apt. # | Date of Birth *(month/day/year)* |
|---|---|---|---|

| City | State | Zip Code | Social Security # |
|---|---|---|---|

**I am aware that federal law provides for imprisonment and/or fines for false statements or use of false documents in connection with the completion of this form.**

I attest, under penalty of perjury, that I am (check one of the following):
☐  A citizen or national of the United States
☐  A Lawful Permanent Resident (Alien # A _____)
☐  An alien authorized to work until ____/____/____
(Alien # or Admission # _____)

Employee's Signature

Date *(month/day/year)*

**Preparer and/or Translator Certification.**  *(To be completed and signed if Section 1 is prepared by a person other than the employee.)  I attest, under penalty of perjury, that I have assisted in the completion of this form and that to the best of my knowledge the information is true and correct.*

| Preparer's/Translator's Signature | Print Name |
|---|---|

| Address (Street Name and Number, City, State, Zip Code) | Date *(month/day/year)* |
|---|---|

**Section 2.  Employer Review and Verification.** To be completed and signed by employer.  Examine one document from List A OR examine one document from List B **and** one from List C as listed on the reverse of this form and record the title, number and expiration date, if any, of the document(s)

| List A | OR | List B | AND | List C |
|---|---|---|---|---|
| Document title: _____ | | | | |
| Issuing authority: _____ | | | | |
| Document #: _____ | | | | |
| Expiration Date (if any): ___/___/___ | | ___/___/___ | | ___/___/___ |
| Document #: _____ | | | | |
| Expiration Date (if any): ___/___/___ | | | | |

**CERTIFICATION - I attest, under penalty of perjury, that I have examined the document(s) presented by the above-named employee, that the above-listed document(s) appear to be genuine and to relate to the employee named, that the employee began employment on** *(month/day/year)* ____/____/____ **and that to the best of my knowledge the employee is eligible to work in the United States.  (State employment agencies may omit the date the employee began employment).**

| Signature of Employer or Authorized Representative | Print Name | Title |
|---|---|---|

| Business or Organization Name | Address *(Street Name and Number, City, State, Zip Code)* | Date *(month/day/year)* |
|---|---|---|

**Section 3.  Updating and Reverification.** To be completed and signed by employer

| A.  New Name *(if applicable)* | B.  Date of rehire *(month/day/year) (if applicable)* |
|---|---|

C.  If employee's previous grant of work authorization has expired, provide the information below for the document that establishes current employment eligibility.

Document Title: _____  Document #: _____  Expiration Date (if any): ___/___/___

I attest, under penalty of perjury, that to the best of my knowledge, this employee is eligible to work in the United States, and if the employee presented document(s), the document(s) I have examined appear to be genuine and to relate to the individual.

| Signature of Employer or Authorized Representative | Date *(month/day/year)* |
|---|---|

Form I-9 (Rev. 11-21-91) N

## LISTS OF ACCEPTABLE DOCUMENTS

| LIST A | | LIST B | | LIST C |
|---|---|---|---|---|
| **Documents that Establish Both Identity and Employment Eligibility** | **OR** | **Documents that Establish Identity** | **AND** | **Documents that Establish Employment Eligibility** |

**LIST A — Documents that Establish Both Identity and Employment Eligibility**

1. U.S. Passport (unexpired or expired)

2. Certificate of U.S. Citizenship *(INS Form N-560 or N-561)*

3. Certificate of Naturalization *(INS Form N-550 or N-570)*

4. Unexpired foreign passport, with *I-551 stamp* or attached INS Form I-94 indicating unexpired employment authorization

5. Alien Registration Receipt Card with photograph *(INS Form I-151 or I-551)*

6. Unexpired Temporary Resident Card *(INS Form I-688)*

7. Unexpired Employment Authorization Card *(INS Form I-688A)*

8. Unexpired Reentry Permit *(INS Form I-327)*

9. Unexpired Refugee Travel Document *(INS Form I-571)*

10. Unexpired Employment Authorization Document issued by the INS which contains a photograph *(INS Form I-688B)*

**LIST B — Documents that Establish Identity**

1. Driver's license or ID card issued by a state or outlying possession of the United States provided it contains a photograph or information such as name, date of birth, sex, height, eye color, and address

2. ID card issued by federal, state, or local government agencies or entities provided it contains a photograph or information such as name, date of birth, sex, height, eye color, and address

3. School ID card with a photograph

4. Voter's registration card

5. U.S. Military card or draft record

6. Military dependent's ID card

7. U.S. Coast Guard Merchant Mariner Card

8. Native American tribal document

9. Driver's license issued by a Canadian government authority

**For persons under age 18 who are unable to present a document listed above:**

10. School record or report card

11. Clinic, doctor, or hospital record

12. Day-care or nursery school record

**LIST C — Documents that Establish Employment Eligibility**

1. U.S. social security card issued by the Social Security Administration *(other than a card stating it is not valid for employment)*

2. Certification of Birth Abroad issued by the Department of State *(Form FS-545 or Form DS-1350)*

3. Original or certified copy of a birth certificate issued by a state, county, municipal authority or outlying possession of the United States bearing an official seal

4. Native American tribal document

5. U.S. Citizen ID Card *(INS Form I-197)*

6. ID Card for use of Resident Citizen in the United States *(INS Form I-179)*

7. Unexpired employment authorization document issued by the INS *(other than those listed under List A)*

**Illustrations of many of these documents appear in Part 8 of the Handbook for Employers (M-274)**

## QUESTIONS AND ANSWERS ABOUT I-9 IMMIGRATION FORMS

**Q.** **Where can I get the Form I-9?**

**A.** There are three copies of the Form I-9 in this book. You can photocopy the forms. You may obtain a limited number of copies from INS, or you may order them in bulk from the Superintendent of Documents at the following address:

> Superintendent of Documents
> U.S. Government Printing Office
> Washington, D.C. 20402
> Tel. (202) 783-3238

**Q.** **Do United States citizens need to prove they are eligible to work?**

**A.** Yes. While United States citizens are automatically eligible for employment, they too must provide the required documents and complete the Form I-9.

**Q.** **Do I need to complete an I-9 for everyone who applies for a job with my company?**

**A.** No. You need to complete I-9s only for people you actually hire. For purposes of the new law, a person is "hired" when he or she begins to work for you.

**Q.** **Do I need to fill out an I-9 for independent contractors or their employees?**

**A.** No. For example, if you contract with another company to provide temporary secretarial services, you do not have to complete I-9s for that company's employees. The other company is responsible for completing the I-9s for its own employees. However, you must not knowingly use contract labor to circumvent the law against hiring unauthorized workers.

**Q.** **What do I do when an employee's work authorization expires?**

**A.** You will need to update the I-9 if you want to continue employing the person. At that time, the employee must present a document that either shows an extension of employment eligibility or that is a new grant of work authorization. If the employee cannot produce such a document, that person is no longer eligible to work. Continuing to employ that person is a violation of the law, even if the employee was previously authorized to work.

**Q.** **As an employer, do I have to fill out all the I-9s myself?**

**A.** No, you may designate someone to fill out the form for you such as a personnel officer, foreman, agent, or anyone else acting in your interest. However, you are still responsible for compliance with the law.

**Q.** **When I review the identity and work authorization documents, should I make photocopies of them?**

**A.** The law does not require you to photocopy documents. However, if you wish to make photocopies, you must retain them with the I-9. Photocopies must not be used for any other purpose.

**Q. What are the requirements for retaining the I-9?**

**A.** You must retain the form for at least three years. If you employ the person for more than three years, you must retain the form for one year after the person leaves your employment.

**Q. Will I get any advance notice if an INS or DOL officer wishes to inspect my I-9s?**

**A.** Yes. The officer will give you at least three days' advance notice before the inspection. He or she will not need to show you a subpoena or warrant at that time. Failure to provide the I-9s for inspection could result in civil penalties.

**Q. What happens if I do everything the new law requires and INS discovers that one of my employees is not actually authorized to work?**

**A.** Unless the government can show that you had actual knowledge of the illegal status of the employee, you will have an affirmative defense against the imposition of employer sanctions penalties if you have done the following things:

- had employees fill out their part of the I-9 when they started to work;
- checked the required documents (they should appear to be genuine and to relate to the individual);
- properly completed the I-9;
- retained the form for the specified time; and
- presented the form upon request to an INS or Department of Labor Officer. You will receive at least three days' advance notice.

**Q. May I specify which documents I will accept for verification?**

**A.** No. You must accept any document or combination of documents listed on the I-9 that appear to be genuine.

**Q. What should I do if the person I hire is unable to provide the required documents within three days?**

**A.** If an employee is unable to provide the required document or documents within three days he or she must at least produce a receipt showing that he or she has applied for the document. The employee must produce the document itself within twenty-one days of the hire.

**Q. What is my responsibility concerning the authenticity of documents?**

**A.** You should examine the documents. If they appear to be genuine on their face and relate to the person, you should accept them. If on their face the documents do not appear to be genuine or relate to the person, you should not accept them. In addition, if the work authorization documents carry restrictions, you should abide by them.

## *Where to Get More Information on Immigration Law and Obtain the I-9 Forms*

You may obtain information from one of the following local INS offices. Direct your letter to the attention of the *Employer Relations Officer.*

**ALABAMA**

75 Spring Street S.W.
Atlanta, GA 30303

**ALASKA**

701 "C" Street, Room D-25 1
Lock Box 16
Anchorage, AK 99513

**ARIZONA**

230 North First Avenue
Phoenix, AZ 85025

**ARKANSAS**

701 Loyola Avenue, Room T-8005
New Orleans, LA 70113

**CALIFORNIA**

300 North Los Angeles Street
Los Angeles, CA 90012

880 Front Street
San Diego, CA 92188

630 Sansome Street
San Francisco, CA 94111

**COLORADO**

1787 Federal Building
1961 Stout Street
Denver, CO 80202

**CONNECTICUT**

JFK Federal Building
Government Center
Boston, MA 02203

**DELAWARE**

601 Market Street
Room 1321, U.S. Courthouse
Philadelphia, PA 19106

**DISTRICT OF COLUMBIA**

4420 North Fairfax Drive
Arlington, VA 22203

**FLORIDA**

7880 Biscayne Boulevard
Miami, FL 33138

**GEORGIA**

75 Spring Street S.W.
Atlanta, GA 30303

**GUAM**

595 Ala Moana Boulevard
Honolulu, HI 96813

**HAWAII**

595 Ala Moana Boulevard
Honolulu, HI 96813

**IDAHO**

Federal Building, Room 512
310 South Park, Drawer 10036
Helena, MT 59626-0036

**INDIANA**

219 South Dearborn Street
Chicago, IL 60604

**IOWA**
Federal Building, Room 1008
106 South 15th Street
Omaha, NE 68102

**KANSAS**
9747 North Conant Avenue
Kansas City, MO 64153

**KENTUCKY**
701 Loyola Avenue, Room T-8005
New Orleans, LA 70113

**LOUISIANA**
701 Loyola Avenue, Room T-8005
New Orleans, LA 70113

**MAINE**
P.O. Box 578, Downtown Station
Portland, ME 04112

**MARYLAND**
101 West Lombard Street
Baltimore, MD 21201

**MASSACHUSETTS**
JFK Federal Building
Government Center
Boston, MA 02203

**MICHIGAN**
333 Mount Elliott Street
Detroit, MI 48207

**MINNESOTA**
927 Main Post Office Building
St. Paul, MN 55101

**MISSISSIPPI**
701 Loyola Avenue, Room T-8005
New Orleans, LA 70113

**MISSOURI**
9747 North Conant Avenue
Kansas City, MO 64153

**MONTANA**
Federal Building, Room 512
310 South Park, Drawer 10036
Helena, MT 59626-0036

**NEBRASKA**
Federal Building, Room 1008
106 South 15th Street
Omaha, NE 68102

**NEVADA**
230 North First Avenue
Phoenix, AZ 85025

**NEW HAMPSHIRE**
JFK Federal Building
Government Center
Boston, MA 02203

**NEW JERSEY**
970 Broad Street
Newark, NJ 07102

**NEW MEXICO**
343 U.S. Courthouse
P.O. Box 9398
El Paso, TX 79984

**NEW YORK**
68 Court Street
Buffalo, NY 14202

26 Federal Plaza
New York, NY 10278

**NORTH CAROLINA**
75 Spring Street S.W.
Atlanta, GA 30303

**NORTH DAKOTA**
927 Main Post Office Building
St. Paul, MN 55101

**OHIO**
1240 East 9th Street, Room 1917
Cleveland, OH 44199

**OKLAHOMA**
Federal Building, Room 6A 21
1100 Commerce Street
Dallas, TX 75242

**OREGON**
511 N.W. Broadway
Portland, OR 97209

**PENNSYLVANIA**
601 Market Street
Room 1321, U.S. Courthouse
Philadelphia, PA 19106

**PUERTO RICO**
GPO Box 5068
San Juan, Puerto Rico 00936

**RHODE ISLAND**
JFK Federal Building
Government Center
Boston, MA 02203

**SOUTH CAROLINA**
75 Spring Street S.W.
Atlanta, GA 30303

**SOUTH DAKOTA**
927 Main Post Office Building
St. Paul, MN 55101

**TENNESSEE**
701 Loyola Avenue, Room T-8005
New Orleans, LA 70113

**TEXAS**
Federal Building, Room 6A 21
1100 Commerce Street
Dallas, TX 75242

P.O. Box 9398
El Paso, TX 79984

2102 Teege Road
Harlingen, TX 78550

2627 Caroline Street
Houston, TX 77004

727 East Durango, Suite A301
San Antonio, TX 78206

**UTAH**
1787 Federal Building
1961 Stout Street
Denver, CO 80202

**VERMONT**
P.O. Box 578, Downtown Station
Portland, ME 04112

**VIRGINIA**
4420 North Fairfax Drive
Arlington, VA 22203

**VIRGIN ISLANDS**
GPO Box 5068
San Juan, Puerto Rico 00936

**WASHINGTON**
815 Airport Way South
Seattle, WA 98134

**WEST VIRGINIA**
601 Market Street
Room 1321, U.S. Courthouse
Philadelphia, PA 19106

**WISCONSIN**
219 South Dearborn Street
Chicago, IL 60604

**WYOMING**
1787 Federal Building
1961 Stout Street
Denver, CO 80202

# THE OBJECTIVE OF WORKERS' COMPENSATION

When accidents happen at work, employers are required to ensure an employee is provided with income protection and medical care.

Workers' compensation is designed to protect employees who suffer work-related injuries or illnesses. Each state governs its own workers' compensation program. Specific benefits vary by state.

The objectives of workers' compensation are:

- To provide income and medical benefits to victims of work-related injuries or illnesses.

- To provide rehabilitation so that injured parties may again become gainfully employed.

- To encourage employer interest in workplace safety and accident/illness prevention.

## *Standard Workers' Compensation Exemptions*

Most states cover all employees under workers' compensation, however, some states exempt the following:

Municipal government employees (or certain categories of government employees such as police officers, firefighters, etc. These employees are usually covered by a special program. Family members working for a family-owned business, religious organizations, or members of the clergy, domestic workers working in private homes, volunteers, self-employed people and agricultural workers.

## *Injuries/Illnesses Covered By Workers' Compensation*

The exact definition of a work-related injury or illness varies by state. Generally, work-related injuries/illnesses are covered as follows:

| | |
|---|---|
| Specific injury/illness: | Resulting from an incident or exposure in the workplace that causes an injury or illness. For example, if an employee injures his or her back lifting a box at work, that is a specific injury. |
| Cumulative injury/illness: | Caused by repetitive activities extending over a period of time. Carpal tunnel syndrome and stress disorders are examples of cumulative injuries/illnesses. |

Some states provide for exclusions from coverage for work-related injury/illness that occur under special circumstances, such as, injuries suffered while under the influence of drugs or alcohol in violation of company policy. Check with your workers' compensation insurance carrier to determine exclusions allowed in your state.

In addition to injuries sustained on the job, most state laws hold employers liable for injuries "arising out of and in the course of employment." Such activities might include an employer sponsored softball game or a bowling league. For example: Employers should be careful to ensure that employees are not pressured to participate in these activities. To avoid liability, employers should emphasize the voluntary nature of such activities, and have employees sign "informed consent" forms which acknowledge their voluntary participation. Check with your workers' compensation carrier regarding such activities.

## Covered Benefits

Generally workers' compensation benefits include:

| | |
|---|---|
| Medical Expenses: | Coverage for medical treatment (including diagnostic testing, doctor visits, surgery, physical therapy or chiropractic treatment, hospitalization, and prescriptions) for injuries or illnesses sustained during the course of employment. |
| Temporary Total Disability: | Provides income benefits while the person is restricted from work due to his or her work-related injury/illness. |
| | The employee's average wage during the pre-injury period is used in the formula to calculate the cash benefits paid by the workers' compensation system. |
| Permanent Partial Disability: | Provides benefits for expected income loss due to a person's permanent partial disability arising from a work-related injury or illness, when the person cannot return to work. |
| Permanent Total Disability: | Provides benefits for workers who have permanent work-related injuries that are totally disabling (with respect to his or her occupation). |
| Rehabilitation: | Provides funds for educational and training expenses, as well as temporary total disability income during retraining when a person cannot return to his or her usual and customary occupation as a result of his or her work-related injury/illness. |
| Death Benefits: | When a work-related accident or exposure results in death, the employee's spouse or dependent children are usually eligible for death/survivor benefits. These may be in the form of a lump-sum payment (for example, a life insurance benefit), or a monthly payment for a specified period of time, for example, monthly payment to dependent children until high school or college graduation. |

Check the law in your state to determine the types of benefits available to your employees.

## Work-Related Injury/Illness Liability

Workers' compensation is intended to be an *exclusive remedy* program. This means that (1) employers accept full responsibility for the injuries/illnesses incurred by their employees arising out of, and in the course of their employment, and (2) employees accept the benefits prescribed by the state in lieu of suing employers for other damages. However, under some circumstances, employees may still sue the employer or other parties for work-related injuries/illnesses for liability in tort. The premise for these claims can be gross negligence or *intentional acts* on the part of the employer. Negligence claims may include:

> *Employer negligence*—Where it can be demonstrated that the employer knowingly allowed a safety hazard to exist that was likely to result in an injury/illness.

> *Fellow employee*—Suits against a fellow employee who the injured party believes caused the injury/illness through his or her intentional acts.

> *Contractors*—Suits against contractors or subcontractors working in the place of employment whose actions caused the injury/illness.

> *Manufacturers*—Suits against manufacturers on whose equipment the employee sustained the injury, or manufacturers of hazardous substances.

## Failure to Carry Workers' Compensation Insurance

When state law requires employers to carry workers' compensation insurance coverage, liability for failure to carry insurance can be extensive. Again, specific liabilities/penalties are defined by your state's laws. However, typical liabilities/penalties include:

- The employee is still entitled to benefits as though the employer had insurance coverage. Such benefits are paid directly by the employer.

- The injured employee may bring a civil lawsuit against the uninsured employer. Since the employer is in violation of state law, negligence and, therefore, liability may be presumed.

- The uninsured employer may be subject to regulatory agency fines and penalties, both civil and criminal.

## Requirements

While requirements vary by state, employers are generally required to:

- Post a visible notice advising employees of their rights under workers' compensation laws.

- Provide employees with the name of the employer's workers' compensation insurance carrier.

- Take accident reports, and submit claim forms for workers' compensation insurance benefits on behalf of employees.

- Notify the insurance carrier of workplace accidents on a timely basis. Most states have claim reporting deadline requirements and assess penalties for late filing. Exceptions may be made if records are kept off site.

- Report a death or serious injury to the appropriate agency (i.e., OSHA) by phone, fax or telegram within 24 hours.

- Maintain an OSHA 200 log of reportable workplace injuries and post it annually (February).

- Cooperate with workers' compensation insurance carriers investigating claims for benefits.
- Protect employees who file or support a claim for workers' compensation insurance benefits from any form of discrimination or retaliation related to the claim.

## Financing of Workers' Compensation

Risk financing is the manner in which an organization finances its obligation to remedy workers' compensation claims.

There are basically three types of risk financing:

1. Assumption of risk, (self-insured or self-funded).
2. Transfer of risk, using a contract or leased employee.
3. Purchase of indemnity insurance.

## Self-Insurance

Self-insurance programs involve the decision to retain risk rather than to insure it, and requires a formalized plan and a system to pay losses as they occur. Accurate loss data records of claims funding and other claims costs must be maintained. Depending on state regulations, a formal self- insurance program may be funded on a "pay as you go" basis from operating cash balances, through systematic payments into a special reserve fund, or through loan instruments such as letters of credit.

## Third-Party Contracting

Some employers choose to transfer risk by contracting with a third party. In this case people are provided on a temporary basis to an employer, and the third parry agency is responsible for providing workers' compensation coverage. Or an employer may retain the services of an independent contractor who is typically not covered by workers' compensation coverage.

## Purchasing Insurance Coverage

The most common approach to workers' compensation coverage is to purchase insurance. Forty-four states allow an employer to choose its workers' compensation carrier; the remaining six states below require employers to insure via monopolistic state compensation funds:

Nevada
North Dakota
Ohio
Washington
West Virginia
Wyoming

The following states offer the employer the choice of insuring through a private carrier or the state fund:

| | |
|---|---|
| Arizona | Minnesota |
| California | Montana |
| Colorado | New York |
| Hawaii | Oklahoma |
| Idaho | Oregon |
| Louisiana | Pennsylvania |
| Maine | Tennessee |
| Maryland | Texas |
| Michigan | Utah |

## *Reform of the Workers' Compensation System*

Recently some states have enacted workers' compensation insurance reforms, including: revised reporting and record keeping requirements; redefined benefit levels; toll-free telephone numbers for reporting safety and health hazards; revised funding arrangements; fraud protection provisions designed to protect employers and the workers' compensation system against fraudulent claims; additional categories of work-related injuries/illnesses including HIV/AIDS, carpal tunnel syndrome, stress or psychological disorders, and prolonged exposure to chemicals or toxins such as radon or electromagnetic exposures.

---

**Manager's Tip**

The workers' compensation system should never be used to get rid of an unwanted employee. The practice is illegal and can increase costs for every employer in the system. Employers must be aware of the consequences of taking such action and avoid retaliatory discharge of an employee. The employer who engages in this practice is subject to severe fines as well as civil lawsuits at both the state and federal levels.

---

## *Workplace Injuries Under FMLA and ADA*

It used to be that an employer's only concern about a workplace injury was whether or not the injury would result in a compensable workers' compensation claim, but now employers have to view every workplace injury not only as a potential workers' compensation claim, but also as a potential Americans With Disabilities Act (ADA) or Family and Medical Leave Act (FMLA) claim.

Because of the potential expense in an ADA action or FMLA leave request, employers need to reconsider how to manage injuries which have occurred in the workplace to minimize their exposure. This includes providing alternative work arrangements for injured employees who continue employment. The ultimate goal is to return employees to work as soon as possible. In addition, employers should concentrate on methods to minimize exposure to workplace injuries.

# DIRECTORY OF STATE WORKERS' COMPENSATION OFFICES

Employment Standards Administration
Office of State Liaison and Legislative Analysis
Division of State Workers' Compensation Programs

**ALABAMA**
Workmen's Compensation
Division of Workmen's Compensation
Department of Industrial Relations
Industrial Relations Building
Montgomery, Alabama 36130
  (205) 261-2868

**ALASKA**
Workmen's Compensation Division
Department of Labor
Post Office Box 1149
Juneau, Alaska 99802
  (907) 465-2790

**ARIZONA**
Workmen's Compensation Division
Industrial Commission
Post Office Box 19070
1601 West Jefferson Street
Phoenix, Arizona 85005
  (602) 255-4661

**ARKANSAS**
Workmen's Compensation Commission
Justice Building
State Capitol Grounds
Little Rock, Arkansas 72201
  (501) 372-3930

**CALIFORNIA**
Division of Industrial Accidents
Department of Industrial Relations
525 Golden Gate Avenue, 6th Floor
San Francisco, California 94102
  (415) 557-3542

**COLORADO**
Division of Labor
Department of Labor and Employment
1313 Sherman Street
Denver, Colorado 80203
  (303) 866-2782

**CONNECTICUT'**
Workers' Compensation Commission
1890 Dixwell Avenue
Hamden, Connecticut 06514
  (203) 789-7783, 579-6235

**DELAWARE**
Industrial Accident Board
Carvel State Office Building, 6th Floor
820 North French Street
Wilmington, Delaware 19801
  (302) 571-2884

**DISTRICT OF COLUMBIA**
Department Director for Labor Standards
D.C. Department of Employment Services
1200 Upshur Street, N.W.
Washington, D.C. 20011
  (202) 576-7100

**FLORIDA**
Division of Workers' Compensation
Department of Labor and Employment Security
Suite 201, Ashley Building
1321 Executive Center Drive, East
Tallahassee, Florida 32301
  (904) 488-2514

**GEORGIA**
Board of Workers' Compensation
Suite 1000, South Tower
One CNN Center
Atlanta, Georgia 30303–2705
  (404) 656-3875

**HAWAII**
Disability Compensation Division
Department of Labor and Industrial Relations
Post Office Box 3769
830 Punchbowl Street
Honolulu, Hawaii 96813
  (808) 548-5414

**IDAHO**
Industrial Commission
317 Main Street
Boise, Idaho 83720
  (208) 334-6000

**ILLINOIS**
Industrial Commission
100 West Randolph Street, 8th Floor
Chicago, Illinois 60601
  (312) 793-6500

**INDIANA**
Industrial Board of Indiana
Room 601, State Office Building
100 North Senate Avenue
Indianapolis, Indiana 46204
 (317) 232-3808

**IOWA**
Workers' Compensation Service
Department of Employment Services
1000 East Grand
Des Moines, Iowa 50319
 (505) 281-5934

**KANSAS**
Division of Workers' Compensation
Landon State Office Building
900 W.W. Jackson Room 651-S
Topeka, Kansas 66612
 (913) 296-344l

**KENTUCKY**
Workmen's Compensation Board
Department of Labor
127 South Building
Highway 127
Frankfort, Kentucky 40601
 (502) 564-5550

**LOUISIANA**
Department of Labor
Office of Workers' Compensation
910 N. Bon Marche Drive
Baton Rouge, Louisiana 70806
 (504) 925-7211

**MAINE**
Workers' Compensation Commission
Deering Building, Station 27
Augusta, Maine 04333
 (207) 289-3751

**MARYLAND**
Workmen's Compensation Commission
6 North Liberty Street
Baltimore, Maryland 21201
 (301) 333-4775 or
toll free 1-800-492-0470

**MASSACHUSETTS**
Industrial Accident Board
100 Cambridge Street
Boston, Massachusetts 02202
 (617) 727-4900

**MICHIGAN**
Bureau of Workers' Disability Compensation
Department of Labor
309 North Washington
Post Office Box 30016
Lansing, Michigan 48909
 (517) 373-3490

**MINNESOTA**
Division of Workers' Compensation
Department of Labor and Industry
Space Center, Fifth Floor
444 Lafayette Road
St. Paul, Minnesota 55101
 (612) 296-6490

**MISSISSIPPI**
Workmen's Compensation Commission
1428 Lakeland Drive
Post Office Box 5300
Jackson, Mississippi 39216
 (601) 987-4200

**MISSOURI**
Division of Workers' Compensation
Post Office Box 58
Jefferson City, Missouri 65102
 (314) 751-4231

**MONTANA**
Division of Workers' Compensation
Department of Labor and Industry
Five South Last Chance Gulch
Helena, Montana 59601
 (406) 444-6500

**NEBRASKA**
Workmen's Compensation Court
State Capitol, Post Office Box 94967
Lincoln, Nebraska 68509–4967
 (402) 471-2568

**NEVADA**
State Industrial Insurance System
515 East Musser Street
Carson City, Nevada 89714
 (702) 885-5284

**NEW HAMPSHIRE**
Workmen's Compensation Division
Department of Labor
19 Pillsbury Street
Concord, New Hampshire 03301
 (603) 271-3176, 271-3171

**NEW JERSEY**
Department of Labor
Division of Workers' Compensation
C.N. 381
Trenton, New Jersey 0862
  (609) 292-2414

**NEW MEXICO**
Workers' Compensation Division
P.O. Box 27198
Albuquerque, New Mexico 87125-7198
  (505) 841-8787

**NEW YORK**
Workers' Compensation Board
180 Livingston Street
Brooklyn, New York 11248
  (718) 802-6934

**NORTH CAROLINA**
North Carolina Industrial Commission
Dobbs Building
430 North Salisbury Street
Raleigh, North Carolina 27611
  (919) 733-4820

**NORTH DAKOTA**
Workmen's Compensation Bureau
Russel Building
4007 North State Street
Bismarck, North Dakota 58501
  (701) 224-2700

**OHIO**
Bureau of Workers' Compensation
246 North High Street
Columbus, Ohio 43215
  (614) 466-2950 or toll free
1-800-282-9536

**OKLAHOMA**
State Industrial Court
1915 N. Stiles
Oklahoma City, Oklahoma 73105
  (405) 557-7600

**OREGON**
Workmen's Compensation Department
201 Labor and Industries Building
Salem, Oregon 97310
  (503) 378-3304

**PENNSYLVANIA**
Bureau of Workers' Compensation
3607 Derry Street
Harrisburg, Pennsylvania 17111
  (717) 783-5421

**PUERTO RICO**
Chairperson
Industrial Commission
G. P. O. Box 4466
San Juan, Puerto Rico 00936
  (809) 781-7576

**RHODE ISLAND**
Department of Workers' Compensation
P.O. Box 3500
610 Manton Avenue
Providence, Rhode Island 02909
  (401) 272-0700

**SOUTH CAROLINA**
Workers' Compensation Commission
1612 Marion Street
P.O. Box 1715
Columbia, South Carolina 29202–1715
  (803) 758-3498

**SOUTH DAKOTA**
Division of Labor and Management
Department of Labor
700 North Illinois Street
Pierre, South Dakota 57501
  (605) 773-3681

**TENNESSEE**
Division of Workers' Compensation
Department of Labor
501 Union Building, Second Floor
Nashville, Tennessee 37219
  (615) 741-2395

**TEXAS**
Industrial Accident Board
200 East Riverside Drive, First Floor
Austin, Texas 78704–1287
  (512) 448-7900

**UTAH**
Workmen's Compensation Division
Industrial Commission
160 East 3rd South
P.O. Box 45580
Salt Lake City, Utah 84145
  (801) 530-6800

**VERMONT**
Department of Labor and Industry
Five Court Street, 3rd Floor
Montpelier, Vermont 05602
  (802) 828-2286

**VIRGINIA**
Industrial Commission
Post Office Box 1794
Richmond, Virginia 23214
  (804) 257-8600 or toll free
1-800-552-4007

**WASHINGTON**
Department of Labor and Industry
General Administration Building
Mail Stop AX-3 I
Olympia, Washington 98504
  (206) 753-6307

**WISCONSIN**
Workers' Compensation Division
Department of Industry, Labor and Human Relations
201 East Washington Avenue
Post Office Box 7901
Madison, Wisconsin 53707
  (608) 266-6827

**VIRGIN ISLANDS**
Division of Workmen's Compensation
Department of Labor
Post Office Box 890
Christiansted
St. Croix, Virgin Islands 00820
  (809) 775-5747

**WEST VIRGINIA**
Workers' Compensation Fund
601 Morris Street
Charleston, West Virginia 25301
  (304) 348-2580

**WYOMING**
Workmen's Compensation Department
122 West 25th Street
Herschler Building
Cheyenne, Wyoming 82002–0700
  (307) 777-7441

# Canada—Federal

**ALBERTA**
Workmen's Compensation Board
9912–l07th Street
Post Office Box 2415
Edmonton, Alberta T5J 255
  (403) 427-1100

**BRITISH COLUMBIA**
Workers' Compensation Board
6951 Westminster Highway
Richmond, British Columbia V7C 1C6
  (604) 273-2266

**MANITOBA**
Workers' Compensation Board
333 Maryland Street
Winnipeg, Manitoba R3G 1M2
  (204) 786-5471

**NEW BRUNSWICK**
Workers' Compensation Board
Post Office Box 160
Saint John, New Brunswick E2L 3X9
  (506) 652-2250

**NEWFOUNDLAND**
Workers' Compensation Board
P.O. Box 9000
Station B
St. John's, Newfoundland A1A 3B8
  (709) 754-2940

**NOVA SCOTIA**
Workers' Compensation Board
Post Office Box 1150
Halifax, Nova Scotia B3J 2Y2
  (2-7341)

**ONTARIO**
Honorable Chairman
Workers' Compensation Board
Two Bloor Street, East
Toronto, Ontario M4W 3C3
  (416) 965-8880

**PRINCE EDWARD ISLAND**
Workers' Compensation Board
60 Belvedere Avenue
Post Office Box 757
Charlottetown, Prince Edward Island
  C1A 7L7

**QUEBEC**
Workers' Compensation Board
524 Rue Bourdages
Post Office Box 1200
Postal Terminal, Quebec GIK 7E2
    (418) 643-5964

**SASKATCHEWAN**
Workers' Compensation Board
1840 Lorne Street
Reginia, Saskatchewan 54P 2L8
    (306) 565-4379

**YUKON**
Workers' Compensation Board
4114 4th Avenue
Suite 300
Whitehorse, Yukon Y1A 4N7

**NORTHWEST TERRITORIES**
Workers' Compensation Board
P.O. Box 8888
Yellowknife, Northwest Territories X1A2R
    (403) 873-7484

# UNEMPLOYMENT COMPENSATION

Unemployment compensation is another legally required benefit that was established years ago as part of the Social Security Act of 1935. Each state operates its own unemployment compensation system, and regulations differ significantly from state to state.

Employers finance this benefit by paying a percentage tax on their total payrolls to state and federal unemployment compensation funds. When an employee is out of work and is actively looking for employment, he or she normally receives up to 26 weeks of pay, at the rate of 50 percent to 80 percent of normal pay. In most states employees may collect unemployment benefits only if they are involuntarily terminated, and they must use up any vacation and severance pay before they can start collecting.

Contact your local unemployment compensation office for details and a copy of your state's regulations.

## Curbing Unemployment Compensation Costs

Unemployment Compensation costs can be one of the most expensive elements of doing business. If you aren't familiar with the laws in the states in which you do business, and don't have the time to monitor this activity, you may want to use an outside organization to report terminations, administer claims, and closely monitor fees and costs. These outside companies more than pay for themselves in dollars saved through effective administration. There are several companies nationwide that do this type of administration. One such company is The Frick Company, 2675 Scott Avenue, St. Louis, MO 63103; 1 (314) 535-3999.

# PERSONAL PRIVACY AND EMPLOYEE RIGHTS

## Personal Privacy Versus the Computer and the HRIS

As more and more personal information on employees is entered into the corporate computer, legal and ethical issues are being raised. In fact, human resource executives, academic experts, congressional committees, and business people have all expressed concern that the use of computers to gather personal information about people may outpace the legal safeguards.

In America, the two most significant gatherers of information on people are the federal government and the individual's employer. Federal laws provide protections against governmental abuses under the concepts of constitutional rights, due process, equal opportunity, individual rights, and safety. Also, government falls under public scrutiny, especially by the press and the television media. The laws that provide safeguards and legal restrictions on government information, however, do not regulate private employers.

Employers can gather all the information on employees they want. There are no controls over employer record keeping, virtually no legal limits on the information that an employer may gather, and no limits on the disclosure of that information to others.

Laws have been passed in some states stating that employees have a right to see their personnel files and may request the company change any information that is in error.

Medical records are another major concern of employees. Even though a doctor takes the Hippocratic Oath, agreeing not to disclose medical information on patients, third party payments and personnel data banks make confidentiality impossible.

Most human resource people can tell horror stories about medical information being used to make a decision on an employee's suitability for promotion. Most human resource people will tell employees not to use medical benefits to pay for psychotherapy if they want to move up in an organization. This is certainly a privacy and an ethical issue that will be challenged in the future.

Employees sign away their rights to privacy when, for example, they sign a medical claims form that says, "I authorize any licensed physician, medical practitioner or other person to disclose information." When you hurriedly sign this statement, you may not realize it, but you are knowingly granting access to any and all medical information in your personnel file.

The issue of personal privacy versus the corporate computer is heating up and employees are beginning to question the invasion of privacy threat of personnel data systems.

## Three Steps to Avoid Invasion of Privacy Lawsuits

It is absolutely essential today to implement corporate privacy policy guidelines. There are three steps you can take to implement workable guidelines and avoid costly litigation in the privacy area.

1. Publish a privacy policy or statement regarding your computer system. Include such areas as controls on operating practices, access of data subjects, and usage control by data subjects. This statement should cover both the system's impact on individual employee privacy and the effect of privacy regulations on the system.

2. Construct a comprehensive privacy plan for all computer systems. A plan will ensure that all necessary privacy controls are integrated into the design of the system. For an existing system, the plan should cover changes in programs, equipment, and procedures.

3. Train employees who work in data systems and in human resources how to handle personal information on employees. Make your privacy policies and procedures well known to all operating personnel and to all employees.

Employees who work with personal information on employees should understand the legal and ethical considerations of employee privacy. Also, employees want to know how their personal information is being treated; because of past abuses, many employees do not trust their employer to maintain confidentiality over personal information. Smart corporate management is open and above-board with employees-telling them exactly what is maintained, where and how it is maintained, and they communicate privacy policies openly to employees.

## Privacy and Home Based Employees

Many employees are working at home using computers and telephones. Television used to be just a device for bringing news and entertainment into the home, but now people hook up their televisions to computers, cable systems, and telephones and are creating new technology called interactive home media, *hometech,* or telecommuting.

Cable is primarily used today for commercial programming, but cable companies are exploring new services that will transform cable into a tremendous network of data available on a daily basis. We will be able to receive electronically stored news, classified ads, yellow pages, weather reports, and stock quotations, and perform interactive transactions such as banking, shopping, making airline reservations, and even have remote medical diagnosis. There will also be monitoring of home security, energy use, opinion polling, and special communications for home workers.

All of this tremendous technical capability also creates privacy dangers that have been largely overlooked. Our old traditional concepts of individual privacy do not account for the new realities of interactive home media.

As more employees choose to work at home and as more companies provide these arrangements, human resource managers must take responsibility in addressing the important issues of both personal privacy and corporate security.

## Protecting the Privacy of Computerized Personnel Records

Most automated personnel systems have protections and safeguards built in, but many human resource information systems that were developed years ago contain information that is contrary to privacy and affirmative action regulations today. You must ensure that the HRIS is cleansed of old, obsolete data. An automated personnel records audit is one way of doing this.

Every change that goes into the system should trigger a profile printout that is given to the employee in order to allow updating and cleansing of wrong information on a regular basis.

There has been an increased use in the last few years of HRIS data in court cases. Most of the time it is used in discrimination cases. Plaintiffs can gain access to the HRIS data through legal processes and attempt to use the data to prove discrimination. The data from computerized systems may be given more credence by a jury and may, therefore, be difficult to rebut.

In the case of *Adams v. Dan River Mills, Inc.,* a case involving alleged racially discriminatory employment practices, the court ordered the defendant, Dan River, to supply the plaintiff with a computerized master payroll file, as well as printouts for the W-2 forms of defendant's employees. The court reasoned:

> The plaintiffs stated that they need the current computer cards or tapes and the W-2 printouts in order to prepare accurate, up-to-date statistics which will be relevant to determining whether or not discriminatory practices have occurred. Furthermore, the plaintiffs contend that the use of this computerized data is the most inexpensive and reliable method which can be used since making the necessary studies with human labor is not only extremely time-consuming and expensive, but also is more susceptible to error.
>
> Because of the accuracy and inexpensiveness of producing the requested documents in the case at the bar, this court sees no reason why the defendant should not be required to produce the computer cards or tapes and the W-2 printouts to the plaintiff.

A plaintiff's attorney can use inaccuracies in a computerized system to weaken a company's defense against an employment discrimination claim. It could also be embarrassing for the human resource department to be the focal point in a lawsuit where the employee- related database they designed, developed, and maintained becomes a helpful tool for a plaintiff.

It becomes more obvious every day how important the management of the human resources information system is. The responsibility transcends just the departmental personnel files.

# AN ADA CHECKLIST FOR EMPLOYERS

The company has long supported equal opportunities for people with disabilities. We support the goals of the Americans with Disabilities Act of 1990 (ADA) because we believe it reflects sound human resource and business practices.

Although this checklist is not intended to be a definitive document on ADA compliance, a "No" answer indicates an area that you may need to examine for improvement.

## HUMAN RESOURCE POLICIES:

|  |  | YES | NO |
|---|---|---|---|
| 1. | Have you communicated to all employees your company's policy and commitment to employment and reasonable accommodation for qualified applicants and employees with disabilities? | ❏ | ❏ |
| 2. | Have training sessions and/or information been made available to current supervisors and managers regarding their ADA responsibilities? | ❏ | ❏ |
| 3. | Is there a process in place to identify the need for reasonable accommodations and other ADA requirements when employees become disabled? | ❏ | ❏ |
| 4. | Is a system in place to maintain confidential medical and health information separately from personnel files? | ❏ | ❏ |
| 5. | Do you provide the same opportunities of employment to all employees in the same job classification (e.g. compensation, benefits, promotion, training, etc.? | ❏ | ❏ |
| 6. | Have you posted notices regarding the individual rights of employees under the ADA? | ❏ | ❏ |

## INTERVIEWING AND HIRING:

|  |  | YES | NO |
|---|---|---|---|
| 7. | Is your application/interviewing process fully accessible to *all* job applicants? | ❏ | ❏ |
| 8. | Have job applications been checked for prohibited questions related to health, disability or workers' comp history, and have interviewers been advised not to ask questions of this nature? | ❏ | ❏ |
| 9. | Do job descriptions within your company identify the essential functions necessary to perform the job? | ❏ | ❏ |
| 10. | Do employment tests and procedures for taking the tests accurately assess only the necessary skills and aptitudes required to perform the essential job functions? | ❏ | ❏ |
| 11. | Are all employer-requested physicals conducted only after a conditional job offer is tendered, and are they required of *all* applicants in that job category? | ❏ | ❏ |
| 12. | Do your post-offer physicals assess only the candidate's ability to perform the essential functions of the offered position? The results of post-offer physicals cannot be used to discriminate against a qualified individual on the basis of disability. | ❏ | ❏ |
| 13. | Are requirements for "reasonable accommodations" understood to be a necessary part of the process when considering an applicant? | ❏ | ❏ |
| 14. | Are managers most likely to be involved with reasonable accommodations aware of the best approach with a disabled person? Have competent external resources been identified that can be used when needed? | ❏ | ❏ |

## OTHER POLICIES:

|  |  | YES | NO |
|---|---|---|---|
| 15. | Have you notified all professional search organizations with whom you have contracts of your intention to fully comply with the ADA? | ❏ | ❏ |
| 16. | Do employees with disabilities have equal access to break rooms, cafeterias, and other facilities (on-site/off-site) provided by you? | ❏ | ❏ |
| 17. | Have you ensured that your company meets its obligations under the Public Accommodations title of the ADA? | ❏ | ❏ |

## SAMPLE ADA ACCOMMODATION LETTER

Date

ADDRESS

Dear Mr./Mrs.:

Thank you for applying for the position of _____ at XYZ Company. We had a number of qualified applicants for the position and have chosen another candidate who met all of the qualifications for the position. After speaking with your contact person, we ascertained that because of your hearing disability you are not able to use a regular telephone or an amplifier on a regular telephone.

The job description for this position states that the physical qualifications for the job require "a normal range of hearing and vision." Frequent telephone discussions with clients, contractors and vendors are an integral part of this job. (See attached job description).

With your experience we feel you could perform some of the essential job functions, but one of the most important functions is use of a telephone. The Company would be willing to make an accommodation for you if you could use an amplifier on our telephone, but the cost of a special telephone system would create an undue financial hardship on the Company and an administrative burden we're not able to accommodate.

We thank you for contacting us and applying for the position, and wish you luck in your job search.

Sincerely,


Human Resources Manager
XYZ Company

# FAMILY AND MEDICAL LEAVE ACT OF 1993 (FMLA)

FMLA requires covered employers to provide up to 12 weeks of unpaid, job-protected leave to "eligible" employees for certain family and medical reasons. Employees are eligible if they have worked for a covered employer for at least one year, and for 1,250 hours over the previous 12 months, and if there are at least 50 employees within 75 miles.

*REASONS FOR UNPAID LEAVE:* Unpaid leave must be granted for *any* of the following reasons:

- to care for the employee's child after birth, or placement for adoption or foster care;
- to care for the employee's spouse, son or daughter, or parent, who has a serious health condition; or
- for a serious health condition that makes the employee unable to perform the employee's job.

At the employee's or employer's option, certain kinds of *paid* leave may be substituted for unpaid leave.

*ADVANCE NOTICE AND MEDICAL CERTIFICATION:* The employee may be required to provide advance leave notice and medical certification. Taking of leave may be denied if requirements are not met.

- The employee ordinarily must provide 30 days advance notice when the leave is "foreseeable."
- An employer may require medical certification to support a request for leave because of a serious health condition, and may require second or third opinions (at the employer's expense) and a fitness for duty report to return to work.

*JOB BENEFITS AND PROTECTION:*

- For the duration of FMLA leave, the employer must maintain the employee's health coverage under any "group health plan."
- Upon return from FMLA leave, most employees must be restored to their original or equivalent positions with equivalent pay, benefits, and other employment terms.
- The use of FMLA leave cannot result in the loss of any employment benefit that accrued prior to the start of an employee's leave.

*UNLAWFUL ACTS BY EMPLOYERS:* FMLA makes it unlawful for any employer to:

- interfere with, restrain, or deny the exercise of any right provided under FMLA;
- discharge or discriminate against any person for opposing any practice made unlawful by FMLA or for involvement in any proceeding under or relating to FMLA.

*ENFORCEMENT:*

- The U.S. Department of Labor is authorized to investigate and resolve complaints of violations.
- An eligible employee may bring a civil action against an employer for violations.

FMLA does not affect any Federal or State law prohibiting discrimination, or supersede any State or local law or collective bargaining agreement which provides greater family or medical leave rights.

*FOR ADDITIONAL INFORMATION:* Contact the nearest office of the Wage and Hour Division, listed in most telephone directories under U.S. Government, Department of Labor.

---

U.S. Department of Labor, Employment Standards Administration                    WH Publication 1420
Wage and Hour Division, Washington, DC 20210                                                  June 1993

# CERTIFICATION OF PHYSICIAN
## UNDER THE FAMILY AND MEDICAL LEAVE ACT OF 1993

| 1. Employee's Name: | 2. Patient's Name (If other than employee): |
|---|---|

**3. Diagnosis** _____
_____
_____
_____

| 4. Date condition commenced: | 5. Probable duration of condition: |
|---|---|

6. Regimen of treatment to be prescribed (Indicate number of visits, general nature and duration of treatment, including referral to other provider of health services. Include schedule of visits or treatment if it is medically necessary for the employee to be off work on an intermittent basis or to work less than the employee's normal schedule of hours per day or days per week):

    a. By Physician: _____
_____
_____

    b. By another provider of health services, if referred by Physician: _____
_____
_____
_____

IF THIS CERTIFICATION RELATES TO CARE FOR AN EMPLOYEE'S SERIOUSLY-ILL FAMILY MEMBER, SKIP ITEMS 7, 8 AND 9 AND PROCEED TO ITEMS 10 THROUGH 14 ON REVERSE SIDE. OTHERWISE CONTINUE BELOW.

Check Yes or No in the boxes below, as appropriate:

    Yes   No

7.  ❏   ❏    Is inpatient hospitalization of the employee required?

8.  ❏   ❏    Is employee able to perform work of any kind? (If "No" skip Item 9.)

9.  ❏   ❏    Is employee able to perform the functions of employee's position? (Answer after reviewing statement from employer of essential functions of employee's position, or, if none provided, after discussing with employee.)

| 15. Signature of Physician: | 16. Date: |
|---|---|

17. Type of Practice (Field of Specialization, if any):

FOR CERTIFICATION RELATING TO CARE FOR THE EMPLOYEE'S SERIOUSLY-ILL FAMILY MEMBER, COMPLETE ITEMS 10 THROUGH 14 BELOW AS THEY APPLY TO THE FAMILY MEMBER AND PROCEED TO ITEM 15 ON REVERSE SIDE.

|  | Yes | No |  |
|---|---|---|---|
| 10. | ❏ | ❏ | Is inpatient hospitalization of the family member (patient) required? |
| 11. | ❏ | ❏ | Does (or will) the patient require assistance for basic medical, hygiene, nutritional needs, safety or transportation? |
| 12. | ❏ | ❏ | After review of the employee's signed statement (See Item 14 below), is the employee's presence necessary or would it be beneficial for the care of the patient? (This may include psychological comfort.) |

13.   Estimate the period of time care is needed or the employee's presence would be beneficial:

### ITEM 14 TO BE COMPLETED BY THE EMPLOYEE NEEDING FAMILY LEAVE.

14.   When Family Leave is needed to care for a seriously-ill family member, the employee shall state the care he or she will provide and an estimate of the time period during which this care will be provided, including a schedule if leave is to be taken intermittently or on a reduced leave schedule:

_____

_____

_____

| Employee Signature: | Date: |
|---|---|

Company/Division/Location:

# 4

# EMPLOYEE
# COMMUNICATIONS

- Making the Personal Connection Is Important to Your Company's Success

- 25 Management/Employee Communications Channels You Can Implement in Your Company

- How to Start an Employee Newsletter

- Sample Employee Handbook

- Employee Handbook Acknowledgment Form

# EMPLOYEE COMMUNICATIONS

## MAKING THE PERSONAL CONNECTION IS IMPORTANT TO YOUR COMPANY'S SUCCESS

Don't rely too heavily on impersonal forms of employee communications if you want the most productive and successful organization possible. The changing makeup of today's workforce is a major contributor to the need for more frequent and personal employee/management communications. The dramatic forces that have been affecting business in the last five years-intense restructuring, mergers and acquisitions, deregulation, global competition, the switch to a service economy-have all had a huge impact on employees and on human resource management. It is becoming more obvious every day that employee communications and a hands-on, positive attitude are needed to successfully manage the diverse workforce of the 1990s.

### 25 MANAGEMENT/EMPLOYEE COMMUNICATIONS CHANNELS YOU CAN IMPLEMENT IN YOUR COMPANY:

1. *Multi-level staff meetings* where workers and supervisors at all levels participate and where their input is sought and used.

2. *Face-to-face communications* every day through walk-arounds and regular non-threatening employee contact.

3. *Frequent informational letters and memos* telling everyone at every level what the company is doing and how current projects are going.

4. *Committees and task forces* that address current issues and problems on a participative basis.

5. *Discussion groups* where there are regular forums, both structured and unstructured, to discuss current issues and company problems, reading discussion groups on topics such as "In Search of Excellence," or "Getting to Yes" (learning how to negotiate).

6. *Employee mass meetings* when there is something of substance to discuss.

7. *Training programs* to address the needs of workers at every level. There may be basic literacy training or more difficult skill building workshops for supervisors on coaching and developing subordinates.

8. *Employee newsletter* published once a month that contains information about the company and employees. Use pictures of employees and company events.

9. *Bulletin boards* for company information and for employee use in selling items or letting each other know about special events.

10. *Social programs,* picnics, Christmas parties, tailgate parties in football season, covered dish lunches where everyone brings the food of their ancestral country (this idea helps foster positive relations with today's diverse workforce).

11. *Athletic programs:* bowling leagues, softball teams. The relaxed atmosphere can create positive communication networks.

12. We are entering an era where the family will once again be the center of activity for many people. Plan *family nights* or a Saturday now and then where you open your plant or offices and let employees bring their children to see where they work. Serve refreshments and encourage the families to linger and get acquainted.

13. *Employee attitude surveys* to give you an idea what employees are thinking and to test the climate. You might want to use an outside consultant to do the survey for you. If you do a survey be sure to give the employees the results and tell them what you intend to do if the survey shows improvements are needed.

14. *Feedback sessions.* If your survey shows that you have some problem areas, it's a good idea to have some small group feedback and discussion sessions. It's a mistake to bury problems. You need to get them out in the open and discuss them.

15. *Brown-bag lunches,* lunch hour movies and mini-seminars. Have local speakers with interesting topics or hobbies come in and talk to employees. Many people will do this free of charge.

16. *Annual report to employees* showing how the company is doing and discussing company benefits and any other human resource items.

17. Run *contests for employees* occasionally. Set sales goals, or build contests around attendance or safety records.

18. Give *service awards* and have service awards dinners for employees at 1 year, 3 years, 5 years, 10 years, and so on.

19. Have an *arts and crafts week.* Let employees bring their artwork or crafts and provide a room for display. Let them sell their items during lunch hours and after work.

20. Start an *employee speakers bureau.* Invite someone from a local speakers group like Toastmasters to come to your offices or plant and help start the group.

21. *Suggestion system* or suggestion box. Give an award each month for the best suggestion. Encourage employees to offer ideas for improving their jobs or increasing production or sales.

22. Once a year *ask each department to prepare an overview* of their department and what they do, for the entire company. This fosters a sense of pride in employees and increases basic knowledge for everyone in the organization.

23. Start an *in-house audio tape library* that employees can use to increase their individual skills. Let them check out tapes and listen to them while commuting to and from work. Tapes could be on improving listening skills or learning how to negotiate. There are hundreds of good subjects. Make audio tapes on the company's history or products.

24. Provide *safety training and classes on CPR or first aid.* Do the training in small groups so that employees learn to work together as a team and to communicate with each other. Design the groups so that participants are from different departments.

25. Start *noontime walking/jogging groups* from different departments in the spring, summer, and fall. It's not only a good idea health-wise, it promotes cross-departmental communications.

Check the chapter on checklists for more ideas on developing new communications programs.

## HOW TO START AN EMPLOYEE NEWSLETTER

Starting an employee newsletter is a challenging assignment. In order for any publication to be successful, it must be attractive and informative for today's wide range of workers.

Readership surveys show that internal publications are the primary source of information for most employees and that the contents of most company newsletters are reliable, accurate, and believable. A survey conducted by the International Association of Business Communicators and Towers, Perrin, Forster and Crosby, of 45,000 personnel at forty organizations in the United States and Canada indicates that a high percentage of people (89 percent) find employee publications believable.

The first thing to do is to define the scope and format of the newsletter. Then establish a budget and a time line for publication.

### *Newsletter Startup Checklist*

❑ Establish the scope of the newsletter. (Is it a total company information tool, or merely an anniversary, birthday, safety award type of publication?)

❑ Establish format (tabloid, newsletter).

❑ Decide on frequency of publication (monthly, quarterly).

❑ Decide on basic contents.

❑ Establish a budget.

❑ Evaluate and decide on the time restrictions of current staff. Will a new person be hired to produce the newsletter?

❑ What outside resources will you use (writers, graphic artists, printers)?

❑ If outside printers are to be used, get three or four quotes on production costs.

❑ Will the publication have to appeal to local employees only, or is there a national or international readership?

❑ Who will have editorial control of the contents? Who will produce the newsletter?

❑ What will be the distribution, and who has distribution control?

❑ How will you measure the newsletter's effectiveness over time?

It's a good idea to set up a news-gathering network from key areas of the business. Ask for volunteers to be reporters, and build a backlog of articles and fillers to have on hand for times when current events are slow. It's also a good idea for the person who does the newsletter to understand design, photography, graphics, and reproduction. Most printers will help in this area.

In planning the newsletter, think about how readability will be measured. How will you determine what employees want to read? What will be the style of the publication? Who will have the editorial and distribution control?

## *Writing for Your Audience*

CASE IN POINT   Linda Brown got a job editing a company newsletter and launched the publication quickly and efficiently, publishing the first issue within her first three weeks on the job. Instead of her first issue being a hit, however, it was a flop! She used the experiences she had gained from her previous employer, not taking the time to assess her new readership. Her previous employer had an older employee population and management that insisted on a formal style. Her writing and graphics followed the formal format she had used before, but the readers in her new company were younger and the company style was more informal. What was accepted and appreciated in her previous company was not accepted at all by her new readers. It is difficult to regroup and gain credibility for a newsletter if you start off on the wrong foot, so audience identification is an important element when starting an employee newsletter.

# SAMPLE EMPLOYEE HANDBOOK

There are pros and cons to having an employee handbook, but many executives and attorneys today feel that a handbook that provides employees with uniform policies and procedures is an important management tool. In a survey of over 600 companies that use handbooks and policy manuals a majority of executives said that among other things, manuals and handbooks pay for themselves by making things work better and eliminating the constant need to interpret "what the policies and procedures are around here."

The key is consistency of treatment, and without set policies and procedures everyone in the company tends to interpret things their own way. A free-wheeling management style tends to get companies into trouble.

The old handbooks and policy manuals tended to be long and full of "legalese." They sounded dry and intimidating. The new, more acceptable style is to keep manuals short and to the point, written in a less formal style. Limit a policy or a procedure to one or two paragraphs and keep the wording simple.

The following model employee handbook may be too brief for your needs. If it is, adapt it to fit your organization.

---

### Manager's Tip

The difference between an employee handbook and a personnel policy manual is *purpose*. The handbook tells employees what procedures to follow and what their benefits are. The personnel policy manual is primarily for supervisors, to help them know and understand the policies in order to manage consistently. The policy manual is a management guide.

# *Employee Handbook*

**Date**

**THIS HANDBOOK SUPERSEDES ALL PREVIOUS HANDBOOKS ISSUED BY THE COMPANY OR ANY OF ITS SUBSIDIARIES**

**Manager's Tip**

Always date your employee handbook and *always* include the above wording. You will need to revise this handbook to fit your policies, procedures, and benefits.

# Employee Guidelines

This handbook provides guidelines related to appropriate handling of matters concerning personnel policies and procedures of _____.
These guidelines are for informational purposes and are not intended to be a legal document or an employment contract. Questions regarding the guidelines should be directed to your immediate supervisor, or to the Human Resources Department. The Company reserves the right to change, modify, suspend, interpret or cancel, in whole or in part, any personnel policy, guideline or practice at any time without advance notice.

# At-Will Employment Relationship

This handbook is not intended to create or constitute an expressed or implied contract between the Company and any one or all of its employees. The Company or the employee may terminate the employment relationship at any time, without prior notice. The Company may terminate an employee for any or no reason with or without the use of progressive discipline. This is called "At-Will employment." apart from the policy of At-will employment and those policies required by law, the Company may change its policies or practices at any time without prior notice.

**Note:**
_____

Use the elements of this handbook that best fit your company needs, however, always use the above paragraphs to reinforce the at-will relationship. You may wish to have your attorney review your handbook before you distribute it to employees.

# Contents

INTRODUCTION
- Your Company
  - Confidential Information and External Communications
  - Code of Conduct
  - Harassment
  - Employees with Disabilities

YOUR JOB
- Introductory Period
- Hours of Work and Overtime
- Attendance
- Absence
- Rest Periods
- Administration
- Scheduling
- Civic Duties
- Jury Duty
- Leaves of Absence
  - Family and Medical Leave
  - Maternity Leave of Absence
  - Military Leave of Absence
  - National Guard
  - Bereavement
  - Absence for Occupational Disabilities
  - Personal Leave of Absence Without Pay
  - Sick Leave

YOUR PAY
- Pay Periods
- Performance Appraisals and Raises
- Overtime

YOUR BENEFITS
- Benefits and Services
- Recognized Holidays
- Holiday Pay
- Vacations

YOUR SAFETY
- Safety
- In Case of Injury
- Security Procedures

JOB OPPORTUNITIES

EMPLOYEE RELATIONS POLICY

PROBLEMS . . . HOW TO SOLVE THEM
- Termination

WHAT ELSE YOU NEED TO KNOW
- Appearance and Attire
- Bulletin Boards
- Business Mileage Reimbursement
- Business Travel
- Inclement Weather Procedures
- Pay For Lost Time Due to Inclement Weather
- Smoking
- Solicitation and Distribution
- Suggestions
- Miscellaneous

OVERVIEW OF EMPLOYEE BENEFITS

ACKNOWLEDGMENT AND RECEIPT OF EMPLOYEE HANDBOOK

# Introduction

We believe that our employees play a major role in our Company's success. We seek to create an atmosphere within the Company that will allow all employees to feel a genuine sense of accomplishment. At no time will we knowingly permit discrimination toward an employee because of age, sex, race, color, religion, national origin, disability, sexual orientation or for any other unlawful reason.

We believe that both the Company and its individual employees should be good citizens. We seek to fulfill our obligations toward our government and toward the community in which we work. We encourage our employees to play a positive role in community endeavors.

Through the contribution of our employees and the recognition of their efforts, we believe that the Company can achieve a level of performance which will provide each of us with a sense of pride. We hope you will enjoy working for our Company. We have established some guidelines to help maintain the harmonious working relationships we feel are important.

# Your Company

(*Put information about your Company here.*)

## Confidential Information and External Communications

How the Company is perceived by its business associates, the media, legislators, regulatory agencies, special interest groups, and the general public is a direct result of the external communications activities carried out by our management and employees. These external relations have a significant impact on our business. In order to present the best image of the Company, it is important that the messages we communicate are consistent with Company philosophy, policies and procedures.

Serious problems could be created for the Company by unauthorized disclosure of internal information about the Company, whether for the purpose of facilitating improper trading in the Company's stock or otherwise. Company personnel should not discuss internal Company matters or developments with anyone outside of the Company, except as required in the performance of regular job duties.

If you are unsure as to what information is confidential, please consult with your supervisor or the Corporate Compliance Department. *Outside inquiries regarding Company business should be referred to the President.*

The President serves as an information channel for news media and for any person or organization outside the Company. He is responsible for approval of press releases, responding to media inquiries, and coordinating interviews with the media.

## Code of Conduct

The Company has a Corporate Code of Conduct that relates to business ethics and conflicts of interest, among other things. The Code is provided to each employee at the time of hire. All employees are required to read the Code, to attend a meeting or watch a videotape that explains the Code in depth, and then to sign an Annual Certification and Compliance Questionnaire. Questions relating to the Corporate Code of Conduct, or possible violations of its provisions, should be referred to the Corporate Compliance Department.

## Harassment

Harassment of any employee in the workplace, based on a person's race, color, sex, religion, national Origin, age, disability or sexual orientation, is unlawful. We fully support equal employment opportunity and will not tolerate discriminatory harassment of its employees. Discriminatory conduct which is sufficiently severe or pervasive as to alter the conditions of employment and which creates an intimidating, hostile, or abusive work environment will be considered harassment pursuant to this policy.

Sexual harassment includes unwelcome sexual advances, requests for sexual favors, sexually degrading or suggestive communications or statements, and other verbal, visual or physical conduct of a sexual nature. No supervisor shall threaten or insinuate, either explicitly or implicitly, that an employee's submission to or rejection of sexual advances will affect the employee's employment, evaluation, wages, advancement, assigned duties or any other term or condition of employment or career development.

Any employee who feels that he/she or someone else is a victim of harassment, including but not limited to any of the conduct listed above, by any employee, customer, client or any other person in connection with his or her employment should report the concern immediately to their supervisor, a member of senior management, or the Director of Human Resources. All complaints will be investigated promptly in as confidential a manner as possible and appropriate corrective or disciplinary action will be taken where warranted.

Any employee who is determined, after investigation, to have engaged in harassment in violation of this policy will be subject to immediate disciplinary action, up to and including discharge.

## Employees with Disabilities

The Americans With Disabilities Act of 1990, as amended, prohibits discrimination on the basis of disability, and protects qualified applicants and employees with disabilities from discrimination in hiring, promotion, discharge, pay, job training, fringe benefits, and other terms and conditions of employment. The law also requires that covered entities provide qualified applicants and employees with disabilities, as defined by the Act, with appropriate reasonable accommodation, if such accommodation does not impose an undue hardship. If you believe that you have been discriminated against based upon disability, contact your supervisor or the Human Resources Department immediately. If you believe you have a qualifying disability and require some reasonable accommodation, also contact your immediate supervisor or the Human Resources Department.

# Your Job

## Introductory Period

There is a 90-day introductory period for all new employees and employees who accept a transfer into a new job. All employees, regardless of status or duration of employment, are required to meet and maintain Company standards for job performance and behavior. Either the employee or the Company may end the employment relationship at will at any time during or after the introductory period, with or without reason or advance notice. Completion of the introductory period does not guarantee employment for any specific period of time. As stated previously, we are an "At-Will" employer.

Benefits go into effect the first day of the month following three months of employment. information regarding benefits will be provided at the New Employee Orientation session.

## Hours of Work and Overtime

*Work Week*—The regular or normal work week consists of 40 hours and begins with the period beginning 12:00 A.M. Monday and ending 168 consecutive hours later on the following Sunday.

*Work Day*—The normal work day for the Company consists of eight hours, excluding lunch periods. Normal hours of business in Denver are 8:30 A.M. to 5:30 P.M. Field locations may have different business hours. Lunch periods are set by each department or subsidiary and may be dictated by the laws in the varying states in which we operate.

*Work Schedules*—Work schedules will be established based upon business needs and objectives and are subject to change at management's request. Employees will be notified in advance of changes in work hours or work schedules.

*Overtime*—All overtime work must be approved in advance by your supervisor.

Nothing in these guidelines should be assumed to be a guarantee of employment for any number of hours or period of time.

## Attendance

You are an essential member of our team . . . and teamwork is the heart of our business. It is important that employees be prompt and regular in attendance. If you are unable to report to work on time because of circumstances beyond your control, you should notify your supervisor as soon as possible on the day you will be absent.

## Absence

The Company and your co-workers depend on you. The success of the Company is dependent on everyone doing their job. When you are absent, it is difficult to fill your shoes. If you need to be away from work, your supervisor must be given advance notice so the vacancy can be filled with a minimum of inconvenience to the operation and to your fellow employees.

If your absence will be longer than one day, your supervisor must be given an expected date of return. Should this date change, notify your supervisor at once. The Company may require medical certification for any absence. When returning to work after an illness of five days or more, a written medical release from your doctor may be required. The Company reserves the right to request a doctor's statement or require the employee to be examined by a physician of the Company's choice. If you are given a conditional medical release, the doctor must state what the conditions of the partial release are and specify any job limitations.

In cases of serious personal illness or other situations in which advance notice is impossible, notify your supervisor as soon as you can. A member of your immediate family may, if necessary, fulfill this obligation.

Tardiness or absenteeism which is considered by the Company to be excessive may result in disciplinary action, up to and including termination. An absence for a period of three consecutive work days without contacting your supervisor to request a leave of absence could be a considered voluntary termination of employment.

## Rest Periods

The Company provides one paid 10-minute break each morning and one paid 10-minute break in the afternoon. Employees who take additional breaks must punch out on the time clock because additional breaks are not paid. Excessive absence from the job during the work day results in lost productivity and could result in an unfavorable performance evaluation or disciplinary action, including termination. Each supervisor establishes the break schedule based on the needs of his or her department, and applicable state regulations.

## Administration

Non-exempt employees must record all hours by submitting a time card or time sheet to their supervisor for approval. Time cards with discrepancies must be corrected prior to each pay period.

Employees must record any vacation, sick pay, personal pay, jury duty, bereavement leaves or any other absence on an Employee Absence Report Form. Your supervisor or the Human Resources Department has these forms.

It is the manager's responsibility to ensure that their employees record all hours correctly on their time cards.

## Scheduling

As the need arises, managers may schedule work days and hours that differ from the standard work days and hours described above. Occasionally, a flex-time schedule may be granted by a manager if the schedule is arranged in advance in writing and benefits the Company as well as the employee. This type of schedule is only for short-term use in order to address a specific employee need. Lunch periods are scheduled by managers. Advance approval of the manager is required when overtime is to be worked or any change in scheduled hours is required.

## Civic Duties

It is Company policy to allow employees reasonable time off without loss of pay to attend to civic duties, such as court appearances on behalf of the Company, voting, witness or jury duty. You may be asked to provide documentary proof of such summons. Your supervisor can provide more information.

## Jury Duty

The Company recognizes jury duty as a civic responsibility of everyone. When summoned for jury duty, you are granted leave to perform your duty as a juror. If you are excused from jury duty during your regular work hours, we expect you to report to work promptly.

You will receive regular pay for the first five days of jury duty if you were scheduled to work and you submit a juror service certificate.

*NOTE:* Jury pay varies from state to state. Check with your supervisor for jury pay at your location.

## Leaves of Absence

For an unpaid leave of absence of more than 10 days, written application must be made on a Leave of Absence Form and must have the department manager's approval.

*Family and Medical Leave:* The Company will comply with The Family and Medical Leave Act of 1993 which became affective August 6, 1993, by providing up to 12 weeks of leave in a 12-month period with the guarantee of the same or an equivalent job upon return to work. Family or medical leave may be taken to care for a newborn or newly adopted child, for your own personal illness, or to care for an immediate family member who is seriously ill. To be eligible, you must be employed for at least 12 months, and have provided 1,250 hours of service during the 12 months before the leave is requested. No more than 12 weeks of Family or Medical Leave may be taken within a 12 month period (measured backward from the beginning of the leave).

If you do not meet the eligibility requirements for a family or medical leave, but need time off because of your medical condition, the Company may grant up to four weeks of unpaid leave, but job reinstatement is not guaranteed.

If the leave is for your own serious medical condition, you must first use your accumulated sick leave; thereafter, or after a 15-day waiting period, you may be paid through the Company's Short-Term Disability program, if eligible. If the leave is to care for the birth or placement of a child, or is to care for a seriously ill family member, you will be paid any accrued vacation time, then accrued sick time, and thereafter your leave would be without pay.

A Leave of Absence Request Form must be completed and approved in advance. The Company will pay their portion of your medical benefits while on an approved Family or Medical Leave. Contact the Human Resources Department in Denver for further details regarding a Family or Medical Leave of Absence.

*Maternity Leave of Absence:* Maternity leave is the same as medical and family leave, and benefits are the same. Maternity leave is compensated in the same manner as any medical disability.

*Military Leave of Absence:* Any regular full-time employee of the Company who enters active duty in the armed forces of the United States will be granted a military leave of absence without pay.

Active military service entered directly from Company employment may result from:

- Being drafted
- Being ordered to active duty, or active duty for training when on reserve status.

An individual returning from military service will be rehired into the former position or into a job of similar status and like pay if the following eligibility criteria are met:

- The individual presents to the company a copy of a certificate of satisfactory completion of military service.
- Application for re-employment is made within 90 days of discharge or from hospitalization continuing after discharge for a period of not more than one year.
- The individual is able to perform the duties of the former or similar position.

*National Guard:* Any regular, fill-time employee, employed seven months or longer, who is a member of a reserve component of the armed forces of the United States, or a member of the National Guard or Air National Guard, will be granted an unpaid two-week leave of absence for annual training duty or for emergency National Guard duty at the call of a state governor. A leave of absence without pay may be granted for any additional time needed to complete annual training or emergency duty.

*Bereavement:* In the event of the death of an immediate family member (spouse, mother, father, siblings, children, grandparents or grandchildren and in-laws), the employee may take up to three consecutive days' paid leave. If the employee must travel out of state, and additional two days may be granted for travel time.

Employees should notify their supervisor immediately upon learning of the death so proper arrangements can be made during the employee's absence. Should additional time be needed and approval is granted by the supervisor, the employee may take vacation time or floating holiday. The employee must make the appropriate notation on the time card.

*Absence for Occupational Disabilities:* An employee who must be away from work due to a work-related illness or injury will fall under the guidelines of the Family and Medical Leave Act. If the employee is unable to return to work within 12 weeks, he/she may be given additional leave under the worker's compensation statutes of the state in which the employee is working. The leave will be unpaid by the Company, and the Company will not pay the employer's portion of the medical insurance premium, while the employee is out and receiving workers' compensation benefits.

If the employee has a work-related injury but can continue to work, time off for medical appointments will be paid by the Company.

*Personal Leave of Absence Without Pay:* The Company may make provisions for a personal leave of absence without pay for an employee who needs more than one month's time off work for a valid reason other than those covered by the above paragraphs. The maximum leave that may be granted is six months.

When an unpaid personal leave of absence is granted, it is given on an individual basis and at the discretion of management, taking into consideration the purpose of the leave, the employee's work record, and the needs of the Company at that particular time. An employee must exhaust all earned unused vacation before an unpaid personal leave will be authorized.

You must be classified as a regular full-time employee and have completed six months of continuous service prior to the effective date of the unpaid personal leave, and you must complete a Leave of Absence Form and have it approved by your supervisor and submit it to the Human Resources Department.

The Company cannot guarantee reinstatement to the former position or to a position with like status and pay, except in the case of Family and Medical Leave or Military Leave. In these two instances, an employee's job or an equivalent job for which the employee is qualified is guaranteed by federal law.

*Employees who are on any approved unpaid leave of absence other than a Family or Medical Leave, which is mandated by state and/or federal law, must pay their own medical, life and dental insurance premiums if they wish to keep their insurance in force while they are gone. Additionally, it should be noted that when an employee who is on an authorized Family Care/Medical Leave mandated by state and/federal law, the Company will pay its portion of medical benefits for a period not to exceed 12 work weeks.*

*Sick Leave:* All regular full-time employees earn 6.67 hours of sick time per month beginning the first day of the month following date of hire. Regular part-time employees who are normally scheduled to work at least 30 hours per week will receive a pro-rated amount. The eligibility requirements for regular part-time employees are the same as for regular fill-time employees. *NOTE:* Change these numbers to fit your plan.

Up to five sick days per year may be used to care for an ill immediate family member.

For each three full days of accrued sick leave in excess of 30 days, the employee will be eligible for one day of vacation. At the employee's anniversary date, any unused "excess" sick leave for the prior year will automatically convert to vacation days at a rate of 3 sick days to 1 vacation day.

An employee should make the appropriate notation for sick pay on their time card or on an Employee Absence Report Form. Where required, attach the doctor's certification to the Form.

Unused sick time is not paid upon termination, except for unused excess sick time which has automatically converted to vacation days.

# YOUR PAY

## Pay Periods

Pay days are on the 15th and the last day of each month. If pay day falls on a holiday or weekend, you will be paid on the last working day preceding the holiday or weekend. Please endorse your check and cash or deposit it within 30 days. If you would like direct deposit of your paycheck, your supervisor or payroll administrator can provide the appropriate forms.

## Performance Appraisals and Raises

Performance is appraised once a year, usually in July. Raises are not guaranteed but are at management's discretion and based on, among other things, management's assessment for job performance and the Company's operating results.

## Overtime

Non-exempt employees are paid one and one-half times their base rate for all hours in excess of 40 hours worked in a week. If you are a regular full-time employee and are asked to work on a Company-recognized holiday you will receive double time for all hours worked on that holiday. Overtime laws vary by state. Ask your supervisor for details for your specific location. Note: In some states like California, overtime must be paid over 8 hours in a day.

# YOUR BENEFITS

## Benefits and Services

As an employee, you will have an opportunity to participate in our many fine benefits programs. A summary of the Company's benefit plans is set forth in the Overview of Employee Benefits in this Employee Handbook.

## Recognized Holidays

We normally observe nine paid holidays per year as follows: New Year's Day, Memorial Day, Independence Day, Labor Day, Thanksgiving Day, day after Thanksgiving Day,

Christmas Day, one floating holiday, and the employee's birthday. The birthday holiday may be taken within 30 days of your birthday. An unused floating holiday or birthday holiday may not be carried forward from year to year, and only the current year's days will be paid on termination.

### Holiday Pay

Regular full-time and part-time employees who are regularly scheduled to work a minimum of thirty (30) hours per week are eligible for holiday pay. To be eligible for holiday pay you must be at work on the scheduled workday before and after a holiday, unless you are on a paid leave of absence, vacation, or are ill. New employees will be eligible for holiday pay after the first day worked.

If your supervisor feels that you have sufficient justification to be off the day before or after a holiday, your absence may be excused and payment of holiday pay will be approved. Written approval must be furnished to the payroll department. Some Company positions, including regular part-time employees, receive prorated holiday pay.

### Vacations

The Company provides a paid vacation benefit to regular full-time and part-time employees who regularly work a minimum of thirty (30) hours per week. Vacation time is prorated for part-time employees who regularly work more than 30 hours per week. A Vacation Request Form must be completed and approved by your supervisor in advance. Each year on your anniversary date, the Company provides the following vacation:

- 2 weeks after 1 year
- 3 weeks after 5 years
- 4 weeks after 10 years

In some states, such as California, vacation benefits accrue immediately when the person is hired. Ask your supervisor about vacation accrual at your location. Earned, unused vacation is paid upon termination.

# YOUR SAFETY

### Safety

Your safety is a concern. We make every reasonable effort to provide you with a safe place to work. We want you to be safe on the job as well as off. Don't take chances. When you think safety, you make things safe for yourself and your fellow employees. If an accident occurs on the job, notify your supervisor immediately. You must complete a First Report of Injury form and give it to your supervisor as soon as you are able but in any case within 48 hours. If immediate medical assistance is required and you cannot reach your supervisor, call 911. Unsafe conditions or employee conduct which jeopardizes your safety or the safety of others should be reported immediately to your supervisor or other management personnel. Such reports will be investigated and appropriate action will be taken, including disciplinary action, where appropriate.

## In Case of Injury

If you are injured on the job in the normal course of your employment, you are directed to report the injury to your supervisor and Human Resources Department immediately, and to seek medical attention from our Health Care Facility. In a life or limb threatening emergency, call 911 and then notify your supervisor immediately. All job site injuries must be reported within 48 hours, or as per state law. If on the day of your work-related injury, you are, in the opinion of your supervisor, unable to work the remainder of the day, you will be compensated. Check with your supervisor for information on reporting accidents and obtaining medical assistance at your specific location.

## Security Procedures

Each Company location has its own set of security procedures. Ask your supervisor for specific information.

Whenever the office fire alarm sounds or there is a bomb threat, everyone in the building is to calmly proceed to the nearest stairway exit and vacate the building. *Never attempt to enter an elevator during an emergency fire alert.*

When leaving your work areas, you are asked to take your personal wallets and purses with you for security reasons. Each supervisor is to check their area to ensure that all personnel have evacuated.

# JOB OPPORTUNITIES

In an attempt to advise employees of job opportunities within the Company, each Division and the Corporate office may post weekly bulletins announcing job vacancies at their specific locations. If you meet the minimum qualifications and would like to be considered for a posted job, contact a Human Resources Representative for a Job Bid form and further information. Following is the Job Line number for our employees: _____.

You must be in a position for six months before asking to be considered for a new job, and you must not be on a performance improvement plan or disciplinary action.

Jobs posted are not necessarily reserved or held exclusively for current employees. The Company reserves the right to hire the candidate that it determines in it's discretion is best suited for the job, and to promote, demote, increase or decrease wages, or take any other actions concerning the terms and conditions of employment without cause or reason and without notice.

# EMPLOYEE RELATIONS POLICY

We hope that your work experience will be rewarding. The Company provides equal opportunity to all applicants and employees regardless of race, color, religion, national origin, sex, age, disability or sexual orientation.

# PROBLEMS: HOW TO SOLVE THEM

We hope all employees share a feeling of pride in the Company, and that your spirit of cooperation and enthusiasm in working for the good of the Company will be apparent in all your relations. We realize however that valid differences occasionally arise. Here is how to handle these differences.

The following complaint procedures have been established. *These procedures may be used by current employees or by terminating employees.*

Step1—Employee discusses the complaint or problem with immediate supervisor. It is expected that every effort will be made to resolve the complaint in a fair and amicable manner at this level.

Step 2—If the employee is not satisfied with this attempt to resolve the complaint or a response (written or verbal) is not received within ten working days, the employee may discuss the matter with the next management level.

Step 3—If the problem still has not been resolved within another ten days at the second level, a formal written complaint may be directed to the President. A determination by the President is final.

At any time, the employee may contact the Director of Human Resources for assistance in resolving a problem.

The Company may impose counseling or disciplinary action which, in its judgment, most effectively addresses the problem. You will be advised of such actions should they occur.

We hope it will not be necessary to discipline or discharge employees. There may be times however, when it becomes necessary to formally correct the performance of individuals and, in some cases, termination could occur. The Company reserves the right to make these decisions, including the right to terminate an employee at any time for any or no reason, with or without use of progressive discipline or performance improvement plans.

## Termination

If it is your intent to resign from employment, two weeks' notice should be provided to the Company. The Company will appreciate the opportunity to make arrangements to cover the vacancy created by your leaving.

# WHAT ELSE YOU NEED TO KNOW

## Appearance and Attire

Our public image is directly dependent on our staff, individually and collectively. People are inclined to judge organizations by the people who represent them. The personal appearance, quality of service and positive attitude of all of our employees are essential to creating and maintaining a favorable public image.

Attire should be conservative, in good taste and promote a business-like professional attitude and image in keeping with your specific job. The best "rule of thumb" is to dress for the position you fill and the people you serve. The Company reserves the right to insist that employees who serve our clients and customers dress professionally. The Company will comply with any state statutes which apply to employee dress codes in states in which we do business.

The Company specifies certain days as casual dress days, however, even on casual days, attire must be in good taste. Managers will be notified of these special days in advance.

## Bulletin Boards

To keep you informed, the Company provides bulletin boards in the lunch rooms at every work site. No material may be posted or removed from bulletin boards `without the approval of the Director of Human Resources.

All applicable federal and state employment laws must remain posted at each location.

## Business Mileage Reimbursement

Unless you are already provided an auto allowance, you will be compensated for mileage on the use of your personal car for Company business at the current rate allowed by the Internal Revenue Service. Your supervisor or the Human Resources Department has special forms for this purpose.

## Business Travel

If you are required to travel out of town to conduct the Company's business, we will pay for your necessary expenditures. Your supervisor will let you know the appropriate procedures for business travel.

## Inclement Weather Procedures

Employees should listen to radio stations or call their supervisor to learn if the offices will be closed when the weather is bad. Employees at other field locations should also check with their supervisor for inclement weather procedures.

## Pay For Lost Time Due to Inclement Weather

- If the Company closes the office, employees will be paid for the hours they missed but were scheduled to work that day.

- If the office is open but attendance "optional," employees who do not work will not be paid for their time off unless they make up the lost time during that same week or use a vacation day.

- If the office is open for business as usual, employees who do not work must use vacation time in order to be paid for the time off, or take the time off without pay.

## Smoking

The Company and all its subsidiaries do not allow smoking in any facility.

## Solicitation and Distribution

Out of respect for the private lives of our employees and our desire to receive the full benefit of your productivity, no person who is not an employee of this Company (except commercial sales people calling on the Company) may come onto the property at any time to solicit for any cause or to distribute material of any kind for any purpose without permission.

Employees may not engage in solicitation or in the distribution of materials of any type for any purpose during working time on Company property, except for that which is necessary to carry out their assigned job duties. However, employees may engage in solicitation during their non-working time and may participate in the distribution of materials on their non-working time in non-working areas as long as standards of neatness are maintained.

An employee is not to enter or remain in work areas except during scheduled working time and a reasonable time before or after scheduled work, or when working scheduled overtime. If an employee wants to enter those working areas at any other time for a legitimate reason, permission must be secured.

## Suggestions

The exchange of ideas within our organization is considered by management to be an asset and is strongly encouraged. Your thoughts concerning ways of increasing productivity, improving the quality of our work products, our projects, safety, and other related matters are welcome. Address your suggestions to the president of the company.

## Miscellaneous

Information regarding employee parking, building access, and facilities may be obtained from your supervisor.

# Overview of Employee Benefits

This is just a summary of the employee benefits. See official plan documents for more detailed information.

| Benefit | Description | Eligibility |
| --- | --- | --- |
| **Holiday Pay** | Nine paid holidays per year, as follows:<br>• New Year's Day<br>• Memorial Day<br>• Independence Day<br>• Labor Day<br>• Thanksgiving Day<br>• Day after Thanksgiving<br>• Christmas Day<br>• Employee's Birthday (must be used within 30 days of birthday)<br>• 1 Floating Holiday<br>If a holiday falls on a Saturday, it will be observed the preceding Friday; if a holiday falls on a Sunday, it will be observed the next Monday. Holiday pay is pro-rated for eligible part-time employees. | Regular full-time or part-time employees. Must be on a paid status to be eligible for holiday pay. |
| **Sick Pay** | Employees earn ten days of paid sick time per year (6.67 hours per month for full-time employees), up to a maximum accrual of 30 days (240 hours). Sick pay is pro-rated for eligible part-time employees. Five days of sick time per year may be used to care for an ill family member. Sick time accrued in excess of 30 days is converted to vacation time, at the rate of one day of vacation for each three full days of sick time. | Accrual begins first of month after hire date for regular full-time and part-time employees who are scheduled to work a minimum of 30 hours per week. |
| **Vacation Pay** | Vacation pay is earned on employee's anniversary date,* and is based on years of continuous service:<br>    2 weeks after 1 year<br>    3 weeks after 7 years<br>    4 weeks after 12 years<br>Vacation time must be scheduled ahead of time and be approved by supervisor; it may be used in increments of half-days. Unused vacation time will carry over from year to year. Vacation pay is pro-rated for eligible part-time employees.<br>(*California employees accrue vacation immediately, based on state law.) | Regular full-time or part-time employees scheduled to work a minimum of 30 hours per week; upon completion of one full year of service. |
| **Other Paid Time Off** | *Bereavement Leave*—Pay will be granted for up to three days leave in the event of death of immediate family member (spouse, mother, father, siblings, children, grandparents, grandchildren and in-laws). Two additional days off may be granted for out-of-state travel.<br>*Jury Duty*—Employees who miss work while performing jury duty will receive the time off with pay for up to a maximum of 30 days, upon submission of proof of jury service. | Regular full-time and part-time employees scheduled to work a minimum of 30 hours per week. |
| **Medical insurance** | Eligible employees may choose one of the two following plans. Cost of health insurance coverage is shared between employer and employee; premiums are deducted from semi-monthly pay.<br>*Designated Provider Program (DPP):* Covered individuals choose a primary care physician (PCP) who will manage-all health care needs. Preventive care is stressed.<br><br>**If PCP and In-Network Used:**<br>• No annual deductible;<br>• No limitations on treatment for pre-existing conditions;<br>• $10 co-pay for doctor's office visit;<br>• $50 for outpatient surgery;<br>• $200 co-pay for hospitalization;<br>• $5 co-pay for generic Prescription drugs from participating pharmacies (supply of 30 days or less); maintenance drugs may be purchased through the mail at discount. | First of month following three months of employment for regular full-time or part-time employees scheduled to work a minimum of 30 hours per week.<br><br>Common-law marriages are not recognized in the states of Arizona, California and Virginia. Subject to change in state legislation.<br><br>May apply for benefits during open enrollment (October 1st of each year). |

| Benefit | Description | Eligibility |
| --- | --- | --- |
| **Medical Insurance,** *continued* | **If Non-Network Provider Used:**<br>• $400 per person annual deductible/$800 per family;<br>• Employee pays 30% of covered charges, up to a maximum of $3,400 per person/$6,800 per family (including deductible);<br>• After maximum out of-pocket expenses are met, covered services are paid at 100%;<br>• Preventive care not covered;<br>• 30% co-insurance for prescription drugs, subject to deductible.<br><br>*Preferred Provider Organization (PPO)*<br>**If Network Provider Used:**<br>• No annual deductible;<br>• $10 per Doctor office visit;<br>• 10% per hospitalization;<br>• Limited preventive care coverage Is provided.<br><br>**If Non-Network Provider Used:**<br>• $200 per person annual deductible/$400 per family;<br>• Employee pays 30% of covered charges, up to maximum of $1,500 per person/$3,000 per family (including deductible);<br>• After maximum out of-pocket expenses have been paid, covered services are paid at 100%;<br>• $5 co-pay for generic prescription drugs; $20 co-pay for brand-name drugs. | |
| **Dental Insurance** | Employees may select one of the following dental plans. Cost of dental insurance coverage is deducted from employee's semi-monthly pay:<br><br>*U.S. Dental* (pre-paid plan):<br>• Must choose dentist within the U.S. Dental Plan network;<br>• $5 co-payment for office visits;<br>• **Basic preventive and diagnostic services** are paid at no charge to employee;<br>• **Restorative services** are provided at no charge or at minimal copayments;<br>• **Extensive services** are provided at reduced fees<br>• **Orthodontic services** are offered at reduced fees.<br><br>*Unilife Dental Plan* (traditional indemnity plan):<br>• Free choice of dentist;<br>• **Preventive procedures** are paid at 100%;<br>• **Restorative procedures** are paid at 805 after the annual deductible of $50 per person has been met;<br>• **Major services** are reimbursed at 50% after the annual deductible of $50 per person has been met; are not available during the first year on the plan;<br>• **Orthodontia services** are available for children after the third year. Are reimbursed at 50% after the lifetime deductible of $50 has been paid;<br>• Maximum annual dental benefit of $750 for first year, $1,000 for second year, and $1,500 per year thereafter. | First of month following three months of employment, for regular full-time or part-time employees scheduled to work a minimum of 30 hours per week.<br><br>May apply for benefits during open enrollment (October 1st of each year).<br><br>Common-law marriages are not recognized in the states of Arizona, California and Virginia. Subject to change in state legislation. |
| **Life Insurance and Accidental Deathand Dismemberment Insurance** | Available as part of Health Insurance package.<br>Company provides $20,000 of life insurance and $20,000 of accident insurance for each eligible employee enrolled in the health insurance plan. scheduled to work a minimum of 30 hours per week. | First of month following three months of employment, for regular full-time or part-time employees |

| Benefit | Description | Eligibility |
|---------|-------------|-------------|
| **Voluntary Term Group Life Insurance Plan** | Employee may purchase coverage up to five times base annual pay (maximum $300,000), in increments of $10,000 for self and spouse. Employee may purchase coverage for eligible children, in increments of $2,500, up to $10,000 maximum<br>$30,000 guarantee issue available if application is made within 30 days of employment.<br>Reduced rates available for non-smokers. | Regular fulltime or parttime employees scheduled to work a minimum of 30 hours per week. No waiting period; coverage begins first of the month after payroll deductions begin.<br><br>Common-law marriages are not recognized in the states of Arizona, California and Virginia. Subject to change in state legislation. |
| **Short Term Disability** | Employees who miss more than 15 days of work due to an illness or injury may receive up to 60% of weekly base pay, to maximum of $500 per week. Benefits end after 150 days away from work, at which time the long term disability benefits may apply. | First of month following three months of employment for regular employees scheduled to work a minimum of 30 hours per week. |
| **Long Term Disability** | Employees who miss more than 150 consecutive work days because of an illness or injury may receive up to 605 of their base monthly earnings, up to a maximum of $4,000 per month, through the long term disability program. | First of month following three months of employment for regular employees scheduled to work a minimum of 30 hours per week. |
| **401 k Plan** | Employee may contribute 1–15% of base pay to retirement account on pre-tax basis, up to statutory limits. Company matching is determined on a year-to-year basis, based on company earnings. Employee has six investment options for contributions. | First of quarter following one full year of employment, for regular full-time employees. |

# Acknowledgment and Receipt
# of Employee Handbook

This employee handbook published (*Date*) supersedes all previous employee handbooks.

I have received a copy of the employee handbook. I understand that I am to read and become familiar with the contents. If I have questions, I understand that I should talk to my Supervisor or the Director of Human Resources.

Further, I understand that:

This handbook is not intended to, nor does it create promises or representations of continued employment. Every employee has an at-will relationship with the Company. This means that I am free to resign my employment at any time, just as the Company is free to terminate my employment, for any or no reason, with or without cause or the use of progressive discipline, at any time.

This handbook represents a summary of the more important company guidelines at the time of publication, and is not intended to be all inclusive. In all instances, the benefit plan texts, trust documents and master contracts, as appropriate, are the governing documents. The employee handbook, personnel policies, benefit plan texts, any trust agreements, or master contracts are not employment contracts.

Apart from our policy of *At-Will* employment and those policies required by law, the Company may change its policies or practices at any time without prior notice. I understand the Company may terminate an employee at any time with or without notice.

Further, I understand that this document will become a part of my personnel file.

_____

Employee Name (Please Print)                    Location/Department

_____

Signature                                        Date

# 5

# PERSONNEL POLICIES

- Keys to Successful Implementation of Personnel Policies
- Checklist for Personnel Policy Manual
- Fifteen Ways to Communicate Your Policies
- Personnel Policy Manual Key Instructions
- Sample Personnel Policy Manual

# PERSONNEL POLICIES

Most organizations today, even small ones, need a set of personnel policies and guidelines. Set policies help managers and supervisors to evenhandedly manage the workforce. This helps the company avoid costly litigation brought by people who feel they were not treated fairly. You don't need a policy to regulate every single event that might occur. What you do need are policies to cover difficult personnel areas like discipline and termination. Policy manuals are mainly for the use of supervisory personnel, to aid in day-to-day management of their people.

## KEYS TO SUCCESSFUL IMPLEMENTATION OF PERSONNEL POLICIES

Planning is the key to success when writing and implementing a personnel policy manual.

### Before Implementation

1. Ask potentially affected department heads to choose a representative to aid in the determination of need, shaping, structure, and implementation of the proposed policy or procedure.
2. Involve representatives from affected departments in all phases.
3. Explore the reasons for the change—advantages and disadvantages—with representatives of affected departments.
4. Evaluate potential alternatives in content and structure with representatives.
5. Determine whether a trial period and subsequent fine-tuning are appropriate.
6. Plan and organize the implementation or revision to ensure smooth transition through clear advance communication and training.

### After Implementation

1. Have the representatives from each affected department oversee and monitor the success of the transition and post-transition phases.
2. Any problem areas that cross departmental lines should be addressed by the committee of representatives.
3. Problems that lie within one department only should be addressed by the representative, department head, and policy initiator.

4. A formal survey throughout affected departments might be conducted six months after implementation in order to assess the workability and success of the newly implemented policy or procedure.

---

**Manager's Tip**
_____

Ask yourself the following questions:
> Does everyone affected clearly know the policy or procedure?
> Is the policy or procedure set up to produce the desired result?
> Are the skills that are necessary for successful administration found or developed in those who will need them?
> Does the policy and procedures manual contain the current information?

# CHECKLIST FOR PERSONNEL POLICY MANUAL

Use the following checklist when writing a personnel policy manual. Issues such as clarity, format, tone, and style should be addressed before you start the process.

## *Review for Clarity, Readability, and Understandability*

- ❏ Review each policy for clarity, readability, and understandability.
- ❏ Consider the education and training levels of the entire work force.
- ❏ Eliminate all ambiguities.
- ❏ Review handbook to ensure that all significant terms are used consistently and correctly.
- ❏ If a significant portion of the work force speaks a language other than English, consider (1) preparing the entire handbook in the foreign language, or (2) including a provision in the handbook that is written in the foreign language and that informs employees where they can obtain assistance if they have difficulty translating or understanding any policies.

## *Issues Regarding Style and Tone: Formal vs. Informal Tone*

### FORMAL

- ❏ References to employees in the third person rather than as "you."
- ❏ Less personal tone.
- ❏ Emphasis on professionalism.

### INFORMAL

- ❏ References to "you" rather than third person or "the employee."
- ❏ Emphasis on brevity.
- ❏ Use of cartoons and pictures.

❏ Avoid too much detail.

❏ Avoid legal and technical terminology.

❏ Tone "folksy" rather than "you're in the army now."

❏ Watch level-don't "talk down" to employees.

## Considerations

❏ Size of work force.

❏ Composition of work force.

❏ Average education levels of employees.

❏ Ability of employees to read and understand English.

❏ Occupations covered by the handbook.

❏ Industry practices and customs.

❏ Practices in the same geographical area.

❏ The impression the employer wishes to convey.

❏ The nature of the work environment.

## Gender References

❏ Check for consistency in all references to gender.

❏ Don't use "he," "she," or "he/she." Change to a plural pronoun and use "employees" or "they."

❏ Avoid references to gender by use of the second person "you" or gender-neutral terms such as "the employee" or "an individual."

## Areas Where Inconsistencies Are Frequently Found

❏ References to gender.

❏ References to employee classifications should be consistent and accurate (part-time employees, and regular full-time employees).

❏ The term used to describe the employer should be used consistently throughout the manual without switching from one term to another.

❏ A handbook should use numbers consistently. A common practice is to spell out numbers from one to one hundred and use numerals from 101 on. Make exceptions where spelling out numbers would be cumbersome, such as for measurements (40 hours; 5 feet). Many practices are "correct"; the important thing is to be precise and consistent.

# FIFTEEN WAYS TO COMMUNICATE YOUR POLICIES

If policies and procedures are not communicated frequently and in a manner that your current work force will accept, they will not be followed or used properly. In addition, any communication program must stay current with changing business conditions.

Following are fifteen ways to communicate with employees:

1. Conduct one-on-one communication between supervisor and employee at least once a month, quarterly, and at the yearly performance review.

2. Publish employee newsletters, articles, and stories about employees who are actively supporting the company and its business plans.

3. Use the media. Show films and slides on topics of current interest. Use video to train employees and for special programs.

4. Have programs during the lunch period, where speakers come in to speak on a variety of subjects pertinent to your business and industry. The company may donate 30 minutes extra if the program helps employees on their jobs, and the investment may be well worth the cost.

5. Some organizations, like U.S. Homes, have started monthly discussion group programs, aimed at managers and professionals. This is used as a management development tool. A particular book will be chosen, all participants read the book, and then a vice- president leads a discussion group on the merits of the principles set out in the book.

6. Sometimes, when companies are going through a particularly difficult time, a question box or telephone hotline will encourage dialogue. The employee doesn't have to give a name. Guarantee a response to all reasonable questions within a few days. You can reply through a special newsletter to all employees. If you do have a question box or hotline, it's important to reply in timely fashion, and you and your top management must agree to be open and honest or these avenues won't work well.

7. Create a communications task force to identify communication problems and suggest solutions. The task force should include people from a variety of functions and all levels in the company. People have more ownership in programs they or their peers help create.

8. To communicate policies and procedures in your own department, route the policy book to staff in your department and ask them to read it.

9. Put an extra copy of the policy manual in your library or in the personnel office, where employees can read it if they want.

10. Implement an orientation program for families so they understand the company, its products, its policies, and the office or plant facilities.

11. Publish an annual report to employees and their families, updating them not only on employee benefit statements, but also on the company's business plans and accomplishments.

12. Use athletic activities and health programs as avenues for employee communication.

13. Start an employee speakers' bureau. Give employees training in public speaking, and select topics that would be of benefit to the company as well as topics the employees choose.

14. If you have extra space that can be used occasionally, have an employee crafts fair where employees can sell their crafts. Make this a communication tool.

15. Set up closed circuit TV/VHF programs to inform employees about important management meetings, and pass on specific information employees may read.

## PERSONNEL POLICY MANUAL KEY INSTRUCTIONS

The policies in the following model personnel policy manual are purposely brief. Review them and rework them to fit your needs. Once you get them on your computer, rework them as the need arises, and keep them current with changes in your organization. You may not need every policy in this manual. Don't create more work for yourself than necessary by having policies that aren't needed.

Having a personnel policy manual will save you and your supervisors and managers untold time spent attempting to define policy verbally everyday throughout the company. Having written policies ensures consistency of treatment and will help you avoid unnecessary litigation. Have your attorney review your manual before implementation.

Use someone on your staff or a personnel consultant to implement the manual. Be sure to let your department heads review all policies, and ask for their input if you want them to be proactive in implementation.

### Note

This personnel policy manual is a sample format. All policies and procedures must conform to the laws in the state in which it will be used and should be reviewed by an attorney familiar with labor and personnel laws prior to being installed.

### Manager's Tip

Instead of using "Personnel Policies and Procedures," you may prefer to call them "Personnel Guidelines." There are two schools of thought: One says, "Make them hard and fast policies." The other says, "They should only be guidelines; let managers manage the company." It's a matter of style, but whether "policies" or "guidelines," they must be administered evenhandedly.

# Personnel Policy Manual

**Note**

Use the policies that fit your needs; you may not need every policy that is in this sample manual. Rewrite the policies to be company-specific. Then have your attorney review your manual before you print, distribute, and implement.

# PERSONNEL POLICIES AND PROCEDURES

This manual is designed as a statement of policy and outline of procedures and guidelines for supervisors to aid in the proper handling of matters concerning company personnel.

The policies and procedures set forth in this manual apply to all employees of _____ Company. However, this manual is not to be interpreted as a legal document or an employment contract. Policies contained herein are only summaries and are not all-inclusive. Managers must still manage day-to-day activities and make policy decisions where there are, at times, no strict guidelines.

Questions regarding these policies and procedures should be directed to _____.

The company reserves the right to alter, change, add to, or delete any of these policies or procedures at any time without notice.

# CONTENTS

- Lunch and Rest Periods
- Maternity Leave of Absence
- Moonlighting
- Orientation, New Employee
- Overtime
- Paydays
- Personnel Records
- Performance Appraisal
- Personal Time Off
- Professional Memberships
- Promotions
- Recreation Activities
- References
- Rehire
- Reinstatement of Benefits
- Relocation
- Safety and Health
- Salary Administration
- Security
- Separation Pay
- Service Awards
- Sick Time
- Smoking Policy
- Suggestion Program
- Signing Authority
- Temporary and Part-Time Employees
- Terminations
- Time Off with Pay
- Unemployment Compensation
- Veterans Reporting Requirements
- Voting
- Work Hours
- Vacation
- Work Rules
- Workers' Compensation

# Absenteeism

Because each employee is an essential member of our team and teamwork is important, we expect employees to be prompt and regular in attendance.

Employees who are unable to report to work on time because of circumstances beyond their control (including illness) are expected to notify their manager within a reasonable period of time on the morning of the absence.

If the absence is going to be longer than one day, the manager should be given an expected date of return. When an employee is returning to work after an illness of over five working days, a medical release from the doctor may be requested.

An absence for a period of three consecutive days without contacting a supervisor or the Personnel Department may be considered justification for termination.

A form is available for use in tracking employee attendance. If it becomes necessary to terminate an employee for absenteeism, the absentee record is an important part of the termination documentation.

# Advertising, Help Wanted

All help-wanted ads should be processed through the Personnel Department using the Help-Wanted Ad form. This will help the company make a uniform presentation in all print media. When an opening occurs and an ad is to be placed, the supervisor should draft the ad so that it contains the appropriate job specifications. The supervisor should send the ad copy to Personnel along with an employment requisition.

# Appearance and Attire

Our public image is directly dependent on our staff, individually and collectively. People are inclined to judge organizations by the people who represent them. The personal appearance, quality of service, and positive attitude of all of our employees are essential to creating and maintaining a favorable public image.

Attire should be conservative, in good taste, and promote a businesslike professional attitude and image in keeping with each specific job. Extreme forms of dress, hairstyle, or makeup are not acceptable. The best rule of thumb is to dress for the position you fill and the people you serve.

**Manager's Tip**

You can only require a specific dress code where the job justifies it. For example, someone who meets the public everyday can be required to dress in more business-oriented attire than a warehouse clerk who doesn't interact with customers.

# BENEFITS

## New Hire Benefits

The company provides medical and life insurance plans, all of which are described in separate brochures. All regular full-time employees are eligible to participate in these benefits after they have passed the 90-day evaluation period.

As employees become eligible, all necessary information will be provided to them.

## Benefits Upon Termination

### *Comprehensive Omnibus Budget Reconciliation Act (COBRA)*

On April 7, 1986, Congress enacted the Comprehensive Omnibus Budget Reconciliation Act (COBRA) which requires that most employers sponsoring group health plans offer employees and their families the opportunity for a temporary extension of health coverage (called "continuation coverage") at group rates in certain instances where coverage under the plan would otherwise end.

Effective January 1, 1987, employees covered by the company's group health plan have a right to choose continuation coverage should they lose their group health coverage because of (1) reduction in hours of employment or (2) termination of employment (for reasons other than gross misconduct on the employee's part).

A spouse or dependent of an employee covered by the company health plan has the right to choose continuation coverage if group health coverage under this plan is also for any of the following reasons:

1. The death of a spouse/parent;
2. A termination of a spouse's/parent's employment (for reasons other than gross misconduct) or reduction in a spouse's/parent's hours of employment;
3. Divorce or legal separation from a spouse/of parent;
4. Dependent ceases to be a dependent child as provided by the plan; or
5. Spouse/parent becomes eligible for Medicare.

Under COBRA, the employee or a family member has the responsibility to inform the personnel department of a divorce, legal separation, a child losing dependent status, Medicare eligibility, or death of an employee covered by the company's group health plan within 14 days of the event.

When the Personnel Department is notified that one of these events has happened, we will notify employees of their right to choose continuation coverage. Under COBRA, the person has at least 60 days from the date coverage would be lost because of one of the events described above to inform the Personnel Department that continuation coverage is desired. If continuation coverage is not chosen, the group health insurance coverage will end.

When continuation coverage is chosen, the company is required to provide coverage which is identical to the coverage provided under the plan to similarly situated employees or family members. The new law requires that employees be afforded the opportunity to maintain continuation coverage for three years unless group health coverage was lost because of a termination of employment or reduction in hours. In that case, the required continuation coverage period is 18 months. However, the new law also provides that continuation coverage may be cut short for any of the following five reasons:

1. The company no longer provides group health coverage to any of its employees;
2. The premium for continuation coverage is not paid;
3. The employee becomes an employee covered under another group health plan;
4. The employee becomes eligible for medicare; or
5. The insured is divorced from a covered employee and subsequently remarries and is covered under the new spouse's group health plan.

The law allows the employer to charge the employee the full premium for the insurance. It also provides that, at the end of the 18-month or three-year continuation coverage period, the employee must be allowed to enroll in an individual conversion health plan provided under the company's group health plan.

# BULLETIN BOARDS

Organizational bulletins announcing the names of newly hired employees, promotions, internal reorganizations, and other pertinent staff data will be posted on all bulletin boards along with other items of interest to employees.

Items intended for placement on bulletin boards must be approved and distributed by the personnel department. (Unless the company has a union: in that case, the union may post bulletins.)

### Manager's Tip

Don't allow employees or outsiders to post things on your company bulletin boards without your permission. Have a separate bulletin board (maybe in the lunch room) for items "For Sale" and other employee generated notices.

# CATASTROPHIC ILLNESS

The company recognizes that employees with life-threatening illnesses, including but not limited to cancer, heart disease, and AIDS, may wish to continue to engage in as many of their normal pursuits as their condition allows, including work. As long as these employees are able to meet acceptable performance standards, and medical evidence indicates that their conditions are not a threat to themselves or others, managers should be sensitive to their conditions and ensure that they are treated consistently with other employees. At the same time, the company has an obligation to provide a safe work environment for all employees. Every precaution should be taken to ensure that an employee's condition does not present a health or safety threat to other employees. Consistent with this concern for employees with life-threatening illnesses, the company offers the following resources available through the personnel department:

- Management and employee education and information on terminal illness and specific life-threatening illnesses

- Referral to agencies and organizations which offer supportive services for people with life-threatening illnesses

- Benefit consultation to assist employees in effectively managing health, leave, and other benefits

## Guidelines

When dealing with situations involving employees with life-threatening illnesses, managers should:

1. Remember that an employee's health condition is personal and confidential. Reasonable precautions should be taken to protect information regarding an employee's health condition.

2. Contact the personnel department if you believe that you or other employees need information about terminal illnesses or a specific life-threatening illness, or if you need further guidance in managing a situation that involves an employee with a life-threatening illness.

3. Contact the personnel department if you have any concern about the possible contagious nature of an employee's illness.

4. Contact the personnel department to determine whether a statement should be obtained from the employee's attending physician to the effect that continued right to require an examination by a medical doctor appointed by the company.

5. If warranted, make reasonable accommodation for employees with life-threatening illnesses consistent with the business needs of the division/unit.

6. Make a reasonable attempt to transfer employees with life-threatening illnesses who request a transfer and are experiencing undue emotional stress.

7. Be sensitive and responsive to co-workers' concerns and emphasize employee education available through the personnel department.

8. No special consideration should be given beyond normal transfer requests for employees who feel threatened by a co-worker's life-threatening illness.

9. Be sensitive to the fact that continued employment for an employee with a life-threatening illness may sometimes be therapeutically important in the remission or recovery process or may help to prolong that employee's life.

10. Employees should be encouraged to seek assistance from established community support groups for medical treatment and counseling services. Information on these can be requested through the personnel department.

**Manager's Tip**

You may or may not want a catastrophic illness policy. Some attorneys say yes, some say no. The consensus of human resource people today, however, is that you should be prepared to deal with major illnesses and have the policy in place.

# COMPLAINT PROCEDURE

Good employee-employer relationships can exist only if employees believe they have been treated equitably and fairly within the management policies, procedures, and actions which influence this relationship. It is recognized that there are occasions when honest differences of opinion can occur regarding the interpretation and application of policies, procedures, and actions.

The following procedure is established to provide an effective and acceptable means for employees to bring problems and complaints to the attention of management.

## Procedure

Step 1—Employee discusses the complaint or problem with immediate supervisor. It is expected that every effort will be made to resolve the complaint in a fair and amicable manner at this level.

Step 2—If the employee is not satisfied with this attempt to resolve the complaint or a response (written or oral) is not received within ten working days, the employee may discuss the matter with the next management level.

Step 3—If the problem still has not been resolved to the employee's satisfaction within another ten days at the second level, a formal written complaint may be directed to the president. A determination by the president is final.

## Documentation

It is understood that any employee who elects to use the employee complaint procedure will be treated courteously and that the case will be handled confidentially at all times. An employee will not be subject to discourteous action or reproach in any form due to use of the complaint procedure.

A complaint documentation file will not become part of an employee's regular personnel file. Complaint documentation will be maintained in a separate file and used only as a basis for recommending changes in management procedures.

Only those members of management with a need to know and who are in the employee's chain of command may have access to complaint procedures documentation.

**Manager's Tip**

This is an important labor relations policy that every company should have. If there is no safe way for employees to file legitimate complaints they will go to outside third parties for assistance.

# CONFIDENTIALITY AGREEMENT

## Policy I

It is the company policy that an Agreement of Confidentiality be signed by all employees. Please read and sign this agreement and return it to the Personnel Department.

### AGREEMENT OF CONFIDENTIALITY

As a condition of employment I understand that I will from time to time be engaged in work on projects that are proprietary and confidential. Because I may have access to or control over various confidential documents, I hereby agree that I will not in any manner reveal or divulge proprietary information to any person outside the company during or after my term of employment.

_____
Signature of Employee

_____
Date

### Manager's Tip

This agreement may or may not hold up in court. However, the consensus is that you may have a better chance of prosecuting a former employee who gives away proprietary information if you have a signed agreement of confidentiality.

# DISABILITY

The company has a short-term disability plan. Use of the plan requires a doctor's statement, and works as follows:

**Short-Term Disability.** Covers illness or injury of seven days or more.

**Accrual.** One day after 90 days of employment, then one day per month thereafter through the first full calendar year, to a maximum of ten days accrual per year. You can accumulate up to 65 days maximum.

**Long-Term Disability.** Long term disability (after 90 days) can be purchased separately by employees from the company's current insurance broker.

### Manager's Tip

This policy should be tailored to your specific needs and your company's budget. Few small companies can afford disability pay, so you may not need this policy.

# DISCIPLINARY ACTION AND WARNING NOTICES

Open communications between management and employees and the establishment of a friendly, cooperative work atmosphere go a long way toward eliminating serious disciplinary problems. If, however, disciplinary problems do arise, supervisors and managers should make every effort to ensure that employees have a thorough understanding of company policies and an awareness of what is expected in the area of job performance.

The purpose of this policy is to provide for progressive, evenhanded disciplinary action. Application of these guidelines must be consistent and equitable so that all employees receive like treatment for similar offenses.

These procedures are meant to assist managers in determining a proper course of action when discipline is needed. They are guidelines, not a substitute for common sense. Documentation of all verbal and written warnings is important in order to avoid the situation of an employee being discharged with no written proof of progressive discipline. In most cases, it is advisable to give an employee at least one documented verbal warning and one written warning before termination.

## Warning Notices

A minimum of two weeks and a maximum of 60 days is suggested as a guideline for determining the length of time between warnings. The warning should be specific in describing what improvement is needed. Copies of the warning should be provided to the employee and to the personnel department.

**Verbal Warning.** Before a written warning is issued, a verbal warning may be given to the employee. A copy or text of the verbal warning should be placed in the employee's personnel file.

**Written Warning.** If improvement is not made within the time period granted in earlier warning, it will be necessary to issue a written warning. Copies of written warnings must be furnished to the personnel department and to the employee. If the employee fails to improve by the date given on the warning, other disciplinary action, including suspension or termination, may result.

**Following the Issuance of a Written Warning.** There should be consultations with the employee to check on progress and improvement in the problem area. These consultations should be accurately documented as to the dates and outcome of the meetings. These meetings with employees should be positive and intended to help the employee improve in the job.

## Repeat Offenses

The procedures described above need not be followed if the employee repeats an offense for which warning has previously been given (in the preceding twelve months). In this case, the employee's supervisor should use discretion in determining the proper course of action. There should be consultation with the next level of management and with the personnel department to determine what actions should be taken.

## Records Retention

Records of verbal or written warnings may be removed from an employee's file after the employee has improved behavior in the problem area to the satisfaction of the manager. Employees should not be unduly penalized in future years for past difficulties and problems. Some human resources people prefer to keep copies or warnings in a separate file not in the employee's regular personnel file.

*If, in the opinion of the company an infraction is serious enough, any and all steps can be bypassed and discharge may occur.*

**Manager's Tip**

This is an area where you must be honest, nondiscriminatory, and evenhanded in policy administration. If you list infractions in your policy you should include a statement that the list is meant for illustrative purposes and is not all-inclusive.

# Drugs at Work

The company will not tolerate the use of alcohol, intoxicants, or illegal drugs at work. An employee found in possession of illegal drugs, using drugs or alcohol at work, or under the influence of alcohol or illegal drugs at work will receive one written warning. The second instance will be grounds for termination.

If there is any doubt about the employee's alcohol or drug use on the job, the company will require a test. The company will help employees who are addicted to alcohol or drugs by referring them to our Employee Assistance Program (EAP). A one-time referral will be paid for by the company. An employee who is referred to our EAP for drug or alcohol rehabilitation must enter the program and stay in it the prescribed time period as a condition of continued employment.

Our company's drug testing policy is aimed at stopping drug abuse through rehabilitation.

**Manager's Tip**

The kind of drug policy you write will depend on the goals you want to achieve. It is a good idea to have a human resource consultant or attorney help you write your policy. The policy should fit your particular needs and reflect your attitude toward drug abuse. Most experts today feel you cannot just fire an employee for drug abuse before trying to help them through rehabilitation. This is one area where you need some expert advice.

# Educational Assistance Program

We recognize that the educational development of employees is important to the company's success, and we encourage employees to engage in personal development activities. For that reason, this policy is established to provide an opportunity for all employees to obtain additional education or training in order to increase their competence in their present jobs and to prepare for advancement in the future.

**Eligibility**

This policy applies to all regular, full-time employees provided their plan of study does not interfere with their work schedule. In addition, the eligible participant must have completed six months of continuous service before starting the course. The maximum course load should be limited to six credit hours at any one time.

Employees already entitled to educational aid extended by a governmental agency (e.g., Veteran's Administration), private agencies, foundations, scholarships, or other such programs may be exempt from this plan. In those cases where such outside aid does not fully cover tuition or other expenses, the company may reimburse the employee for any differences covered by our plan if the employee meets all other requirements. The course must be business-related and approved by the supervisor. After successful completion of the approved course, an employee must submit receipts for tuition and books required for the course, and the company will reimburse the employee for those expenses. Successful completion will be defined as obtaining a grade of C or better.

# EMERGENCY PROCEDURES

The company has the following emergency procedures in place in case of crisis:

FIRE:

BOMB THREAT:

TERRORIST OR CRAZED PERSON ENTERING THE BUILDING:

MEDIA CRISIS:

OTHER:

**Manager's Tip**

Every company should try to identify the types of crisis that might occur and what procedures employees should follow in the case of each crisis. We are living in a time when crisis is commonplace; advance planning can save lives and considerable expense. The company should maintain current records that contain an emergency contact and next of kin on each employee.

# EMPLOYEE HANDBOOK AND AGREEMENT

It is company policy to provide each employee with an employee handbook setting out key company policies and procedures. This employee handbook should not be considered as an employment contract or a guarantee of employment. Each employee must sign an Employee Agreement that specifically states he or she realizes that neither the employee handbook nor the personnel policy manual constitutes an express or implied contract or assurance of continued employment, or that just cause is required for termination. (See Employee Agreement attached.)

The employee handbook should contain the date it was issued and further state that all previous editions are superseded by the current publication.

# EMPLOYEE AGREEMENT

This employee handbook and the personnel policy manual describe only the highlights of the company policies, procedures, and benefits. In all instances the official benefit plan texts, trust agreements, and master contracts as appropriate are the governing documents. Your employee handbook is not to be interpreted as a legal document or an employment contract. Employment with the company is at the sole discretion of the company and may be terminated with or without cause at any time for any reason. Nothing in this handbook or in the personnel policy manual constitutes an express or implied contract or assurance of continued employment, or that just cause is required for termination.

Understood and Agreed:

_____
(Employee's Signature)

_____
Date

**Manager's Tip**
_____

This employee agreement is to be signed and returned to the personnel department to be placed in the employee's personnel file when an employee handbook is provided to the employee. Note that in the past some courts have ruled that employee handbooks may be considered employment contracts.

# EMPLOYMENT OF SPOUSE

It is company policy not to discriminate in employment and personnel actions with respect to employees, prospective employees, and applicants on the basis of marital status. No employee, prospective employee, or applicant will be denied employment or benefits of employment solely on the basis of marital status. However, the company retains the right to:

- Refuse to place one spouse under the direct supervision of the other spouse where there is the potential for creating an adverse impact on supervision, safety, or morale.

- Refuse to place both spouses in the same department, division, or facility where there is the potential for creating an adverse effect on supervision, safety, security, or morale, or conflict of interest.

The company will allow the transfer of spouses between departments in order to accommodate married employees.

**Manager's Tip**

Policies on nepotism or restriction on the employment of relatives are almost a thing of the past. Employees are taking these cases to court and winning, so you may not want this policy.

# EQUAL EMPLOYMENT OPPORTUNITY

It is the intent of the company to establish by policy our commitment to afford equal employment opportunity to qualified individuals regardless of their race, color, religion, sex, national origin, age, physical or mental handicap, or veteran status and to conform with the content and spirit of applicable Equal Opportunity and Affirmative Action laws and regulations. This policy is intended to apply to those actions related to both employees and applicants for employment.

## Guidelines

In keeping with the intent of this policy, the company will adhere strictly to the following practices:

- Recruitment, hiring, and promotion of individuals in all job classifications will be conducted without regard to race, color, religion, national origin, age, sex, physical or mental handicap, or veteran status, except where a bona fide occupational qualification exists.
- Employment and promotional decisions will be made in such a manner as to further the principle of equal employment opportunity when possible, based upon selection criteria that are job related.

## Implementation

Overall responsibility for the development and execution of our affirmative action program and equal opportunity compliance is the responsibility of our managers; however, the day-to-day administration of the program is the responsibility of the equal opportunity coordinator. The equal opportunity coordinator will provide the president with quarterly and special activity and progress reports. Our Affirmative Action Plan is available in the personnel department for review by all employees.

## Recordkeeping

In order to fulfill recordkeeping requirements, applicant and hire logs should be maintained by each office that interviews and hires employees.

**Manager's Tip**

Reserve the right to fill the job with the most qualified person. EEO policy should include information as to which company official is responsible for enforcement of the policy.

# TO BE POSTED ON THE EMPLOYEE BULLETIN BOARDS AND INCLUDED IN THE EMPLOYEE HANDBOOK AND PERSONNEL POLICY MATERIAL

## EQUAL EMPLOYMENT OPPORTUNITY POLICY

It is the policy of _____ to afford equal employment opportunity to qualified individuals regardless of their race, color, religion, sex, national origin, age, physical or mental handicap, or veteran status, and will conform to all applicable state and federal laws and regulations. In keeping with the intent of this policy, the Company will adhere to the following personnel practices:

- Recruitment, hiring and promotion of individuals in all job classifications will be conducted without regard to race, color, religion, national origin, age, sec, physical or mental handicap, or veteran status, except where a bona fide occupational qualification exists. All employment decisions will be made in such a manner as to further the principle of equal employment opportunity.

- Promotional decisions will be made in accordance with the principles of equal employment opportunity through the use of valid job related criteria.

- All other personnel actions such as compensation, benefits, transfers, promotions, training and development, educational assistance and social and recreational programs will be administered without regard to race, color, religion, national origin, age, sex or physical or mental handicap, or veteran status, except where a bona fide occupational qualification exists.

Overall responsibility for the development and execution of our Affirmative Action Program is delegated to _____ as EEO/AAP Coordinator. The EEO/AAP Coordinator will provide the president with regular EEO activity reports.


_____          _____
Date                                                            President

# Employee Assistance Program

The company has an outside employee assistance program (EAP) which is available for use by employees who have alcohol or drug abuse problems, or serious personal problems they cannot cope with. To use the program you can either contact your manager to get permission to seek outside help through the EAP, or if you have a substance abuse problem you can call the EAP directly without fear of losing your job. The number is _____.

For further information on the EAP contact the personnel department. The EAP is provided by the company to assist troubled employees in seeking help to keep their jobs.

### Manager's Tip

Excessive absenteeism and poor performance are reasons to insist an employee get help. You may want to make use of the EAP a condition of employment. Be sure you have used progressive discipline and counseling and are being fair with the employee, and check first on the laws and court cases in your state.

# Exit Interviews

It is company policy to conduct exit interviews for terminating employees. The interview is conducted in the personnel department. Its purpose is to enable the company to identify conditions which may contribute to terminations and to formalize the reason for termination for unemployment compensation purposes.

Pertinent comments made by terminating employees will be discussed with appropriate management personnel in order to improve and update our policies and procedures.

When employees voluntarily terminate, they will be asked to sign a separation form stating the reason for terminating and that it is a voluntary termination. See attached separation form.

### Manager's Tip

The reason you need the separation form signed is so that if employees try to collect unemployment when they terminate voluntarily you can send the signed form to the unemployment commission to show the terminations were voluntary. This can save a lot of money on your unemployment compensation account.

# External Communications

How the Company is perceived by its clients, business associates, the media, legislators, regulatory agencies, special interest groups, and the general public is a direct result of the external communications activities carried out by our management and employees. These external relations have a significant impact on our business.

In order to present the best image of the Company, it is important that the messages we communicate are consistent with our philosophy, policies and procedures. Before discussing confidential or sensitive information with anyone outside of the Company, questions regarding what constitutes confidential or sensitive information or Company confidential information should also be discussed with your supervisor.

The President serves as the information channel for news media and is responsible for approval of all press releases, responding to media inquiries, and coordinating interviews with the media.

# EVALUATION PERIOD

The evaluation period is the time allowed all newly hired employees to demonstrate their qualifications for the job. The evaluation period for all employees is up to 90 days. However, passing the evaluation period is not a guarantee of future employment. At the end of the 90-day evaluation period, employees will be formally evaluated by management.

The following regulations apply to new employees during the time their status is being evaluated:

- The employee is eligible for all benefits as defined and outlined in the Employee Benefits Statement.

- Employees may be transferred or promoted within their organizational unit.

- Previous employees must satisfy the evaluation requirements upon rehire.

- The company reserves the right to hire and fire at will.

---

**Manager's Tip**

---

*Evaluation period* used to be called the *probationary period* before courts ruled that there is somehow an implicit agreement that one becomes a permanent employee after passing the probationary period.

Also, we now use the term *regular employment* rather than *permanent employment* because the word *permanent* implied that the employee was promised permanent employment.

In a non-union company there is really no need for an evaluation period any more because employee's rights are protected from the first day of employment. Most companies like the idea of such a period, however, because supervisors will pay more attention to the employee's performance during the initial months on the job and decide not to retain poor performers.

It's a good idea to use the words "up to 90 days" rather than "the first 90 days," because some organizations have interpreted the latter to be a guarantee of employment for the maximum number of days, regardless of how poorly the employee is performing.

# FUNERAL-TIME OFF

See "Time Off With Pay"

# Garnishments

Employees are expected to conduct their personal financial affairs in such a manner that the company will not be served by garnishments. *Garnishment* refers to any legal procedure through which the earnings of an individual are required to be withheld for payment of a debt. However, under the Federal Consumer Credit Protection Act as well as the laws of some states, employers are prohibited from discharging employees as a result of a garnishment.

## Guidelines

### Contested Garnishments

In the case of contested garnishments (particularly false claims), employees are entitled to resist garnishments by every legal means, and this policy may not be used to force them to settle against their will. However, unless a court release is obtained within legally prescribed time limits, the company must remit the required amount to the court.

### Wages Subject to Garnishment

Only disposable earnings are subject to garnishment. Disposable earnings are defined as that part of an employee's earnings remaining after all legally required deductions.

All disposable earnings owed to the employee on the date and time of the garnishment is received are to be used in determining the amount to be sent to the court. This includes checks written but not yet mailed.

In addition to regular pay, the Internal Revenue Service has legislative authority to levy paid time off, floating holidays, and vacation that has accrued but has not been taken.

### Calculating and Processing Garnishments

Garnishment actions will be calculated and processed in accordance with applicable federal and state laws and regulations and will be handled by the accounting department.

# Gifts and Gratuities

No employee shall accept, receive, or benefit from any gift, gratuity, present, property, or service of any kind or nature regardless of value, which may be directly or indirectly offered as a result of, or in anticipation of, an employee's position or performance of duties with the company. Exceptions include:

- Unsolicited advertising or promotional materials of nominal intrinsic value such as pens and calendars
- Awards for meritorious civic service contributions
- Unsolicited consumable items that are donated to an entire work group during holidays and are consumed on the premises

# HARASSMENT

The company will not tolerate any form of harassment including sexual harassment or hazing. A supervisor who harasses or solicits favors (including sexual favors) from an unwilling subordinate in return for promotions, increased wages, continuance of the job, or any similar promise will be terminated.

Likewise, unwelcome sexual propositions between employees may also constitute sexual harassment and will not be tolerated.

If an employee feels he or she is being harassed and cannot for whatever reason discuss the problem with the appropriate supervisor or manager, a discussion should take place between the employee and the Personnel Manager. A second option would be to use the Employee Assistance Program hotline. The number is _____.

A report of sexual or other harassment will be treated seriously, and a thorough investigation will be conducted. An employee who files a complaint will be treated fairly and courteously at all times.

# HIRING PROCEDURES

All positions must be approved prior to being filled, and it is the company's policy to coordinate all hiring with the Personnel Department.

When a replacement or additional regular full-time employee is needed, you must complete a requisition for help. If it is a new position for which there is no job description, a standard Job Description Form must be completed. Please forward these forms to the Personnel Department along with information on any advertising you plan to do. Once the proper salary grade has been assigned and the necessary approvals are granted, you may start the interviewing process. Sample forms for new hires are attached.

Before you hire you must complete:

- Requisition for Help
- Job Description

After approval to hire is received, you must complete:

- Employment Application
- W-4

# HOLIDAYS

We recognize certain days of religious and historic importance as approved paid holidays. These are:

| | |
|---|---|
| New Year's Day | Labor Day |
| Memorial Day | Thanksgiving (2) |
| Independence Day | Christmas (2) |

## Eligibility

All regular full-time and regular part-time employees are eligible for paid holidays.

## Rules

Employees must be at work on their scheduled workdays before and after a holiday in order to receive holiday pay unless on:

- Paid leave of absence
- Long-term disability
- Vacation

**Note:**
_____

If a paid holiday occurs during a vacation, an additional day may be added to the vacation period to compensate for that holiday.

An employee's manager may approve an employee's being off on a scheduled workday before or after a holiday. In this case the employee will receive holiday pay.

When a holiday falls on Saturday, it is observed the preceding Friday. When a holiday falls on Sunday, it is observed the following Monday.

# HOURS OF WORK

## Work Hours

Work hours are 8:00 A.M. to 5:00 P.M., Monday through Friday. Flex-time hours may be established at the supervisor's discretion within the time frame of 7:30 A.M. to 5:30 P.M.

## Lunch Period

(Check state wage and hour laws to determine your policy.)

## Break Period

No official break period is established. However, the company will permit brief, occasional breaks when needed by an employee and upon approval of the supervisor. (Check your state laws on this policy also.)

## Compensation

Employees will be paid their regular base rate of pay for 40 hours worked in a week. Overtime worked in excess of these hours will be paid at time and one-half the regular rate. Overtime will be paid within the same pay period in which it is worked. Salaried employees are not paid overtime but may occasionally receive compensatory time. Compensatory time must be taken in the same pay period in which it is worked. Lunch periods are not paid, but breaks, if taken according to policy, are paid.

## Scheduling

As the need arises, supervisors may schedule work days and hours that differ from the standard set forth above. Flex-time may be granted by supervisors if the schedule is arranged with the employee. Lunch periods are scheduled by supervisors. Advance approval of the supervisor is required when overtime is to be worked or any change in scheduled hours is required.

## Time Records

Nonexempt employees are required to complete time cards reflecting the exact time worked.

## Responsibility

Supervisors are responsible for scheduling work hours that will provide maximum coverage of the department during the regular work day. At the same time, needs of the employee should be given consideration. Flexibility of the hours worked will be at the discretion of the supervisor. When overtime is necessary, employees are required to work as requested; however, advance notice should be given.

Employees may receive written warnings for abuse of the work schedule. Repeated abuse as determined by the supervisor could result in termination.

# IMMIGRATION REFORM AND CONTROL ACT COMPLIANCE

It is company policy to conform to the Immigration Reform and Control Act of 1986. We are required to verify the work authorization, identify, and citizenship of all employees and applicants for employment who are hired. Government Form 1-9 must be completed on every new employee and the forms must be retained in the personnel department.

## Employer Review and Verification

Following are the methods by which the Personnel Department will verify documents:

Examine one document from those in List A and check the correct box, or examine one document from List B and one from List C and check the correct boxes. Provide the Document Identification Number and Expiration Date for the document checked in that column.

## List A-Identity and Employment Eligibility

- United States passport
- Certificate of Naturalization
- Unexpired foreign passport with attached employment authorization
- Alien Registration Card with photograph
  Document Identification # _____
  Expiration Date (if any) _____

## List B-Identity

- A state driver's license or I.D. card with a photograph, or information, including name, sex, date of birth, height, weight, and color of eyes.
  Specify state _____
- U.S. Military Card
- Other (Specify document and issuing authority)

  _____

  Document Identification # _____
  Expiration Date (if any) _____

## List C-Employment Eligibility

- Original Social Security Number Card (other than a card stating it is not valid for employment)
- A birth certificate issued by state, county, or municipal authority bearing a seal or other certification.
- Unexpired INS Employment Authorization
  Specify Form _____
  Document Identification # _____
  Expiration Date (if any) _____

### Manager's Tip

Independent contractors who work with the company from time-to-time are not required to complete I-9 forms. I-9 forms must be retained for three years after the date of hire, or for one year after the date of termination.

**U.S. Department of Justice**
Immigration and Naturalization Service

OMB No. 1115-0136
**Employment Eligibility Verification**

Please read instructions carefully before completing this form. The instructions must be available during completion of this form. **ANTI-DISCRIMINATION NOTICE. It is illegal to discriminate against work eligible individuals. Employers CANNOT specify which document(s) they will accept from an employee. The refusal to hire an individual because of a future expiration date may also constitute illegal discrimination.**

**Section 1. Employee Information and Verification.** To be completed and signed by employee at the time employment begins

| Print Name: Last | First | Middle Initial | Maiden Name |
|---|---|---|---|

Address (Street Name and Number) | Apt. # | Date of Birth (month/day/year)

City | State | Zip Code | Social Security #

I am aware that federal law provides for imprisonment and/or fines for false statements or use of false documents in connection with the completion of this form.

I attest, under penalty of perjury, that I am (check one of the following):
☐ A citizen or national of the United States
☐ A Lawful Permanent Resident (Alien # A _____)
☐ An alien authorized to work until ___/___/___
(Alien # or Admission # _____)

Employee's Signature | Date (month/day/year)

**Preparer and/or Translator Certification.** (To be completed and signed if Section 1 is prepared by a person other than the employee.) I attest, under penalty of perjury, that I have assisted in the completion of this form and that to the best of my knowledge the information is true and correct.

Preparer's/Translator's Signature | Print Name

Address (Street Name and Number, City, State, Zip Code) | Date (month/day/year)

**Section 2. Employer Review and Verification.** To be completed and signed by employer. Examine one document from List A OR examine one document from List B and one from List C as listed on the reverse of this form and record the title, number and expiration date, if any, of the document(s)

| List A | OR | List B | AND | List C |
|---|---|---|---|---|
| Document title: _____ | | _____ | | _____ |
| Issuing authority: _____ | | _____ | | _____ |
| Document #: _____ | | _____ | | _____ |
| Expiration Date (if any): ___/___/___ | | ___/___/___ | | ___/___/___ |
| Document #: _____ | | | | |
| Expiration Date (if any): ___/___/___ | | | | |

**CERTIFICATION** - I attest, under penalty of perjury, that I have examined the document(s) presented by the above-named employee, that the above-listed document(s) appear to be genuine and to relate to the employee named, that the employee began employment on (month/day/year) ___/___/___ and that to the best of my knowledge the employee is eligible to work in the United States. (State employment agencies may omit the date the employee began employment).

Signature of Employer or Authorized Representative | Print Name | Title

Business or Organization Name | Address (Street Name and Number, City, State, Zip Code) | Date (month/day/year)

**Section 3. Updating and Reverification.** To be completed and signed by employer

A. New Name (if applicable) | B. Date of rehire (month/day/year) (if applicable)

C. If employee's previous grant of work authorization has expired, provide the information below for the document that establishes current employment eligibility.
Document Title: _____ Document #: _____ Expiration Date (if any): ___/___/___

I attest, under penalty of perjury, that to the best of my knowledge, this employee is eligible to work in the United States, and if the employee presented document(s), the document(s) I have examined appear to be genuine and to relate to the individual.

Signature of Employer or Authorized Representative | Date (month/day/year)

Form I-9 (Rev. 11-21-91) N

## LISTS OF ACCEPTABLE DOCUMENTS

| LIST A | | LIST B | | LIST C |
|---|---|---|---|---|
| **Documents that Establish Both Identity and Employment Eligibility** | **OR** | **Documents that Establish Identity** | **AND** | **Documents that Establish Employment Eligibility** |

**LIST A — Documents that Establish Both Identity and Employment Eligibility**

1. U.S. Passport (unexpired or expired)

2. Certificate of U.S. Citizenship *(INS Form N-560 or N-561)*

3. Certificate of Naturalization *(INS Form N-550 or N-570)*

4. Unexpired foreign passport, with *I-551 stamp or* attached *INS Form I-94* indicating unexpired employment authorization

5. Alien Registration Receipt Card with photograph *(INS Form I-151 or I-551)*

6. Unexpired Temporary Resident Card *(INS Form I-688)*

7. Unexpired Employment Authorization Card *(INS Form I-688A)*

8. Unexpired Reentry Permit *(INS Form I-327)*

9. Unexpired Refugee Travel Document *(INS Form I-571)*

10. Unexpired Employment Authorization Document issued by the INS which contains a photograph *(INS Form I-688B)*

**LIST B — Documents that Establish Identity**

1. Driver's license or ID card issued by a state or outlying possession of the United States provided it contains a photograph or information such as name, date of birth, sex, height, eye color, and address

2. ID card issued by federal, state, or local government agencies or entities provided it contains a photograph or information such as name, date of birth, sex, height, eye color, and address

3. School ID card with a photograph

4. Voter's registration card

5. U.S. Military card or draft record

6. Military dependent's ID card

7. U.S. Coast Guard Merchant Mariner Card

8. Native American tribal document

9. Driver's license issued by a Canadian government authority

**For persons under age 18 who are unable to present a document listed above:**

10. School record or report card

11. Clinic, doctor, or hospital record

12. Day-care or nursery school record

**LIST C — Documents that Establish Employment Eligibility**

1. U.S. social security card issued by the Social Security Administration *(other than a card stating it is not valid for employment)*

2. Certification of Birth Abroad issued by the Department of State *(Form FS-545 or Form DS-1350)*

3. Original or certified copy of a birth certificate issued by a state, county, municipal authority or outlying possession of the United States bearing an official seal

4. Native American tribal document

5. U.S. Citizen ID Card *(INS Form I-197)*

6. ID Card for use of Resident Citizen in the United States *(INS Form I-179)*

7. Unexpired employment authorization document issued by the INS *(other than those listed under List A)*

**Illustrations of many of these documents appear In Part 8 of the Handbook for Employers (M-274)**

Form I-9 (Rev. 11-21-91) N

# JOB POSTING

## Policy 1

The company is generally committed to providing promotional opportunities to employees who have demonstrated exemplary job progress and self-motivation. In an attempt to advise employees of job openings, bulletins will be posted announcing job vacancies as the need arises. Employees who meet the standards and are interested in being considered for posted jobs should contact the Personnel Manager for an application and further information about the job. Those employees selected for consideration of a posted job will be contacted by the Personnel Manager and will receive an interview.

Jobs posted are not necessarily reserved or held exclusively for current employees. The company may concurrently advertise or otherwise recruit qualified persons in the appropriate labor market, and may, at its discretion, hire from outside the company. The company reserves the right to hire the most qualified person for the job.

## Policy 2

It is the policy of the Company to post all open positions for a period of five working days and to entertain bids from current employees before we go outside the company to fill a position. Jobs are posted up through manager level.

The only exception to this policy will be situations where an internal department candidate is being groomed and developed to fill a higher level position through promotion. In that instance the job will not be posted if the employee is ready for promotion.

Samples of job postings are attached to this policy.

### Manager's Tip

A few years ago, it was unthinkable to post open positions in a nonunion salaried environment. But over the past few years, with Equal Employment Opportunity, the need for companies to maximize their human resources, and increasing concern for individual career progression, job posting has become quite common.

Here are some pros and cons of posting open positions:

**Pros**
- Fewer employees look for new jobs or transfers because they find suitable jobs through the posting system.
- The program makes upward mobility easier.
- It creates better morale by making employees aware of open positions.
- Employees have more control over career progression.
- It assists with affirmative action programs.
- It affords better use of the human resources.

**Cons**
- The program lengthens the process of filling jobs.
- It creates a chain reaction, and more jobs have to be filled.
- Employees who don't get jobs require counseling and may become disgruntled.

# JOB POSTING FORM

Date  _____

## POSITION ANNOUNCEMENT

The _____ Corporation is recruiting for the following position:

| | |
|---|---|
| **TITLE:** | **HUMAN RESOURCE SECRETARY** |
| **REPORTS TO:** | Human Resource Director |
| **SUMMARY** | Provides secretarial support and coordinates a variety of |
| **OF DUTIES:** | human resource activities including screening applicant inquiries, scheduling meetings and interviews, processing benefit paperwork. Responsible for maintaining confidential employee records and files. |

**REQUIREMENTS:**

| | |
|---|---|
| **EDUCATION:** | High school diploma or equivalent. Some college or business courses preferred. |
| **EXPERIENCE:** | Two years of secretarial experience preferably in a human resource department. |
| **SKILLS:** | Ability to type 60 w.p.m. on a word processor. Knowledge of Word Perfect preferred. Strong organizational skills, good grammar, and spelling competency. Must have ability to communicate with a variety of people, work independently, and maintain strict confidence of personnel information. |

CLOSING DATE:  _____

Interested applicants should submit an application form and letter of interest to: Employment Manager, (list address and phone).


THE _____ CORPORATION IS AN EQUAL OPPORTUNITY EMPLOYER

# JOB BID FORM

Name _____    Date _____

Current Department  _____

Current Supervisor _____

Job Applying for_____    Dept._____

Your qualifications for the job:  _____

_____

_____

_____

_____

Other qualifications such as degrees, licenses, etc.

_____

_____

_____

_____

_____
Employee Signature

--------------------------------------------------------------------------------

## TO BE COMPLETED BY PERSONNEL DEPARTMENT

Date employee was interviewed_____

Did this employee get the job?  _____ yes  _____ no

Why didn't employee get the job  _____

_____

Has employee's supervisor been notified?_____

Has employee been notified?_____

_____
Personnel Representative

**Jury Duty**

See "Time Off with Pay."

# LAYOFF

It is company policy to avoid layoffs when possible. It may, however, be necessary from time-to-time when there are adverse business conditions to lay people off or to eliminate jobs.

In the event of either a layoff or job elimination, the company reserves the right to retain those employees with the best performance rather than those with the most seniority. If jobs are to be eliminated they will be those jobs the company least needs to effectively run the remaining operations. The company will take performance, job importance, and seniority into consideration in a layoff, but retains the right to make the final decision based on business and economic needs and will not provide bumping or recall rights to employees who are terminated.

The company will comply with the Worker Adjustment and Retraining Notification Act that became effective on February 4, 1989. We do employ more than 100 full-time workers and therefore will give 60 days advance notice of facility closings or major layoffs as follows:

- When closing a facility or discontinuing an operating unit with 50 or more workers;
- When laying off 50–499 workers (and these workers comprise at least 33 percent of the total work force at a single site of employment); or
- When laying off 500 or more workers at a single site of employment.

Notice will be provided as follows:

- To each employee to be laid off or, if represented by a union or unions, to the employee's union representatives. Notice will be mailed to the employee's last known address.
- We will mail notice to the local government's chief elected official.

### Manager's Tip

*Bumping* refers to letting an employee bump a lower level or less tenured employee down the line out of their job. *Recall* relates to calling a laid-off employee back to work when business picks up rather than hiring a new employee. You want to reserve the right to make those decisions.

# LEAVES OF ABSENCE

Personal leaves of absence for reasons other than civic duties, military duty, or work-related injury/illness are granted on an individual basis at the sole discretion of the company, but always taking into consideration the purpose of the leave, the employee's work record, and the needs of the company at that particular time. A personal leave of absence may be granted as a result of illness, accident, pregnancy, or for any other reason of a personal nature not specifically covered under other policies. The leave must be approved by the employee's supervisor and department manager.

All personal leaves are without pay unless otherwise approved by the employee's supervisor and department manager. The company does not normally guarantee reinstatement to the former position or to a position with like status and pay. However, if work loads permit, the position may be held open if the employee's supervisor and department manager approve. This concession must be made in writing and requires personnel department approval.

Upon return from the approved leave, if no prior guarantee of reinstatement has been made, every effort will be made to reinstate the employee in a comparable position. If reinstatement is impossible, the returning employee will have continuous service rights, so long as the employee follows the rules and procedures outlined in this policy, and meets the eligibility requirements of company benefit plans.

## Length of Leave

This policy applies to requests for time off from work exceeding one month. Approved time off from work for a period of one month or less for a reason other than active military or reserve duty will be considered an excused absence. The maximum personal leave granted under this policy is six months.

## Family and Medical Leave Act

The Family and Medical Leave Act of 1993 provides that eligible employees may take up to 12 work weeks of unpaid leave within a prescribed 12-month period for the care of a newborn or newly adopted child, or for the serious health condition of the employee or the employee's spouse, son, daughter or parent. To be eligible, employees must be employed for a total of 12 months, and have provided 1,250 hours of service during the previous 12-month period. No more than 12 work weeks of Family or Medical Leave may be taken within a 12-month period (measured backward from the beginning of the leave), except where applicable state law requires otherwise. In all instances the company should comply with applicable federal and state law.

If an employee does not meet the eligibility requirements for a Family or Medical Leave but needs time of because of his/her own medical condition, the company should grant up to four weeks of unpaid leave; however, job reinstatement does not need to be guaranteed.

If the leave is for an employee's serious medical condition, the employee should first exhaust any accrued sick leave. If the leave is related to the birth or placement of a child, or is to care for a seriously ill family member, the employee should be paid any accrued vacation time, then accrued sick pay, and, thereafter, the remainder of the leave would be without pay. (*Note:* In California, a female employee on a pregnancy disability leave will have the option of substituting accrued vacation leave, but shall not be required to use her vacation time.)

The employee should be required to provide medical certification to support a request for leave based upon a serious health condition and may require second and third opinions, at the company's expense. Medical certification for returning to work will be required upon the employee's return to work from a leave based upon a serious medical condition.

The company will require certification from the health care provider if the leave is to take care of a child, parent or spouse who has a serious health condition. If the company grants a leave, the employee should be reinstated to the same or comparable job at the end of the leave subject to any defense the company may assert under law. The company should pay its portion of the employee's medical benefits while the employee is on an approved Family or Medical Leave. The employee must pay his or her portion of the premium during the leave period. If the employee fails to return to work after the expiration of the leave, the company may seek to recover from the employee the insurance premiums it paid during the leave period.

Where the Family or Medical Leave is foreseeable, the employee should notify the company no less than thirty days prior to the commencement of the leave. Intermittent or reduced leaves may be permitted in some circumstances. Your supervisor or the Human Resources Department can provide more information. A Leave of Absence Request Form must be completed and approved in advance.

*Pregnancy Medical Disability Leave:* Pregnancy leave is treated as a Family and Medical Leave, and benefits are the same, except where state law requires additional leave be granted. (*Example:* State of California requires the company to provide a maximum of 88 work days in addition to the 12 work weeks.) The company should comply with the laws of each state in which it does business. Maternity leave should be compensated in the same manner as any medical disability.

## Military Leave

The company will pay the difference between the employee's regular rate of pay and their military pay for a period of up to ten working days for summer military duty. The company will grant leaves of absence for longer periods of military duty in accordance with the Veterans Re-employment Act. See the personnel department for details of the law.

## Medical Leave (Not FMLA)

The company may grant a medical leave of absence for an employee if all of their sick leave has been used. (Some companies have short-term and long-term disability policies. Write this policy to fit your company benefits.) A doctor's certificate may be required before an employee may return to work after a medical leave.

When an employee is on a medical leave the company will continue payment of medical insurance benefits. Employees on a medical leave will retain their seniority and benefit eligibility rights.

## Benefit Status While on Personal Leave of Absence

The company does not provide benefit coverage for employees while on an unpaid, nonmedical leave of over 30 days. The employee can, however, make arrangements to pay for their medical coverage while on an approved leave. Failure to return from an approved leave may result in the employee's termination.

### Manager's Tip

Maternity leave regulations require that employers provide employees on maternity leave the same benefits they provide to workers on any type of disability leave.

The Veterans Reemployment Rights Act requires that employees be granted a leave of absence to perform military obligations. No employee should be denied retention of employment or any promotion because of military obligations. Employees on a military leave of absence are entitled to participate in insurance and other benefits offered by the employer to the same extent as employees granted other types of leave. Employers are not required to pay employees who are on active duty in the armed forces.

Upon completion of military service, employees must be restored to their former position or a position of like seniority, status, and pay. This assumes that the employees are still qualified to perform the duties of the former position and that they make an application for reemployment within 90 days after discharge from military service 3 l days after reserve service.

Seniority status, pay, and vacations must be credited as if the employee had not been absent. Employers may not require employees to use earned vacation for summer encampment or military training call-ups (Veterans Reemployment Rights Act).

A simple sentence stating that "veteran reemployment rights are determined by law" may be all that is required in an employee handbook or policy manual.

Review this entire policy carefully and change it to fit your company's needs. If in doubt about how your specific policy should be written, have a labor attorney help you with it.

# CERTIFICATION OF PHYSICIAN UNDER THE FAMILY AND MEDICAL LEAVE ACT OF 1993

| 1. Employee's Name: | 2. Patient's Name (If other than employee): |
|---|---|

3. Diagnosis _____

_____

_____

_____

| 4. Date condition commenced: | 5. Probable duration of condition: |
|---|---|

6. Regimen of treatment to be prescribed (Indicate number of visits, general nature and duration of treatment, including referral to other provider of health services. Include schedule of visits or treatment if it is medically necessary for the employee to be off work on an intermittent basis or to work less than the employee's normal schedule of hours per day or days per week):

   a. By Physician: _____

_____

_____

   b. By another provider of health services, if referred by Physician: _____

_____

_____

_____

IF THIS CERTIFICATION RELATES TO CARE FOR AN EMPLOYEE'S SERIOUSLY-ILL FAMILY MEMBER, SKIP ITEMS 7, 8 AND 9 AND PROCEED TO ITEMS 10 THROUGH 14 ON REVERSE SIDE. OTHERWISE CONTINUE BELOW.

Check Yes or No in the boxes below, as appropriate:

    Yes  No

7.  ❏   ❏   Is inpatient hospitalization of the employee required?

8.  ❏   ❏   Is employee able to perform work of any kind? (If "No" skip Item 9.)

9.  ❏   ❏   Is employee able to perform the functions of employee's position? (Answer after reviewing statement from employer of essential functions of employee's position, or, if none provided, after discussing with employee.)

| 15. Signature of Physician: | 16. Date: |
|---|---|

17. Type of Practice (Field of Specialization, if any):

FOR CERTIFICATION RELATING TO CARE FOR THE EMPLOYEE'S SERIOUSLY-ILL FAMILY MEMBER, COMPLETE ITEMS 10 THROUGH 14 BELOW AS THEY APPLY TO THE FAMILY MEMBER AND PROCEED TO ITEM 15 ON REVERSE SIDE.

Yes    No

10. ❏    ❏    Is inpatient hospitalization of the family member (patient) required?

11. ❏    ❏    Does (or will) the patient require assistance for basic medical, hygiene, nutritional needs, safety or transportation?

12. ❏    ❏    After review of the employee's signed statement (See Item 14 below), is the employee's presence necessary or would it be beneficial for the care of the patient? (This may include psychological comfort.)

13. Estimate the period of time care is needed or the employee's presence would be beneficial:

ITEM 14 TO BE COMPLETED BY THE EMPLOYEE NEEDING FAMILY LEAVE.

14. When Family Leave is needed to care for a seriously-ill family member, the employee shall state the care he or she will provide and an estimate of the time period during which this care will be provided, including a schedule if leave is to be taken intermittently or on a reduced leave schedule:

_____

_____

_____

Employee Signature:                              Date:

Company/Division/Location:

# LEAVE REQUEST/RETURN FROM LEAVE FORM

Date _____

Employee's
Name _____

Social Security
Number _____

Job Title _____

Date Hired _____

LEAVE REQUEST

**REASON FOR LEAVE:**

( ) Personal disability

( ) Family illness (name) _____

( ) Military

( ) Family death (name) _____

( ) Training conference

( ) Other (explain) _____

( ) Compensatory time off

_____

( ) Jury duty

_____

**LEAVE REQUESTED:**

|  | A.M. | Total number of |
|---|---|---|
| From: Date _____ Time _____ | P.M. | hours requested: _____ |
|  | A.M. | Total number of |
| To:   Date _____ Time _____ | P.M. | days requested: _____ |

Regular Work Shift: _____

_____

Employee Signature: _____ Date: _____

- - - - - - - - - - - - - - - - - - - - - - - - - - - - - - - - - - - - - - -

I recommend that this
leave be approved:

( ) With pay
( ) Without pay

Authorized Signature: _____ Date: _____

RETURN FROM LEAVE

**ABSENT:**

|  | A.M. |  |
|---|---|---|
| From: Date _____ Time _____ | P.M. | Total number of |
|  | A.M. | working days absent: _____ |
| To:   Date _____ Time _____ | P.M. |  |

( ) Excused/warranted

( ) Not excused/not warranted (explain) _____

**EMPLOYEE:**

( ) Resumed part-time work

( ) Resumed full-time work

( ) Resumed modified duty (explain) _____

( ) Other (explain) _____

Affirmed by: _____ Date: _____

# LUNCH AND REST PERIODS

See "Hours of Work."

# MATERNITY LEAVE OF ABSENCE

See "Family Medical Leave Act."

# MOONLIGHTING

For some time it has been company policy that employees be asked not to hold second jobs or to "moonlight" outside the organization.

Because many of the states in which we operate have laws that make it illegal to prohibit employees from engaging in lawful occupations wherever and whenever they see fit, our policy on moonlighting has been changed.

We do not approve of executives and officers of the company holding second jobs, but we do not put such restrictions on hourly nonexempt personnel.

# ORIENTATION—NEW EMPLOYEE

It is company policy to provide each new employee with a thorough orientation to the company and its policies and procedures.

Following are a number of the areas that will be covered in the orientation:

- Introduction to the company
- Discussion of organizational structure, key employees, office locations
- Review of policies, procedures, and the employee handbook
- Review of benefits and signing of all necessary forms
- Introduction to managers and co-workers

# OVERTIME

All hourly nonexempt employees who are requested to work overtime will be paid time and one-half for all hours worked in excess of 40 in a work week with the exception of the State of California where overtime is paid over 8 hours in a day. Overtime must be approved in advance by the appropriate supervisor. Salaried exempt employees who work exceptional amounts of overtime may occasionally receive compensatory time off.

Vacation, holidays, and sick pay will not be treated as hours worked in the calculation of overtime.

# Paydays

The pay period at the company is Monday through Sunday and paydays are Thursdays. When a payday falls on a holiday, employees will be paid on the last work-day before the holiday.

The company posts on all bulletin boards a notice of our regular paydays and the time and place of payment.

### Manager's Tip

Some states require companies to post this information on their bulletin boards.

# Personnel Records

Employee personnel records are maintained in the Personnel Department. Managers and supervisors should not maintain separate files in their desks.

When changes occur in any of the following categories, please notify the Personnel Department so that they can be reflected promptly in the handling of your pay benefits:

- Name
- Address
- Telephone number
- Marital status
- Number of dependents
- Beneficiaries
- Educational progress

The Personnel Department: (1) collects, uses, and retains only that personnel information which is required for business or legal reasons; (2) restricts the internal availability of personnel information to those with a business need to know; (3) releases personnel information outside the company only with employee approval, except to verify employment or to satisfy legitimate investigatory or legal requirements. All records concerning employment are company property and are maintained in the Personnel Department. Employees may review their personnel file. Requests to view the records should be made to the Personnel Manager.

# Performance Appraisal

It is company policy to conduct performance reviews with all employees once a year. The appraisal is intended to be an employee development activity to assist and motivate employees to attain their maximum potential.

The objectives of the program are:

- To motivate and guide employees toward greater self-development and improved performance by discussing significant strengths and areas needing improvement in a positive, constructive manner
- To provide an objective and uniform means for supervisors to make merit salary determinations based on an assessment of employee performance
- To identify training needs and succession planning activities
- To provide a record of employee progress

The appraisal will be conducted by the employee's immediate supervisor and reviewed by the department manager.

# PERSONAL TIME OFF

The company recognizes that occasionally employees need personal time off. If you do need some time off for personal reasons, it may be granted at the discretion of your manager. However, it will be without pay unless you have paid vacation days coming. Employees should give advance notice if possible in order to allow adequate scheduling in their department. Personal time off without pay is granted at the discretion of the company taking into account departmental work loads and responsibilities.

### Manager's Tip

More companies are providing some paid personal time off in order to help families cope with sick children or conduct personal business that can't be done on weekends.

# PROFESSIONAL MEMBERSHIPS

It is the policy of the company to provide memberships in professional and technical organizations for employees. We feel these memberships aid employees in doing their jobs and provide professional growth opportunities.

## Eligibility

Only regular full-time employees are eligible for company-sponsored or company-paid memberships in professional or technical organizations. These memberships will be determined by the position held by the employee, the need for the membership from a business standpoint, and the benefits to be derived by the Company.

## Company-Sponsored Memberships

Company-sponsored memberships are those in which the company is responsible for acquiring the membership, paying directly for all costs of the membership. This type of membership is transferable and is the sole property of the Company.

## Approval

All memberships paid by the company require the approval of the president. At least annually, a list of employee memberships will be prepared for the president's approval.

## Number of Memberships

Employees are expected to limit their professional memberships so that they may participate actively and therefore benefit fully from each membership.

# PROMOTIONS

It is company policy to promote current employees rather than hiring from outside the company whenever possible. The purpose of our in-house training and development programs is to help employees experience their full potential.

## Guidelines

When position vacancies occur, supervisors will assist the Personnel Department in determining whether there are eligible candidates within the company. Candidates for promotion will be selected on the basis of their qualifications and work records without regard to age, sex, race, color, religion, mental or physical handicap, or national origin. The standards will apply to all employees.

Service with the company may be a factor considered in the process of selecting a candidate for promotion. However, it will not be the deciding factor when determining which candidate is chosen. Promotions will always be based on ability, potential, and actual performance.

The company reserves the right to hire or promote at its discretion and in its best interests.

# RECREATION ACTIVITIES

It is the intent of the company to encourage social and recreational activities which will assist in maintaining good working relationships among our employees and with other members of the community. To this end, management will give consideration to requests for modest financial assistance to such programs, provided that participation is open to all employees.

## Eligibility for Financial Support

Determination of activities to be sponsored will be made on the basis of overall employee interest and cost to the company. As a general practice, it is desirable that the cost of such activities be shared with the participating employees.

In the best interest of employees, sponsorship will generally be limited to activities in which only our employees participate. In the event there is an insufficient number of participants to complete a roster, remaining positions may be filled by persons outside the company. If during the program or season, however, there are additional employees interested in participating, outside team members will be replaced unless otherwise restricted by program or association regulations.

Grants for financial assistance may be made for the following items:

1. Entry fees and other pertinent and reasonable association charges.
2. Cost for uniforms or other athletic equipment. These costs will be shared with employees.

## Approval Procedures

Employees who wish to start or participate in a program should first consult with their immediate supervisor.

Requests for financial assistance for recreational activities should be made in writing to the Personnel Manager, stating the activity, participants' names, association charges or entry fees, projected total shared costs for uniforms, equipment, or both, and the requested company contribution.

## Waiver of Liability

The company, its officers, and management assume no liability for the actions of participants while participating in company supported recreational activities, including a reasonable period of time preceding and following such activity, or for policies of the association, except as expressly set forth as company policy or benefits (for example, medical insurance programs for employees). Employees participating in recreational activities will be asked to sign a waiver of liability.

# WAIVER OF LIABILITY

I, (*Employee Name*) hereby release (*Company Name*) from any and all liability connected with my participation in company recreational activities. I acknowledge that I am participating in these activities on my own time and of my own choice.

_____
Employee

_____
Date

_____
Witness

# REFERENCES

It is the policy of the company to verify the facts and information which applicants furnish regarding their qualifications. The Personnel Manager is authorized to do this by telephone or with a reference letter. Applicants release employer from all liability when they sign our application for employment. Employment reference procedures are as follows:

- A reference check may be made by telephone. In this case, the details are recorded and retained in the employee's personnel file.

- Reference letters may be mailed to selected employers listed on the application.

- An individual will not be hired prior to verification of previous employment.

- Falsification of information on an employee's application may be considered cause for discharge.

- A verification of college degrees is always conducted.

It is the policy of the company to Cooperate with other businesses requesting information regarding previous employment of an individual as follows: The Personnel Manager is authorized to reply to telephone inquiries by verifying dates of employment and termination and job titles only. Salaries are not verified by telephone. Employment verification information for home loans and so forth, may be obtained upon written request to the Personnel Manager. No one in the company is authorized to provide personal references on former employees.

### Manager's Tip

There has been a flurry of lawsuits in the past few years in which employers gave references on past employees and were later sued for slander because the person giving the information said something negative about the former employee. When the employee didn't get the new job, and heard about the past employer's comments, he brought suit against the company. Be careful of what information you provide on former employees.

# REHIRE

The company may, at its discretion, rehire former employees. It will do so only after a thorough review of the employee's past personnel records and only by approval of the appropriate vice-president or the CEO.

The guidelines for reinstating the employee's benefits and seniority are as follows:

- Reinstatement of benefits and seniority may take place if the employee was gone from the company one year or less and is at the discretion of the employee's manager and the appropriate departmental vice-president.

- Employees will not be given credit for vacation pay or pension accruals during the time they were gone. The employee will start earning credit toward vacation and other benefits again on date of rehire.

# LETTER REGARDING REHIRE AND REINSTATEMENT OF BENEFITS

Ms. Kathleen Kane
1918 North Parkway
Colorado Springs, Co 80906

Dear Kathleen:

We appreciate your responding to our recent advertisement for an insurance administrator and letting us know that you would like to come back to work for American Insurance Company.

We have discussed your return with Jane Ackerman, Human Resources Director, and she agrees that according to our personnel policies you can be reinstated to your old position. Because your lapse in employment was less than one year we have agreed to treat it as a leave of absence and not as a termination and rehire for the purpose of computing your future vacation and retirement benefits.

Our rehire policy states that employee benefits can be reinstated if the time an employee is gone from the Company is less than one year.

It is our policy, however, to require a signed agreement before you can be reinstated. That agreement is attached to this letter. Please sign the agreement and bring it to work when you return on December 9.

We are pleased that you are coming back to work for American Insurance Company.

Sincerely,

John L. Macon
Vice-President, Administration

Enclosure: Agreement

## ACKNOWLEDGMENT AND AGREEMENT

This Acknowledgment and Agreement is made by and between American Insurance Company ("the Company") and Kathleen Kane ("Kane").

## RECITALS

1. Kane was employed with the Company from June 20, 1987 until May 1, 1997, at which time she terminated her employment.

2. Kane became reemployed with the Company on December 9, 1997, and has worked continually with the Company or its subsidiaries since that time.

3. Kane desires to have her lapse of employment (May 1, 1997 to December 9, 1997) be treated as a leave of absence and not as a termination and rehire for the purposes of future vacation and retirement benefits.

4. The Company is willing to treat such lapse in employment as a leave of absence for said purposes upon certain conditions, as enumerated below.

## AGREEMENT

The company and Kane agree and/or acknowledge as follows:

1. Kane acknowledges that as of this date, she knows of no claim which she may have against the Company or any of its subsidiaries, agents, or employees under any common law rights or under Title VII of the Civil Rights Act of 1964 (42 U.S.C. Sec. 2000 et seq.), the Colorado Fair Employment Act found under C.R.S. 24-34-401 et seq., or the Age Discrimination and Employment Act of 1967 (29 U.S.C. Sec. 621 et seq.), and, to the fullest extent possible hereby releases and holds the Company, its agents, employees, and subsidiaries, harmless from any and all liabilities and claims which she may have against such parties at the present time.

2. For its part, the Company shall treat the lapse of employment (May 1, 1997 through December 9, 1997) as a leave of absence for purposes of future computation of retirement and vacation privileges.

3. Kane acknowledges that she makes no claim for any benefits whatsoever which may have accrued to her during the lapse of employment (including but not limited to vacation pay, benefits, retirement contributions, and health insurance coverage).

ALL OF WHICH IS DATED THIS 9TH DAY OF DECEMBER, 1997

_____
Kathleen Kane
AMERICAN INSURANCE COMPANY

By:    _____
John K. Smith

# RELOCATION

It is the policy of the company to pay the reasonable expenses incurred by employees as a result of a transfer from one location to another, when such transfer is made for the benefit of the company. Specific benefits will be finalized with the employee's manager and the Personnel Department and will be put in writing. A copy of the approved relocation benefits memorandum will be placed in the employee's personnel file.

# SAFETY AND HEALTH

The company is concerned about the safety and health of all of its employees and will strive to maintain the highest level of personal safety for employees.

We will make every effort to provide working conditions that are as healthy and safe as possible, and employees are expected to be equally conscientious about workplace safety, including using proper work methods and reporting potential hazards. Unsafe work conditions in any work area that might result in an accident should be reported immediately to a supervisor. The company's safety policy and practices will be strictly enforced including possible termination of employees found to be willfully negligent in the safe performance of their jobs.

If an employee is injured in connection with employment, regardless of severity of the injury, the employee must immediately notify the supervisor, who will see to necessary medical attention and complete required reports. In any case of serious injury, employees will receive prompt medical attention followed by the filing of necessary reports.

## General Safety Rules

The following general safety rules apply in all company work places. Each work unit may prepare separate safety rules applicable to the specific nature of work in their area but not in conflict with these rules.

- No employee will be assigned to work under unsafe conditions or with unsafe tools or equipment. In the event that such a condition develops, it will be immediately reported to the supervisor, who will determine and initiate corrective action if necessary.

- Employees should pay strict attention to their work. Practical joking and horseplay will not be tolerated.

- Warning signs and signals posted to point out dangerous conditions are to be obeyed by employees.

- Employees will not take shortcuts through or over dangerous places.

- Extreme caution should be exercised by employees operating any type of power equipment.

- Employees should not jump from truck beds, platforms, fences, or other elevated places unless absolutely necessary to the performance of duty.

- Because of the hazard inherent in running, employees should refrain from running unless it is absolutely necessary to the performance of duty.

- Employees will use safety equipment appropriate to the job, such as safety glasses, gloves, toe guards, and hard hats.

- Employees will avoid wearing loose clothing and jewelry while working on or near equipment and machines.

- All accidents, regardless of severity, personal or vehicular, are to be reported immediately to the supervisor.

- Operators and passengers in a business vehicle equipped with seat belts must wear them when the vehicle is in operation, and all employees operating vehicles will observe all local traffic laws.

- In all work situations, safeguards as required by state and federal Safety Orders are provided in the Personnel Department.

**Manager's Tip**

Tailor these rules to your particular organization. Enlist the help of supervisors and managers from all departments to ensure they meet your company's specific needs.

# SALARY ADMINISTRATION

It is company practice to pay an equitable salary competitive with that paid by other companies in our field and our location and commensurate with the value of service performed. A salary range is set for each position according to the level of responsibility relative to similar positions in other business environments.

Your specific salary level within that range is determined primarily by your performance on the job. Appropriate salary adjustments may occasionally be made within the assigned range for each job. The size and frequency of such salary adjustments are based on careful evaluation of your job performance in your present assignment and on .the financial ability of the company to make pay adjustments.

Performance reviews are given once a year. All promotions and merit increases are based on performance.

Your salary is a confidential matter between you and the company and is not a topic for discussion with anyone other than your manager. You may be assured, however, that all personnel who have similar responsibilities are paid within the same salary range. Salaries will vary somewhat within any salary range based upon length of service, ability, and performance.

# SECURITY

Today, violence in the workplace is a very real concern. The security of the company, its facilities, and employee property are important. We ask that our employees be vigilant in their work areas and make sure that unauthorized people are not wandering around unattended. Employees should keep purses and other personal items in drawers where they are not readily accessible. Keys to offices and combinations to company safes should be protected. If you see unauthorized people in your work area, please call a security guard.

Computer security is of special concern and all employees are asked to strictly adhere to computer security guidelines.

### Manager's Tip

It is important to write security guidelines to fit the specific needs of each individual organization. Consider the following:

- Size of company
- Location
- Type of business
- Number of employees
- Industry needs
- Union or non-union

Draft a policy you think will fit your needs and then run it by the managers in each key functional area for their input before you finalize it.

# SECURITY CHECKLIST

❑ Screen applicants for potential security risks: Use a company such as Filofax or Avert. Check with previous employers.

❑ Provide policies and procedures for terminating employees caught stealing company or employee property.

❑ Hire a security guard on staff or on an occasional contract basis to check on security of buildings, equipment, parking lots, and so forth.

❑ Install an alarm system to protect facilities.

❑ Mark company equipment and property for theft prevention and recovery.

❑ Perform a regular inventory of equipment and supplies. Put someone in charge of issuing supplies and make that person responsible for them.

❑ Depending on company size, value of equipment, and building access, require employee identification badges.

❑ Provide procedures for monitoring visitors entering your facilities. Require visitors to sign in and out and require that they wear identification badges while on the premises.

❑ Provide written instructions to receptionists on how to handle crisis situations such as a person entering the buildings with a gun. Provide emergency numbers.

❏ Establish a formal evacuation plan for fire, bomb threats, terrorist situations, shootings, and the like.

❏ Develop written security guidelines for bomb threats.

❏ Develop a community relations program. Work with local community leaders and create a "good citizen" public image in the immediate area of the facility. Get to know local officials. Locate closest police station.

❏ Provide emergency first aid stations in several locations and post first aid information in accessible areas. Include fire, police, and ambulance numbers.

❏ Communicate company security policies and procedures to employees.

❏ If there is a high incidence of theft, consider hiring an undercover detective service.

❏ Analyze computer security. Establish guidelines for computer entry.

❏ Audit cash flow and other monetary procedures.

❏ If there is an area of significant loss, form a risk management committee to review the problem.

❏ Maintain emergency phone numbers on all employees in the central location in each facility.

# SEPARATION PAY

When jobs are eliminated or the company must undergo a reduction in force, it is our policy to provide separation pay to those employees being terminated. The company will provide one week of separation pay for each year of service up to a maximum of 12 weeks.

Separation pay is designed for situations where an individual's job has been eliminated or the employee is being laid off. It does not apply to discharges, resignations, retirements, or situations where the company has been acquired, merged, or ceases to operate.

### Manager's Tip

Eligibility for separation pay can be granted across the board or can be based on any of the following:

- Length of service
- Management position vs. nonmanagement position
- Level of salary
- Company's ability to pay

Many companies have eliminated separation or severance pay when they are experiencing adverse economic conditions.

# SERVICE AWARDS

The company recognizes employees for longevity of service at five-year intervals, as follows:

1 year award—Company pin

3 year award—Desk Set with scissors and letter opener

5 year award—Gold Cross pen and pencil set

10 year award—Clock-radio with employee's name on a small plate in the front

15 year award—VCR

20 year award—Color television set

## Annual Presentation of Awards

The presentation of service awards will be made at a time and date set by the president.

# SICK TIME

You are granted up to 40 hours per year sick time. Sick time is a privilege extended by the company to prevent inconvenience or the hardship in loss of pay when an employee is ill. This time may be used for family medical appointments or illness. When possible, you are requested to schedule doctor's appointments with a minimum of inconvenience to your department. Illness should be reported during the first hour of absence. Sick time can be taken only after the 90-day evaluation period, although accrual is retroactive to the beginning of employment. We hope you will use this time only when needed. Sick time not used will be paid in cash on December 10 of each year and may not be carried over from year to year. Unused sick time is not paid upon termination.

# SMOKING POLICY

As a result of the changing attitudes of employees and the fact that a majority of current employees do not smoke, the company has taken action at this time to install a no-smoking policy. A variety of national reports, including one from the Surgeon General's office, verify the fact that smoking is a serious health hazard to smokers and to nonsmokers who work around smokers.

Smoking is not permitted in any of our buildings except in private offices and in certain designated smoking areas. We wish to be considerate of both nonsmokers and smokers and to fairly address issues surrounding this no-smoking policy. Any employee who wishes to discuss the policy may do so at any time by contacting the personnel manager.

We are confident that implementation of this policy will go smoothly. We will all try to remain sensitive to the needs of both smokers and nonsmokers in order to maintain a caring attitude toward one another.

If problems arise as a result of this policy, a task force of employees, both smokers and nonsmokers, will be convened to arbitrate and resolve the issues.

### Manager's Tip

This policy or any policy you end up using may create as many problems as it resolves. Smoking issues are very emotional. You can expect further state and local regulations and more litigation from both smokers and nonsmokers. The key is to try and meet the needs of both smoking and nonsmoking employees.

# SUGGESTION PROGRAM

The company provides an employee suggestion box in the lunch room. We welcome employee suggestions. We are all working to better ourselves and the company, and employee suggestions are one way of helping us all achieve our goals.

When an employee signs the suggestion form and asks for a response, a reply will be provided within five working days of receipt.

If an employee has suggestions to help the company or their department but does not wish to sign the form no response can be given. However, if the suggestion results in positive change we will make note of that change in the company newsletter.

# SIGNING AUTHORITY

It's the company's intent that those employees in management positions have sufficient authority to carry out the responsibilities required of each position. However, it's also necessary that the president be informed as to the extent of obligations to which the company is being committed.

The company assumes no responsibility or liability for any financial obligation that has been executed by an employee who is not an approved officer of the company.

Whenever it is deemed necessary that the company be committed by means of a space or equipment lease to an extent greater than $250, appropriate review is required. Capital expenditures over $250 also require executive review. That review will include having legal counsel review and approve of the general terms and conditions of the document. Further, the manager should send to the office of the president a written explanation of why the equipment, space, or capital expenditure is needed, the terms and conditions of the obligation, and the approval of the head of the division. If no further discussion is necessary, the president will initial the memorandum, sign the required legal documents, and return the package to the originator so that the transaction can proceed.

When the purchase or lease of equipment or other capital expenditures are anticipated, the Purchasing Department must be involved. The items may be available from storage or from a vendor with whom a price has been negotiated based on the company's purchasing volume.

This policy also covers all employee compensation arrangements. Salaries are determined by the evaluation of job description, job evaluation, and the company's ability to pay. All commission, incentive, or bonus arrangements must be reviewed by the Personnel Manager and approved by the president of the parent company before a commitment is made.

Any violation of this policy may be considered cause for disciplinary action or termination. The company reserves the right to take any action necessary to recover costs and expenses that may be incurred in the case of violation of this policy.

# SIGNING AUTHORITY (ALTERNATIVE POLICY)

It is the company's intent that those employees in management positions have sufficient authority to effectively carry out their required responsibilities. However, it is also necessary that the president and chief financial officer of the Company be informed of the obligations to which the company is being committed. Therefore, we have approved two levels of authority as follows:

|  | APPROVAL AUTHORITY | DOLLAR COMMITMENT |
|---|---|---|
| LEVEL II | Branch Managers<br>Department Heads | Up to $500.00 |
| LEVEL I | President and CEO<br>Chief Financial Officer | Anything over $500.00 |

Any contract that the company is considering entering into must be reviewed and approved by our legal counsel.

When the purchase or lease of equipment or other relevant capital expenditures are anticipated, the Purchasing Department should become involved. The item may be available from our storage areas or from a vendor with whom a price has been negotiated based on the company s total buying volume.

This policy also covers all employee compensation arrangements including new hires, promotions, raises, advances, and bonus agreements. Violation of this policy may be cause for termination. The company reserves the right to take any action necessary to recover costs and expenses that may be incurred in the case of a violation of this policy.

# TEMPORARY AND PART-TIME EMPLOYEES

## Temporary Part-Time Employees

Temporary part-time employees are needed from time to time to perform a variety of duties. Temporary part-time employees may be obtained by running an ad or by using a temporary service. Call the Personnel Department for assistance in obtaining temporary help.

Temporary part-time employees do not receive company benefits and should not be on the company payroll for long periods of time.

## Regular Part-Time Employees

Regular part-time employees are sometimes added to the payroll. The schedule of a regular part-time employee should not be more than 30 hours per week. If a regular part-time employee works at least 30 hours per week for an extended period, the employee may be eligible for some company benefits. Employees who work over 1,000 hours must receive pension benefits according to ERISA regulations.

# TERMINATIONS

When termination of an employee is indicated, it is the responsibility of the supervisor to follow the procedures set forth in this policy. The maintenance of accurate records and a thorough investigation of the reasons for termination are necessary to ensure fair compliance with Equal Employment Opportunity guidelines and to determine the employee's eligibility for unemployment Compensation. In order to document the exact reason for a voluntary termination, an exit interview should be done and a separation form completed. Please send all records of terminated employees and termination forms to the Personnel Department as soon as possible.

The rules and procedures for handling terminations vary according to the voluntary or involuntary nature of the termination, the length of the employee's service, and the general circumstances surrounding the termination. These rules do not apply to temporary employees, since they can be terminated without notice and are not eligible for the benefits afforded permanent full-time employees until they have worked 1,000 hours. All terminations should be reviewed by the Personnel Manager.

## General Rules

Resignation notice period will be two weeks only, regardless of length of service. An extension of this two-week period will require appropriate management level approval.

Failure to report for three consecutive days may be grounds for voluntary termination. The terminated employees are ineligible for rehire, unless there are extenuating circumstances, in which case the Personnel Manager should be consulted.

## Termination Procedures

Supervisor collects all company property (keys, credit cards, books, equipment) as directed in the Personnel Manual. All terminating employees will receive a letter advising them of their insurance conversion rights, including letters required by government regulation under COBRA.

### Voluntary Terminations

All forms associated with a voluntary termination must be received in Accounting within twenty-four hours after the employee gives notice. The employee's final check will be provided on the next normal payday, unless the employee requests it sooner.

The time card must be transmitted to Accounting on the employee's final day. An exit interview will be conducted on all voluntary terminations, and a separation form will be completed.

### Involuntary Terminations

All forms associated with an involuntary termination should be processed in advance so the employee can be given the last paycheck at the time of termination. Employees being involuntarily terminated must be paid immediately.

## TIME OFF WITH PAY

### Funeral Leave

Up to three days of paid leave may be given to an employee for the purpose of attending the funeral of a member of the immediate family. Immediate family is defined as spouse, children, parents, and siblings (grand, step, and in-laws included). Additional time, if needed, must be arranged through the supervisor and reviewed by the Personnel Department. Time off to attend the funeral of someone other than a relative may be arranged with the employee's supervisor.

### Jury Duty

The company will continue the employee's regular rate of pay for jury service up to a maximum of ten days. Proof of service must be submitted.

### Voting Time

NOTE: Write this policy in accordance with the laws in your state.

## UNEMPLOYMENT COMPENSATION

The company is a covered employer and pays taxes for unemployment insurance purposes in this state. An employee who is separated from the company may be entitled to unemployment insurance benefits, if certain requirements (prescribed by the state) are met. Employee information regarding state unemployment insurance benefits is posted on company bulletin boards and is available in the Personnel Department. It is the responsibility of supervisors, managers, and the human resources personnel to ensure that an exit interview and a separation form are completed on terminating employees in order to determine whether a terminating employee is eligible for unemployment compensation.

**Manager's Tip**

When the termination is voluntary and the employee signs the separation form, the form can be sent to the Unemployment Compensation Department if the employee tries later to file for unemployment. A person may collect unemployment only when termination is involuntary.

# VETERANS REPORTING REQUIREMENTS

Employed veterans must be reported to the Department of Labor by all companies doing business with the federal government. The report is VETS-100, and it must include the total number of new employees hired during the year, the number of disabled veterans, and the number of veterans with service during the Vietnam War, their job categories and place of hire. The company complies with this federal reporting requirement.

# VOTING

See "Time Off with Pay."

# WORK HOURS

See "Hours of Work."

# VACATION

All regular full-time employees who have completed the 90-day evaluation period earn vacation as follows:

2 weeks after 1 year

3 weeks after 5 years

4 weeks after 10 years

If an employee desires to take a week's vacation before it is earned, this can be granted with supervisor's approval. A form must be signed by employees stating that if they quit before the vacation is earned, the pay will be withheld from the last check. (See attached form.) Accrued unused vacation is payable on termination.

Employees must take earned vacation each year or forfeit it. Unused vacation may not be carried over or paid. Occasional exceptions to this policy may be approved by the supervisor. However, the company feels employees need time off the job for rest and relaxation.

**Manager's Tip**

You can design your own vacation policy, but keep it as simple as possible.

**MEMO TO:** Payroll Department

I have requested that I be allowed to take _____ days of vacation from _____ to _____. These days are unearned and I agree that if I quit before this vacation time is earned, the company is authorized to withhold the unearned pay from my final check.

_____
Employee Signature

_____
Date

_____
Supervisor Signature

_____
Date

# WORK RULES

Any group of people working together must honor rules for their common good and safety and maintain a consistent standard of action for all. Therefore, some rules have been established to protect employee rights against arbitrary actions by others. They are intended not to restrict, but to provide a uniform policy upon which to base actions and decisions.

The severity of any problem at work will determine whether verbal or written warning, suspension, or termination is appropriate. In most cases, before a written warning is issued a verbal warning will be given to the employee. If improvement is not made within the time period granted in earlier warnings, it will be necessary to issue a written warning. Copies will be furnished to the Personnel Department and to the employee. If the employee fails to improve by the date given on the warning or suspension, termination of employment could result.

Upon notification by the manager, the Personnel Department will remove records of verbal or written warnings from an employee's personnel file after the employee has improved in the problem area to the satisfaction of the manager. We feel employees should not be unduly penalized in future years for past difficulties.

The following work rules apply to employees while on company property. Violation of the rules may be grounds for termination:

1. Theft, vandalism, or careless destruction of company property, or property belonging to a fellow employee is prohibited.

2. Drinking, using, possessing, or selling intoxicants, narcotics, or illegal drugs on company property is prohibited.

3. Use or possession of firearms is prohibited.

4. Making fraudulent statements on employment applications or job records is prohibited.

5. Employees may not solicit for any purpose or sell anything during working hours or in work areas unless specifically authorized by their supervisor.

6. Gambling during working time or on company property is prohibited.

7. Insubordination or willful disregard of a supervisor's instructions is prohibited.

8. Fighting on company property is prohibited.

9. Excessive absenteeism is grounds for dismissal.

10. Failure to observe proper work schedules with regard to starting times, meal times, and quitting times, is prohibited.

The above list of work rules is not all-inclusive and may be amended at any time without notice. Note: Some experts advise now that this section be eliminated. Check with your attorney.

# WORKERS' COMPENSATION

In accordance with applicable state laws and regulations, certain employees are eligible for workers' compensation benefits. These benefits are available in the event of an accident or illness resulting from an employee's occupation and which requires medical treatment, hospitalization, or loss of work time.

Promptness in reporting an injury cannot be overemphasized. In the event of an accident or illness resulting from a covered employee's occupation, the company must complete a report of the accident or illness. This report will assist in the determination of any liability.

Workers' compensation bulletins are posted on bulletin boards throughout the company, and forms are available in the Personnel Department.

## Reporting Requirements

It is the joint responsibility of covered employees and their supervisors to report any job- related injury or illness. Each worksite will comply with local and state regulations concerning the recording and filing of information on covered employee injuries and illnesses. State laws and regulations vary to the extent that no attempt will be made in this policy to define the various regulations.

## Definition of "Covered Employees"

Employees in most occupational classifications, are eligible for benefits under the applicable state worker's compensations laws and regulations.

**Manager's Tip**

Be sure to check on the worker's compensation law in your state and write your policy to conform.

# 6

# COMPENSATION AND BENEFITS

- How Compensation Programs Are Changing
- Designing and Evaluating Your Compensation Program
- Job Descriptions and Job Evaluations: How to Choose the Best System for Your Company
- The DOs and DON'Ts of Writing Job Descriptions to Describe Physical and Mental Demands
- Understanding "Essential Job" Functions Under the Americans with Disabilities Act (ADA)
- Sample Statements That Can Be Used in Job Descriptions
- Sample Job Description
- The Three Most Common Methods of Job Evaluation
- Making Job Evaluation Simple but Effective
- Model of Wage Grades and Rates for a Small Company
- Sample Job Descriptions
- Model Salary Program
- Pay for Performance and Performance Management
- Employee Benefits
- Glossary of Benefits Terms
- Work and Family Benefits
- Examples of Employee Benefits

# COMPENSATION AND BENEFITS

Most compensation programs are taking on a new look today. The entire area of compensation and benefits is changing dramatically in the U.S. The key terms are *flexible* and *multiple compensation strategies.* Pay-for-performance is in, and most companies are moving away from a single policy or pay line and one compensation system for the whole company.

More businesses are using one-time lump-sum pay increases that don't increase base pay, and many factories are going to all-salaried plants. Some companies are moving to two-tier wage programs and a variety of new pay structures. They are not all working well, but the idea is that companies are trying all types of new programs.

## HOW COMPENSATION PROGRAMS ARE CHANGING

Here are eleven items to consider when developing your strategies for new salary programs.

1. Consider developing and implementing plans that marry compensation systems to company goals. Find more tangible ways of linking employee productivity goals to corporate profits and thereby actualizing pay-for-performance objectives.

2. The move to multiple-compensation objectives allows a company to save in some areas by putting that money into programs that will provide a better return on investment. For example: an organization might announce its intention to move to a third quartile pay level in hard-to-fill technical jobs but remain at first quartile pay levels in staff jobs where the first quartile is externally competitive.

3. Many companies have moved to multiple policy lines in salary programs. For example, there may be one policy line for hourly nonexempt employees, another for salaried exempt professionals, and still a third for executives.

4. There is a trend to salaried manufacturing plants. Some companies feel productivity increases at salaried plants. Dow Chemical, TRW, Rockwell International, and Dana Corp. have all tried this concept. Companies still pay overtime to workers, but they have eliminated time clocks and treat all levels of employees as salaried, attempting to increase self-worth and self-esteem.

5. Many organizations are developing innovative pay-for-performance programs and taking them seriously. More union contracts are linking scheduled pay increases to specific measurable productivity improvements. Even the teaching profession has experienced new incentive programs. One school board links pay to performance

by paying salary incentives of up to $7,000 based on measurable performance improvements.

6. Deferred compensation is becoming more popular. Management employees and professionals who have the option more and more prefer to defer taking pay increases until retirement.

7. Gain sharing is replacing profit sharing in many organizations. Gain sharing is more of an industrial engineering approach that supports the idea of affordability and makes sense in many businesses.

8. Comparable worth claims are becoming more frequent as more women enter the workforce. This emotional issue will continue to plague companies that employ large numbers of low-paid female workers. Be sure new programs are designed with this in mind.

9. High-tech industries are often more innovative in terms of pay, benefits, and perks. These differences will begin to run over into other industries, like the information and service industries, as more high tech people cross over to work for service and information companies.

10. More companies are considering implementing lump sum pay increases that don't increase base pay. The auto, aerospace, and insurance industries already have plans in effect. One-time lump sum pay increases need not increase base pay, which has been accelerating at any incredible rate in some industries.

11. There is a move by many organizations to two-tier pay in labor contracts. American Airlines claims it has saved over $100 million per year with its two-tier contract. Labor unions and employees do not approve of two-tier contracts that penalize new workers by paying them much less than long-term employees doing the same job, but companies that have two-tier pay programs say they have gone to them out of necessity to remain in business.

What is most obvious today is that compensation programs are no longer market driven. The key issue is affordability. The whole compensation and benefit scene is a collage of changing, innovative thought and programming.

## DESIGNING AND EVALUATING YOUR COMPENSATION PROGRAM

It is almost easier to design a new salary program than to reevaluate or revise your current one to fit your changing needs. Whether designing a new plan or revising an old one, you need a checklist or an audit procedure to identify your specific compensation needs. You must look internally and externally at all the issues, problems, and opportunities you face.

### Compensation Program Evaluation Checklist

If you have not performed a thorough audit of compensation before, here is a fairly standard procedure to use with tips on completing the project so that the information obtained will be most relevant to your actual compensation picture.

Answer the following questions:

❑ Who are your competitors and what will your competitive posture be? What is your current position?

❑ What is your company's preferred mix of pay? How does base salary compare with bonuses, benefits, and other components? If your salaries appear to be "low," it may be because your fringe benefits package is so expensive. In many companies benefits are costing 37 percent to 40 percent of payroll, and management cannot afford to increase base pay and still provide benefits.

❑ How could you better relate salary to individual effort and good performance? Can you set performance standards in most jobs, and then relate pay incentives to productivity gains?

❑ What emphasis should you give to performance rather than seniority or cost of living (COLA) increases? Most companies are putting more emphasis on productivity and pay for performance, and in most cases have eliminated COLAs altogether.

❑ Should you change from a profit sharing program to a gain sharing plan? This is more of an industrial engineering approach, but it works well in many companies. You will need some help from experts in the compensation industry to research and design a plan that will fit your specific needs. Companies like the Hay Group in Philadelphia, or Hewitt Associates in Lincolnshire, Ill. can be very helpful.

❑ Have you looked seriously at market conditions for your industry, your region, and your specific business? Many businesses today can't afford to have market-driven compensation programs. Affordability is the key issue.

❑ Do you pay attention to practices of your industry? Should the same policies apply to all locations? If your company has been involved in mergers and acquisitions, your overall policies probably need a critical review. Check with human resource directors in similar organizations and with your industry associations to ensure your practices are competitive.

❑ Do you need a change in the policy itself, or do you just need to update a policy that is basically sound? By reviewing your policies on a regular basis, you may find policies that cost you money could be eliminated as times change.

❑ Review your relocation and transfer practices. Consider the real necessity of assignments to high-cost living either in the United States or overseas if you have international operations.

❑ Overseas employee policies need review. Some companies are changing policies that were set up for United States expatriates in favor of using local nationals whenever possible to eliminate the high cost of relocation of American employees. Relocation is an expensive issue.

## Job Description

- ❏ Are there current job descriptions for every job? Job descriptions should be revised as jobs change.

- ❏ Do descriptions support job evaluations, provide guides for selection and recruiting, meet EEO and other legal requirements? Do they stress job content?

- ❏ Who writes your job descriptions? Is the person trained? Do you know what the job really entails?

- ❏ Are descriptions reviewed by higher management?

- ❏ Do you have a regular updating schedule so that if the job is split or downsized the job descriptions and job evaluations are revised?

## Job Evaluation

- ❏ Are the job evaluation (JE) factors appropriate to the tests to which your program is likely to be subjected?

- ❏ Are factors defined sufficiently and have you looked at relationships?

- ❏ Are evaluators trained and knowledgeable? Watch out for a "down bias" in ratings of jobs that are held by minorities and women.

- ❏ Do employees have an appeal mechanism if they don't agree with the evaluation? Most employee handbooks provide an employee complaint procedure. Be sure you have one.

- ❏ What does it cost to administer? Some plans are so complex that there are unreasonable costs to administer the plans. If your plan is too complex, review and simplify it to cut costs of administration. If you don't have time to do it, hire a consultant to assist you with the project.

- ❏ Is your plan market-oriented or job/content-oriented? Can you defend a market- based approach? Job evaluation plans that are market-oriented have been ruled in some courts to be discriminatory against women. It is best to use a specific job/ content-oriented evaluation program to avoid charges of sex or pay discrimination.

## Salary Structure

- ❏ Check compa-ratios: Where are the majority of your jobs placed within your salary ranges? Are compa-ratios very low or very high? Extremes can be a danger signal. Compute compa-ratio by dividing employees' current salary by the salary midpoint. A compa-ratio of 80 percent places employees at minimum of the salary range, 100 percent at midpoint, and 120 percent at maximum of range.

- ❏ Check internal relationships. Watch for signs of compression. Particularly watch where this problem is arising—in hourly operations or in professional categories?

❏ Has the plan been kept up to date with the minimum wage and wage-hour regulations?

❏ Do you review geographic and industry differentials regularly to ensure the plan is competitive?

❏ Do you pay shift differentials? Are they competitive in your industry?

❏ Are survey sources still relevant? Periodically review and evaluate sources. If you feel survey data are weak, consider starting a new survey group to compare relevant data.

❏ Check communications: How much do you tell employees about the plan, and how good a job do you do? Do you get feedback from employees on your plan?

## Policies

❏ Check written policies on hiring, promotion, transfers. Do the same rules apply to individuals in all departments?

❏ How good are merit guide rules? Have they flattened out so that, in effect, most people are getting "average" raises, thus turning your "merit" program into a longevity system?

❏ What basis are you using for making these individual determinations: merit? performance? cost of living? a combination? What proportion of the raise is allocable to each factor?

❏ Measure whether your program is in fact doing what your policy says. Do this by going back to increases that were given and see how they check out against the employees' performance. Can you defend your choices?

❏ If your system is truly performance-related, do you follow through to check performance ratings?

❏ What is your timing for giving raises: annual, semiannual? Is this policy working well?

❏ When individuals are promoted, are promotional raises substantial enough to reward them for their extra effort and responsibility?

❏ Do promotional raises get all the employees into the range of the new job? Check to see that women employees are treated the same as males in promotional increase percentages. In some companies women always fall below the range after a promotion and men always fall above. This should not be allowed to happen.

❏ Do you periodically check policies and philosophical objectives to be sure your practices and procedures are on target?

After you've completed the checklist you will have covered most of the issues facing you when you design your plan. If you are a small organization you will not need as sophisticated a plan as you would if you employed over 300 people. For example, if you are a small company (fewer than 100 people), you can use the short form job description.

Also, you can use the simplified job grade system rather than the more difficult and time-consuming point factor evaluation system. Samples of these plans follow.

# JOB DESCRIPTIONS AND JOB EVALUATIONS: HOW TO CHOOSE THE BEST SYSTEM FOR YOUR COMPANY

Job descriptions and job evaluations are the underpinnings of an effective compensation program. If you are a mid-size or large organization you need to create a program that includes in-depth job descriptions and a point-factor job evaluation program that will hold up in case of litigation. If you are a small company, the long job descriptions and point-factor evaluation process may not be necessary.

The job description is the most important document in the compensation program. Ask yourself three important questions before you begin to write the job description:

1. How will the job descriptions be used?
2. What kind of job descriptions do you want, long or short forms?
3. Are you capable of maintaining updates on an ongoing basis?

## Preparing Job Descriptions

The first step in preparing your job descriptions is the collection of data. This should be done systematically, by gathering important facts about the job. There are four key data elements: skill requirements, effort, responsibility, and working conditions.

In order to include all of the key data elements, follow these seven steps:

1. *Principal job duties and responsibilities.* Determine and record any function that takes up 5 percent or more of the employee's time.
2. *Output.* Determine what results are expected by the job, quantitative and qualitative.
3. *Reporting relationships.* Determine all reporting relationships, upward and downward. Include an accurate and current organizational chart.
4. *Skill requirements.* Determine all skill, ability, or training requirements, including formal education (degree), specialized training (certification), specialized skills (licensing), and amount of experience.
5. *Effort.* Include the physical and mental effort required to perform the job.
6. *Responsibilities.* Determine and record in detail how much independent judgment is allowed and used, the impact of the job on the organization, whether the job has responsibility for the supervision of others, and whether it has responsibility for policy design and administration.
7. *Working conditions.* Include any unpleasant or dangerous working conditions, travel required (determine percentage of time), or abnormal working times or workdays.

## Methods of Collecting Data

There are several methods available to the job analyst collecting the key data elements for job descriptions. Interviews are often conducted on a one-to-one basis with the job incumbent. This method produces high-quality data but is very expensive. It is most suitable for collecting data on senior management jobs. Direct observation also produces high-quality data. But it's time-consuming and methods-oriented, slanted to the incumbent's way of doing things. This method is recommended for use with short-cycle, production-type jobs.

The fastest and least expensive method of data collection is the questionnaire. It's also considered the best general-purpose method. If possible, have the entire group of employees that hold the job fill out the questionnaire at the same time. This gives a fuller picture of how the job is performed and doesn't damage morale by singling out employees to be surveyed.

When the data collection is completed and you begin to write the job descriptions, remember to:

- Keep in mind the primary use of the job description (compensation, legal defense).

- Make sure all personnel jargon is removed.

- Review the description in light of legal requirements.

## Job Descriptions and the Law

To help make sure job descriptions won't run afoul of the law, remember to focus on job content, not the incumbent. Keep your descriptions up to date with periodic review. Do an immediate follow-up when job duties change. Keep your records accurate. Don't include unreasonable requirements or expectations. Some specific tips are as follows:

- Make sure your job descriptions don't include such phrases as, "This job requires a young, aggressive . . . or, "a training position for a recent college graduate." Such statements in your job descriptions could get you into trouble under the Age Discrimination in Employment Act.

- Keep educational and experience requirements job-related. The EEOC considers such requirements to be employment "tests," and they are subject to the uniform guidelines on testing. Requirements that aren't job-related can get you into trouble under Title VII of the Civil Rights Act.

- Make sure your job descriptions' references to health requirements, working conditions, and effort are proper and accurate. Job descriptions that don't fully explain physical activities won't help you if you're charged with violating the Rehabilitation Act.

- When developing your wage and salary programs, use only complete and accurate descriptions of job content. When the content of two or more jobs is similar, grade and range should be similar.

# THE DOs AND DON'Ts OF WRITING JOB DESCRIPTIONS TO DESCRIBE PHYSICAL AND MENTAL DEMANDS

No one likes to write job descriptions, but here are some guidelines and some DOs and DON'Ts that can speed the process.

## DOs

- Focus on job content—the essential job functions, not extraneous information.

- List only the requirements that are necessary now; you can focus on expectations when the employee has mastered the current job.

- Keep education and experience job related. This is essential for regulatory reasons, but it also ensures the incumbent has the background to succeed in the position.

- Describe physical and mental requirements and working conditions. Medical group practices do not have the demanding physical or working conditions of a mining operation, but every job has some critical environmental factors. For example, a clerical position may require sitting at a switchboard/reception desk most of the day, or at a word processor. Working conditions may be stressful, such as in an emergency outpatient clinic.

- Keep records of job analysis information. You will want to refer to them when you begin your next revision cycle or in case of equal employment opportunity (EEO) action.

- Build flexibility into the job description. Ensure that it is a true position description which is tailored to fit the job incumbent.

- Allow an opportunity to broaden job responsibilities. Again, turning the job description into a position description provides the means for developing the employee through increased responsibility.

- Use job descriptions that focus on results. For example, instead of the duty being typing, it should be typing and completing the letter to company standards. Use results-oriented language.

## DON'Ts

- Don't focus on the incumbent. The job analysis and job description are about the job, not the person.

- Don't list desirable requirements. List necessary requirements.

- Don't use potentially discriminatory methods or terminology. Avoid possible discrimination with wording that adversely impacts someone regarding race, age, gender, handicap, veteran status, or religion. Unfortunately, job descriptions are a way in which unintended bias and resistance to change may perpetuate unfair employment and pay practices.

- Don't be vague. Job descriptions must be as specific as possible.

- Don't detail every activity of the job holder. A job description is a list of tasks for which the employee is responsible.

- Don't make them too long. Although the job description includes much information, present it as briefly as possible. An outline format works well.

- Don't use the common phrase that ends so many job descriptions, "and other tasks as assigned." This phrase kills the intent of a well-developed job description-to precisely define the content and requirements of an employee's work. By using the phrase, the employee is subject to demands that may affect successful job performance. A better phrase is "and other tasks as negotiated." This implies that the employee and supervisor communicate about new job needs and prioritize workload.

## TIPS

- Rank order essential job functions. Put the most important first, followed by the less important and lastly by occasional duties so the employee is clear about priorities.

- Develop a graphic representation of job duties showing priority duties, with the amount of time allocated for duties. The total should add up to 100 percent. However, ensure every job picture includes room for occasional duties and contingencies. For example, 10 percent of time is allocated for extra, unexpected duties.

- Provide an organizational chart that shows where this position fits into the "big picture." This graphic also helps reporting structure, interpersonal relationships and the overall thrust of the organization.

- Use action verbs when writing duty descriptions.

- Avoid sexist language, such as using only masculine terms like "he," "him," etc. Preferably, construct sentences so that pronouns are not required. If necessary, use "he/she," "they/them" or neutral/genderless words. Do not specifically state or generally infer that certain jobs are "male" or "female" jobs.

- Use quantitative words. The employee should be given a frame of reference as a performance measure. For example, must type 40 words per minute or must lift 50 pounds.

- Avoid ambiguous words. Be as clear as possible. For example, instead of saying "handles files," say, "sets up files according to the organization's procedures, pulls and refiles files daily, and makes new files as needed."

- Avoid brand name/proprietary words unless critical to the duty. If the employee is expected to do general photocopying, say so instead of "xeroxing," unless you have a complex Xerox machine that requires specific experience.

- Limit the use of the word "may"; it is a vague word. Instead, say what you mean. For example, "Periodically the employee substitutes for the receptionist." Don't say "may substitute."

# UNDERSTANDING "ESSENTIAL JOB" FUNCTIONS UNDER THE AMERICANS WITH DISABILITIES ACT (ADA)

The term "essential functions" means the fundamental job duties of the position the individual with a disability holds or desires. According to the Regulations, a job function may be considered essential for any of several reasons, including but not limited to the following:

- the function may be essential because the reason the position exists is to perform that function;
- the function may be essential because of the limited number of employees available among whom the performance of that job function can be distributed; and/or
- the function may be highly specialized so that the incumbent in the position is hired for his or her expertise or ability to perform the particular function.

The Guidelines state that, once it is determined that the individual who holds the position is actually required to perform the function the employer asserts is an essential function, the inquiry will then center around whether removing the function would fundamentally alter that position. The Regulations list several kinds of evidence that are relevant to determining whether a particular job function is essential. These factors include, but are not limited to:

- the employer's judgment as to which functions are essential
- written job descriptions prepared before advertising or interviewing applicants for the job
- the amount of time spent on the job performing the function
- the consequences of not requiring the incumbent to perform the function
- the terms of a collective bargaining agreement
- the work experience of past incumbents in the job and/or
- the current work experience of incumbents in similar jobs.

Consideration is given to the employer's judgment as to what functions of the job are essential as a matter of business necessity and, if an employer has prepared a written job description before advertising or interviewing applicants for the job, the description will be considered as evidence of the essential functions of the job.

# SAMPLE STATEMENTS THAT CAN BE USED IN JOB DESCRIPTIONS TO DESCRIBE PHYSICAL AND MENTAL DEMANDS

## Typical Physical Demands

- Requires prolonged sitting, some bending, stooping, and stretching. Requires eye–hand coordination and manual dexterity sufficient to operate a keyboard, photocopier, telephone, calculator, and other office equipment. Requires normal range of hearing and vision to record, prepare and communicate appropriate reports. Requires lifting boxes up to 50 pounds. Requires dexterity and data entry skills.

- Requires prolonged standing, bending, stooping, and stretching. Requires occasional lifting up to 40 pounds. Requires exposure to machines, chemicals, and solvents. Requires manual dexterity and eye–hand coordination for data input. Must be able to operate simple to complex and heavy duty machinery. Requires normal range of hearing and vision.

- Requires frequent sitting, standing, bending, or stooping for prolonged periods. Requires lifting up to 75 pounds. Requires vision correctable to within the normal range and to operation of fork-lift and heavy equipment. Requires working in areas which are not ventilated or air-conditioned. Requires eye–hand coordination sufficient to operate machinery such as a truck or fork-lift  Requires full range of body motion including handling and lifting, manual and finger dexterity and eye–hand coordination. Requires standing and walking for extensive periods of time. Occasionally lifts and carries items weighing up to 50 pounds. Requires corrected vision and hearing to normal range. Requires working under stressful conditions or working irregular hours.

- Frequent mobility and/or sitting required for extended periods of time. Some bending and stooping required. Requires occasional lifting up to 50 pounds of boxes or paper. Requires manual dexterity to operate computer keyboard, calculator, copier machine, and other office equipment. Requires eyesight correctable to 20/20 to read numbers, reports, and computer terminals. Requires hearing within normal range for telephone use. Occasional high stress work may require dealing with customers/clients.

- Requires sitting, standing, bending, and reaching. May require lifting up to 50 pounds. Requires manual dexterity sufficient to operate standard office machines such as computers, fax machines, calculators, the telephone, and other office equipment. Requires normal range of hearing and vision.

- Requires sitting, standing and bending and a normal range of hearing and vision.


## Typical Mental Demands

- Must understand vague and implicit instructions, and react favorably in all work situations. Must be mentally adaptable and flexible in dealing with a variety of people. Is frequently called upon to handle difficult situations.

- Must be able to deal with a variety of emotions and frustrations in making business decisions. Emotional stability and personal maturity are important attributes in this position.

- Must be able to analyze many variables and choose the most effective course of action for the organization at any given point in time. Must handle novel and diverse work problems on a daily basis.

- Must be able to communicate providing verbal feedback in a professional manner. Must be able to analyze causes of interpersonal conflict and resolve complex communications issues (i.e., undefined roles, objectives, and information gaps).

- Must be able to resolve problems, handle conflict, and make effective decisions under pressure. Must have a long attention span in order to listen to people, perceive the *real* problems, and bring issues to a successful conclusion.

- Must be able to accurately code data, must be knowledgeable in office procedures, and able to answer questions in a professional and friendly manner. Must be able to balance accounts and compile computer reports. Requires public contact and excellent interpersonal skills. Must be able to make effective decisions in manager's absence.

- Ability to give, receive, and analyze information, formulate work plans, prepare written materials, and articulate goals and action plans. Must understand people and be able to communicate effectively with them.

- Ability to receive and analyze data and input into the computer.

- Ability to do simple math calculations, input data into the computer, and analyze data as requested.

## Equipment to Be Used

- Must be able to operate computer and other office machines such as fax, calculator, telephone, and so on.

## Working Conditions

- May be required to work some overtime. Works in typical office setting.

---

**Manager's Tip**

You may mix the descriptions on these two pages or add information as needed.

# SAMPLE JOB DESCRIPTION

| | | | |
|---|---|---|---|
| **JOB TITLE:** | Human Resources Director | **FLSA STATUS:** Exempt | |
| **JOB CODE:** | 409 | **DATE:** | |
| **DIVISION:** | Human Resources | **REVISION NO.:** | |
| **REPORTS TO:** | President & CEO | **REVISION DATE:** | |

## POSITION SUMMARY:

This position is responsible to the President and CEO for the direction, coordination and overall management of the Human Resource (HR) function. The Director must identify, plan and implement strategic objectives for the HR Department including an annual human resource plan, to ensure the organization's overall effectiveness. The Director is responsible for recruiting, employment, affirmative action, compensation, benefits, labor relations, management training and development, as well as employee relations and communications. This responsibility includes ensuring compliance with all federal, state and local government regulations as they relate to the human resources function.

## ESSENTIAL JOB FUNCTIONS:

- Responsible for the implementation and ongoing maintenance of all human resource policies and procedures.
- Responsible for recruiting and employment to ensure positions are filled in a timely manner.
- Develop and implement compensation programs within the budget guidelines of the Company. Ensure that the program includes objective and defensible elements for job evaluation, and an employee salary program that includes internal fairness and external competitiveness in our industry.
- Provide guidance and expertise to employees and management in resolving personnel problems.
- Provide leadership with regard to the Company's Affirmative Action Program. Manage the implementation of the Americans with Disabilities Act and The Civil Rights Act, guidelines to ensure that these programs are implemented and reviewed annually, and that all supervisors receive the information and training needed in order to comply with all government regulations pertaining to the human resources function.
- Maintain current working knowledge of benefit laws and IRS requirements to ensure the Company's compliance. Maintain benefit programs for the Company. Manage the benefits function in an effective manner to ensure timely resolution of benefit claims and employee benefits problems.
- Develop, implement and conduct management or other human resources related training programs to ensure the organization is up-to-date on management techniques, and that professionals (CPAs, Attorneys, and so on) can maintain their credentials.
- Ensure compliance with all regulatory and legal requirements.
- Manage human resources administrative functions including personnel files, an applicant tracking system and all other personnel actions and administrative responsibilities of the HR function.
- Design and implement employee communication programs in order to ensure ongoing, positive up and down communications throughout the organization.

THIS JOB DESCRIPTION DOES NOT CONSTITUTE A CONTRACT FOR EMPLOYMENT

JOB TITLE: Human Resources Director
DATE:
PAGE 2 of 3

### ESSENTIAL JOB FUNCTIONS: (cont'd)

- Manage the human resources of the organization in an effective manner, institutionalizing positive human resources procedures and policies, thus assisting in the prevention of litigation or costly labor relations problems.
- Delegate responsibility to appropriate staff members to ensure that the day-to-day human resource functions are carried out. Personally manage the human resources staff members who are responsible for the administrative areas of the Human Resources Department.
- Responsible for encouraging the growth of the human resources staff

### JOB REQUIREMENTS:

**EDUCATION:**     Bachelor's Degree in Business or Human Resource Management, or ten years experience in human resource management.

**EXPERIENCE:**    A minimum of ten years of successful human resource experience in developing, implementing and managing HR programs, benefit contract negotiations, compensation programs, familiarity with governmental regulations and complex organizational structures, as well as training and development.

**SKILLS:**        Strong leadership, management and organizational skills, as well as understanding of multi-disciplinary programs. An ability to integrate and harmonize diversified functions, including the administrative function. Effective consultative skills as well as executive and managerial skills. Understanding, influencing and serving others are important attributes in this position. The ability to select, develop and motivate people and create a positive work environment. The ability to resolve human resource problems quickly and effectively, and determining appropriate courses of action for the organization in the human resources area. Must display a high degree of emotional maturity while keeping difficult situations in proper perspective. Must be flexible and have well-developed interpersonal skills. Must excel in personal interactions with the human resources staff and employees at all levels of the Company.

### SUPERVISORY RESPONSIBILITIES:

Supervise the human resources staff.

### EQUIPMENT TO BE USED:

Must be able to operate computer and other office machines such as fax, calculator, telephone, and so on.

### TYPICAL PHYSICAL DEMANDS:

Requires sitting, standing, bending and reaching. May require lifting up to 50 pounds. Requires manual dexterity sufficient to operate standard office machines such as computers, fax machines, calculators, the telephone and other office equipment. Requires normal range of hearing and vision.

THIS JOB DESCRIPTION DOES NOT CONSTITUTE A CONTRACT FOR EMPLOYMENT

JOB TITLE: Human Resources Director
DATE:
PAGE 3 of 3

## TYPICAL MENTAL DEMANDS:

Must be able to analyze many variables and choose the most effective course of action for the organization at any given point in time. Must handle novel and diverse work problems on a daily basis. Personal maturity is an important attribute. Must be able to resolve problems, handle conflict and make effective decisions under pressure. Must have a long attention span in order to listen to people, perceive the *real* problems and bring issues to a successful conclusion. Must relate and interact with people at all levels in the Company.

## WORKING CONDITIONS:

Occasionally called upon to work overtime or odd schedules. Works in a typical office setting.

REVIEWED BY: _____

DATE: _____

THIS JOB DESCRIPTION DOES NOT CONSTITUTE A CONTRACT FOR EMPLOYMENT

## THE THREE MOST COMMON METHODS OF JOB EVALUATION

*The classification method* of job evaluation is used by most civil service systems. Before the jobs are evaluated, a decision is made as to the number of pay grades that are needed, and then job descriptions are written for each class of jobs in the structure.

*The ranking method* of job evaluation is one of the easier methods. A list of jobs to be evaluated is established, and the jobs are then ranked in relation to each other on an overall basis. The overall judgment is made on the value of each job in relation to all other jobs on the list. This method works best in smaller companies.

*The point method* of job evaluation reviews three or four job factors that are common to all the jobs being evaluated and then rates each job in relation to each factor on a numerical scale. Points are given for each factor, looking at the degree to which the job possesses each factor. There are usually four or five factors reviewed. They might be education, know-how, safety, responsibility for budgeted dollars, management skills, and so on. The points are added, and a total point factor is assigned to each job. Jobs are then related to each other on the basis of the total point scores, and total points can be related to wage and salary ranges. To arrive at a salary range, points usually apply to a dollar formula, which will place the job at a particular place on a salary policy line. For example:

Job points = 500

Policy line formula = $50 per point + $10,000

Multiply through, and you get a salary range midpoint of $35,000 for a job worth 500 points.

If the measured worth of a job fits an established job grade schedule, a range of point totals (for example, 401 to 500 points) could be assigned a specific salary grade (for example, a grade 12 in a 20-grade system).

## MAKING JOB EVALUATION SIMPLE BUT EFFECTIVE

There seems to be a trend today of hiring qualified compensation people and implementing your own salary programs in-house. One area, however, where we do see outside consultants used most in human resource management is the area of job evaluation. Consultants in this area are expensive, but there are good reasons for considering an outside expert:

- Trial and error is an expensive way to attempt to install a salary program. The errors can cost more than the consultant.

- The consultant can devote full time to the project, and if there are time constraints this is a real plus.

- Top management's commitment is essential to the successful installation of a job evaluation program, and executives may be more amenable to an outside expert with prestige in the field.

- You can utilize the expert to the fullest in the job evaluation process by seeing that your staff is trained as the installation is implemented.

- The consultant should provide an operating guide for use of the system, and cooperation between your staff and the consultant can ensure that the program and the guide are tailored specifically to your company.

The fact that the consultant is an impartial third party should aid the installation. One of the foremost consultants in the job evaluation field today is the Hay Group of Philadelphia, Pennsylvania. They install the Hay Guide Chart Profile method of job evaluation, which is popular in many larger organizations throughout the country. There are many other proprietary systems available.

## The Hay Guide Chart Profile Method of Job Evaluation

The two key elements for measuring job content under the Hay Guide Chart Profile method are (1) a thorough understanding of the content of the job to be measured, and (2) the comparison of one job with another in order to determine the relative value.

It's almost impossible to measure an entire job against another entire job, so elements that are present in all jobs are measured. These elements are:

- *Know-how.* The sum total of all knowledge and skills, however acquired, needed for satisfactory job performance.
- *Problem solving.* The amount of original thinking required by the job for analyzing, evaluating, creating, reasoning, and arriving at conclusions.
- *Accountability.* The person's responsibility for actions and for the consequences of those actions.

The most important aspect of the Hay job evaluation method is understanding the job. This understanding usually comes from the job description, so it's important that the job description be current and complete and captures the essence of the job—what it's expected to accomplish, why it's needed, what results are to be achieved, and so on.

Whether you use the Hay job evaluation or another system of your own design, there are several essential elements to consider.

## Essential Elements of Job Evaluation

Job evaluation (JE) is a systematic method for comparing jobs in an organization to determine a reasonable and effective order or hierarchy. A good job evaluation program will give you an accurate measure of differences in accountabilities and duties of the jobs in your company so that reasonable salary differentials can be made between them.

Performance is irrelevant to job evaluation. It is not meant to judge the performance of the employee being observed. Its purpose is to measure *what* is done, not *how well* one particular person performs.

The goal of JE is to offer a solution to the basic management problem of pay inequity. When employees feel there is no logical connection between their compensation and their jobs, dissatisfaction and poor performance can easily result. Job evaluation works on the premise that a basic pattern controls the wage relationships between jobs in every company. JE helps you discover what that pattern is, and it produces an *explain-*

*able* system for comparing the relative worth of similar or widely differing jobs—routine, observable jobs with easily defined tasks, as well as jobs requiring the performance of non observable, highly cognitive tasks.

The following are important goals and benefits of a sound job evaluation program as reported by Prentice-Hall in their *Compensation Service:*

- To simplify and make rational the relatively chaotic wage structure likely to result from chance, custom, and individual biases; to eliminate favoritism and discrimination.

- To justify existing pay rates and relationships between jobs (internal equity).

- To provide a factual guideline for judging the relevance of job applicants' backgrounds to available jobs.

- To aid performance review. (Only by knowing what the job consists of can the quality of performance be measured.)

- To attract and hold capable employees by setting pay in line with rates for comparable jobs in other firms (external equity).

- To provide work incentives and boost morale. (Only by studying jobs can you recognize superior performance.)

- For unionized firms, to provide a rational basis for setting negotiated rates.

- For non unionized firms, to remove a common cause of low morale and dissatisfaction when employees perceive an inequity exists. If there is a perception of inequity, it might encourage unionization drives.

- To safeguard a company's prerogative to grant salary increases during periods of government wage control (incomes policy).

- To develop a policy of equal pay for equal work consistent with federal law.

How can you determine whether your firm is in sufficient need of a JE plan to justify a large commitment in capital and manpower? Here are some rules of thumb that may help you decide:

- *How large is your company?* If your CEO can't have personal knowledge of all the jobs in the organization, salary decisions must be delegated to others. Job evaluation will keep these decisions objective, consistent, and justifiable. Many JE experts feel that the critical point is somewhere between 500 and 1,000 employees. However, many smaller offices and manufacturing firms install programs covering only 50 or 100 people. It depends on the complexity of the organization and the jobs.

- *How fast is your firm growing?* Regardless of size, you may need a JE plan because of your company's growth or expansion. If former organizational patterns, recruiting techniques, or pay practices are no longer applicable, a JE program can provide a flexible system in which to grow.

- *Are you having a recruiting or turnover problem?* If you find your company is attracting low-quality job applicants or losing many employees, your pay rates may be to blame. Inconsistencies in pay, both internal (among jobs in your organization) and external (when compared with your competitors), may be the culprits.

- *How is employee morale?* Even if recruiting or turnover problems haven't materialized, productivity and costs can be adversely affected if employees are dissatisfied with existing pay relationships.

If your answers to these questions indicate that you need a formal program, your next step is to make all of the top decision-makers in your organization share your awareness.

The decision to undertake a job evaluation program must be arrived at by the top operating officers of the firm without undue sales pressure from you and with full knowledge of all that is involved. The initiator of the program, whether a personnel executive or some other manager, should never try to minimize the costs of the JE program. A lack of honesty at this state can undermine the program later. The plan will cost money, it will take managers and staff away from their normal duties, and it will interfere with the operating routine of the workers. To indicate otherwise, either directly or indirectly, in an effort to sell the program is unwise. The decision to install a JE program must be made with the full knowledge by all concerned that there will be inconveniences. The job of the initiator is to show that the benefits of the plan will far outweigh any temporary annoyances. The formation of a top management committee to approve the establishment of the JE plan can be of great help in gaining acceptance of the concept. Participation in the plan should begin at this level and continue downward throughout the organization.

If your company has a compensation specialist, he or she can be invaluable in the early stages of the plan. The compensation department will be intimately involved with the plan and can offer strong support to the claim that the plan will be soundly administered after its installation.

### Manager's Tip

The point factor job-evaluation system has had the most success for companies that have become involved in litigation. There are many good books on job evaluation, including the Prentice-Hall *Compensation* publication, which is published monthly; the Society for Human Resource Management Handbook, *Motivation and Commitment,* Volume II, published by the Bureau of National Affairs, Inc., Washington, D.C. 20037, and *Recruitment and Retention* published by AMACOM Books.

## MODEL OF WAGE GRADES AND RATES FOR A SMALL COMPANY

If your company is small, you needn't go to the time and expense of completing a lengthy job evaluation program. The simplest way for you to proceed is to create a job grade system, such as the following:

| *Grade* | *Job Title* |
| --- | --- |
| 1 | Courier, Mail Clerk, Accounting Clerk III |
| 2 | Accounting Clerk II, Typist, Data Entry II, Payroll Clerk |
| 3 | Secretary, Accounting Clerk I, Data Entry I, Purchasing Expediter |

*Note: Your grade structure should run to the top salary level, usually vice president*

Then you need to create wage ranges, for example:

| Grade | Min | Mid | Max |
|-------|-----|-----|-----|
| 1 | $5.75/hr. | $7.20/hr. | $8.65/hr. |
| 2 | $6.75 | $8.45 | $10.15 |
| 3 | $7.75 | $9.70 | $11.65 |

This is a simple but effective way to establish grades and pay ranges.

If there is not a local salary survey group that provides wage information on a regular basis, you can do your own survey by calling other companies in your industry and asking them to participate in a survey. Then share the information.

### Manager's Tip

Be careful when exchanging raw salary data. It could be misconstrued as "wage fixing." It's a good idea to use an outside consultant to gather the data and provide it to the group.

### *Sample Job Description*

**Position:**
Accounting Assistant

**Basic Function:**
Assists Accounting Manager in a variety of functional accounting activities. Performs a number of ongoing responsibilities in accordance with standard accounting procedures under general supervision and guidance.

**Dimensions:**
Provides accounting assistance to:
- (1)  Accounting Manager
- (1)  Internal Auditor
- (1)  Sales Manager -FP
- (6)  Data Entry Operators

**Principal Accountabilities:**
1) Preparation of ROA for Data Entry
2) Weekly Sales & Margin Analysis on PC
3) Income Statement Account Reconciliations
4) Administrative and Clerical Activities for General Accounting Department
5) Bank Statement Reconciliation

Incumbent needs good analytical skills and knowledge of computer systems

**Principal Interactions:**
Inside the Company:     90 People
Outside the Company:   10 banks, finance companies, customers

**Knowledge/Education Requirements:**
Bookkeeping/accounting background—Bachelors degree helpful but not mandatory
3 years experience

**Level of Authority:**
No supervisory responsibilities.

**Reports to:**
Accounting Manager

**Typical Physical Demands:**
Requires prolonged sitting, some bending and stooping. Manual dexterity sufficient to operate a computer keyboard and calculator. Requires normal range of hearing and vision. Must be able to lift up to 40 pounds.

Note

You may wish to use some of these job descriptions as samples in your own organization. Change them to fit your needs. Ask your employees for input. The job description can't be written in a vacuum if it is to be a valuable tool.

*Job Description**

JOB TITLE: President

DATE:

**Position Description**
Under policy direction of the Board of Directors, performs a wide range of difficult to complex management activities related to finances and accounting, marketing and promotion of services, staffing and personnel operations, and discretionary activities that serve to support effective business operations. Uses considerable independent judgment in decisions that influence operations. Advises and assists the Board of Directors in planning, policy, and operations matters.

**Responsibilities**
1. Directs the development and implementation of corporate goals, objectives, policies, and procedures; directs and ensures proper coordination of all administrative affairs; prepares and submits to the Board of Directors reports of finances, staffing, programs, and other administrative activities; prepares agenda and documents, attends and participates in Board of Director meetings to receive general direction.
2. Develops and implements organizational and program plans; researches applicable laws, pending legislation, and regulations; prepares reports, correspondence, memos, records, and forms; evaluates activities and interacts with representatives of comparable firms; develops and prepares forms, records, charts, and other operational materials, and implements operations systems to achieve effective workloads and workflow.

---

*This job specification should not be construed to imply that these requirements are the exclusive standards of the position. Incumbents may be required to follow any other instructions, and to perform any other related duties, as may be required.

3. Directs and carries out the marketing plan and supervises the sales force to ensure annual marketing objectives are achieved.

4. Prepares and delivers formal presentations before various public and private concerns; attends meetings, conferences, and seminars requiring periodic to frequent commute travel.

5. Secures the services and products of outside sources such as business insurance, security systems, vehicles and equipment, office supplies and furnishings, and legal or other advisory/support services.

6. Performs immediate supervision of department heads and key support staff, and maintains official records.

7. Works with the Controller to prepare the annual budget and approves subsequent modifications and transfers; monitors and evaluates accounting systems, audits of accounts, and internal control methods; establishes the method and means of determining fiscal accountability; reviews and approves accounts payable, payroll, and other financial warrants, requisitions, purchase orders, receipts, and records or reports.

8. Works with the Human Resource Director to develop personnel policies and procedures. Reviews job specifications, performance, and disciplinary determinations; conducts staff meetings and wage surveys and initiates wage increases based on performance; hears and resolves complaints and grievances as necessary.

## Employment Standards

**Education/Experience:** Any combination of education and experience that would provide the required skill and knowledge for successful performance would be qualifying. Typical qualifications would be equivalent to a master or bachelor degree from an accredited college or university with major coursework in business management and five years experience performing responsible general administrative work.

**Knowledge of:** Principles and practices of business management and marketing including personnel practices and employment laws, program budgeting, general accounting, and fiscal management practices; office procedures and business operating systems; and the appropriate methods and means of dealing with human behavior in a variety of business circumstances.

**Skill at:** Communicating effectively, verbally and in writing, in a diverse range of audiences and settings; persuasion and negotiation of conflicts and problems; assessing operational, program, staffing, and fiscal needs; interpreting legal documents and government regulations; evaluating fiscal and financial reports, forms, and data; analyzing complex written documents; identifying and resolving administrative problems; working long and irregular hours, and under pressure conditions; delegating responsibility and achieving results through subordinates; and maintaining order in an environment of changing priorities.

## *Job Description**

JOB TITLE: Controller

DATE:

### Position Description

Under general direction of the President, oversees the operations in connection with financial matters including accounts receivable and payable, payroll, and auditing; trains and supervises department staff; develops and initiates systems, policies, and procedures for transacting financial matters; and ensures that the financial system is accurate, efficient, and in accordance with professional accounting practices and governmental regulations.

### Responsibilities

1. Develops and implements the Accounting Department's goals, policies, procedures, methods, projects, and controls.

2. Directs accounting activities including maintenance of general ledgers, analysis of computer-generated data, and review of payroll records.

3. Prepares monthly reports as required by state and federal regulations, profit-loss statements, annual corporate tax returns, and special financial reports, studies, and analyses.

4. Develops and maintains internal audit control system; develops and administers the cash management program.

5. Provides data, reports, and other information to assist in the preparation of the annual budget.

6. Forecasts revenues, expenditures, and year-end balance.

7. Plans, designs, implements, and modifies the data processing system.

8. Prepares and revises the fiscal operations procedure manual.

9. Coordinates with other departments concerning short- and long-range fiscal needs and plans.

10. Responds to requests for information.

11. Supervises daily accounting operations, especially the verification and signing of payroll and cash disbursements.

12. Selects, trains, supervises, and evaluates accounting staff.

### Employment Standards

**Education/Experience:** Any combination of education and experience that would provide the required skill and knowledge for successful performance would be qualifying. Typical qualifications would be equivalent to:

1. Possession of a bachelor degree in accounting or business administration with an accounting concentration from an accredited college or university; and

2. Four years of progressively responsible experience in accounting, of which two years were in a supervisory capacity.

---

*This job specification should not be construed to imply that these requirements are the exclusive standards of the position. Incumbents may be required to follow any other instructions, and to perform any other related duties, as may be required.

**Knowledge of:** Principles, practices, and methods of accounting and auditing; principles and practices of financial administration including budgeting and reporting; modern office practices, procedures, methods, and equipment; modern principles and practices in operations procedures and data processing; application of data processing in the maintenance of accounting records and financial administration; budget preparation, program analyses, and revenue forecasting; principles and practices of organization, administration, budget, and management; and reports accounting practices required by state and federal regulations.

**Skill at:** Planning, coordinating, and directing a complex financial operation; developing, revising, and installing accounting systems and procedures; interpreting and applying appropriate laws and regulations; preparing various financial statements, reports, and analyses; communicating clearly and concisely orally and in writing; selecting, supervising, training, and evaluating assigned staff.

**Desirable Qualifications:** Possession of a Certified Professional Accountant (CPA) certificate.

## *Job Description**

JOB TITLE: Human Resource Director

DATE:

### Position Description

Responsible for the management of the Human Resource and Employee Relations function which includes recruiting, employment, affirmative action, compensation, benefits, labor relations, management training and development, and employee communications. Responsible for ensuring compliance with all federal, state, and local laws and regulations as they relate to the personnel function.

### Responsibilities

1. Responsible for human resource planning and staffing. Seeing that the company has the people they need in the required positions in a timely manner.

2. The Human Resource Director must work closely with the Deputy Director for Administrative Services and the other deputy directors to manage the human resource and employee relations functions to ensure the maximum productivity within the corporation's budget limitations. This means keeping jobs filled and employees motivated through the corporation's compensation, benefits, and communications activities.

3. Develop and implement competitive compensation program within the budget restrictions of the company. Ensure the program includes objective and defensible elements for job evaluation and a salary program that includes internal fairness and external competitiveness in our industry.

*This job specification should not be construed to imply that these requirements are the exclusive standards of the position. Incumbents may be required to follow any other instructions, and to perform any other related duties, as may be required.

4. Maintain competitive benefit programs for the company. Manage the day-to-day benefits activity throughout the organization in current manner. Ensure timely resolution of benefits claims and employee requests. Maintain current working knowledge of benefits laws and IRS requirements to ensure the company compliance with laws and regulations regarding benefits.

5. Work closely with other directors to develop needed management or other business-related training programs. For example, the Human Resource Director should be able to design, implement, and personally conduct such training programs for supervisors as "How To Hire, Discipline, and Terminate Employees in Order to Avoid Unnecessary Litigation."

6. The Human Resource Director must be able to design and implement employee communications programs in order to ensure on-going, positive up and down communications throughout the organization.

7. Manage the development and implementation of the company's affirmative action program. Ensure the program is updated annually and that all supervisors and directors receive the training they need to comply with the spirit and the letter of the company's affirmative action program. Provide leadership to conduct AAP recruiting activity to ensure women, minorities, and ethnic groups are represented in the company's workforce pursuant to the objectives of the AAP.

8. Maintain a current working knowledge of all state, federal, and local laws as they pertain to the Human Resource function in order to ensure compliance in a timely manner.

9. Maintain all personnel policies, procedures, and employee handbooks in a current manner. Write and rewrite policies as needed. The policies and procedures are meant to assist supervisors and directors in getting their jobs done as quickly and as efficiently as possible. Therefore, the personnel policies should assist in that process, not delay it.

10. Provide guidance and expertise to employees, supervisors, directors, deputy directors, and the executive director in the management of the total human resources of the organization in a positive, flexible, and competent manner.

11. Responsible for encouraging the growth and development of the human resource staff.

## Employment Standards

**Education/Experience:** Bachelor degree in business or human resource management. Applicant must have minimum of five years of human resource management experience.

**Knowledge of:** Principles and practices of effective human resources management and personnel administration.
**Skill at:** Strong managerial experience in the HR field. Strong human relations skills.

*Job Description*\*
_____

JOB TITLE: Branch Manager

DATE:

**Position Description**

Under general direction performs a wide range of difficult to complex administrative activities; coordinates and directs operations and personnel so as to ensure efficient and profitable operations; uses independent judgment within the framework of established policies and objectives in decisions affecting branch activities; makes recommendations and assists in the formulation of branch objectives, policies, and plans.

**Responsibilities**

1. Plans, examines, analyzes, and evaluates branch operations.
2. Prepares reports and records for management review.
3. Evaluates current procedures, practices, and precedents for accomplishing branch activities and functions.
4. Identifies and resolves operational problems; develops and implements alternative methods for work improvement.
5. Coordinates branch activities with interrelated activities of other branches or departments for optimum efficiency and economy.
6. Prepares periodic budget estimates and reports.
7. Orders supplies and equipment as needed.
8. Reviews branch audit reports to ensure operational efficiency and quality control.
9. Develops relationships with customers, businesses, and community and civic organizations to promote goodwill and generate new business.
10. Directs and coordinates, through subordinate personnel, branch activities and functions, utilizing knowledge of established policies, procedures and practices.
11. Initiates personnel actions such as recruitments, selections, transfers, promotions, and disciplinary or dismissal measures.
12. Resolves work grievances or submits unsettled grievances to next in chain of command for action; prepares work schedules; assigns or delegates responsibilities.
13. Gives work directives, resolves problems, and sets deadlines to ensure completion of branch operational functions.
14. Interprets and disseminates policy to workers and evaluates employee performance.

**Employment Standards**

**Education/Experience:** Any combination of education and experience that would provide the required skill and knowledge for successful performance would be qualifying. Typical qualifications would be equivalent to:

1. Possession of a bachelors degree in business administration with a management or financial concentration from an accredited college or university; and

_____
\*This job specification should not be construed to imply that these requirements are the exclusive standards of the position. Incumbents may be required to follow any other instructions, and to perform any other related duties, as may be required.

2. Three years of progressively responsible business experience of which two years were in a supervisory and planning capacity.

**Knowledge of:** Principles, practices, and methods of accounting and financial administration including budgeting, auditing, reporting, and quantitative analysis skills; modern principles and practices of organization, administration, budget, and management; financial and personnel reports and practices required by state and federal regulations.

**Skill at:** Planning, coordinating, and directing varied and complex administrative operations; speaking clearly and effectively; writing legibly and effectively; collecting, analyzing, and interpreting data from a wide variety of sources and taking appropriate action; selecting, supervising, training, and evaluating employees.

## *Job Description**

JOB TITLE: Data Processing Manager

DATE:

### Position Description

Under general supervision plans, coordinates, controls, supervises, and participates in the provision of activities and services relating to information system design, programming and documentation, data processing operations, and data communications; provides highly technical and responsible staff assistance.

### Responsibilities

1. Participates in the development and implementation of goals, objectives, policies, and priorities for the Data Processing Department.
2. Plans, coordinates, and manages the activities involved in the study of problems, the development and analysis of alternative solutions, and the programming, testing, implementation, computer processing, procedures, and forms design of the selected solutions.
3. Establishes work standards, assigns schedules, reviews staff work, directs training, and interprets policies, purposes, and goals to subordinates; administers all work rules, disciplinary actions, and employment practices.
4. Establishes and maintains production schedules and records, consults with manufacturers' representatives to define equipment and software needs; prepares requests for proposals, reviews and evaluates proposals.
5. Prepares and administers the division budget.
6. Orders necessary data processing supplies and materials.
7. Assists other department managers and staff in using computers and computer software.

### Employment Standards

**Education/Experience:** Any combination of education and experience that would provide the required skill and knowledge for successful performance would be qualifying. Typical qualifications would be equivalent to:

---

*This job specification should not be construed to imply that these requirements are the exclusive standards of the position. Incumbents may be required to follow any other instructions, and to perform any other related duties, as may be required.

1. Possession of a bachelor degree in business administration or computer science from an accredited college or university; and

2. Three years of increasingly responsible experience in computer operations, programming, and system development and design of which two years were in a supervisory capacity.

**Knowledge of:** Principles and techniques of systems analysis and programming; operating principles, methods, and practices of computers and related equipment. Must know the company's programming language, principles of organization, administration, budget, and personnel management.

**Skill at:** Planning, organizing, assigning, supervising, and reviewing data processing activities and services; designing systems and performing necessary programming and documentation; establishing and maintaining production schedules; operating computer equipment; communicating clearly and concisely, orally and in writing; selecting, supervising, training, and evaluating assigned staff.

## *Job Description\**

JOB TITLE: General Duties and Responsibilities of Supervisors

DATE:

The functions of individual office, plant, and general supervisors vary widely. There are a number of duties and responsibilities, however, which are common to most supervisors. Some of the more common ones are listed below:

1. Plans and schedules the work of a section, department, or organization for the most effective utilization of employees, equipment, and material within budgetary, cost, and quality standards.

2. Estimates manpower requirements. Requisitions and selects qualified employees necessary to perform work.

3. Assigns employees to jobs. Instructs them in proper performance of work and familiarizes them with company rules and regulations.

4. Maintains discipline of employees under their supervision in accordance with established rules and regulations. Initiates appropriate disciplinary action.

5. Assumes responsibility for the proper application of established employee relations and wage and salary administration policies, safety and health regulations, and union agreements.

6. Initiates action and approves or recommends approval of promotions, merit increases, transfers, leaves of absence, and other personnel changes.

7. Coordinates the functions performed under his/her supervision with those performed under other supervision.

8. Arranges for proper maintenance of machines, equipment, and facilities for which they are responsible.

9. Prepares reports concerning departmental activities.

---

\*This job specification should not be construed to imply that these requirements are the exclusive standards of the position. Incumbents may be required to follow any other instructions, and to perform any other related duties, as may be required.

*Job Description**

JOB TITLE: Accountant

DATE:

### Position Description

Under general supervision performs a variety of professional accounting work; compiles, prepares, and maintains financial data and records ensuring that all financial data are recorded in accordance with generally accepted accounting principles and consistent with established policy and procedures.

### Responsibilities

1. Performs professional accounting work in accordance with prescribed accounting system and generally accepted principles of accounting. Establishes and maintains accounts.

2. Prepares monthly journal entries and accounting corrections to ensure accurate accounting records; and checks general ledger from books of detail entries.

3. Assists in the preparation, analysis, and review of estimates of revenues, reimbursements, expenditures, fund conditions, or other proprietary and budgetary accounts.

4. Analyzes and verifies financial reports and statements, accounts, and records of expenditures and revenues.

5. Assists with the preparation of accounting and management control reports. Prepares and files all necessary state and federal reports.

6. Handles asset transfers among activities.

7. Organizes, directs, and controls the retention of historical accounting and legal records, ensuring that all information is safely stored and available on short notice.

### Employment Standards

**Education/Experience:** Any combination of education and experience that would provide the required skill and knowledge for successful performance would be qualifying. Typical qualifications would be equivalent to:

1. Possession of a bachelor degree in accounting or business administration from an accredited college or university; and

2. Two years of professional accounting experience.

**Knowledge of:** Principles, practices, and methods of modern accounting and auditing; principles and practices of financial administration including reporting; modern office practices, procedures, methods, and accounting equipment.

**Skill at:** Examining and verifying financial documents and reports; developing accounting procedures and forms; working independently from general instructions; communicating clearly and concisely, orally and in writing; assisting in supervision and training of clerical personnel.

---

*This job specification should not be construed to imply that these requirements are the exclusive standards of the position. Incumbents may be required to follow any other instructions, and to perform any other related duties, as may be required.

*Job Description\**
_____

JOB TITLE: Executive Secretary

DATE:

## Position Description

Under general supervision, performs a variety of complex, responsible, and confidential secretarial and administrative duties requiring a thorough knowledge of organizational procedures and precedents; supervises office clerical staff; provides clerical assistance to designated staff members, and performs related work as required. This position requires the ability to work independently, exercising judgment and initiative.

## Responsibilities

1. Screens visitors, telephone calls, and mail directed to the appropriate executive.
2. Independently responds to letters and general correspondence of a routine nature; responds to complaints and requests for information.
3. Assists in preparation of routine personnel, budget, payroll, and purchasing reports.
4. Researches, compiles, and analyzes data for special projects; prepares routine reports.
5. Maintains appointment schedules and calendars; makes travel arrangements; arranges meetings: assists in agenda preparation, gathers information, and contacts meeting participants.
6. Trains, supervises, assigns duties to, and evaluates subordinates; provides clerical assistance to designated staff members.
7. Takes and transcribes dictation from shorthand notes or dictaphone recordings.
8. Takes, edits, and types meeting minutes and distributes copies.

## Employment Standards

**Education/Experience:** Any combination of education and experience that would provide the required skill and knowledge for successful performance would be qualifying. Typical qualifications would be equivalent to:

1. High school diploma.
2. Graduation from an accredited business school or two years of college.
3. Three years of increasingly responsible secretarial and clerical experience.

**Knowledge of:** Correct English usage, grammar, spelling, and punctuation; modern office methods and procedures, equipment, and filing systems; business letter and report writing techniques; proofreading; statistical and recordkeeping principles and procedures; principles of supervision, training, and performance evaluation.

_____

*This job specification should not be construed to imply that these requirements are the exclusive standards of the position. Incumbents may be required to follow any other instructions, and to perform any other related duties, as may be required.

**Skill at:** Performing responsible secretarial and clerical work requiring independent judgment with speed and accuracy; learning, interpreting, and applying organizational policies, laws, rules, and regulations; taking responsibility for the compilation and organization of reports; composing correspondence on own initiative; typing accurately from a clear copy at a speed of 65 words per minute; taking dictation at a speed of 100 words per minute and transcribing it accurately; making arithmetic calculations with speed and accuracy; meeting the public tactfully and courteously and answering questions in person and over the telephone; communicating effectively with all segments of the community.

**Desirable Qualifications:** Fundamental accounting or bookkeeping knowledge plus good interpersonal skills.

## *Job Description\**

JOB TITLE: Receptionist

DATE:

### Position Description

Under general supervision operates a multi-line telephone console, gives routine information to the public; greets the public; performs routine clerical work such as typing, filing, and mail processing; performs related work as required.

### Responsibilities

1. Receives calls and gives information to callers, screens and routes calls to appropriate destination. Obtains and records caller's name, time of call, nature of business, and person called upon.
2. Greets visitors, staff, and others in a professional and courteous manner. Ascertains nature of business and directs visitors or callers to appropriate department or person.
3. Types reports, business correspondence, memos, schedules, and other statistical and financial data. Adds and checks columns of figures; checks and tabulates simple statistical or accounting data.
4. Maintains various files, listings, and records.
5. Reads and routes incoming mail; prepares outgoing mail; maintains records of long distance calls; may schedule appointments.
6. Operates office machines, including calculator, copy machine, and computer.

### Employment Standards

**Education/Experience:** Any combination of education and experience that would provide the required skill and knowledge for successful performance would be qualifying. Typical qualifications would be equivalent to:

1. Sufficient formal or informal education to assure the ability to write well, to use simple business math at a level required for successful job performance.

---

*This job specification should not be construed to imply that these requirements are the exclusive standards of the position. Incumbents may be required to follow any other instructions, and to perform any other related duties, as may be required.

2. One year of work experience in an organization performing duties comparable to a telephone switchboard operator and/or general clerk/typist.

3. Graduation from an accredited business school with courses in business practices and typing.

**Knowledge of:** Operation of a multi-line telephone console; correct English usage, spelling, grammar, and punctuation; office practices, procedures, and equipment.

**Skill at:** Operating a multi-line telephone console; performing routine clerical work; learning to operate office appliances and learning office methods, rules, and policies; understanding and carrying out verbal and written directions; typing at a speed of not less than 40 words per minute from clear copy; making arithmetic calculations; maintaining working relations with staff and public; recognizing and maintaining confidentiality of work materials as appropriate; working independently in the absence of supervision.

**Desirable Qualifications:** Excellent interpersonal skills.

# MODEL SALARY PROGRAM

The sample salary program on the next page can be adapted to fit your actual needs. You may not want to use all the formal wording and written explanation. If not, simplify it and make it work for you. The idea is to get across to employees that you have a formal plan, that it is internally equitable and externally competitive, and this is how it works.

If you don't have someone on staff who can write and implement a salary program for you, seek outside assistance from a human resources consultant or a compensation consultant.

Today's workers are more vocal and more active in wanting to know exactly how their company benefits and compensation programs work and that they are fair. This type of formal program needs to be well thought out, easy to understand, and fair and equitable in its implementation.

*Sample*

# Salary Program

_____
(Company Name)

EFFECTIVE _____ (Date) _____

## CONTENTS

# BACKGROUND AND OBJECTIVES
# OF THE SALARY PROGRAM

_____
(*Company Name*)

## Broad Objectives of the Program

The company's salary program is part of the organization's total management activity and helps attain the following overall management objectives:

- Attract and retain qualified people
- Provide incentive for performance by rewarding performance on the basis of results achieved
- Ensure equitable compensation regardless of sex, race, or handicap

## Specific Program Objectives

The program is designed and administered to fulfill these specific salary program objectives:

*Internal Fairness.*   This assures fair salary treatment in line with your position and the effectiveness of your performance.

*External Competitiveness.*   The salary structure is maintained at a competitive level in the job market in which we hire.

*Pay for Performance.*   The program provides the means for recognizing and rewarding individual performance.

*Centralized Program Administration.*   The salary program is administered under overall company management guidelines.

*Flexible Program Management.*   The salary program is flexible enough to be easily adapted to organizational change. It is responsive not only to internal organizational change but also to changes in the job market.

## INTERNAL FAIRNESS AND EXTERNAL COMPETITIVENESS

It is our intention that your salary be fair for the position you hold and your performance in it. We also consider its value with respect to other positions in our organization.

The salary program achieves internal fairness and external competitiveness through four basic and interacting devices:

- Position descriptions
- Position evaluation
- Actual pay practice
- Outside market information

# POSITION DESCRIPTIONS

## Preparation and Structure

A position description exists for each individual job in the organization. The descriptions were developed using information gathered from the people performing the jobs and from their supervisors. Each job incumbent and supervisor then reviewed and approved the descriptions. Our position descriptions include eight key elements of a job.

*Basic Function.*   This includes a brief description of the job.

*Dimensions.*   The purpose of this information is to show who the position assists and who it impacts on a daily basis and, when applicable, its budget impact.

*Principal Accountabilities.*   This is a list of the end results the position is expected to produce. Accountabilities identify what the job is held accountable for, not how it is accomplished. The pay-for-performance philosophy emphasizes achieving results, not generating activity.

*Human Relations and Other Skills.*   This describes the level of interpersonal skills needed to reach positive, long-term results.

*Principal Interactions.*   Describes the main internal and external interactions.

*Knowledge, Education, and Experience.*   This is a statement of the basic knowledge, education, and experience needed to perform the job.

*Level of Authority.*   This shows levels of responsibility, including supervision and budget authority.

*Reports to.*   Shows the level of the job in the organization.

The total position description is concerned only with position content and end results, not the qualifications of the incumbent.

## Uses of Position Descriptions

Position descriptions serve a number of useful purposes, including the following:

**Position Evaluation**

*Organization Analysis.*   Position descriptions contain valuable information for study and analysis of operating needs and organization structure and design.

*Communication.*   Your description serves as the basis for you and your immediate supervisor to reach a common understanding of your position. This is useful in day-to-day activities and for the long-range planning of your performance.

*Performance Management and Pay for Performance.*   The content of the job description, and specifically the accountabilities, are vital ingredients in planning and measuring your job performance for both pay for performance and performance management.

## Access to Position Descriptions

Every employee should receive a copy of the current position description from his/her supervisor.

# POSITION EVALUATION

## Purpose and Method

The purpose of position evaluations is to relate the value of your position to other positions in the organization and to job market data. While positions can be evaluated in many ways, the company uses a point factor method to provide an objective means of measuring position content. An experienced job evaluation consultant performed the evaluations. The *job* is evaluated, *not the person* who holds it. The evaluator considers what the position actually is, as described in the position description, not what it should be or might become in the future.

The evaluation of the job is accomplished using the following criteria:

*   Knowledge—What the individual in the position needs to know to perform satisfactorily.

*   Ability to solve—What thinking is required to perform the job.

*   Accountability—What the position contributes toward achieving the goals of the organization, including fiscal responsibility.

*   Human relations and other skills—What level of interpersonal skills are needed to influence positive long-term results.

Other evaluation considerations are: knowledge, education, experience, and level of authority.

## Outside Salary Surveys

Determining external competitiveness at the outset of a compensation study and maintaining it once a compensation program has been implemented require an effective methodology to determine:

- What current salary levels are
- What the job market actually is at any point in time

Our primary source of information on the external job market is from other similar organizations. Other surveys are also used. In combination, these surveys enable us to compare our salary structure with positions of equivalent value.

At least once each year, we review our salary structure both internally and against current marketplace data. Any adjustments necessary to maintain internal fairness and external competitiveness are then made.

# PAY FOR PERFORMANCE

## The Salary Range

The company's salary range achieves internal fairness through:

- Preparation of accurate position descriptions
- Evaluation of those positions
- Analysis of actual salaries being paid

The company's salary range achieves external competitiveness through:

- Use of outside salary surveys to ensure our knowledge of competitive pay practices
- Establishment of salary ranges that represent our desired salary policy

In general terms, the minimum of the salary range is an appropriate pay zone for the performance level of learners or newcomers to a position. The area between the minimum and the midpoint is a pay zone for a level of good, solid job performance.

The salary program is linked to merit. It does not provide a system of regular, periodic, or automatic increases in which, rigidly and mechanically, an individual moves from minimum to maximum over a specified period of years and at a specified rate.

A fully adequate level of performance is the good, solid performance that is desired and, in fact, expected of any employee.

## Merit Increases

The company pays for performance in two ways:

- Through merit increases, which are salary increases within the salary range of the position you now hold, based on your job performance level
- Through promotions to positions of greater responsibility

Our main concern here is merit increases, since these are the most directly related to our salary program policy.

Your performance is appraised at least annually by your immediate supervisor through the performance appraisal system, with your active participation. It is by means of this system that the level of your performance is determined for granting merit increases.

Raises are also based on the organization's ability to provide increases based on its profits and expenses, productivity, and overall financial condition.

# PERFORMANCE APPRAISAL

## The Performance Appraisal System

Under our performance appraisal system, your performance is appraised at least annually by your supervisor to:

- Determine your performance level as the basis for identifying performance improvement needs
- Permit you and your supervisor to discuss past performance and plan your future performance on the basis of your needs and the organization's expectations

Performance appraisal is therefore an important activity in the total salary administration process. It involves you and your immediate supervisor discussing your performance and determining how you might make it even better in the coming year. Improved performance is ultimately reflected in a higher salary.

# SUMMARY

The company's salary program has been carefully developed and aims to do the following:

- Assure that a proper relationship is maintained between the salary for your position and the salary of other positions within the organization. This is accomplished through carefully and jointly prepared position descriptions and the evaluation of each position against uniform criteria.
- Establish a salary range for your job which compares favorably with the salary range of other similar organizations in our area.
- Provide salary opportunity tied to the level of your performance. Your efforts and successes are recognized with pay directly related to performance.
- Assist you in attaining your best performance by involving you and your immediate supervisor in the performance appraisal system. In the final analysis, good salary administration must rest with the immediate supervisor. This plan provides a means for effectively discharging that responsibility.
- Facilitate fair but flexible management of the program throughout the organization.

# (SAMPLE GRADES FOR A LEGAL CENTER)

## SALARY PROGRAM
## GRADES AND POSITIONS LIST

### Effective _____

|  | Grade | Position title |
|---|---|---|
| *Nonexempt* | 1 | Clerk |
|  | 2 | Administrative Assistant |
| *Exempt* | 3 | Financial Manager |
|  |  | Office Manager |
|  |  | Ombudsman Specialist |
|  | 4 | Paralegal |
|  |  | Program Specialist |
|  |  | Director of Development |
|  | 5 | Legal Services Developer |
|  | 6 | State Ombudsman |
|  | 7 | Senior Attorney |
|  | 8 | Supervising Attorney |
|  | 9 | Executive Director |
|  |  | Director Legal Services |

# PAY FOR PERFORMANCE AND PERFORMANCE MANAGEMENT

Most organizations today feel they can only pay for effective performance on the job. Few businesspeople can afford to pay employees just for showing up and filling a desk or a spot on a production line eight hours a day. Pay-for-performance programs are fairly easy to initiate and Certainly have an impact on the bottom line.

The following information will help you start a pay-for-performance program, including how to set goals and objectives and how to give constructive feedback in a performance appraisal meeting. A sample appraisal form is also provided.

---

**Manager's Tip**

---

Without a human resource/personnel background, you may need to hire a personnel consultant to help you set up your pay-for-performance program. Once you establish your program and train your supervisors and managers they can manage it over time.

## *Ten Keys to an Effective Pay-for-Performance Program*

1.  Total commitment from top management.

2.  A thoughtful and complete plan of action.

3.  A timetable for installation and follow-through.

4.  A budget for a pay-for-performance program (not the usual merit budget).

5.  Specific, objective criteria for each job (identified by including the employee in the process). Establish key result areas (KRAs).

6.  KRAs tie the employees' job objectives and achievements to the organization's overall strategic plans. (Linking the employee's bottom line to the organization's bottom line.)

7.  A performance management program that includes performance appraisals and ongoing performance feedback throughout the organization.

8.  A plan that provides up and down communications on the program and measures supervisor and employee acceptance on an ongoing basis.

9.  A system to monitor the program through periodic, ongoing reports, on the program and how well it's working, including measures of productivity. You can track increases or decreases in productivity by shift, by floor, by department, etc. Some measures may be:

    *   Increase in number of clients served/units produced

    *   Decreases in complaints

    *   Less staff needed per shift

    *   Decrease in turnover

    *   Long-term achievement of organizational goals

10. A feeling on the part of both the employees and management that your mutual goals are being attained.

Manager's Tip
_____

A normal merit budget for increases may be anywhere from 3 percent to 5 percent. In a pay-for-performance program you need perhaps 7 percent to 10 percent for increases in order to differentiate between levels of performance. The top performers should get a much larger increase than the fully adequate or even above-average performers.

## *How to Start . . .*

First, decide what effective job performance is. Start by establishing key results areas (KRAs) for each job. Review the job description and update it to reflect true job content.

Then, agree on a plan to achieve the KRAs. The plan is the appraisal form itself. The form is completed by the supervisor and the employee at the beginning of each year. It is the yearly "Action Plan" agreed upon by both parties.

The management group must decide what it can afford to pay for achievement (achieving the KRAs). In some organizations, performance appraisal programs and pay raises are purposely not given at the same time. However, in a pay-for-performance program both events must occur simultaneously in order to achieve your goals. The pay increase range needs to be broad enough to take into account good, excellent, and outstanding performers-probably a range of 5 percent to 15 percent.

Remember, it's important to tie the employee's performance objectives to the organization's overall objectives.

### EXAMPLE:

*Organizational Objective:* Increase same family usage of our facility when a hospital stay is required.

*Employee Objective:* Raise patient satisfaction through better individual service.

How will you know when your objective is achieved?

*Organization:* When there is an increase in the hospital's repeat business.

*Employee:* When there is an increase in repeat business and patient comments and feedback are positive.

## *What Is Meant by Goals?*

The appraisal process starts when the employee and supervisor reach a mutual understanding of what needs to be accomplished. If expectations are not clearly stated, mutually understood, and presented in measurable terms, performance will be difficult to evaluate.

Goals are methods by which job expectations can be established. Those responsible for performance appraisals need a good understanding of goals and how to use them during the appraisal process.

A goal is a statement of results which are to be achieved. Goals describe:

1. Conditions that will exist when the desired outcome has been accomplished;
2. A time frame during which the outcome is to be completed; and
3. Resources the organization is willing to commit to achieve the desired result.

Goals should be challenging but achievable and established with the participation of those responsible for meeting them. Here is an example:

> "To increase the flow of invoices through the Accounting Department to a minimum of 150 per day by June 1. The total cost increase to accomplish this should not exceed $750."

Once a goal is accomplished, a new goal can be established to emphasize the next set of desired results.

## Setting Objectives

The following steps will help you set and reach your objectives:

- Review sources for setting objectives:
    - —Organization plans, objectives, strategies
    - —Key results areas
    - —Job descriptions
    - —Discussion with subordinates
    - —Previous performance plan and objectives
- List all objectives which can be established within each of the key results areas.
- Review the list with the employee to clarify meaning, priority, and preliminary thoughts on specific objectives.
- Develop one or more draft objectives, including those of a continuing and project nature for each key results area.
- Set a rough action plan for each objective.
- Make modifications.
- Develop a detailed action plan for each objective.
- Carry out action plans.
- Periodically review plans and results.

Setting objectives is a two-way process. It involves both the employee and the supervisor. If all the objectives are set by the supervisor with no input from the employee, results will be disappointing.

## Management by Objectives (MBO)

Management by objective contains four key elements:

**JOB REVIEW AND AGREEMENT**   The employee and the supervisor review the job description and key elements of the employee's job.

**DEVELOPMENT OF PERFORMANCE STANDARDS**   Specific standards of performance are mutually agreed upon. This phase identifies a satisfactory level of performance that is specific and measurable.

**SETTING OBJECTIVES**    Objectives are established by the employee in conjunction with, and guided by, the supervisor.

**ONGOING PERFORMANCE DISCUSSIONS**    The employee and the supervisor use the objectives as a base for continuing discussions about the employee's performance. Although a formal review session may be scheduled, the employee and the supervisor do not necessarily wait until the appointed time for a performance discussion. Objectives may be modified and progress discussed at any time during the year.

**APPRAISAL BENEFITS**

| *Use Appraisal For:* | *What You Learn—Issues Identified* |
|---|---|
| *Staffing:* | |
| Recruitment | Identifying current needs |
| Selection | Criteria for selection |
| Placement | Current placement data |
| Transfer | Individual skills for new assignment |
| Promotion | Identifying Outstanding performers |
| Termination | Identifying inadequate performers |
| Human resource inventory | Skill and succession data |
| *Rewarding:* | |
| Benefits | Flexibility |
| Salary structure | Compensation inadequacies |
| Merit | Comparative data on performance |
| Intrinsic | Motivation through objective-selling, feedback, and participation |
| *Changing:* | |
| Organizational climate | Appraisee evaluation |
| Organizational structure | Reorganization data |
| Management styles | Identify need for change |
| Policies | Feedback |
| Communication | Feedback |
| *Developing:* | |
| Rotating | Judgments on learning |
| Training | Identifying individual development needs |
| Counseling | Career planning-performance evaluation |

## *The Appraisal Interview*

Once appraisals have been completed on employees, it is important that they be communicated. The results should be discussed with employees so they have a clear understanding of how they stand in the eyes of the immediate supervisor and the organization. The emphasis in the appraisal interview should be on counseling and developing, not on "telling" the employee what the rating is.

The appraisal interview presents both an opportunity and a difficult situation. It is an emotional experience for the supervisor and for the employee. The supervisor must communicate both praise and constructive criticism. A major concern is how to emphasize the positive and still discuss improvements that are needed. Following are some ideas for the appraisal interview:

| **Do** | **Don't** |
|---|---|
| • Prepare in advance | • "Lecture" the employee |
| • Focus on performance and development | • Mix performance appraisal and salary or promotion issues |
| • Be specific about reasons for ratings | • Concentrate on the negative |
| • Decide on specific steps to be taken for improvement | • Do all the talking |
| • Consider your role in the subordinate's performance | • Be overly critical or "harp" on a failing |
| • Reinforce the behavior you want | • Feel it's necessary that you agree on everything |
| • Focus on the future performance | • Compare the employee to others |

## Constructive Feedback

The key to an effective performance appraisal interview lies in the ability of the supervisor to listen and to give constructive feedback. Following are eleven characteristics of positive feedback:

1. It is *descriptive* rather than evaluative. By describing one's own reactions, it leaves the individual free to use it or not to use it as he sees fit. By avoiding evaluative language, it reduces the need for the individual to respond defensively.

2. It is *specific* rather than general. To be told that one is "dominating" will probably not be as useful as to be told that "in the conversation that just took place, you did not appear to be listening to what others were saying."

3. It is focused on *behavior* rather than on our perceptions. Thus we might say that a person "talked more than anyone else in this meeting" rather than "the person is a loud-mouth."

4. It takes into account the *needs of both the receiver and the giver of feedback*. Feedback can be destructive when it serves only our own needs and fails to consider the needs of the person on the receiving end. We too often give feedback because it makes us feel better or gives us a psychological advantage. It is directed toward behavior which the receiver can do something about.

5. It is directed toward *behavior which the receiver can do something about*. Frustration is only increased when a person is reminded of some shortcoming over which the person has no control.

6. It is *solicited* rather than imposed. Feedback is most useful when the receiver actively seeks it.

7. It is *well-timed*. In general, feedback is most useful at the earliest opportunity after the given behavior. Feedback presented at an inappropriate time may do more harm than good.

8. It involves *sharing of information,* rather than giving advice. By sharing information, we leave people free to decide in accordance with their own goals and needs. When we give advice we tell them what to do and to some degree take away their freedom to decide for themselves.

9. It considers the *amount of information the receiver can use* rather than the amount we would like to give. When we give more than can be used, we are often satisfying some need of our own rather than helping the other person.

10. It concerns *what is said and done, or how,* not why. The "why" takes us from the observable to the inferred and involves assumptions regarding motive or intent. Telling people what their motives or intentions are tends to alienate them. It does not contribute to learning or development.

11. It is *checked to ensure clear communication.* One way of doing this is to ask the receiver to elaborate on what you've said to ensure the message is clear.

## *List of Phrases for Use with Performance Appraisals*

### Communication Skills

Communicates effectively with credibility and confidence.

Excels in interpersonal communications and interactions.

Effectively communicates objectives, ideas, and concepts.

Communicates confidence with peers, subordinates, and superiors.

Conveys a positive impression which reflects favorably with the public.

Encourages open communications to achieve mutual understanding.

### Competency

Combines technical competence with dependability and loyalty.

Is professionally competent.

Effectively applies skills and abilities to the position.

Demonstrates strong personal competence on the job.

### Cost Management

Effectively controls costs through the judicious use of personnel, materials, and equipment.

Projects and follows through with realistic budget data.

Displays sound judgment in managing and controlling expenses.

Ensures expenditures are in the best interests of the company.

Monitors budget variances and makes appropriate adjustments.

# PERFORMANCE
# APPRAISAL WORKSHEET

**STRICTLY
CONFIDENTIAL**

DATE OF THIS REPORT

EMPLOYEE NAME

REPORT OF PERFORMANCE
FROM                    TO

DEPARTMENT          POSITION TITLE

TIME IN THIS CLASSIFICATION          EMPLOYMENT DATE
YRS._____ MOS._____

## INSTRUCTIONS

1. All employees should be appraised at least annually.
2. Use in conjunction with the Merit Review Program.
3. Review employee's work performance for the entire period; refrain from basing judgment on recent events or isolated incidents only.
4. Do not allow personal feelings to govern your rating. Disregard your general impression of the employee.
5. Consider the employee on the basis of the standards you expect to be met for the job. Place a check by the area you feel best describes the employee's performance since the last appraisal.
6. REASON MUST BE GIVEN FOR EACH FACTOR TO SUBSTANTIATE AREA CHECKED

**QUALITY OF WORK**—Consider standard of workmanship, accuracy, neatness, skill, thoroughness, economy of materials, organization of job.

☐ FULLY MEETS JOB REQUIREMENTS       ☐ UNSATISFACTORY DOES NOT MEET MINIMUM REQUIREMENTS       ☐ MEETS MINIMUM REQUIREMENTS       ☐ EXCEEDS JOB REQUIREMENTS       ☐ OTHER (Specify)

Reason: _____

**VOLUME OF WORK**—Consider use of time, the volume of work accomplished and ability ot meet schedules, under normal conditions.

☐ DOES NOT MEET JOB REQUIREMENTS       ☐ EXCEEDS JOB REQUIREMENTS       ☐ MEETS MINIMUM JOB REQUIREMENTS       ☐ FULLY MEETS JOB REQUIREMENTS       ☐ OTHER (Specify)

Reason: _____

**ADAPTABILITY**—Consider ability to meet changing conditions and situations, ease with which the employee learns new duties and assignments.

☐ IMPROVEMENT NEEDED       ☐ SATISFACTORY       ☐ OUTSTANDING       ☐ VERY GOOD

Reason: _____

**JUDGMENT**—Consider ability to evaluate relative merit of ideas or facts and arrive at sound conclusions, ability to decide correct course of action when some choice can be made.

☐ VERY GOOD       ☐ NEEDS MUCH IMPROVEMENT       ☐ SATISFACTORY       ☐ OUTSTANDING

Reason: _____

**JOB KNOWLEDGE AND SKILL**—Consider understanding of job procedures and methods, ability to acquire necessary skills, expertness in doing assigned tasks and utilization of background for job.

☐ FULLY MEETS JOB REQUIREMENTS       ☐ IMPROVEMENT NEEDED       ☐ MEETS MINIMUM JOB REQUIREMENTS       ☐ EXCEEDS JOB REQUIREMENTS

Reason: _____

**ATTITUDE**—Consider coopertion with supervisor and co-workers; receptiveness to suggestions and constructive criticisms; attitude toward Company; enthusiasm in attempts to improve performance.

☐ EXCEEDS JOB REQUIREMENTS ☐ FULLY MEETS JOB REQUIREMENTS ☐ MEETS MINIMUM JOB REQUIREMENTS ☐ IMPROVEMENT NEEDED

Reason: _____

_____

_____

**TEAM EFFORT—LEADERSHIP**—Consider ability to inspire teamwork, enthusiasm to work towards a common objective, desire to assume responsibility, ability to originate or develop ideas and get things started, ability to train others.

☐ DOES NOT MEET JOB REQUIREMENTS ☐ EXCEEDS JOB REQUIREMENTS ☐ MEETS MINIMUM JOB REQUIREMENTS ☐ FULLY MEETS JOB REQUIREMENTS

Reason: _____

_____

_____

**SELF-DEVELOPMENT ACTIVITIES OF THIS EMPLOYEE (To be completed during interview)**

_____

_____

_____

### PRESENT STATUS—NEEDS—PLAN OF ACTION

**OVERALL EFFECTIVENESS**—Considering the amount of experience on present job, check the rating which most nearly describes _total_ current performance.

☐ EXCEEDS JOB REQUIREMENTS ☐ DOES NOT MEET JOB REQUIREMENTS ☐ FULLY MEETS JOB REQUIREMENTS ☐ MEETS MINIMUM JOB REQUIREMENTS

**WHAT ASPECTS OF PERFORMANCE, IF NOT IMPROVED, MIGHT HINDER FUTURE DEVELOPMENT OR CAUSE DIFFICULTY IN PRESENT CLASSIFICATION (WEAKNESSES OF EMPLOYEE)?**

_____

_____

**WHAT ARE GREATEST STRENGTHS OF EMPLOYEE?** _____

_____

Forward completed performance appraisal to designated approval authority before reviewing with subject employee. After appraisal is approved, review contents of appraisal with subject employee and complete section concerning specific plans to improve performance. Have employee sign the form and then forward original appraisal to the _Personnel Department_—retain copy for your files.

GIVE SPECIFIC PLANS YOU AND YOUR EMPLOYEE HAVE MADE TO IMPROVE WORK PERFORMANCE

_____

_____

_____

| EVALUATED BY: | TITLE: | DATE: |
|---|---|---|
| APPROVED: | TITLE: | DATE: |
| EMPLOYEE'S SIGNATURE (Does not necessarily indicate concurrence) | TITLE: | DATE: |

## CREATIVITY

Demonstrates creative ability in managing the department.

Excels in creative thinking and effective problem solving.

Creates satisfying solutions while conforming to organizational policies.

Originates, develops, and implements constructive ideas.

Encourages an environment for creative excellence.

Initiates fresh ideas.

## DELEGATING

Delegates to maximize organizational strengths.

Recognizes the importance of working through subordinates.

Delegates with clearly defined responsibility and authority.

Delegates to motivate subordinates.

## DEPENDABILITY

Consistently accurate and dependable.

Consistently achieves results when confronted with major responsibilities and limited resources.

Can be counted on to achieve results in difficult circumstances.

A self-starter who displays a strong personal commitment to successfully completing projects.

## DEVELOPMENT

Excels in selecting and developing potential talent.

Deals effectively with different levels of employees.

Effectively plans for future career development and accomplishment.

Successfully demonstrates ability to develop employees.

Inspires subordinates to reach their fullest potential.

Encourages employees to acquire appropriate skills and knowledge.

## GOALS AND OBJECTIVES

Effectively implements departmental goals and objectives.

Excels in formulating and achieving goals and action plans.

Sets, obtains, and manages organizational goals.

Formulates realistic objectives.

Establishes relevant objectives and performance standards.

Excels in planning, forecasting, and determining courses of action.

## LEADERSHIP

Projects self-confidence, authority, and enthusiasm.

Demonstrates natural leadership ability.

Displays the strengths of an exceptional leader.

Inspires confidence and respect.

Effectively uses power and influence.

Inspires the cooperation and confidence of others.

Promotes harmony and teamwork.

## LOYALTY AND DEDICATION

Places organizational interests ahead of personal goals.

Is committed to organizational goals.

Displays a high degree of honesty, loyalty, and integrity.

## MANAGEMENT ABILITY

Is effective at planning, organizing, motivating, and controlling resources.

Displays the qualities that make a manager effective on the job.

Recognizes the difference between managing and doing.

Excels at resolving interdepartmental conflicts.

Effectively manages change.

Maximizes the use of company resources.

Uses personnel effectively and efficiently.

## MATURITY

Displays a high degree of emotional maturity.

Keeps situations in proper perspective.

Displays superior emotional adjustment and stability.

## MENTAL CAPACITY

Understands both theoretical and practical concepts.

Thinks fast on the feet.

Uses common sense to reach workable conclusions.

Grasps the most difficult concepts.

Is alert, quick, and responsive.

Thinks logically—uses common sense.

## ORGANIZATION

Builds organizational effectiveness.

Maximizes organizational productivity.

Encourages organizational action.

Makes effective use of organizational resources.

Overcomes organizational blocks.

Keeps organizational levels to a minimum.

### PERFORMANCE QUALITIES

Demonstrates positive self-concepts.

Turns negatives into positives.

Maintains an optimistic outlook when faced with difficulties.

Competes with confidence—extremely self-confident.

Demonstrates credibility.

### PERSONALITY AND APPEARANCE

Displays natural charm and a cheerful disposition.

Is stable, patient, and steady.

Is relaxed, confident, and enjoyable to be with.

Polished and poised; displays social grace.

Uses humor constructively.

## EMPLOYEE BENEFITS

Most employers, unless they are very small, provide some benefits to their employees. You are probably already providing more benefits than you realize. The following table provides an identification of various types of employee benefits companies offer.

Employee benefits are so highly regulated by the federal government that the average businessperson cannot begin to design, purchase, and install their own benefits program. It's a good idea to ask other business people you know and trust to recommend a personnel or benefits consultant to assist you in choosing a benefits package to fit your organization.

### *Benefit Consultants*

Hewitt Associates
100 Half Day Road
Lincolnshire, IL 60015
(212) 345-7000

William M. Mercer, Inc.
3500 Texas Commerce Tower
2200 Ross Avenue
Dallas, TX 75201
(214) 220-6524

Watson Wyatt Worldwide
999 Eighteenth Street
Suite 2900
Denver, CO 80202
(303) 298-7878

## Benefit Costs

Although benefits are generally not considered part of an individual's compensation for tax purposes, they do represent a significant expenditure from the organization's point of view. Every two years the U.S. Chamber of Commerce surveys a large number of industries to determine the extent of benefit payments. In the most recent survey, an employer in American industry averaged paying 39 percent of total payroll in benefits. The significance of this figure is that the average employee earns $15,191 per year and receives $5,924.49 in benefits per year. The amount of benefits provided varies significantly. An employee in the hospital industry averages $64.60 per week in benefits, while an employee in the chemical manufacturing industry receives $135.79 per week in benefits.

Because benefits are so expensive, it is important for a company that provides even a few benefits to do a good job of communicating to their employees just what is provided. Use an annual report to let employees know what you are doing for them in this area.

The key to keeping benefits costs down is to monitor usage, institute prevention and health programs, use HMOs or PPOs where possible, and install flexible benefits programs. Provide a certain dollar amount of benefits and let the employee choose the ones most needed. Don't pay for a lot of fixed benefits your employees don't need or use. Many organizations have started passing on some of the costs of providing benefits to the employees, but this practice is not well accepted. Many employees can't afford the costs of their benefits any more than the employer can.

The benefits area is a difficult one to understand, and it is highly regulated. The following glossary of benefits terms will help you deal with administrators and consultants in the field.

# GLOSSARY OF BENEFITS TERMS

**American Academy of Actuaries (AAA).** A national association of actuaries based in Washington, D.C. Acting in an advisory capacity, the AAA formed a task force after passage of the Tax Reform Act of 1986 to study ways to value benefits under Section 89. A report produced by that task force was completed in April 1988. It presently constitutes the most thorough methodology for valuing benefits, although it lacks the force of law or regulation and has not been endorsed or approved by the Treasury Department.

**Average employer-provided benefit.** The total value of all employer-provided benefits received by employees under all plans being tested, divided by the total number of employees, whether or not they are covered under the plans being tested. The average benefits for highly compensated employees and non-highly compensated employees are calculated separately.

**Blue Book.** The general explanation of every major tax reform act that is prepared after the legislation is enacted by the Joint Committee on Taxation. Because the Blue Book is prepared after enactment of the legislation, it is not considered by courts or the Internal Revenue Service to be as authoritative as pre-enactment legislative history. However, the Blue Book frequently clarifies issues that were not adequately discussed in the legislative history and also may point out where the statute needs to be technically corrected.

**Bright-line test.**   Any clear standard, such as a dollar maximum on an excludable benefit or the new mathematical nondiscrimination tests of Section 89, that when applied to a given set of facts will always yield the same result. The nondiscrimination rules of prior law were vague standards that were applied differently by different employers and/or different revenue agents.

**Cafeteria plan.**   An employer-maintained benefit plan under which participating employees may choose between at least one taxable benefit (usually cash) and at least one nontaxable benefit. Also referred to as a "flexible benefits plan."

**Cash or deferred arrangement (CODA).**   A type of profit-sharing or stock bonus plan under which an employee may defer current compensation into an account on a pretax basis. Also referred to as "salary reduction" plans under Section 401(k).

**Classification test.**   A requirement under Section 89 that a plan must be made available to employees in a manner that does not discriminate in favor of highly paid employees.

**COBRA.**   The Consolidated Omnibus Budget Reconciliation Act of 1985. This law includes the federal mandate that requires employers to offer continuation health coverage to certain former employees.

**"Code" or "IRC."**   The Internal Revenue Code.

**Comparable plan rules.**   A Section 89 testing provision that involves comparing the value of coverage offered under different health plans. An employer may combine either a group of health plans or a group of health benefits that have been desegregated into separate plans, as long as the least valuable benefit available under any plan is at least 95 percent of the most valuable benefit available.

**Compensation.**   TAMRA modified the definition of compensation by specifying that: (1) compensation need not be determined on the basis of the plan limitation year used for qualified retirement plan purposes, and (2) the definition should not include either accrued compensation or any amounts received while the employee is not a participant in the plan.

**Concentration tests.**   Nondiscrimination rules that apply to cafeteria plans, dependent care plans, educational benefit plans, and group legal services plans which prohibit excessive percentages of plan benefits from being provided to employees who own five percent or more of the employer.

**Conference report.**   The explanation of the statutory provisions of a tax bill. The conference report is prepared by members of the House Committee on Ways and Means and the Senate Finance Committee after differences in the two versions of the bill as initially passed by the House of Representatives and the Senate have been eliminated in conference. Unlike a Blue Book, the conference report on a bill is considered by the courts and the Internal Revenue Service to establish binding precedents for interpreting vague or ambiguous statutory provisions.

**Constructive receipt.**   An income tax principle that requires money or property to be included in income at the time the person has an unrestricted right to receive the money or property, even if the person may decide not to actually claim the money or property until a later date.

**Controlled group.** A group of corporations, each of which is at least 80 percent owned (either directly or through one or more chains of subsidiary corporations) by a common parent corporation, or by a group composed of five or fewer individuals, estates, or trusts.

**Core benefits.** Generally defined as all accident and health benefits except coverage for dental, vision, psychological, and orthodontic expenses and elective cosmetic surgery (which are defined as "non-core benefits"); disability insurance; low-level non-elective medical reimbursement coverage; and health insurance plans that are funded entirely through salary reduction amounts. Section 89 does not specifically define core benefits.

**Cost modification factors.** Under Section 89 as amended by TAMRA, employers may modify their actual costs (for purposes of valuing employer-provided health benefits) based on variables such as historic costs, geographic differences, demographic characteristics, utilization rates, and multiemployer plan considerations.

**De minimize benefit.** A fringe benefit provided to employees or independent contractors that has a value so small as to make accounting for it unreasonable or administratively impracticable. Meals eaten at certain company cafeterias that meet special standards (including nondiscrimination rules) are classified as de minimize benefits.

**Deemed family coverage.** Under TAMRA, employers may deem family coverage to be available to employees without families, if such coverage is offered to them at no charge, and the employer does not use the rule to evade the nondiscrimination rules. The rule was designed to relieve employers from the burden of determining which employees have families.

**Defined benefit plan.** An employer-provided retirement plan in which employer contributions are determined by actuarial calculations based on projected benefits. Mini- mum contributions are required by law, and benefits are usually paid monthly.

**Defined contribution plan.** An employer-provided retirement plan that involves contributions made by the employer to individual employees' accounts, usually based on compensation. Benefits are based on an employee's account balance upon retirement, and are usually paid in a lump sum.

**DEFRA.** Deficit Reduction Act of 1984.

**Dependent care plans.** Employer-provided assistance to employees through (1) cash reimbursements for dependent care expenses incurred by employees, (2) payments directly to daycare centers, or (3) on-premises dependent care facilities. This care must be provided to children or other dependents under age 18, or other older dependents, including spouses, who are physically or mentally unable to care for themselves, and must enable the employee to be gainfully employed.

**Determination letter.** A letter from the Internal Revenue Service formally recognizing that an employee benefit plan satisfies the Code requirements governing exclusion of benefits provided under the plan.

**Determination year.** The current plan year.

**Discriminatory excess.** The amount of an employer-provided benefit that exceeds the "highest permitted benefit" under Section 89 (see below). In other words, the amount of nontaxable employer-provided benefits that would have to be purchased with after-tax employee dollars in order to pass Section 89's discrimination tests.

**Disregard rule.** Permits employers to disregard employees with core coverage from another employer. Under Section 89 as amended by TAMRA, employers must offer employees core coverage before they can be disregarded. TAMRA also permits employers to offer free core coverage as an alternative to collecting sworn statements.

**DRG.** Diagnostic Related Group.

**Dual-service personnel.** Unless exceptions are established in future regulations, employees who perform services for more than one line of business cannot be treated as belonging to a stand-alone line of business, but rather must be allocated among the employer's other lines of business.

**EBRI.** Employee Benefit Research Institute.

**Elective contribution.** Contributions to employee benefit plans made as a result of an employee's choice. A pre-tax elective contribution results from an employee's election under a cafeteria plan to reduce salary or forego a bonus before the compensation is received, in order that the employer would instead contribute to a welfare benefit plan selected by the employee. These pre-tax elective contributions are treated under the Code as employer contributions that would not be taxable to the employee as long as the rules (such as nondiscrimination rules) governing exclusion of that benefit are satisfied. An after-tax elective contribution, by contrast, is a contribution made by an employee out of salary that has already been taxed.

**Employee benefits.** Under Section 89, "benefits" include accident and health plans, group term life plans, welfare benefit plans, cafeteria plans, tuition reimbursement, group legal services, dependent care, educational assistance, miscellaneous fringe benefits, employee achievement awards, and continuation of health care benefits. A qualified retirement plan is not treated as a benefit under Section 89.

**Employer-provided subsidy.** Health benefits other than those provided through salary reduction or elective employee contribution.

**ERISA.** Employee Retirement Income Security Act of 1974.

**ESIC codes.** The Enterprise Standard Industrial Classification codes. A listing of two-digit codes contained in a manual produced by the Statistical Policy Division of the Office of Management and Budget (OMB) that could be used to help employers demonstrate the differences and similarities in their products and services for determining separate lines of business.

**Excess benefit.** See *Discriminatory excess.*

**Excludable employees.** Employees who may be excluded from Section 89's nondiscrimination tests (provided that once the exclusion categories are established, they are applied uniformly) include employees who are subject to a collective bargaining agreement, employees with less than six months of service (one year for non-core benefits), employees who work fewer than 17.5 hours per week or six months per year, employees who are under 21 during the entire plan year, and nonresident aliens with no U.S.-source income.

**Exclusion reversal rules.**   Rules designed to prevent employers from applying any of the various employee exclusion categories unless the exclusion is applied uniformly to all employees in the excludable class. TAMRA provides that multi-employer plan entry standards that govern benefits for newly hired, part-time, seasonal, or under-age employees will not trigger these rules.

**401(k) ADP/ACP tests.**   Mathematical nondiscrimination tests governing cash or deferred arrangements that prohibit the average compensation deferral percentages for all highly compensated employees from exceeding, by more than fixed amounts, the average deferral percentages for all non-highly compensated employees. The "compensation deferral percentage" is the contribution to the Section 401(k) plan on behalf of each employee, divided by that employee's compensation.

**Family member.**   Under Section 89, "family members" are defined as an employee's spouse, lineal ascendants and descendants, and their spouses.

**The Family Support Act.**   Signed into law on October 13, 1988, this law makes major changes in the nation's welfare system. These changes are financed in part by various tax provisions, including altering the present relationship between the child care credit and the dependent care exclusion as of January 1, 1989. As a result of these changes, the new law will have a major impact on the notices that employers must send to employees that describe the dependent care exclusion.

**FICA.**   Federal Insurance Contributions Act (a.k.a. Social Security).

**50-Employee test.**   A rule requiring that all employees must be allocated to a particular line of business or operating unit, each of which must contain at least 50 nonexcludable employees. To comply, employers may be forced to aggregate otherwise distinct, but small, lines of business with unrelated groups of employees.

**Flexible benefits.**   See *Cafeteria plans.*

**Form 5500.**   An IRS form covering a plan's financial activity that must be filed with an employer's tax return annually.

**Former employees.**   TAMRA exempts employers from having to test benefits provided to employees who separated from service before 1989 with respect to benefits provided as of Dec. 3 i, 1988, and with respect to certain nondiscriminatory increases in those benefits made after Dec. 31, 1988.

**Geographically separate businesses.**   An employer's businesses can be tested separately under the line of business rules if they are geographically separate-such as in different states or different cities.

**Good faith compliance standard.**   In the absence of Treasury regulations, employers must make a "good faith effort" to comply with Section 89 using a reasonable interpretation based on the statute and its legislative history and considering the likely position on unclear issues that would be taken by the IRS and the courts. An employer would not be acting in good faith if he or she consistently resolves unclear issues in his or her own favor.

**Grandfathered.**   A term used to describe individuals or entities that are exempted from a new statutory rule, most commonly using a cut-off date to determine eligibility.

**Group legal services plan (GLSO).** An employee benefit that offers legal services (or reimbursement for same) to plan participants, such as divorce actions, traffic offenses, and estate planning. Congress is currently considering a retroactive extension of GLSO's nontaxable status under Code Section 120, which expired on Dec. 31, 1987.

**Group term life insurance.** General life insurance (other than travel or accident insurance) provided by an employer to a group of employees under a policy carried directly or indirectly by the employer that provides insurance benefits based on uniform factors such as age, years of service, compensation, or position.

**Headquarters employees.** Under Section 89, headquarters employees must be allocated for testing purposes to one line of business in accordance with the performance of their services. Thus, if a majority of a headquarters employee's services are performed for a particular line of business or operating unit, the employee must be allocated to that line of business or operating unit. Employees performing services for more than one line of business or operating unit may be allocated on a pro rata basis or to any one line of business.

**Health maintenance organization (HMO).** An organization that provides a range of health care services for a specific group of individuals for a fixed periodic fee.

**Helper health plans.** Under Section 89 as amended by TAMRA, plans that are outside the allowable percentage range for plan comparability can be aggregated with other plans (for purposes of passing the 80-percent benefits test), provided that each helper plan actually provides health coverage to a percentage of non-highly compensated employees that is equal to at least 80 percent of the percentage of highly compensated employees who are covered under the plan.

**Highest permitted benefit.** To determine the highest permitted benefit, the nontaxable benefits of all highly compensated employees in a discriminatory plan are reduced until the plan becomes nondiscriminatory.

**Highly compensated employee.** During the previous plan year, five-percent owners, employees who earned over $75,000 in compensation, employees who earned over $50,000 in compensation and were among the top-paid 20 percent of employees, and officers of the company who earned more than $30,000. Every employer must have at least one officer who is treated as a highly compensated employee. Former employees are treated as highly compensated employees if they were highly compensated at the time of separation or at any time after attaining age 55.

**HII.** Health Insurance Institute.

**Indemnity.** Predetermined benefits that are paid in the event of a loss covered by insurance.

**Key employees.** Officers of an employer whose compensation is more than $45,000, and individuals who fall into one of three groups of highly compensated employees who hold ownership interests in the employer: (1) employees with the ten largest owner- ship interests (at least 0.5 percent ownership); (2) employees whose compensation is at least $150,000 and who own at least one-percent interests; and (3) employees who own at least five-percent interests.

**Leased employees.**   Under Section 89, leased employees are treated as employees of the organization for which they provide services. A person is a "leased employee" if he or she has been performing services for a recipient employer under one or more agreements with a leasing organization for a period of at least a year (six months in the case of core health benefits), and the services provided are of a type historically performed by employees in the business field of the employer.

**Look-back year.**   The plan year prior to the current plan year.

**Line of business.**   See *Separate line of business.*

**Lineal ascendant.**   For Section 89 purposes, a parent of an employee.

**Lineal descendent.**   For Section 89 purposes, a child of an employee.

**Medicare Catastrophic Coverage Act of 1988.**   A law passed during the 100th Congress that expands the Medicare system to include benefits for catastrophic illnesses. The controversial "maintenance of effort" provision in the law requires that employers pass on to employees most of the health insurance savings in 1989 and 1990 that may result from the Act's expansion of Medicare benefits.

**Multi-employer plan.**   A collectively bargained defined benefit plan to which more than one employer contributes and which is administered by a joint employer/union board.

**Non-core benefits.**   See *Core benefits.*

**Nondiscriminatory terms test.**   Under this test, the plan being tested must not contain any provision relating to eligibility to participate that explicitly or implicitly discriminates in favor of highly compensated employees. For example, a plan that is designed to suit special needs of certain highly compensated employees violates this rule.

**Nontaxable benefit.**   A benefit whose value is excludable from an employee's gross income for tax purposes.

**Normal working hours.**   For purposes of classifying part-time employees, TAMRA recognizes that an employee is considered to normally work the average number of hours that were worked during the period in the testing year prior to the testing date. If the period is less than 60 days, an employee is considered to normally work either (1) the average number of hours worked during the prior testing year; or (2) if the employee did not work at least 60 days during the prior testing year, the average number of hours the employee is scheduled to work as of the testing date, during the longer of (a) the next 60 days, or (b) the period between the testing date and the end of the testing year.

**OBRA.**   Omnibus Budget Reconciliation Act.

**OMB.**   Office of Management and Budget.

**Open-season rule.**   Beginning in 1990, no non-highly compensated employee can be disregarded in testing incremental family coverage separately, even if the employee's sworn statement includes single status, unless the employer informs the employee that he or she has the right, should the employee ever have a family, to elect health coverage for the family without regard to whether it is open season at the time.

**Operating unit.** A business that includes all the employees necessary for the preparation of property for sale to customers, or for the provision of services to customers, such as a manufacturing plant or a beauty parlor. Operating units that meet the "geographic separateness" standard can be tested separately from each other under the line of business rules.

**Permissive aggregation.** Under Section 89's comparable plan rules, health plans with different values may be aggregated (at an employer's choice) for purposes of the 80-percent alternative benefits test and the 50-percent eligibility test.

**Plan permanency.** One of the requirements for plan qualification included in Section 89(k). Under this requirement, a plan must be established "with the intention of being maintained for an indefinite period of time." This rule is drawn from an existing "permanent program" requirement for qualified retirement plans. The employer may reserve the right to amend or terminate a plan. However, such abandonment of a plan within a few years after its establishment for any reason other than business necessity is considered evidence that the plan is not a permanent, bona fide program for the exclusive benefit of employees.

**Plan year.** The 12-month period (or shorter period, in the case of an initial plan year) used as the fiscal year of an employee benefit plan. Typically, employees' benefit elections must be made (or changed) prior to the beginning of the plan year.

**Preferred provider organization (PPO).** An arrangement to provide medical care in which an insurer or third-party payor contracts with a group of physicians to provide care at lower than customary fees in return for a predetermined volume of patients and prompt payment.

**Private letter ruling (P.L.R.).** An opinion letter issued by the Internal Revenue Service in response to specific questions and factual situations presented by an individual taxpayer. While a P.L.R. can be relied upon as an authoritative ruling only by the taxpayer to whom it is issued, they are often cited by other taxpayers since they may indicate the IRS' position on a particular issue. User fees must be paid before the IRS will consider a taxpayer's request for a P.L.R.

**Pro-rata allocation.** Employees who do not perform a "majority of services" for one line of business may be allocated on a proportionate basis among different lines of business.

**Qualification requirements.** Under Section 89, an employee benefit plan must meet five standards or "qualification requirements": (1) the plan must be in writing; (2) employees' rights under the plan must be enforceable; (3) employees are provided with reasonable notification of their benefits; (4) the plan is maintained for the exclusive benefit of employees; and (5) the plan is intended to be maintained indefinitely. If a plan does not meet all five requirements, covered employees lose their favorable tax status.

**Reasonable classification test.** When organizing a company into separate lines of business, employers must demonstrate that the plan being tested is available on an employer-wide basis. The reasonable classification test examines the facts and circumstances of each case to determine whether the plan unduly benefits highly compensated employees.

**Reasonable notification.** One of the requirements for plan qualification included in Section 89(k). The term "reasonable notification" is not defined in the legislative history of Section 89. However, the IRS is not likely to establish a new standard that differs from similar requirements that are already in force under the Employee Retirement Income Security Act of 1974 (ERISA). The ERISA rules allow employers to provide employees with plan notices by mail or by posting them on a bulletin board. The rules also specify what information should be provided (and/or cross-referenced) in the notice itself.

**Rule of convenience.** A provision in a statutory requirement that is intended to ease the administrative burden of the requirement.

**Qualified benefit or plan.** A general term that applies to a benefit that is provided free by the employer and meets applicable qualification requirements under tax law.

**Safe harbor.** A provision in a statute or regulation that exempts specific types of individuals or organizations from one or more of the statute's requirements.

**Salary reduction.** An election by an employee to reduce his or her salary in exchange for contribution by the employer of an equivalent sum to a cash or deferred arrangement or a cafeteria plan. Also see *Elective contribution*.

**Section 89 coalition.** A group of employers, employer organizations, insurance companies, and organized labor formed in the Spring of 1988 to lobby Congress for a one year delay in Section 89's effective date. The coalition proposed a series of changes in the law that were included in TAMRA.

**Self-employed individuals.** Under Section 89, self-employed individuals are treated as employees.

**Self insurance.** A group insurance program that provides benefits financed entirely by the employer through a self-insurance reserve fund, under an "administrative services only" contract, or under a retrospectively rated premium contract with a commercial carrier. Under a self-insurance program, there is no shifting of insurance risk to a commercial carrier.

**Separate line of business.** Under Section 89, a business entity that is part of a larger organization, has at least 50 employees, and satisfies the Treasury Department's guidelines or obtains a determination letter or private letter ruling certifying it as a separate line of business.

**Separate plans.** Generally, every plan that is not substantially the same is considered to be separate under Section 89. A separate health plan has one or more of the following: separate levels of coverage, separate levels of employee contribution, or different coinsurance and deductible levels. Additionally, employee-only coverage is separate from family coverage, and former employees' plans are separate from current employees' plans.

**Simplified employee pension (SEP) plan.** A simple form of defined contribution plan, available only to employers with twenty-five or fewer employees, in which an employer may contribute to employees' Individual Retirement Accounts under a set formula. Employees may also contribute to an SEP on a salary-reduction basis.

**Single plan.** Under Section 89, two or more plans that are identical except for the employees they cover may be tested as a single plan. In addition, group term life plans that vary their coverage according to employees' compensation and identical health plans that proportionately reduce the benefits of employees who work fewer than 30 hours a week also may be tested as one plan.

**Sole proprietor.** Under Section 89, a sole proprietor is treated as his or her own employer.

**Special scrutiny.** If an employer cannot satisfy the general tests to prove the genuine separateness of its business lines or operating units, but nevertheless wishes to test these businesses separately under Section 89, the Internal Revenue Service will look more closely at the facts and circumstances of each particular case and issue private letter rulings, if requested, under "special scrutiny" standards to be outlined in regulations.

**Statutory plan.** Any plan that includes health or group term life insurance on a mandatory basis. In addition, employers may elect to treat group legal services, educational assistance, and dependent care plans as statutory plans.

**Summary plan description (SPD).** A brief, clear description of provisions in an employee benefit plan that is distributed to employees whenever a plan is adopted or amended.

**Supplemental plan.** A health plan providing benefits in addition to those provided under the employer's basic health plan. In applying the permissive aggregation rules, supplemental coverage should be added to the basic coverage for valuation purposes before plans are tested for comparability.

**Table I rates.** Relatively low, safe-harbor rates for valuing group term life insurance premiums under Reg. 1.79-3(d).

**TAMRA.** The Technical and Miscellaneous Revenue Act of 1988 (P.L. 100-647). This law includes technical corrections to the Tax Reform Act of 1986. Substantive changes to Section 89 designed to ease the compliance burden were incorporated in the law.

**Tax expenditure.** The revenue that is lost to the government as the result of a tax exemption.

**Taxable year.** The fiscal year used for tax purposes. Almost all individuals use the calendar year as their taxable year.

**Tax Reform Act of 1986.** One in a series of laws that modified the Internal Revenue Code. TRA 1986 added Section 89 to the Code.

**TEFRA.** Tax Equity and Fiscal Responsibility Act of 1982.

**Testing day.** Under Section 89 as amended by TAMRA, employers must test their plans on only one day per year (as opposed to every day under prior law). The testing day may be any day in the testing year, including the last day of the year. The date must be the same for all plans of the same type being tested together. The annual date need not be an actual date (e.g., Jan. 1) but may also be determined using a fixed method (e.g., the last day of the first two-week pay period ending in the testing year). If a testing date is not specified, the IRS assumes the testing date to be the last day of the testing year.

**Testing year.** Employers may designate a common 12-month period as the testing year to be used in testing plans that may have non-uniform plan years. The testing period is subject to the same consistency requirement that applies to the testing date. In general, the testing year must be the same for all plans of the same type. Designation of a testing period may not result in any period being disregarded for purposes of Section 89. If a testing date is not specified, the IRS assumes the testing year to be the calendar year.

**Top-heavy plan.** A qualified retirement plan that has accrued excessive benefits for "key employees" and meets other tests provided by Code Section 416.

**Top-paid group.** The highest paid 20 percent of an employer's workforce.

**"Top 100" rule.** An employee who is not among the 100 employees earning the highest compensation during a plan year will not be treated as (1) receiving compensation above $75,000; (2) receiving compensation above $50,000 and being in the "top- paid group" (see above); or (3) an officer receiving compensation above $45,000 in the plan year if he or she failed to meet one of those three criteria in the preceding plan year.

**Transition period.** Under Section 89, a period of time that begins on the date an employer becomes or ceases to be a member of a controlled group or an affiliated service group and ends on the last day of the first plan year beginning after the change in status.

**Tuition reduction program.** Programs under which schools provide current and retired employees (and their dependents) discounts of up to 100 percent on tuition for education below the graduate level at either the employer school, or at another educational institution covered by a student exchange agreement.

**Utilization rates.** In valuing employer-provided health benefits, employers may take into account differences in the use of certain health care features that are common to different coverages. This adjustment must be made by estimating the cost of each plan with the common features as if the usage had been distributed evenly among all plans.

**Valuation.** See *Valuing benefits.*

**Valuing benefits.** Under Section 89, the process of determining the total value of coverage under health and group term life plans. For all other plans, the value of the employer- provided benefit is calculated.

# WORK AND FAMILY BENEFITS

In a survey of 259 major U.S. employers, Hewitt Associates found that:

- 56 percent of employers offer some kind of childcare assistance to employees. Most common is dependent care spending accounts.
- 31 percent of employers offer elder care assistance; usually a dependent care spending account.
- 56 percent of employers offer flexible scheduling arrangements, usually a flextime program.
- Only 5 percent of employers have paid parental leave programs, but 42 percent have unpaid parental leave policies.
- 77 percent offer employee assistance programs (EAPs). EAPs are most commonly provided through an outside provider.

With the changing structure of the family and with more two-career couples, work and family benefits are becoming increasingly important.

## EXAMPLES OF EMPLOYEE BENEFITS

| Required Security | Voluntary | Time Off | Insurance | Financial | Recreational | Retirement |
|---|---|---|---|---|---|---|
| 1. Worker's compensation | 1. Severance pay | 1. Birthdays | 1. Medical | 1. Credit union | 1. Bowling league | 1. Social security |
| 2. Unemployment compensation | 2. Supplemental unemployment benefits | 2. Vacation time | 2. Dental | 2. Profit-sharing or 401(k) | 2. Company newsletter | 2. Pension funds |
| 3. Old age, survivors', and disability insurance | 3. Leave of absence | 3. Company-subsidized travel | 3. Survivor benefits | 3. Company provided housing or car | 3. Professional memberships | 3. Early retirement |
| 4. State disability insurance | | 4. Holidays | 4. Accidental dismemberment insurance | 4. Legal services | 4. Club memberships | 4. Preretirement counseling |
| 5. Medicare hospital benefits | | 5. Sick pay | 5. Travel accident insurance | 5. Purchase discounts | 5. EAP counseling | 5. Retirement gratuity |
| 6. Benefits portability | | 6. Military reserve | 6. Group insurance | 6. Stock plans | 6. Company-sponsored events | 6. Retirement annuity plan |
| | | 7. Election day | 7. Disability insurance | 7. Financial counseling | 7. Childcare services | 7. Benefits for retired employees |
| | | 8. Social service sabbatical | 8. Life insurance | 8. Moving expenses | 8. Cafeteria | 8. Disability retirement benefits |
| | | 9. Funeral leave | 9. Misc. medical insurance | 9. Tuition assistance | 9. Season tickets | |
| | | 10. Jury duty pay | | 10. Discounts on company products | 10. Service awards | |

# 7

# HANDLING DISCIPLINE AND DISCHARGE

- Performance Improvement
- Determining Discipline and Discharge Policy
- Sample Discipline Policy
- Discipline and Discharge Forms
- Sample Letters on Discipline

# Handling Discipline and Discharge

Business people should take a long, serious look at the changing trend in the law relating to "employment at will." As business people, we have had a long period where we could run our own show and fire people for any reason other then causes covered by the Civil Rights Act or the Federal Labor Relations Law. For years the right to do so was unquestioned.

It's a different story today, however, as courts in some states have ruled that statements made to employees may constitute employment contracts and can, in some cases, eliminate our ability to terminate at will.

The main issue in disciplinary action is *just cause*. It's generally held that you must have *just cause* for enforcing discipline. Just cause definitions vary, but it's a good idea to ask yourself the following questions before you terminate an employee:

- Did we adequately communicate the policy or procedure involved in the disciplinary action?

- Has the employee been warned orally, in writing, or both of the consequences of his or her action?

- Did we investigate the misconduct? Was the investigation thorough and fair?

- Has the policy or procedure that was violated been violated by other employees? Was disciplinary action taken in those cases? If so, what action was taken?

- Have we reviewed the employee's personnel record to see if this is the first time discipline has been administered?

- Is the planned discipline too tough or too light? Does the discipline fit the severity of the situation? Is it being used as a corrective/learning experience or as a punitive action?

The key to appropriate discipline is equal treatment and internal consistency.

## PERFORMANCE IMPROVEMENT

Before you take disciplinary action, you may want to try a more positive approach by giving an employee a performance improvement memorandum. This sometimes works better than immediately issuing a disciplinary notice. It puts the employee on notice that you are serious when you ask for improvement in performance, and it documents that discussion. If you decide to use a performance improvement memorandum, be specific in detailing the poor performance and in listing exactly what you expect in the way of improvement. Establish a time frame for improvement and follow-up to make sure the employee is performing to established standards. A sample performance improvement memorandum follows.

351

## MEMORANDUM

**TO:**        Employee Name

**FROM:**      Supervisor

**DATE:**

**SUBJECT:**   Performance Improvement Plan

This memo is notification that your performance has not been acceptable for the following reasons:

1.

2.

3.

4.

You have had a verbal warning about your performance and this written warning will serve as notice that the following actions must be taken:

1.

2.

3.

4.

We expect you to perform your job requirements in a timely, professional and conscientious manner at all times.

This plan will be in effect for the next 30 days and there must be immediate and sustained improvement or further action up to and including termination could occur.

Nothing contained herein is, or shall be construed as an employment contract. Your employment with the Company has been, and if continued, remains employment-at-will.

I have received a copy of this memo on the date below:

Received

_____          _____
Employee                                    Date


_____          _____
Supervisor                                  Date

# DETERMINING DISCIPLINE AND DISCHARGE POLICY

Discipline and discharge are the two toughest areas to manage in any organization. The way your supervisors and managers handle these issues will impact your bottom line.

You must have a discipline and discharge policy in order to ensure that everyone is treated fairly and that there is due process. By this we mean that employees facing discipline or discharge should be aware of the employer's conduct or performance expectations, that they have a copy of the handbook setting out the work rules and that they are given a chance to present their side of the story and defend themselves against charges of misconduct. Other issues in due process are:

- *Forewarning*—Before discipline or discharge takes place employees should be made aware of their misconduct. A series of warnings, usually one oral and one written, should be made.

- *Reasonableness of rule and penalty*—An employer should be able to show that the work rule violated by an employee is reasonable and was reasonably applied. Additionally, the penalty assessed against the employee should reflect the seriousness of the offense and be consistent with progressive discipline principles.

- *Evenhanded enforcement*—Employees who commit similar acts or cause similar problems should be subject to similar penalties.

- *Timeliness*—Discipline should be imposed in a timely manner.

# SAMPLE DISCIPLINE POLICY

The following model discipline and discharge policy can be adapted to your organization. Word it to fit your needs. Be sure that your policy is reasonable and is enforced in an evenhanded manner.

If you have no other policies in your policy manual, you must have a policy and a procedure on discipline and discharge in order to avoid costly litigation.

Consider holding mandatory workshops for all your supervisors and managers to train them in your discipline policy and procedures. If you cannot conduct an in-house workshop or find a local workshop, write to the American Management Association at 135 West 50th Street, New York, New York 10020. Ask for their seminar catalog.

---

*Sample Discipline Policy*
_____

**Policy**

Open communications between management and employees and the establishment of a friendly, cooperative work atmosphere go a long way toward eliminating serious disciplinary problems. If, however, disciplinary problems do arise, supervisors should make every effort to ensure that employees have a thorough understanding of company policies and an awareness of what is expected in the area of job performance.

The purpose of this policy is to provide guidelines for disciplinary action. Application of these guidelines must be consistent and equitable so that all employees receive like treatment for similar offenses.

## Procedures

The procedures described below are meant to assist supervisors and managers in determining proper course of action when discipline is needed. They are guidelines, not a substitute for common sense. Documentation of all verbal and written warnings is important to avoid the situation of an employee being discharged with no written proof of earlier warnings. In most cases, it is advisable to give an employee at least one documented verbal warning and one written warning before termination.

## Warnings

You should use your own judgment in determining the length of time between warnings. A minimum of thirty days and a maximum of ninety days is suggested as a guideline. The warning should be specific in describing what improvement is needed. Copies of the warning should be forwarded to the senior officer of the employee's department and to the affirmative action coordinator in the human resource department for follow-up.

1. *Verbal Warning.* Before a written warning is issued, a verbal warning may be given to the employee. This verbal warning should be recorded.

2. *Written Warning.* If improvement is not made within the time period granted in earlier warnings, it will be necessary to give a written warning. This may be done in the form of a memo. In such cases, signature of the employee acknowledges receipt of the written warning but may not indicate concurrence with the information contained in the warning. Copies of written warnings should go into the files and a copy should go to the employee. If the employee fails to improve by the date given on the warning, other disciplinary action, including termination, may result.

3. *Consultation.* Following a written warning, you should consult with the employee to check on progress and improvement in the problem area. Consultations should be documented accurately as to the dates and outcomes of the meetings.

The employee's file will be purged if after twelve months have elapsed, the employee has improved and there have been no subsequent warnings.

## Consistency of Treatment

If there is one guideline that cannot be stressed enough, it is consistency and equality of treatment of all employees.

## Suspension

Some companies employ progressive disciplinary procedures that include suspensions. Suspensions work best when the problem is not serious enough to warrant discharge, but the supervisor needs to take action.

## Evaluation

An evaluation period (formerly called probationary period) also is utilized by some organizations to give the employee time to change behavior. The key here is to identify the best disciplinary situation for your specific organization and your work force.

The key to discipline is to make it as positive as possible, to allow the employee to retain self-respect. The objective is to correct problem behavior and, when the employee has corrected behavior, to wipe the slate clean.

**Manager's Tip**

Set up a tracking system to ensure that proper follow-up occurs on any disciplinary action. Follow through-if you don't, you might have to reinstitute the disciplinary procedures with a new time period.

## DISCIPLINE AND DISCHARGE FORMS

When completing discipline or termination forms, you must be thorough, honest, and to the point. You must "tell it like it is" in terms of stating the facts, but eliminate judgments and blame. You may end up explaining these issues and your forms to top executives or to regulatory people such as hearing examiners or attorneys. Don't be frightened of the issues, but take them seriously and spend the time you need to complete adequate documentation.

## SUPERVISOR'S CHECKLIST FOR EFFECTIVE DISCIPLINE
## (COMPLETE BEFORE TAKING ACTION)

Employee's Name _____     Date _____

Length of Service _____ Department_____

**INCIDENT**

Employee(s) involved _____

_____

What happened?—Provide an accurate statement of what happened.

_____

_____

_____

How did it happen?

_____

_____

_____

What are the facts?—Be specific—no opinions.

_____

_____

_____

_____

Has the employee had a chance to tell his/her side of the story? . . . . . . . . . . . . . ❏ Yes   ❏ No

Explain_____

_____

_____

Did you talk to the employee in private? . . . . . . . . . . . . . . . . . . . . . . . . . . . . ❏ Yes   ❏ No

Was the employee aware of the rule or procedure? . . . . . . . . . . . . . . . . . . . . . ❏ Yes   ❏ No

Was the rule published in writing and communicated to all employees? . . . . . . . ❏ Yes   ❏ No

How consistently has the rule been enforced? _____

_____

What needs to be corrected?

_____

_____

_____

What has been done in similar cases?

_____

_____

_____

Has this violation been previously overlooked?. . . . . . . . . . . . . . . . . . . . . . ❑ Yes  ❑ No

Did the employee have any previous warning? . . . . . . . . . . . . . . . . . . . . . . ❑ Yes  ❑ No

What is the employee's past record?

_____

_____

_____

Can you back up this record with facts. . . . . . . . . . . . . . . . . . . . . . . . . . . . ❑ Yes  ❑ No

What is appropriate and justifiable discipline?
   ❑ Verbal warning
   ❑ Written warning
   ❑ Placed on probation
   ❑ Discharge

Will corrective action prevent a recurrence and encourage better performance? . . ❑ Yes  ❑ No

Which persons did you check with before taking disciplinary action?
   ❑ Your Manager        ❑ Human Resource Department        ❑ Other
                                                            _____

                                                            _____

## FOLLOW-UP ACTION

What follow-up action is necessary?

_____

_____

_____

_____

_____

Have you recorded this incident and put a copy in the personnel file? . . . . . . . . ❑ Yes  ❑ No

# DISCIPLINARY WARNING NOTICE

Employee's Name  _____    Date  _____

Department  _____  Position/Title  _____

---

**REASON FOR NOTICE:**

_____

_____

_____

---

**ACTION TAKEN ON THIS NOTICE:**

❏ Verbal Warning

❏ First Written Warning
  Discussion            _____

                        _____

                        _____

---

**NEXT STEP:**

❏ Second Written Warning

❏ Termination

❏ Other (specify)       Discussion  _____

                        _____

                        _____

---

**SUPERVISOR'S COMMENTS:**

_____

_____

_____

---

**EMPLOYEE'S COMMENTS:**

_____

_____

_____

_____

---

**EMPLOYEE'S SIGNATURE** _____

**SUPERVISOR SIGNATURE** _____

---

*NOTE:* **If, in the opinion of the Company, an infraction is serious enough, any and all steps may be bypassed and discharge may occur at any time.** A copy of this notice must be given to the employee and a copy placed in the employee's personnel file.

# EMPLOYEE WARNING NOTICE

Employee Name: _____

Social Security
Number: _____

Position Title: _____

Date of
Warning: _____

**TYPE OF
PROBLEM**

( ) Tardiness
( ) Absenteeism
( ) Insubordination
( ) Other: _____
_____
_____

( ) Quality of Work
( ) Quantity of Work
( ) Neatness

( ) Carelessness
( ) Safety
( ) Intoxication or Drinking

Problem Occurred on:    Date _____    **WARNING**    ( ) First Date: _____

Time _____    **NOTICE:**    ( ) Second Date: _____

Place _____           ( ) Final

_____

| COMPANY STATEMENT | WARNING DECISION |
|---|---|
| 1. Describe in detail what the employee has done | 1. Explain in detail what the employee must do to improve performance or change behavior. |
| 2. Cite how this interferes with work environment, employee performance, business operations or the well being of other employees. | 2. Cite date that improvements are to be required. |
| 3. Cite verbatim the rule, policy, law, standard, or regulation that was violated. | 3. Cite consequences if improvements are not achieved by date specified. |
| | APPROVED BY:_____ |
| | TITLE: _____ |
| | DATE: _____ |

**Attach separate page if needed for more detailed explanations.**

EMPLOYEE COMMENTS: _____
_____
_____

_____
Employee's Signature                 Date

_____
Supervisor's Signature              Date

Manager's Tip
_____

The Employee Consultation Form can be used for many types of consultations, not only for discipline or discharge. You may want to modify the form and use it for general employee counseling sessions.

The key issue with all of these forms is that you have documentation of discussions and warnings. You keep copies for the personnel files, and you also give copies to the employee. If you were to end up in a regulatory hearing, the first thing a hearing examiner would ask you is whether you provided the employee with a copy of the warning notice.

## EMPLOYEE CONSULTATION FORM

NAME _____ Dept._____

Type of Problem _____

Date of Problem _____

First Warning

Second Warning

Third Warning

Suspension. . . . From _____ To _____ Return to Work _____

Discharge

_____

Description of Problem: _____

_____

_____

_____

Disciplinary action to be taken: _____

_____

_____

_____

_____

_____

_____

Employee's statement: _____

_____

_____

_____

_____


Signed _____        Date _____
            Supervisor


Signed _____        Date _____
            Employee
            Signature acknowledges receipt only

# SEPARATION NOTICE

COMPANY NAME _____

EMPLOYEE NAME _____

SS # _____ JOB TITLE _____

DATES OF EMPLOYMENT: Start_____ Last_____ Previous dates of employment _____

WORKING HOURS_____ AM PM TO_____ AM PM WORKING DAYS _____

RATE OF PAY_____ per _____ PAID OVERTIME? Yes____ No____ UNION INVOLVED? Yes____ No____

AMOUNT OF PAY GIVEN IN LIEU OF NOTICE, IF ANY _____

VOLUNTARY QUIT _____ DISCHARGED _____ LACK OF WORK ____

WHAT WAS THE FINAL CIRCUMSTANCE LEADING TO SEPARATION? _____

_____

_____

_____

WHAT OTHER CIRCUMSTANCES, IF ANY, WERE TAKEN INTO CONSIDERATION? _____

_____

_____

_____

EMPLOYEE'S COMMENTS   (Continue on back) _____

_____


_____              _____
Employee's Signature                          Immediate Supervisor's Signature


                                              Title: _____
Date: _____        Date: _____
                                              Phone: _____

WOULD YOU REHIRE THIS INDIVIDUAL?
Yes _____        No _____              _____
                                             Witness

Attached are supportive documents as applicable (warning notices, application forms, doctor's statements, etc.)
This form should be completed immediately at separation time.


Note _____

By completing this form and having the terminating employee sign it, you have documentation
showing the type of termination. If the employee agrees that it is a voluntary termination, he/she
may not collect unemployment compensation if it is not due on voluntary terminations under
the laws of your state.

# CHECKLIST FOR TERMINATION

**(Attach All Termination Documentation)**

Employee Name _____ Dept. _____ Date _____

Complete all areas of the form.

_____        Voluntary

_____        Involuntary

_____        With Notice

_____        Reason _____

                _____

_____        Eligible for Rehire?

_____        Vacation Pay Paid?

_____        Letter of Resignation/Separation Notice Completed

_____        License information

_____        Return of all Company property, including keys and parking
                pass, telephone codes, credit cards, personnel manual, and so
                on.

_____        Paycheck delivered to employee at time of termination

                _____
                Supervisor

                _____
                Date

# EXIT INTERVIEW FORM

Employee Name_____     Employee Number _____

Department/Company _____

Job Title _____     Job Code _____

Termination Date _____

## VOLUNTARY TERMINATION

1.  Because your termination was *voluntary,* we would like to know your reasons for leaving the company.

    _____

    _____

    _____

    _____

    _____

2.  Did you experience any dissatisfaction during your employment at _____? If so, please describe.

    _____

    _____

    _____

    _____

    _____

3.  What recommendations would you suggest to make this a better company?

    _____

    _____

    _____

    _____

    _____

4.  What did you like most about working here?

    _____

    _____

    _____

    _____

Are there any other comments—positive or negative—that you would like to make? If so, please do so in the space below. (Feel free to use the back of this form or attach another sheet.)

_____

_____

_____

_____

_____

_____

_____

_____

_____

_____

**Thank you for completing this form. Your comments will be helpful to us
in our future planning as we are constantly striving to improve in all areas.**

Please sign below:

_____          _____
Employee's Signature                                    Date


- - - - - - - - - - - - - - - - - - - - - - - - - - - - - - - - - - - - - - - - - - - - - - - - - - -

**For Human Resources Department Use Only**

_____Keys and access card checked in                    _____Final check given to employee

_____Termination form presented to employee            _____Insurance conversion discussed

_____Prescription card returned

# SAMPLE LETTERS ON DISCIPLINE

Letters or memos on discipline or discharge are the most difficult ones most managers have to write in the course of their jobs. The following model letters will provide you with ideas and formats to help you get started. Modify the letters to fit your specific needs. All letters come from *The Personnel Manager's Complete Model Letter Book,* by Mary Cook, Prentice Hall 1989, and are used by permission of the publisher.

## *Tips for Disciplinary Action or Discharge Letters*

- Get the facts right and state them succinctly.
- Act on and write about first-hand information only, not hearsay.
- Get directly to the point. Don't be vague and don't get "on your soapbox."
- Provide the reasons for discipline or termination but don't agonize over the details.
- Convince the employee there is only one course of action, and help the employee to understand the reasons behind the discipline or termination.

Be careful of statements made to employees in writing. Such statements might be construed as inappropriate or even illegal and later used against your company.

## DISCIPLINARY ACTION: SUSPENSION WITHOUT PAY

Date

Mr. John Simpson
60241 Green Lane
Montgomery, AL 36130

Dear John:

This letter is to inform you that you are hereby suspended from your job without pay for three working days commencing March 15. This disciplinary action is being taken based on the following facts:

- You fell asleep on your job on February 26 and left power equipment in the plant unattended for over an hour.
- This is the second such incident in 30 days.

Your conduct as described above constitutes sufficient cause for disciplinary action. In addition, you have been disciplined in the past for the same problem.

Your formal disciplinary action is:

- Suspension without pay for three consecutive working days beginning March 15.

A copy of this letter will be placed in your personnel file. You have the right to respond in writing to this information or arguments rebutting this suspension. If you choose to respond, you have until 5:00 P.M. on April 1 to do so. Your response, if any, will be given consideration. It is assumed that you have waived the right to respond if you do not take advantage of the above alternative.

The purpose of this suspension is to impress upon you the seriousness with which we regard the above violation of employment and to give you the opportunity to reflect upon your future compliance with our employment standards. One more violation of the conditions of your employment will result in termination.

Sincerely,


Karen True
Director Human Resources

## DISCIPLINARY ACTION: SIX-MONTH EVALUATION

Date

Dale L. Bradley
8796 Dawn Drive
Brooklyn, NY 11210

Dear Dale:

The purpose of this letter is to describe the events that have occurred over the past several weeks which have resulted in the need for disciplinary action, and to inform you of the conduct required on your part for continued employment with ROC.

On Thursday, January 19th, you left your work assignment in Washington, D.C. without permission from your supervisor, and traveled to Miami, Florida, for personal reasons. On February 1st, you submitted your expense report to your supervisor and falsified the dates that you were on the job in Washington, D.C.

Inconsistencies between your expense report and the hotel receipt were noticed by our supervisor. When questioned about this, you admitted that you had left Washington, D.C. and then falsified the expense statement.

As we discussed, such acts of deception are unacceptable and will not be permitted by either myself or the executive management of ROC. Accordingly, I am placing you on disciplinary notice for a period of six months from the date of this letter. During this period, l will carefully monitor your work activities.

Any further incidents observed during this period that are contrary to acceptable standards of behavior could result in your dismissal.

Dale, we want you to succeed, and we hope that your acknowledgment of the seriousness of this situation will have a positive result on your future at ROC.

Sincerely,

Stanley Bishop
Human Resources Director

# 8

# Safety, Accident Reporting, and OSHA Regulations

- Occupational Safety and Health Administration's Leading Violations
- Employer Obligations for Reporting Occupational injuries and Illnesses Under OSHA
- Sample Guide to Accident and Injury Reporting
- Accident Reporting Forms
- Glossary of Occupational Safety and Health Terminology

# SAFETY, ACCIDENT REPORTING, AND OSHA REGULATIONS

All organizations have a responsibility to maintain a safe workplace. Some of the areas of accident prevention are proper engineering controls, preventive maintenance, and employee safety training. The following are some basic safety procedures:

- Plants and manufacturing facilities must have good preventive maintenance programs for production and other equipment.
- Supervisors should be required to inspect work areas every day. This can be an informal inspection but should be seriously carried out.
- Worker-management teams using checklists should inspect monthly or quarterly.
- Formal plant and office safety audits should be completed annually with ultimate reporting responsibility to top management.
- Management should encourage employees to report hazards and provide an avenue for them to do so.
- Training and retraining on a regular basis including employees and supervisors should be mandatory.
- Offices and plants should be clean, well designed, and controlled for noise, heat, dust, fumes, and hazardous waste.
- OSHA has toughened exposure limits on 376 toxic chemicals in the workplace. OSHA's Hazards Communication Standards require every workplace in the country to identify hazardous substances on the premises, list them, and train employees in their use. This law applies to all employers—from accountants to zookeepers.

## OCCUPATIONAL SAFETY AND HEALTH ADMINISTRATION'S LEADING VIOLATIONS

The ten most common workplace OSHA violations according to Department of Labor Statistics are:

1. No posting of the OSHA notice of employer obligations.
2. No grounding of electrical equipment connected by cord and plug.
3. No machinery guards at point of operation.
4. No guards for pulleys.

5. No guards for live parts of electrical equipment.

6. No enclosures for blades of fans in use less than 7 feet above floor of working level.

7. No guards for belt, rope, and chain drives.

8. Disorderliness in aisles and passageways.

9. No guards for vertical and inclined belts.

10. Not maintaining a log and summary of job injuries and illnesses.

# EMPLOYER OBLIGATIONS FOR REPORTING OCCUPATIONAL INJURIES AND ILLNESSES UNDER OSHA

The Occupational Safety and Health (OSHA) Act of 1970 requires covered employers to prepare and maintain records of occupational injuries and illnesses. The Bureau of Labor Statistics of the U.S. Department of Labor is responsible for administering the recordkeeping system established by the act. The OSHA Act and record keeping regulations in 29 CFR 1904 provide specific recording and reporting requirements which comprise the framework of the OSHA recording system.

Some employers may be subject to additional record keeping and reporting requirements not covered in this report. Many specific standards and regulations of the Occupational Safety and Health Administration (OSHA) have additional requirements for the maintenance and retention of records for medical surveillance, exposure monitoring inspections, and other activities and incidents relevant to occupational safety and health, and for the reporting of certain information to employees and to OSHA. For information on these requirements employers should refer directly to the OSHA standards and regulations or contact their OSHA regional office.

## Annual Survey of Occupational Injuries and Illnesses

Section 8(c)(2) of the Act requires employers to make periodic reports of deaths, injuries, and illnesses which have been recorded on the OSHA injury and illness records. This periodic reporting is accomplished through the Annual Survey of Occupational Injuries and Illnesses conducted by the Bureau of Labor Statistics.

The annual survey provides measures of the occurrence and the extent of recordable occupational injuries and illnesses. Injuries and illnesses are reported as either fatalities, lost workday cases, or nonfatal cases without lost workdays.

Measures produced by the survey include incidence rates and numbers of occupational injuries and illnesses. Incidence rates relate the numbers of injuries, illnesses, or lost workdays to a common base of exposure. They show the equivalent number of injuries and illnesses or lost workdays per 100 full-time workers. This common base enables accurate interindustry comparisons, trend analysis over time, and comparisons among firms regardless of size.

This survey is conducted on a sample basis, and firms required to submit reports of their injury and illness experience are contacted by BLS or a participating state agency.

A firm not contacted by its state agency or BLS need not file a report of its injury and illness experience. Employers should note, however, that even if they are not selected to participate in the annual survey for a given year, they must still comply with the record keeping requirements as well as with the requirements for reporting fatalities and multiple hospitalization cases.

Participants in the annual survey consist of two categories of employers: (1) employers who maintain OSHA records on a regular basis; and (2) a small, rotating sample of employers who are regularly exempt from OSHA record keeping. The survey procedure is different for these two groups of employers.

**Participation of Firms Regularly Maintaining OSHA Records** When employers regularly maintaining OSHA records are selected to participate in the Annual Survey of Occupational Injuries and Illnesses, they are mailed the survey questionnaire in February of the year following the reference calendar year of the survey. The survey form, the Occupational Injuries and Illnesses Survey Questionnaire, OSHA No. 200-S, requests information about the establishment(s) included in the report and the injuries and illnesses experienced during the previous year. Information for the injury and illness portion of the report form can usually be copied directly from the totals on the log and summary, OSHA Form 200, which the employer should have completed and posted in the establishment by the time the questionnaire arrives. The survey form also requests summary information about the type of business activity and number of employees and hours worked.

**Participation of Normally Exempt Small Employers and Employers in Low-Hazard Industries** A few regularly exempt employers (those with fewer than 11 employees and those in designated low-hazard industries) are also required to participate in the annual survey in order to produce injury and illness statistics that are comparable in coverage to the statistics published in years prior to the reference calendar year of the survey. These employers must maintain injury and illness records for the coming year.

## SAMPLE GUIDE TO ACCIDENT AND INJURY REPORTING

If you are a small company with only one location, you may not need a formal guide to accident and injury reporting. However, if you have more than one location and are a fast-growing business, you may want to provide uniform guidelines so that all supervisors at all of your locations will handle injury reporting in the same manner.

Having such a guide could save money and unnecessary delay should a crisis arise. Even one single automobile or truck accident that an employee or supervisor mishandles could cost hundreds of thousands of dollars. As you grow you'll want to consider a more formal risk management program, but if you are still a small or medium-sized organization the guide that follows will be helpful. Modify the guide to fit your specific needs. Review your accident insurance policies and federal and state regulations as you rewrite this guideline to ensure you are in compliance in each area.

# Guide to Accident and Injury Reporting

_____
(COMPANY NAME)


_____
(DATE)


## CONTENTS

- Purpose
- Definitions
- General
- Accident Reporting
- Physical Examination
- Injury Report/Investigation Form
- Accident Reporting Forms

# PURPOSE

The purpose of this guide is to provide a source of information for the supervisor to assist in complying with corporate policy and federal and state laws concerning the reporting of work related injuries.

# DEFINITIONS

- For the purpose of this guide, a work *injury* is any injury including occupational disease and other work-connected disability which arises out of and in the course of employment.

- A *day of disability* (lost time) is any day on which an employee is unable, because of injury, to perform effectively throughout a full shift the essential functions of a regularly established job which is open and available to him/her.

- American National Standard Z16.1, Method of Recording and Measuring Work Injury Experience, shall be used as a reference in all work-related injuries or illnesses.

# GENERAL

In order to comply with both workers compensation and OSHA regulations, certain forms must be completed and procedures and time guidelines followed.

# ACCIDENT REPORTING

## Fatality

1. Report immediately by telephone to the supervisor or the Personnel Department and to the police department where the death occurred.
2. Follow up with written report of injury using Injury Report and Investigation Form, and the OSHA Form 200 and send copies to the Personnel Department.

## Medical Treatment for Accident or Injury

- Employees will be notified by a bulletin board posting and verbally by their supervisors that injuries occurring in the course of regular employment must be immediately reported to their supervisor.

- Emergency first aid treatment will be given by a supervisor certified in first aid. It will be the duty of the supervisor providing first aid to determine whether further medical treatment is warranted.

- Injuries requiring the attention of a person qualified to administer first aid, a nurse, or physician must be reported by phone to the Personnel Department within 24 hours.

- Completion of the Injury Report, the Investigation Form, and OSHA Form 200 is required in these cases and is to be forwarded to the Personnel Department within 24 hours of injury.

# PHYSICAL EXAMINATION

The following employees must be found physically fit by a company physician before being allowed to return to work:

- All employees returning to work after absence for work-related accident or injury.

- All employees returning to work after absence of 30 working days because of illness, injury, or disability regardless of cause. The Personnel Department at its discretion may require a physical examination for anyone who has been absent from work with a contagious disease.

- Employees in jobs running machinery or critical quality control equipment when returning to work after drug or alcohol abuse rehabilitation.

# INJURY REPORT/INVESTIGATION FORM

Data provided on the Injury Report and Investigation Form is required for the completion of other reports and forms for workers compensation.

## Procedure

The Injury Report and Investigation Form is divided into eight sections. The responsibility for completion and information required is as follows:

*Section 1:*  The basic information is to be supplied by the supervisor, who may find it necessary to check the employee personnel file for complete and accurate information.

*Section 2:*  This section is to be completed by the injured employee, in his or her own handwriting, describing the events and conditions contributing to the injury. If the employee is unable to write as a result of the injury an oral statement may be obtained and entered on the form by the supervisor.

***Section 3:*** The medical disposition of the employee must be entered in this section by the supervisor or attending physician.

***Section 4:*** After a thorough investigation of the accident and its probable cause, the supervisor completes this portion.

***Section 5:*** The supervisor is to check the appropriate square or squares indicating the unsafe act or unsafe conditions which contributed to the accident. Company management wants to ensure that any unsafe work areas or equipment are immediately attended to and brought up to standard.

***Section 6:*** Again, the supervisor is to show why the unsafe act or conditions existed and what steps are to be taken to correct the situation. The estimated completion date sets goals and is intended to create a commitment to remedy the situation causing the accident or injury.

***Section 7:*** The name of the person responsible for assuring the recommended action is taken.

***Section 8:*** The department head and personnel safety representative are to sign indicating their satisfaction that the information is complete and an effective remedy has been implemented.

Complete the form and forward to the Personnel Department within 72 hours of injury.

# ACCIDENT REPORTING FORMS

The following are sample forms for use in safety reporting. Modify them to fit your specific needs. Ask your supervisors to help design the forms. They will have to use them and will be more likely to accept them if they took part in their design and implementation. It is a good idea to form a safety committee comprised mainly of supervisors. Ask them to meet on a regular basis to review safety problems and accident report forms. Keep the committee small and workable and ask for feedback to management on safety issues.

**Manager's Tip**

All safety and accident reports must be filled out completely and accurately. You never know when the incident might blow up into a major case costing hundreds of thousands of dollars. Your documentation then becomes all-important and directly impacts your bottom-line. Insist that your supervisors be thorough in creating documentation records and maintaining files.

## INJURY REPORT AND INVESTIGATION FORM

**1**

DATE: _____ OFFICE: _____ STATE: _____

EMPLOYEE'S NAME: _____ AGE: _____ DATE OF BIRTH: _____ ____ SEX: M F

ADDRESS: _____ SOC. SEC. NO. _____

DATE OF INJURY: _____ TIME: _____ DATE INJURY REPORTED: _____

DEPARTMENT ASSIGNED: _____ SUPERVISOR'S NAME: _____

DATE HIRED: _____ LENGTH OF TIME ON PRESENT JOB: _____

**2**

DID YOU HAVE AN INJURY IN THE COURSE OF YOUR EMPLOYMENT? YES: _____ NO: _____

DESCRIBE HOW ACCIDENT OCCURRED: (WHAT, HOW, OBJECT OR SUBSTANCE INVOLVED) _____

_____

_____

_____

_____

_____

_____

_____

_____ EMPLOYEE'S SIGNATURE: _____ DATE: _____

**3**

| DISPOSITION | YES | NO |
|---|---|---|
| DISABLING INJURY: | | |
| SENT TO HOSPITAL | | |
| SENT TO COMPANY DOCTOR | | |
| RETURN TO REGULAR JOB | | |
| RETURN TO LIGHT DUTY JOB | | |
| RECORDABLE ON OSHA FORM 100 | | |

ESTIMATED DAYS OF DISABILITY: _____

DATE TO RETURN TO WORK: _____

INITIAL MEDICAL DIAGNOSIS: _____

_____

IF HOSPITALIZED, NAME & ADDRESS OF HOSPITAL:

_____

_____

**BODY PART INJURED**

☐ EYE
☐ HEAD
☐ CHEST
☐ BACK
☐ ABDOMEN
☐ ARM
☐ HAND - FINGER
☐ LEG
☐ FOOT - TOE
☐ RESPIRATORY SYSTEM
☐ _____

**TYPE OF INJURY**

☐ LACERATION
☐ ABRASION
☐ PUNCTURE
☐ BURN
☐ FRACTURE
☐ STRAIN - SPRAIN
☐ AMPUTATION
☐ FOREIGN BODY
☐ HERNIA
☐ CONTUSION
☐ _____

ATTENDING PHYSICIAN OR MEDICAL ATTENTION: _____

**4**

SUPERVISOR'S DESCRIPTION OF ACCIDENT AFTER INVESTIGATION: (Note if employee was wearing required personal protective equipment)

_____

_____

_____

_____

SUPERVISOR'S SIGNATURE      DATE

**8**

EMPLOYEE RELATIONS (Signature)    DATE     FUNCTIONAL HEAD (Signature)     DATE

**ALL ACCIDENTS ARE THE RESULT OF UNSAFE ACTS AND/OR UNSAFE CONDITIONS.
INVESTIGATE THOROUGHLY AND CHECK THE APPROPRIATE CAUSES BELOW.**

| YES | NO | UNSAFE ACT | UNSAFE CONDITION | YES | |
|---|---|---|---|---|---|
| | | LACK OF SKILL OR KNOWLEDGE | IMPROPER MATERIAL STORAGE | | |
| | | UNSAFE ACT OF OTHER | CONGESTION - LACK OF SPACE | | |
| | | PHYSICAL LIMITATION OR MENTAL ATTITUDE | IMPROPER AND/OR WORN TOOLS AND EQUIPMENT | | |
| | | FAILURE TO USE PROPER TOOLS OR EQUIPMENT | UNSAFE DESIGN AND/OR CONSTRUCTION | | |
| | | FAILURE TO WEAR PERSONAL PROTECTIVE EQUIPMENT | UNSAFE CONDITION OF MACHINE | | |
| | | UNAWARE OF HAZARDS | IMPROPER GUARDING | | |
| | | SHORT CUT TO SAVE TIME OR EFFORT | IMPROPER JOB PROCEDURE | | |
| | | UNSAFE MATERIAL HANDLING | UNSAFE FLOORS, RAMPS, STAIRWAYS | | |
| | | OTHER: | IMPROPER LIGHTING | | |
| | | | OTHER: | | |

(5)

**WHAT WAS DONE UNSAFELY?**

**WHAT UNSAFE CONDITION EXISTED?**

**WHY WAS IT DONE THAT WAY?**

**WHY DID THESE CONDITIONS EXIST?**

(6)

**HOW WILL WE CONTROL THE ABOVE?**

**HOW WILL WE CORRECT THESE CONDITIONS?**

**ESTIMATED COMPLETION DATE:**

**ESTIMATED COMPLETION DATE:**

**WHO WILL ASSUME RESPONSIBILITY FOR CONTROL?
BE SPECIFIC:**

**WHO WILL ASSUME RESPONSIBILITY FOR CORRECTION?
BE SPECIFIC:**

(7)

**U.S. Department of Labor**

For Calendar Year 19 _____          Page ____ of ____

| Company Name | Form Approved |
|---|---|
| Establishment Name | O.M.B. No. 44R 1453 |
| Establishment Address | |

| Extent of and Outcome of INJURY | | | | | | Type, Extent of, and Outcome of ILLNESS | | | | | | | |

| Fatalities | Nonfatal Injuries | | | | | Type of Illness | | | | | | | Fatalities | Nonfatal Illnesses | | | | |
|---|---|---|---|---|---|---|---|---|---|---|---|---|---|---|---|---|---|---|
| Injury Related | Injuries With Lost Workdays | | | | Injuries Without Lost Workdays | CHECK Only One Column for Each Illness (See other side of form for terminations or permanent transfers.) | | | | | | | Illness Related | Illnesses With Lost Workdays | | | | Illnesses Without Lost Workdays |
| Enter DATE of death.  Mo./day/yr. | Enter a CHECK if injury involves days away from work, or days of restricted work activity, or both. | Enter a CHECK if injury involves days away from work. | Enter number of DAYS away from work. | Enter number of DAYS of restricted work activity. | Enter a CHECK if no entry was made in columns 1 or 2 but the injury is recordable as defined above. | Occupational skin diseases or disorders | Dust diseases of the lungs | Respiratory conditions due to toxic agents | Poisoning (systemic effects of toxic materials) | Disorders due to physical agents | Disorders associated with repeated trauma | All other occupational illnesses | Enter DATE of death.  Mo./day/yr. | Enter a CHECK if illness involves days away from work, or days of restricted work activity, or both. | Enter a CHECK if illness involves days away from work. | Enter number of DAYS away from work. | Enter number of DAYS of restricted work activity. | Enter a CHECK if no entry was made in columns 8 or 9. |
| (1) | (2) | (3) | (4) | (5) | (6) | (a) | (b) | (c) | (d) | (e) | (f) | (g) | (8) | (9) | (10) | (11) | (12) | (13) |
| | | | | | | | | | | (7) | | | | | | | | |
| | | | | | | | | | | | | | | | | | | |
| | | | | | | | | | | | | | | | | | | |
| | | | | | | | | | | | | | | | | | | |
| | | | | | | | | | | | | | | | | | | |
| | | | | | | | | | | | | | | | | | | |
| | | | | | | | | | | | | | | | | | | |
| | | | | | | | | | | | | | | | | | | |
| | | | | | | | | | | | | | | | | | | |
| | | | | | | | | | | | | | | | | | | |
| | | | | | | | | | | | | | | | | | | |
| | | | | | | | | | | | | | | | | | | |
| | | | | | | | | | | | | | | | | | | |
| | | | | | | | | | | | | | | | | | | |
| | | | | | | | | | | | | | | | | | | |

INJURIES          ILLNESSES

Certification of Annual Summary Totals By _____ Title _____ Date _____

FOLD

OSHA No. 200          **POST ONLY THIS PORTION OF THE LAST PAGE NO LATER THAN FEBRUARY 1.**

Bureau of Labor Statistics
Log and Summary of Occupational
Injuries and Illnesses

| NOTE: | This form is required by Public Law 91-596 and must be kept in the establishment for *5 years*. Failure to maintain and post can result in the issuance of citations and assessment of penalties. *(See posting requirements on the other side of form.)* | | **RECORDABLE CASES:** You are required to record information about every occupational **death**; every nonfatal occupational **illness**; and those nonfatal occupational injuries which involve one or more of the following: loss of consciousness, restriction of work or motion, transfer to another job, or medical treatment (other than first aid). *(See definitions on the other side of form.)* | | | |
|---|---|---|---|---|---|
| Case or File Number | Date of Injury or Onset of Illness | Employee's Name | Occupation | Department | Description of Injury or Illness |
| Enter a nonduplicating number which will facilitate comparisons with supplementary records. | Enter Mo./day. | Enter first name or initial, middle initial, last name. | Enter regular job title, not activity employee was performing when injured or at onset of illness. In the absence of a formal title, enter a brief description of the employee's duties. | Enter department in which the employee is regularly employed or a description of normal workplace to which employee is assigned, even though temporarily working in another department at the time of injury or illness. | Enter a brief description of the injury or illness and indicate the part or parts of body affected.<br><br>Typical entries for this column might be: Amputation of 1st joint right forefinger; Strain of lower back; Contact dermatitis on both hands; Electrocution—body. |
| (A) | (B) | (C) | (D) | (E) | (F) |
|  |  |  |  |  | PREVIOUS PAGE TOTALS ➡ |
|  |  |  |  |  |  |
|  |  |  |  |  |  |
|  |  |  |  |  |  |
|  |  |  |  |  |  |
|  |  |  |  |  |  |
|  |  |  |  |  |  |
|  |  |  |  |  |  |
|  |  |  |  |  |  |
|  |  |  |  |  |  |
|  |  |  |  |  |  |
|  |  |  |  |  |  |
|  |  |  |  |  |  |
|  |  |  |  |  | TOTALS (Instructions on other side of form.) ➡ |

OSHA No. 200

**Instructions for OSHA No. 200**

I. **Log and Summary of Occupational Injuries and Illnesses**

Each employer who is subject to the recordkeeping requirements of the Occupational Safety and Health Act of 1970 must maintain for each establishment a log of all recordable occupational injuries and illnesses. This form (OSHA No. 200) may be used for that purpose. A substitute for the OSHA No. 200 is acceptable if it is as detailed, easily readable, and understandable as the OSHA No. 200.

Enter each recordable case on the log within six (6) workdays after learning of its occurrence. Although other records must be maintained at the establishment to which they refer, it is possible to prepare and maintain the log at another location, using data processing equipment if desired. If the log is prepared elsewhere, a copy updated to within 45 calendar days must be present at all times in the establishment.

Logs must be maintained and retained for five (5) years following the end of the calendar year to which they relate. Logs must be available (normally at the establishment) for inspection and copying by representatives of the Department of Labor, or the Department of Health, Education and Welfare, or States accorded jurisdiction under the Act.

II. **Changes in Extent of or Outcome of Injury or Illness**

If, during the 5-year period the log must be retained, there is a change in an extent and outcome of an injury or illness which affects entries in columns 1, 2, 6, 8, 9, or 13, the first entry should be lined out and a new entry made. For example, if an injured employee at first required only medical treatment but later lost workdays away from work, the check in column 6 should be lined out, and checks entered in columns 2 and 3 and the number of lost workdays entered in column 4.

In another example, if an employee with an occupational illness lost workdays, returned to work, and then died of the illness, the entries in columns 9 and 10 should be lined out and the date of death entered in column 8.

The entire entry for an injury or illness should be lined out if later found to be nonrecordable. For example: an injury or illness which is later determined not to be work related, or which was initially thought to involve medical treatment but later was determined to have involved only first aid.

III. **Posting Requirements**

A copy of the totals and information following the fold line of the last page for the year must be posted at each establishment in the place or places where notices to employees are customarily posted. This copy must be posted no later than *February 1 and must remain in place until March 1.*

Even though there were no injuries or illnesses during the year, zeros must be entered on the totals line, and the form posted.

The person responsible for the *annual summary totals* shall certify that the *totals are true* and complete by signing at the bottom of the form.

IV. **Instructions for Completing Log and Summary of Occupational Injuries and Illnesses**

**Column A  —  CASE OR FILE NUMBER.** Self-explanatory.

Column B  —  DATE OF INJURY OR ONSET OF ILLNESS.
For occupational injuries, enter the date of the work accident which resulted in injury. For occupational illnesses, enter the date of initial diagnosis of illness, or, if absence from work occurred before diagnosis, enter the first day of the absence attributable to the illness which was later diagnosed or recognized.

Columns
C through F —  Self-explanatory.

Columns
1 and 8  —  INJURY OR ILLNESS-RELATED DEATHS.
Self-explanatory.

Columns
2 and 9  —  INJURIES OR ILLNESSES WITH LOST WORKDAYS.
Self-explanatory.

Any injury which involves days away from work, or days of restricted work activity, or both must be recorded since it always involves one or more of the criteria for recordability.

Columns
3 and 10  —  INJURIES OR ILLNESSES INVOLVING DAYS AWAY FROM WORK. Self-explanatory.

Columns
4 and 11  —  LOST WORKDAYS—DAYS AWAY FROM WORK.
Enter the number of workdays (consecutive or not) on which the employee would have worked but could not because of occupational injury or illness. The number of lost workdays should not include the day of injury or onset of illness or any days on which the employee would not have worked even though able to work.
NOTE:  For employees not having a regularly scheduled shift, such as certain truck drivers, construction workers, farm labor, casual labor, part-time employees, etc., it may be necessary to estimate the number of lost workdays. Estimates of lost workdays shall be based on prior work history of the employee AND days worked by employees, not ill or injured, working in the department and/or occupation of the ill or injured employee.

Columns
5 and 12  —  LOST WORKDAYS—DAYS OF RESTRICTED WORK ACTIVITY.
Enter the number of workdays (consecutive or not) on which because of injury or illness:
(1)  the employee was assigned to another job on a temporary basis, or
(2)  the employee worked at a permanent job less than full time, or
(3)  the employee worked at a permanently assigned job but could not perform all duties normally connected with it.

The number of lost workdays should not include the day of injury or onset of illness or any days on which the employee would not have worked even though able to work.

Columns
6 and 13 — INJURIES OR ILLNESSES WITHOUT LOST WORKDAYS. Self-explanatory.

Columns 7a
through 7g — TYPE OF ILLNESS.
Enter a check in only *one* column for each illness.

TERMINATION OR PERMANENT TRANSFER—Place an asterisk to the right of the entry in columns 7a through 7g (type of illness) which represented a termination of employment or permanent transfer.

## V. Totals

Add number of entries in columns 1 and 8.
Add number of checks in columns 2, 3, 6, 7, 9, 10, and 13.
Add number of days in columns 4, 5, 11, and 12.
Totals are to be generated for each column at the end of each page and at the end of each year. *Only* the yearly totals are required for posting.

If an employee's loss of workdays is continuing at the time the totals are summarized, estimate the number of future workdays the employee will lose and add that estimate to the workdays already lost and include this figure in the annual totals. No further entries are to be made with respect to such cases in the next year's log.

## VI. Definitions

OCCUPATIONAL INJURY is any injury such as a cut, fracture, sprain, amputation, etc., which results from a work accident or from an exposure involving a single incident in the work environment.
NOTE: Conditions resulting from animal bites, such as insect or snake bites or from one-time exposure to chemicals, are considered to be injuries.

OCCUPATIONAL ILLNESS of an employee is any abnormal condition or disorder, other than one resulting from an occupational injury, caused by exposure to environmental factors associated with employment. It includes acute and chronic illnesses or diseases which may be caused by inhalation, absorption, ingestion, or direct contact.

The following listing gives the categories of occupational illnesses and disorders that will be utilized for the purpose of classifying recordable illnesses. For purposes of information, examples of each category are given. These are typical examples, however, and are not to be considered the complete listing of the types of illnesses and disorders that are to be counted under each category.

7a. **Occupational Skin Diseases or Disorders**
Examples: Contact dermatitis, eczema, or rash caused by primary irritants and sensitizers or poisonous plants; oil acne; chrome ulcers; chemical burns or inflammations; etc.

7b. **Dust Diseases of the Lungs (Pneumoconioses)**
Examples: Silicosis, asbestosis, coal worker's pneumoconiosis, byssinosis, siderosis, and other pneumoconioses.

7c. **Respiratory Conditions Due to Toxic Agents**
Examples: Pneumonitis, pharyngitis, rhinitis or acute congestion due to chemicals, dusts, gases, or fumes; farmer's lung; etc.

7d. **Poisoning (Systemic Effect of Toxic Materials)**
Examples: Poisoning by lead, mercury, cadmium, arsenic, or other metals; poisoning by carbon monoxide, hydrogen sulfide, or other gases; poisoning by benzol, carbon tetrachloride, or other organic solvents; poisoning by insecticide sprays such as parathion, lead arsenate; poisoning by other chemicals such as formaldehyde, plastics, and resins; etc.

7e. **Disorders Due to Physical Agents (Other than Toxic Materials)**
Examples: Heatstroke, sunstroke, heat exhaustion, and other effects of environmental heat; freezing, frostbite, and effects of exposure to low temperatures; caisson disease; effects of ionizing radiation (isotopes, X-rays, radium); effects of nonionizing radiation (welding flash, ultraviolet rays, microwaves, sunburn); etc.

7f. **Disorders Associated With Repeated Trauma**
Examples: Noise-induced hearing loss; synovitis, tenosynovitis, and bursitis; Raynaud's phenomena; and other conditions due to repeated motion, vibration, or pressure.

7g. **All Other Occupational Illnesses**
Examples: Anthrax, brucellosis, infectious hepatitis, malignant and benign tumors, food poisoning, histoplasmosis, coccidioidomycosis, etc.

MEDICAL TREATMENT includes treatment (other than first aid) administered by a physician or by registered professional personnel under the standing orders of a physician. Medical treatment does NOT include first-aid treatment (one-time treatment and subsequent observation of minor scratches, cuts, burns, splinters, and so forth, which do not ordinarily require medical care) even though provided by a physician or registered professional personnel.

ESTABLISHMENT: A single physical location where business is conducted or where services or industrial operations are performed (for example: a factory, mill, store, hotel, restaurant, movie theater, farm, ranch, bank, sales office, warehouse, or central administrative office). Where distinctly separate activities are performed at a single physical location, such as construction activities operated from the same physical location as a lumber yard, each activity shall be treated as a separate establishment.

For firms engaged in activities which may be physically dispersed, such as agriculture; construction; transportation; communications; and electric, gas, and sanitary services, records may be maintained at a place to which employees report each day.

Records for personnel who do not primarily report or work at a single establishment, such as traveling salesmen, technicians, engineers, etc., shall be maintained at the location from which they are paid or the base from which personnel operate to carry out their activities.

WORK ENVIRONMENT is comprised of the physical location, equipment, materials processed or used, and the kinds of operations performed in the course of an employee's work, whether on or off the employer's premises

# Accident/Injury Report

**Supervisor must complete report and return to the Human Resource Department within 24 hours.**

Name: _____    SSN: _____ - _____ - _____

Date of Accident: Day_____ Mo._____ Yr._____

Time of Accident: _____am/pm

Place of Accident: _____

Witnesses: (if any)            First Aid Given? _____Yes _____No

Name _____    By Whom? _____

Address: _____    Hospitalized? _____Yes _____No

_____    Physician: _____

Phone No.: _____

Nature and extent of injuries: _____

_____

How did accident/injury occur? (Be specific; use extra sheet if necessary): _____

_____

_____

Job or activity engaged in at time of injury (Be specific): _____

_____

_____

Describe any unsafe conditions, methods or practices related to the accident: _____

_____

_____

_____      _____

Employee's Signature            Date

_____      _____

Supervisor's Signature            Date

_____      _____

Department/Company            Location

# SUPERVISOR'S REPORT OF ACCIDENT INVESTIGATION
## CONFIDENTIAL REPORT—FOR CORPORATE USE ONLY

Injured Employee _____ Date of This Report _____

Job Title_____ Dept_____ Age_____ Sex_____ Length of Employment _____

Date and Time of Accident_____ Exact Location _____

Description of Accident (Detail what employee was doing and what tools, equipment, structures, or fixtures were involved). _____

_____

_____

_____

_____

_____

_____

_____

Nature of Injuries _____

_____

Was report to supervisor of first aid given immediately?_____Explain _____

_____

_____

Check accident causes on this report; Comment Fully (Use back of this sheet if you need more space).

_____

_____

_____

_____

_____

_____

_____

_____

What should be done, and by whom to prevent recurrence of this type of accident in the future?_____

_____

_____

_____

_____

Supervisor's Signature_____Date _____

Comments By Department Head or Safety Manager _____

_____

_____

_____

_____

# XYZ COMPANY

---

**Workers' Compensation
Employee Verification Form**

---

I have been notified by my employer of the procedure to follow in the event I incur a work-related injury or illness. I understand that my employer has designated _____ medical centers as primary providers for all work related injuries and illnesses. I understand that if I do not receive my medical care for work-related injuries and illnesses from _____ medical centers, I may be financially responsible for that care. See attached maps for _____ medical center locations.

I have been informed that authorization is required from my employer before I access medical care for non-emergency, work-related injuries and illnesses.


_____

Name of Employee (Please Print)


_____          _____

Signature of Employee                             Date


_____          _____

Signature of Human Resources Administrator         Date

## QUARTERLY SAFETY PERFORMANCE RECORD

For the Period: _____

| LOCATION | CURRENT QUARTER | | | YEAR-TO-DATE | | | LATEST NATIONAL RATES |
|---|---|---|---|---|---|---|---|
| | HOURS WORKED | LOST WORK DAY INJURIES | INCIDENCE RATE | HOURS WORKED | LOST WORK DAY INJURIES | INCIDENCE RATE | |
| | | | | | | | |
| | | | | | | | |
| | | | | | | | |
| | | | | | | | |
| | | | | | | | |
| | | | | | | | |
| | | | | | | | |
| | | | | | | | |
| | | | | | | | |
| | | | | | | | |
| TOTALS | | | | | | | |
| REMARKS | | | INCIDENCE RATE LOST WORK DAY INJ = | No. OF CASES x 200,000 / HRS. WORKED | | | |

$$\text{INCIDENCE RATE LOST WORK DAY INJ} = \frac{\text{No. OF CASES} \times 200,000}{\text{HRS. WORKED}}$$

# GLOSSARY OF OCCUPATIONAL SAFETY
# AND HEALTH TERMINOLOGY

The following glossary of occupational safety and health terminology is provided as a quick reference for supervisors, managers, and others who must complete safety records or deal with OSHA officials. Most business people today need a basic understanding of safety and health language.

**Annual summary.** Consists of a copy of the occupational injury and illness totals for the year from the OSHA No. 200, and the following information: The calendar year covered; company name; establishment address; certification signature, title, and date.

**Annual survey.** Each year, BLS conducts an annual survey of occupational injuries and illnesses to produce national statistics. The OSHA injury and illness records maintained by employers in their establishments serve as the basis for this survey.

**Bureau of Labor Statistics (BLS).** The Bureau of Labor Statistics is the agency responsible for administering and maintaining the OSHA record keeping system and for collecting, compiling, and analyzing work injury and illness statistics.

**Certification.** The person who supervises the preparation of the Log and Summary of Occupational Injuries and Illnesses, OSHA No. 200, certifies that it is true and complete by signing the last page of, or by appending a statement to that effect to, the annual summary.

**Cooperative program.** A program jointly conducted by the states and the federal government to collect occupational injury and illness statistics.

**Employee.** One who is employed in the business of his or her employer affecting commerce.

**Employee representative.** Anyone designated by the employee for the purpose of gaining access to the employer's log of occupational injuries and illnesses.

**Employer.** Any person engaged in a business affecting commerce who has employees.

**Establishment.** A single physical location where business is conducted or where services or industrial operations are performed; the place where the employees report for work, operate from, or from which they are paid.

**Exposure.** The reasonable likelihood that a worker is or was subject to some effect, influence, or safety hazard; or in contact with a hazardous chemical or physical agent at a sufficient concentration and duration to produce an illness.

**Federal Register.** The official source of information and notification on OSHA's proposed rule making, standards, regulations, and other official matters, including amendments, corrections, insertions, or deletions.

**First aid.** Any one-time treatment and subsequent observation of minor scratches, cuts, burns, splinters, and so forth, which do not ordinarily require medical care. Such treatment and observation are considered first aid even though provided by a physician or registered professional personnel.

**First report of injury.** A workers compensation form which may qualify as a substitute for the supplementary record, OSHA No. 101.

**Incidence rate.** The number of injuries, illnesses, or lost workdays related to a common exposure base of 100 full-time workers. The common exposure base enables one to make accurate interindustry comparisons, trend analysis over time, or comparisons among firms regardless of size. This rate is calculated as:

$$N/EH \times 200,000$$

where:

N = number of injuries and/or illnesses or lost workdays

EH = total hours worked by all employees during calendar year

200,000 = base for 100 full-time equivalent workers (working 40 hours per week, 50 weeks per year).

**Log and Summary (OSHA No. 200).** The OSHA record keeping form used to list injuries and illnesses and to note the extent of each case.

**Lost workday cases.** Cases which involve days away from work or days of restricted work activity, or both.

**Lost workdays.** The number of workdays (consecutive or not), beyond the day of injury or onset of illness, the employee was away from work or limited to restricted work activity because of an occupational injury or illness.

1. *Lost workdays—away from work.* The number of workdays (consecutive or not) on which the employee would have worked but could not because of occupational injury or illness.

2. *Lost workdays—restricted work activity.* The number of workdays (consecutive or not) on which, because of injury or illness: (1) the employee was assigned to another job on a temporary basis; (2) the employee worked at a permanent job less than full time; or (3) the employee worked at a permanently assigned job but could not perform all duties normally connected with it.

   The number of days away from work or days of restricted work activity does not include the day of injury or onset of illness or any days on which the employee would not have worked even though able to work.

**Low-hazard industries.** Selected industries in retail trade; finance, insurance, and real estate; and services which are regularly exempt from OSHA record keeping. To be included in this exemption, an industry must fall within an SIC not targeted for general schedule inspections and must have an average lost workday case injury rate for a designated 3-year measurement period at or below 75 percent of the U.S. private sector average rate.

**Medical treatment.** Includes treatment of injuries administered by physicians, registered professional personnel, or lay persons (i.e., nonmedical personnel). Medical treatment does not include first aid treatment (one-time treatment and subsequent observation of minor scratches, cuts, burns, splinters, and so forth, which do not ordinarily require medical care) even though provided by a physician or registered professional personnel.

**Occupational illness.** Any abnormal condition or disorder, other than one resulting from an occupational injury, caused by exposure to environmental factors associated with employment. May include acute and chronic illnesses or diseases which may be caused by inhalation, absorption, ingestion, or direct contact. The following categories should be used by employers to classify recordable occupational illnesses on the log in the columns indicated:

### Column 7a. Occupational skin diseases or disorders

Examples: Contact dermatitis, eczema, or rash caused by primary irritants and sensitizers or poisonous plants; oil acne; chrome ulcers; chemical burns or inflammations

### Column 7b. Dust diseases of the lungs (pneumoconioses)

Examples: Silicosis, asbestosis, and other asbestos-related diseases, coal worker's pneumoconiosis, byssinosis, siderosis, and other pneumoconioses

### Column 7c. Respiratory conditions due to toxic agents

Examples: Pneumonitis, pharyngitis, rhinitis or acute congestion due to chemicals, dusts, gases, or fumes; farmer's lung

### Column 7d. Poisoning (systemic effects of toxic materials)

Examples: Poisoning by lead, mercury, cadmium, arsenic, or other metals; poisoning by carbon monoxide, hydrogen sulfide, or other gases; poisoning by benzol, carbon tetrachloride, or other organic solvents; poisoning by insecticide sprays such as parathion, lead arsenate; poisoning by other chemicals such as formaldehyde, plastics, and resins

### Column 7e. Disorders due to physical agents (other than toxic materials)

Examples: Heatstroke, sunstroke, heat exhaustion, and other effects of environmental heat; freezing, frostbite, and effects of exposure to low temperatures; caisson disease; effects of ionizing radiation (isotopes, X-rays, radium); effects of nonionizing radiation (welding flash, ultra-violet rays, microwaves, sunburn)

### Column 7f. Disorders associated with repeated trauma

Examples: Noise-induced hearing loss; synovitis, tenosynovitis, and bursitis; Raynaud's phenomena; and other conditions due to repeated motion, vibration, or pressure

### Column 7g. All other occupational illnesses

Examples: Anthrax, brucellosis, infectious hepatitis, malignant and benign tumors, food poisoning, histoplasmosis, coccidioidomycosis

**Occupational injury.** Any injury such as a cut, fracture, sprain, or amputation which results from a work accident or from a single instantaneous exposure in the work environment. Note: Conditions resulting from animal bites, such as insect or snake bites, and from one-time exposure to chemicals are considered to be injuries.

**Occupational injuries and illnesses, extent and outcome.** All recordable occupational injuries and illnesses resulting in either:

1. Fatalities, regardless of the time between the injury, or the length of illness, and death;

2. Lost workday cases, other than fatalities, that result in lost workdays; or

3. Nonfatal cases without lost workdays.

**Occupational Safety and Health Administration (OSHA).** OSHA is responsible for developing, implementing, and enforcing safety and health standards and regulations. OSHA works with employers and employees to foster effective safety and health programs which reduce workplace hazards.

**Posting.** The annual summary of occupational injuries and illnesses must be posted at each establishment by February 1 and remain in place until March 1 to provide employees with the record of their establishment's injury and illness experience for the previous calendar year.

**Premises, employer's.** Consist of the employer's total establishment; they include the primary work facility and other areas in the employer's domain such as company storage facilities, cafeterias, and restrooms.

**Recordable cases.** All work-related deaths and illnesses, and those work-related injuries which result in: loss of consciousness, restriction of work or motion, transfer to another job, or require medical treatment beyond first aid.

**Record keeping system.** Refers to the nationwide system for recording and reporting occupational injuries and illnesses mandated by the Occupational Safety and Health Act of 1970 and implemented by Title 29, Code of Federal Regulations, Part 1904. This system is the only source of national statistics on job-related injuries and illnesses for the private sector.

**Regularly exempt employers.** Employers regularly exempt from OSHA record keeping include: (1) all employers with no more than 10 full- or part-time employees at any one time in the previous calendar year; and (2) all employers in retail trade; finance, insurance, and real estate; and services industries; i.e., SICs 52-89 (except building materials and garden supplies, SIC 52; general merchandise and food stores, SICs 53 and 54; hotels and other lodging places, SIC 70; repair services, SICs 75 and 76; amusement and recreation services, SIC 79; and health services, SIC 80). (Note: Some state safety and health laws may require these employers to keep OSHA records.)

**Report form.** Refers to survey form OSHA No. 200-S which is completed and returned by the surveyed reporting unit.

**Restriction of work or motion.** Occurs when the employee, because of the result of a job-related injury or illness, is physically or mentally unable to perform all or any part of his or her normal assignment during all or any part of the workday or shift.

**Single dose (prescription medication).** The measured quantity of a therapeutic agent to be taken at one time.

**Small employers.** Employers with no more than 10 full-time and/or part-time employees among all the establishments of their firm at any one time during the previous calendar year.

**Standard Industrial Classification (SIC).** A classification system developed by the Office of Management and Budget, Executive Office of the President, for use in the classification of establishments by type of activity in which engaged. Each establishment is assigned an industry code for its major activity which is determined by the product manufactured or service rendered. Establishments may be classified in 2-, 3-, or 4- digit industries according to the degree of information available.

**State (when mentioned alone).**   Refers to a state of the United States, the District of Columbia, and U.S. territories and jurisdictions.

**State agency.**   State agency administering the OSHA record keeping and reporting system. Many states cooperate directly with BLS in administering the OSHA record keeping and reporting programs. Some states have their own safety and health laws which may impose additional obligations.

**Supplementary Record (OSHA No. 101).**   The form (or equivalent) on which additional information is recorded for each injury and illness entered on the log.

**Title 29 of the Code of Federal Regulations, Parts 1900–1999.**   The parts of the Code of Federal Regulations which contain OSHA regulations.

**Volunteers.**   Workers who are not considered to be employees under the act when they serve of their own free will without compensation.

**Work environment.**   Consists of the employer's premises and other locations where employees are engaged in work-related activities or are present as a condition of their employment. The work environment includes not only physical locations, but also the equipment or materials used by the employee during the course of his or her work.

**Workers' compensation systems.**   State systems that provide medical benefits and/or indemnity compensation to victims of work-related injuries and illnesses.

# 9

# LABOR RELATIONS

- Key Issues in Labor Relations
- Questions and Answers on Retaining Union-Free Status
- What You Should Know About Plant Closings and Layoffs/Sample Labor Relations Letters
- Arbitration of Employment Disputes

# LABOR RELATIONS

The pros and cons of unionization will be debated forever. Whether you are pro-union or against unions is immaterial, what you need to determine in your particular business venture is whether you think your company needs union representation. Most business people feel that they do not need an outside third party telling them how to run their company. However, if employees perceive that they are not being treated fairly, or paid a competitive wage, they may seek third party representation and they have that right.

## KEY ISSUES IN LABOR RELATIONS

When does a company need labor relations assistance? When should a small company that is growing formalize personnel policies? When does a company need someone assigned full time to personnel administration and human resource management? There's no simple answer to these questions but the following list will assist any businessperson in determining when a formal human resource management program is needed. When you start asking yourself if you need full-time personnel assistance or an HRM consultant do the following:

Systematically review the current policies (written or unwritten) that are followed in the organization. Are there frequent problems with any of the policies?

- Review the cost of carrying out your policies and procedures. Are the costs reasonable?

- The largest costs of doing business for most small organizations (fewer than 150 people) are employee costs. Review the costs of hiring, retaining, and replacing employees.

- Can existing policies be modified or strengthened by putting them in writing and distributing them to the employees? If they were in writing, would they save managers time from constantly interpreting policy?

- Are policies and current practices consistent with federal, state, and local laws and regulations?

- Are processes available so that employees clearly understand what is expected of them and how they are doing in meeting those expectations?

- What are the lines of up-and-down communication in the organization? Are they open and working? How do you know?

- Do you have a healthy labor relations climate, or do you have ongoing problems?

- Can you use an HR consultant on a part-time basis or do you need a full-time HR manager on staff?

If you do not have a human resource manager, perhaps it is time to hire one. Ask yourself these questions:

1. Is human resource leadership needed?
2. Is authority to make personnel decisions so diffused that it is perceived as unfair and unequal across the company?
3. Are personnel decisions either too inflexible or too loose?
4. Is effective manpower planning done? Do you have the people you need when you need them?
5. Are people receiving the training they need?
6. Are jobs filled from within, including promotions? Is there effective succession planning? Are open jobs posted, or does the company always go outside to fill jobs? If so, employee morale could be affected.
7. Do you have a lot of EEO charges? If so, in which departments and in which jobs? EEO charges can be an indication of human resource problems that should be resolved before they go too far.
8. Are you complying with all state and federal regulations?

These are just some of the questions that should be answered when considering whether to install a full human resource department or to hire a human resource professional. Keep in mind that you may not need a full-time HR manager on staff. Many small and mid-size companies use a personnel consultant part time until they get big enough, (about 250 to 300 employees) to have a full-time person.

## QUESTIONS AND ANSWERS ON RETAINING UNION-FREE STATUS

**Q.** What does it really mean to a company to remain union-free?

**A.** It means the company maintains full control of its operations. It means the human resource function can be administered in an open environment, with direct communication with employees and without third-party intervention.

**Q.** What is the key element in remaining union-free?

**A.** There are many things that foster a union-free environment, but probably the most important is competitive pay. We've all seen the articles that say pay is far down on the list of priorities for employees, but pay is very important. There are naturally other things that make an employee happy in the job, including:

- Good communications up and down in the company
- Job enrichment
- Participatory management
- A fair and impartial supervisor

- Pleasant work and working conditions
- Good pay and benefits

**Q.** How far can a company go in saying a union could do more harm than good?

**A.** It used to be that you walked a fine line between what was permissible and what was not permissible. You needed to be as strong as you could be in saying that a union may not do employees as much good as it claimed, but on the other hand, if you went too far, you ran the risk of having your statements viewed by the National Labor Relations Board as threats, and the company could be ordered to bargain on the grounds that a fair election could not be held. In June 1982, the Board began to announce policy-changing decisions that have affected basic rules of labor law. For example, the National Labor Relations Board will not rule at all now on whether campaign statements made by either side were accurate or inaccurate. The NLRB will continue, however, to set elections aside if:

- Either side uses threats, promises, or the like which interfere with employees' free choice.

- Either side uses a forgery that leaves voting employees unable to tell whether what they are reading is propaganda.

- Official NLRB documents are altered so it appears the board itself is endorsing one side or the other.

The decision that brought about this NLRB change was *The Midland National Life Insurance Company* decision on August 4, 1982.

Another significant decision of the NLRB in 1982 was the *Materials Research* decision, which held that all employees, union or nonunion, have the right to bring help to a meeting or interview that the employee fears may end in discipline. It is incumbent on the employee to ask permission to bring someone to the meeting; however, management has no obligation to advise the employee of the right to help.

## What to Do and What Not to Do When the Union Organizer Demands Recognition

A union gains the right to represent your employees:

1. by a secret ballot election conducted by the labor board;
2. by voluntary recognition; or
3. by board-ordered recognition.

In any case, you are required to bargain in good faith with the union over wages, hours, and other terms and conditions of employment.

The union has a right to demand recognition in an appropriate bargaining unit as long as a majority of your employees has signed authorization cards. You have a right to demand a labor board election if you have a good-faith doubt that the union represents a majority of your employees in a unit appropriate for bargaining.

Even when a union does represent a majority of your employees and even when you have a good-faith doubt of its majority, the union can file refusal to bargain charges against you, and the NLRB will order you to bargain without an election if management takes steps to undermine or destroy the union majority by threats or promises to your employees or by committing unfair labor practices that tend to undermine the union's majority.

A union that wants to organize or unionize a group of employees usually tries to persuade the employees to sign authorization cards or a petition. If 30 percent of the employees in an appropriate bargaining unit sign such cards or petitions, the union may petition the National Labor Relations Board for a secret-ballot election in which all eligible employees in the group or unit may vote on whether they want to be represented by the union. However, if more than 50 percent of the employees sign cards or a petition, the union may demand immediate recognition and bargaining from the employer without having to file a petition and prove its majority status in the secret-ballot election. The employer may be forced to accede to this demand and to bargain with the union without an election if the employer makes the wrong move and commits unfair labor practices when the first union contact is made.

A union that has obtained signed authorization cards or a petition from a majority of the employees sometimes demands both recognition and bargaining from the employer and files a petition for an election. Even if the union loses the election, it then may seek an order from the NLRB requiring the employer to recognize and bargain with the union. Thus, the employer's actions after receiving a demand for bargaining must be carefully planned even if the union has also filed a petition for an election.

Once a union has obtained signed authorization cards or a petition from a majority of the employees in an appropriate unit, it almost always will make a demand on the employer for immediate recognition and bargaining. This demand may or may not be a prelude to or be accompanied by the filing of a petition for an election with the NLRB. However, in either case, the manner in which the demand is presented to the employer may vary. It may be by (1) letter, (2) telegram, (3) telephone, (4) personal visit by union representatives, or (5) a combination of these methods.

If and when a demand for recognition is made in person by a union organizer, *do not:*

- Ask to see the cards.
- Look at any lists of employees.
- Discuss, look at, review, count, or accept any cards or even flip through them if they are handed to you or deposited on your desk.
- Review or comment upon any offered document that may be or purports to be a labor agreement.
- Look at, discuss, or review any writing or paper they may attempt to hand you or deposit on your desk.
- Refuse to talk to or meet with union representatives if they are already in your presence.
- Poll or interview your employees to ascertain whether they signed cards.
- Engage in objectionable conduct that may tend to undermine the union's majority.
- Threaten employees, directly or by implication.
- Make promises, directly or by implication.
- interrogate employees about union activities or the union campaign.

When a demand is made, *do:*

- Arrange to have a witness with you if at all possible. There is no need to have a secretary present to record or transcribe what was said during the visit.

- Remain calm and dignified. Keep your cool.

- Ask questions. You run the show, and if you have difficulty, ask them to leave and not return until they can act courteously and in a businesslike manner. Be a good listener! Do not engage in small talk about matters having nothing to do with the purpose of the visit. Do not talk about children, sports, hunting, fishing, the weather, or the state of the nation. The less said, the better. Keep the meeting short.

- When the union representatives identify themselves, either get their calling cards or, carefully and specifically, in their presence, put down their names, addresses, and exactly who it is they claim to represent.

- Ask them to state their business. Obtain, but do not give, information. If and when they claim in any form to represent your employees, state clearly, "I have good-faith doubt that your union does, in fact, represent an uncoerced majority of our employees in an appropriate bargaining unit."

If the union organizer suggests that you agree on a professor, federal mediator, or someone like that to check the cards for the purpose of verifying the union's majority, stand firm on the ground that you believe justice would be better served by utilizing the orderly processes of the governmental agency set up to handle them and to make the necessary determinations.

Should the cards be put on your desk or thrown at you in leaving, you should have someone witness that you put them in an envelope at the moment and sealed them without looking at them.

On receipt of any letter, answer the letter in a reasonable period of time. The letter should state your "good-faith doubt that the union does, in fact, represent an uncoerced majority of the employees in a unit appropriate for bargaining."

**Q.** What are employee, management, and union rights?

**A.** Employee rights include:

- The right to form and join a union.
- The right to vote the way they want.
- The right to vote join or not join a union.

Management rights include:

- The right to wage a campaign and to talk about union negatives.
- The right to run your own business.
- The right of free speech.
- The right to answer false and misleading charges.

Union rights include:

- The right to organize and make promises.
- The right to bring charges against the employer. The right to picket for a certain period of time.

Labor relations is a difficult and highly regulated area of human resource management. If you are having labor problems it is a good idea to retain a labor attorney.

There are also excellent consulting groups around the U.S. that provide labor relations assistance. One such organization is Mountain States Employers Council in Denver, Colorado, 303-839-5177.

# WHAT YOU SHOULD KNOW ABOUT PLANT CLOSINGS AND LAYOFFS/SAMPLE LABOR RELATIONS LETTERS

The Worker Adjustment and Retraining Notification Act requires employers of 100 or more full-time workers to give 60 days advance notice of closings or major layoffs. It became effective in February 1989, and impacts employers who are closing a facility or an operating unit with 50 or more workers, or who will be laying off over 50 employees. Please note that there is a layoff checklist in the checklist section of this book.

The following letters and memos are provided to give you a start at writing documents regarding layoffs and reductions in force. You should modify them to fit your specific needs.

# LETTER TO BRANCH PERSONNEL MANAGER ON PREPARING FOR A LAYOFF

Date

Ms. Gwen Chavez
Personnel Manager
The Aimes Company
1839 W. 19th Avenue
Chicago, IL 89000

Dear Gwen:

I am following up on our telephone conversation regarding the impending layoff at our Los Angeles facility.

Layoffs are certainly unpleasant, but if you prepare ahead of time and account for all contingencies in advance, you can manage a smooth transition.

The following are items to consider when preparing for a layoff:

- How many people will be involved?
- What departments are involved?
- What will be the layoff criteria? Performance, seniority, job elimination? If it is a job elimination, it may be a reduction in force, rather than a layoff, which means there may be no recall rights involved.
- Prepare a layoff policy, stating criteria decided upon and what regular pay, severance, and vacation pay will be paid.
- Determine how much advance notice will be given.
- Before a reduction in force, some companies poll employees to determine whether anyone wishes to quit voluntarily. If any employees do, the company gives them severance pay.
- Ask employees of retirement age if they wish to take early retirement and receive severance pay.
- Decide when the layoff notice is given whether employees will be allowed time to look for a job before the layoff date.
- Develop a seniority list.
- Review lists of company property held by employees who will be laid off.
- Draft letters from management to employees regarding the layoff.
- Prepare a press release. Send it to the newspapers after employees have been notified.
- Have appropriate benefits people make arrangements regarding medical and life insurance coverage. Review pension plans if you have such benefits. Provide insurance conversion forms and send COBRA notifications.
- Prepare an information sheet to hand out to employees regarding what benefits they will have and for how long.
- Decide on the amount of severance and unused vacation that will be paid to each employee.
- Prepare an out placement program that includes workshops in writing a resume and interviewing.
- Provide employees with information on how to collect unemployment insurance.
- Contact employers in the area to find out if they have any employment opportunities.

A layoff or reduction in force is never pleasant, but if you have a game plan it makes the whole effort much easier.

Sincerely,

Fred K. Adams
Director, Human Resources

## MEMO TO EMPLOYEES REGARDING A REDUCTION IN FORCE

Date

**TO:**     All Salt Lake City Employees

**FROM:**   Raymond C. Davidson
            President, Davidson Corporation

**SUBJ:**   REDUCTION IN FORCE

---

You will recall that a very stringent cost-improvement program was implemented at Davidson Corporation with the expectation that the economy would recover by midyear. Unfortunately, that has not occurred, and the economic outlook continues to be uncertain.

Therefore, it is necessary at this time to take a most difficult step and reduce the number of our employees. The reduction in force will take place immediately, and affected employees at the Salt Lake City operation will be informed by their managers.

Terminated employees will be paid through September and will receive severance pay according to their years of service. We have made arrangements to provide medical and hospitalization coverage for these employees through October and will provide job counseling and assistance in preparing résumés.

Any questions concerning these actions should be directed to your immediate manager or to the Human Resources Department.

We expect market conditions to improve and hope that the remaining organization will permit us to fully meet the demands of these expected improvements. It is important to note that this is a permanent reduction in force, not a temporary layoff situation.

We are sorry to be losing many good employees and wish you the best of luck in finding new positions. The company will be providing out placement services including resume preparation classes. Ask your manager about these benefits.

In addition, you will be receiving a letter in the next few days telling you about your medical benefits and the costs of continuation for the next 18 months.

If you have other questions, please ask your immediate supervisor.

## LETTER TO EMPLOYEE REGARDING A REDUCTION IN WORKFORCE

Date

Mr. Fred L. Fine
14390 32nd Avenue
Los Angeles, CA 90031

Dear Fred:

Due to current economic conditions and our inability to finalize several of our current projects on a timely basis, we have found it necessary to have a reduction in force, and we are terminating your employment effective October 8. The company agrees to pay you, however, for an additional 30 days through November 7; all unused and accrued vacation; and severance pay at the rate of two weeks for each year of service up to a maximum of 26 weeks.

You understand and agree that this severance payment is in lieu of all other payments and benefits due you as a result of your employment at Macro-Software Company and its affiliate companies except those payments and benefits specifically identified in this letter.

In addition to termination pay, severance pay, and vacation pay, the company will pay your medical insurance coverage through December. All other benefits cease October 8. You will have the right to continue medical coverage at your own expense for an additional 18 months.

The company is also prepared to provide job search counseling and résumé assistance to those employees who request it. Please notify us no later than October 15 if you wish to receive these services.

A letter reviewing specific details of your particular benefits and severance pay will be mailed to your home on October 10.

We wish you the best of luck in your future career endeavors.

Sincerely,


Fred K. Adams
Director, Human Resources

## LETTER OF NOTIFICATION OF LAYOFF

Date

Ms. Julie Waltham
250 Mt. Aubum Street
Cambridge, MA 02138

Dear Julie:

Due to current economic conditions and our inability to finalize on a timely basis several new projects, we have found it necessary to have a reduction in force, and we are terminating your employment, effective Friday, July 30. However, in view of your ten years of service to the Company, we agree to pay you an additional 30 days through August 31, plus all unused accrued vacation, and severance pay as follows:

| | |
|---|---|
| Unused vacation | $1,000 |
| Severance pay = one week's pay for each year of service | $5,000 |
| Total | $6,000 |

You will receive all severance and vacation pay in one check on Friday, July 30.

You understand and agree that this severance payment is in lieu of all other payments and benefits due you as a result of your employment by Webster-Stone Company and its parent or affiliate companies, except those payments and benefits specifically identified in this letter.

You will receive your normal pay checks on August 5 and August 20, and your final check for August on September 5. Normal direct deposit procedures will apply for the August 5 check if you have already chosen that option. For other people, it will be sent to their homes. Please complete the attached instruction to Payroll for the checks of August 20 and September 5. If applicable, make sure your final time card is filled out, signed, and forwarded to Payroll immediately.

In addition to termination pay, severance pay, and vacation pay, the Company will pay your medical insurance coverage for the months of August and September. All other benefits will cease as of July 30.

The Company is also prepared to provide out placement assistance to those individuals who request it. Please contact Ruth Span, ext. 2902, by August 6 to participate in our outplacement service.

For more specific details on your benefit coverage, refer to the attached summary. If you have any questions, please contact me.

Sincerely,


Linden Blue
Vice-President, Human Resources

Attachments

Read and accepted:


_____          _____
Employee Signature                                        Date

## LETTER OF TERMINATION—REDUCTION IN FORCE

Date

Mr. Kenneth W. Long
537 Washakie Avenue
Rockville, MD 20852

Dear Kenneth:

Please be advised that we are terminating your employment, effective February 15 due to a need to reduce our workhorse. In view of your year of service to the Company we agree to pay you the following severance:

| | | |
|---|---|---|
| Regular wages | | $1,116.76 |
| Vacation (none—already taken in November) | | |
| Severance Pay | | $1.030.77 |
| | | $2,147.53 |
| Less: | FIT | -632.05 |
| | FICA | -143.88 |
| | Savings Bond | -25.00 |
| Net: | | $1,346.60 |

If you desire, you may continue your medical insurance coverage at your expense under COBRA regulations. The choice to continue must be made within sixty days of your termination. If it is your desire to continue coverage, contact Mary Bell in the benefits office for additional information.

You understand and agree that this severance payment is in lieu of all other payments and benefits due you as a result of your employment by RMSE and its parent or affiliate companies.

Sincerely,


Myrna Browne
Personnel Manager

Read and accepted:


_____          _____
Kenneth W. Long                          Date

# ARBITRATION OF EMPLOYMENT DISPUTES

In the last few years, employers have seen a number of employment laws passed, including the Americans with Disabilities Act, Family and Medical Leave Act, Small Business Job Protection Act, and the Health Insurance Portability and Accountability Act. In addition to these relatively new laws, there has been unprecedented litigation activity related to Title VII claims, the Age Discrimination in Employment Act, state discrimination laws, and a number of common law claims. Compounding this problem for companies is the fact that, in addition to the enormous number of cases being filed by disgruntled ex-employees, juries seem to be awarding larger and larger damage amounts to plaintiffs in these cases.

More often today, employers are seeking alternatives to the slow and very expensive process of litigation. The attraction of alternative dispute resolution (ADR) has been tempting employers for some time. One of the dispute methods thought to be a viable and preferable alternative to litigation is binding arbitration. Only recently, however, have the courts provided much guidance as to the effectiveness and legitimacy of arbitration.

In 1991, the Supreme Court issued a landmark decision in *Gilmer v. Interstate Johnson Lane Corp.* This case and those that have followed have profoundly affected the resolution of employment law disputes. In light of these cases, many employers are turning to binding arbitration in an effort to avoid costly litigation. Although many questions remain unanswered by the Supreme Court, a substantial body of law is developing in lower courts that suggests arbitration may provide a viable alternative to litigation.

# 10

# PERSONNEL LETTERS AND MEMOS

- Letter to Applicant Confirming Employment Offer
- Replies to Applicants
- Applicant Rejection Letter
- Sample ADA Accommodation Letter
- Letter Requesting Employment Verification
- New Employee Welcome
- New Employee Orientation Schedule
- Orientation Schedule
- Employee Secrecy Agreement
- Confidentiality Agreement
- Letter to New Employee Regarding Conflict of Interest
- Letter Regarding Rehire and Reinstatement of Benefits
- Job Sharing Proposal
- Confirmation of Transfer Decision
- To Employee Regarding Request for a Leave of Absence
- Letter to Branch Manager on Use of Independent Contractors
- To Employees Informing of an Impending Layoff
- Notification of Layoff
- Letter to Employees Regarding Notice of Plant Closing
- To All Employees Regarding Company Relocation
- Letter Informing Employee of Being Placed on 60-Day Performance Improvement Plan
- Unacceptable Work Performance—Must Improve

*continued,*

- Letter Informing Employee of Disciplinary Action
- Letter to Employee Regarding Suspension Without Pay
- Written Warning for Excessive Absenteeism
- Letter to Employee on Termination for Excessive Absenteeism
- Termination for Theft of Company Property
- To Employee with a Substance Abuse Problem
- Letter to Employee on Termination for Intoxication on the Job
- Memorandum to All Employees Regarding Drug Testing
- Department Managers on Turnover Analysis
- Request for Additional Salary Budget
- Reviewing Company Policy on Salary Increases When Employee Is on Leave of Absence
- To Employee Regarding Company Privacy Policy
- To Human Resources Manager Regarding Employee Privacy
- Letter to Personnel Manager Regarding Corporate Procedures for Employees Wishing to File a Complaint
- Memorandum to Division Manager Regarding Sexual Harassment
- To Manager Regarding Sexual Harassment Complaint
- To Employee Regarding Her Sexual Harassment Complaint
- To EEOC Regarding Allegation of Age Discrimination Charge
- To Employees Covering Annual Report of Employee Benefit Plans
- Letter Questioning Claims Processing Time
- Letter to Employee Requesting 401(k) Hardship Withdrawal
- Memorandum to Employees Announcing a New Company Benefit
- Confirming Company Participation in Support of Employee Bowling League
- To Employees Regarding United Way Drive
- Sample COBRA Letter to Employees: Summary of Rights and Obligations Regarding Continuation of Group Health Plan Coverage
- Sample COBRA Letter to Terminating Employee or Dependent
- Sample Alternative COBRA Letter to Employees
- Condolences on Death of Employee's Spouse

# Letter to Applicant Confirming Employment Offer

Date

Mr. Scott Lever
2109 South Hoyt Way
Albuquerque, NM 87197

Dear Mr. Lever:

Thank you for giving us the opportunity to discuss a professional position with our firm. It was a pleasure meeting you and discussing your personal and professional goals and the ways in which employment with our firm might help you achieve them.

We take great pleasure in welcoming our employment offer to you as an assistant on our professional accounting staff Your starting salary will be $3,000 per month. In addition, you will be compensated for overtime hours as an accounting staff person. The agreed upon starting date is July 6.

I believe that the dedication and ability you have shown in preparing for the accounting profession will start you on the right foot, and with your ongoing commitment, will allow you to achieve your goals. We do let all new employees know that we are an "at will" employer and either the employee or the employer may terminate the employment relationship at any time with or without prior notice.

Again, we're delighted that you have accepted our employment offer and we look forward to seeing you in July. In the interim, if you have any questions please feel free to call us.

Sincerely,


Karen West
Human Resource Manager

## REPLIES TO APPLICANTS

Date

Mr. Stephen L. Lipscomb
380 South Corona
Albuquerque, NM 87108

Dear Mr. Lipscomb:

Thank you for your inquiry regarding our advertisement for a plant manager.

Although we are impressed with your abilities and accomplishments, we have filled the position with another candidate whose experience is better suited to our current needs. The information you submitted will be retained for one year, and you will be contacted if an appropriate position becomes available within that time.

Your interest in New Mexico Equipment Company is very much appreciated.

Sincerely,


Ruth L. Aspen
Employment Manager

## REPLIES TO APPLICANTS

Date

Mr. Daniel M. Norton
10840 Foothill Road
Golden, CO 80401

Dear Mr. Norton:

Thank you for your inquiry regarding employment opportunities with the Brown Construction Company.

Unfortunately, we do not anticipate any openings for construction workers at the time you expect to graduate. However, the information that you submitted will be retained for one year, and you will be contacted should an appropriate position open within that time.

Your interest in our company is appreciated, and we wish you success in your job search.

Sincerely,


James C. Wade
Human Resources Manager

REPLIES TO APPLICANTS

Date

Mr. R. O. Hibler
639 North Miller Drive
Salt Lake City, UT 84120

Dear Mr. Hibler:

Your letter to Mr. James C. Smith, president of Rocky Mountain Energy Company, regarding employment opportunities with our company has been referred to me for response.

Your skills and background are impressive; however, at this time we do not have an open position that would fit your qualifications. We will keep your résumé on file and will contact you if an appropriate position should become available.

In the meantime, another possibility might be our corporate audit staff. If you are interested, you may contact or send your résumé to Mr. Charles Billing, Assistant Controller, Lancaster Corporation, 1416 Gilpin Street, Omaha, Nebraska 68179.

Sincerely,



Andrew E. James
Human Resources Manager

## APPLICANT REJECTION LETTER

Date _____

Dear _____:

Thank you for your response to our recent advertisement for the position of _____
_____.

We appreciated the opportunity to review your credentials and were pleased that you are interested in employment with the _____ Company.

We have narrowed our search to those few applicants who have the specific qualifications and experience we need for this position. Although your credentials do not specifically meet our current needs, we will retain your résumé for six months in the event that an appropriate career opportunity becomes available.

Thanks again for your interest. We wish you the best of luck in your job search.

Sincerely,



Vice President
Human Resources

## SAMPLE ADA ACCOMMODATION LETTER

DATE

ADDRESS

Dear Mr./Mrs. _____:

Thank you for applying for the position of _____ at XYZ Company. We had a number of qualified applicants for the position and have chosen another candidate who met all of the qualifications for the position. After speaking with your contact person, we ascertained that because of your hearing disability you are not able to use a regular telephone or an amplifier on a regular telephone.

The job description for this position states that the physical qualifications for the job require "a normal range of hearing and vision." Frequent telephone discussions with clients, contractors, and vendors are an integral part of this job (see attached job description).

With your experience we feel you could perform some of the essential job functions, but one of the most important functions is use of a telephone. The Company would be willing to make an accommodation for you if you could use an amplifier on our telephone, but the cost of a special telephone system would create an undue financial hardship on the Company and an administrative burden we're not able to accommodate.

We thank you for contacting us and applying for the position and wish you luck in your job search.

Sincerely,


Human Resources Manager
XYZ Company

## LETTER REQUESTING EMPLOYMENT VERIFICATION

Date

Mr. John Smith
Personnel Director
Financial Services Corporation
815 16th Street NW
Washington, DC 20006

Ref:  Employment Verification
Carol L. Mills

Dear Mr. Smith:

The person identified above is being considered for employment and has signed our employment application form authorizing this inquiry. We would appreciate a statement of your experiences with this person when she was employed by your company. Please provide the information requested on the bottom of this letter and return the letter to us in the enclosed self-addressed stamped envelope at your earliest convenience. Your reply will be held in strict confidence. We sincerely appreciate your cooperation and will reciprocate with employment information on your applicants should the need arise.

Sincerely,

John Watson
Velcare Corporation

------------------------------------------------------------------------------

CONFIDENTIAL

Applicant Name and Address: _____

_____

Name and Location of Former Company: _____

_____

Dates Employed: _____

General Work Record: _____

## NEW EMPLOYEE WELCOME

Date

Ms. Joan Garcia
13150 Walnut Street
Glendale, CA 91201

Dear Joan:

Welcome to Lincoln Energy Corporation. We are looking forward to working with you and hope you will enjoy your part-time position with our company. You'll want to review the enclosed *Things to Know* guidelines.

Lincoln is the mineral resources exploration and development subsidiary of the National Energy Corporation. Other subsidiaries of National are Overland Industries and Front Range Technology Corporation.

Our organization is highly integrated and comprised of many departments, including exploration, engineering, land acquisition, human resources, accounting, data processing, drafting, marketing, law, and mineral economics. As a result, a variety of challenging opportunities are offered to those who have the skills and desire to fill our positions.

We try to provide challenging opportunities for growth for our full-time employees, and as these full-time positions become available we welcome your application for employment. Should you decide to seek permanent employment at the Lincoln Energy Corporation, you may contact our Human resources department and a staff member will be pleased to discuss career opportunities with you.

Sincerely,

John Swenson
Director of Human Resources
Enclosure: *Things to Know*

## NEW EMPLOYEE ORIENTATION SCHEDULE

Date

Mr. James C. Maddox
342 Magnolia Street
Denver, CO 80202

Dear Jim:

I am enclosing a copy of the orientation schedule for your first week of employment at Rocky Mountain Energy Company.

The orientation program has been developed to assist you in learning about the Employee Relations Department and our current projects as quickly as possible.

We are looking forward to working with you and to making your first week on the job productive and enjoyable.

Welcome to the company, and to the employee relations group.

Sincerely,

Mary F. Cook
Director, Employee Relations

## ORIENTATION SCHEDULE

**James C. Maddox**

*April 11th (Monday)*

| | | |
|---|---|---|
| 8:15–10:00 | | New Employee Orientation |
| 10:00–11:00 | Larry White | Review of current Organizational Development activities |
| 11:45 | John King | Lunch |
| 1:30–2:30 | Mary Cook | Review of current Employee Relations activities |
| 2:30–3:30 | John King | Overview of Recruiting, Employment, and Affirmative Action program |
| 3:30–5:00 | Dick Brown | Overview of Compensation, Benefits, Approval Package processes, etc. |

*April 12th (Tuesday)*

| | | |
|---|---|---|
| 8:30–noon | (Auditorium) | Attend Managers' Administrative Overview presentation |
| Noon | (Open) | Lunch |
| 2:00–4:30 | Mary Cook | Introductions around the company |

*April 13th (Wednesday)*

| | | |
|---|---|---|
| 8:30–10:30 | Mary Cook | Discussion of Succession Planning and Management Development |
| 11:45 | Dan Smith | Lunch |
| 1:30-2:30 | Dan Smith | Review of Training and Management Development programs |
| 2:30–5:00 | (Open) | |

# NEW EMPLOYEE ORIENTATION

*NOTE: All employees must attend an orientation session.*

---

Employee's Name: _____ SSN: _____

Job Title: _____ Dept.: _____ Date: _____

---

HUMAN RESOURCES DEPARTMENT: The information checked below has been given or explained to the employee.

---

*Compensation and Benefits*

- Time sheet/card ( )
- Payroll procedures ( )
- Insurance Program Booklet ( )
- Voice Booklet ( )
- Educational Assistance ( )
- Credit Union ( )
- Stock Purchase Plan ( )
- Savings Bond Plan ( )
- Sick Benefits—A&S— ( )
  Limitations, and so on

*Leaves, Promotions, and Transfers*

- Performance Evaluations ( )
- Promotions ( )
- Transfers ( )
- Vacations ( )
- Holidays ( )
- Absences—Tardiness ( )
- Jury Duty ( )
- Leaves of Absence—
  Maternity—Medical &
  Family, and so on ( )

*General*

- Code of Conduct ( )
- Employee Handbook ( )
- Complaints and Grievance
  Procedures ( )
- I.D. or Entrance Card ( )
- Introduction to the Department ( )
- Parking Facilities ( )
- Safety Guidelines ( )
- First Aid and Requirements
  for Reporting Injury ( )
- Bulletin Boards/Company Events ( )
- Voluntary Resignation Notice ( )
- Termination Procedures ( )

**SUPERVISOR:** The following is a checklist of information necessary to orient the new employee to the job in your department. Please check off each point as you discuss it with the employee and return to the Human Resources Department to be placed in the employee's personnel file.

*Welcome The New Employee*

- Review copy of employee's application. Be familiar with employee's experience, training, and education.                                ( )
- Review job description with employee, including the duties, responsibilities, and working relationships.                               ( )
- Discuss with the employee the unit organization and the department division organization. Explain the function of your department/division as related to the total organization and how the employee fits in.   ( )
- Confirm that employee has a copy of employee handbook, and has read and understands it.                                                ( )

*Introduce Employee to Co-Workers*

- Indicate to each co-worker the new employee's position.                ( )
- Explain the functions of each person as you introduce the new employee.   ( )

*Show New Employee Around the Facility*

- Tour the department, plant, or company.                               ( )
- Explain where lavatories, coffee areas, and parking facilities are located.   ( )
- Explain the various departments within the organization.              ( )

*Introduce the New Employee to Job*

- Insure that new employee's working area, equipment, tools and supplies are prepared and available.                                     ( )
- Explain the levels of supervision within the department.              ( )
- Provide new employee with necessary or required training.             ( )
- Explain use of:   Telephone (personal/company calls)                  ( )
                    Copy machines                                       ( )
                    Company vehicles                                    ( )
                    Mail procedures                                     ( )
                    Supply procedures                                   ( )
                    Personal expense reimbursement                      ( )
- Explain hours of work/overtime/call-in procedures.                    ( )
- Give new employee department telephone number.                        ( )
- Review location of department's first aid equipment.                  ( )
- Explain housekeeping responsibilities.                                ( )

*Future follow-up*

- Set date and time within one week to cover any questions or concerns ( )
  of the new employee.

---

Supervisor's Signature                           Employee's Signature

Supervisor's Title                               Date

Department

Date

*Note:* Return this form to the Human Resources Department.

## MEMO TO MANAGEMENT PERSONNEL
## REGARDING EMPLOYEE SECRECY AGREEMENT

DATE: _____

TO:        All Management Personnel

FROM:      Jonathan A. Magneson
           Chief Executive Officer

SUBJ:      EMPLOYEE SECRECY AGREEMENT

Because of the highly confidential and proprietary nature of our products, as of January 1 we will require that an employee secrecy agreement be signed by all employees currently employed and by those hired after the above date. Following is a copy of this agreement. If you have any questions regarding this new policy please contact me directly (extension 5108).

**EMPLOYEE SECRECY AGREEMENT**

I, _____, am an employee of _____ Company. As part of my duties, I have access to trade secrets of my employer such as _____. All knowledge and information I gain from these trade secrets as well as the trade secrets themselves, including all unpatented inventions, designs, know-how, trade secrets, technical information and data, specifications, blueprints, transparencies, test data, and additions, modifications, and improvements thereon which are revealed to me shall for all time and for all purposes be regarded by me as strictly confidential and held in trust by me. I will not reveal or disclose the trade secrets to any other person, firm, corporation, company, or entity now or at any time in the future unless my employer instructs me to do so in writing. This secrecy protection will continue even if I no longer am employed by _____. I understand that if I reveal the trade secrets to unauthorized persons I personally may be subject to penalties and lawsuits for injunctive relief and money damages as well as possible criminal charges by my employer.

I acknowledge that I have read and understood the contents of this Agreement and freely sign it with the intent to be legally bound hereby.


_____          _____
EMPLOYEE SIGNATURE                        DATE


_____          _____
WITNESS                                   DATE

## Confidentiality Agreement

The nature of services provided by the (*organization's name here*) requires that information be handled in a private, confidential manner.

Information about our business or our employees or clients will not be released to people or agencies outside the company without our written consent; the only exceptions to this policy will be to follow legal or regulatory guidelines. All memoranda, notes, reports, or other documents will remain part of the company's confidential records.

Personal or identifying information about our employees (such as names, addresses, phone numbers or salaries) will not be released to people not authorized by the nature of their duties to receive such information, without the consent of management and the employee.

I agree to abide by this Confidentiality Agreement.

_____

Name

_____

Witness

_____

Date

**Manager's Tip**

This form can be used for organizations that have goods or services of a proprietary nature, but it doesn't fit all situations. Adjust accordingly, or have it reviewed by legal counsel.

## LETTER TO NEW EMPLOYEE REGARDING CONFLICT OF INTEREST

Date

Mr. Marvin Williams
1023 Fourteenth Street
West Chester, PA 19382

Dear Marvin:

During the course of your employment with Johnston Services, Inc. you will meet and come in contact with many of the company's clients.

As a tenet of your faith in and loyalty to the firm, and as part of our employment arrangement with you, kindly sign, date, and return to us the enclosed copy of this letter thereby indicating that:

In the event you leave our employment for any reason whatsoever and within a period of two (2) years from the date on which your employment is terminated you serve a client of Johnston Services, Inc. in your individual capacity, as partner or stockholder in another firm, or an employee of another individual or firm, or in any other manner in a professional capacity (the character of such services being similar to those services previously rendered to such a client or clients by Johnston Services, Inc.), you will pay to Johnston Services, Inc. an amount (determined on the accrual basis) equal to the latest year's fee earned by Johnston Services, Inc. from such client or clients. For purposes of the foregoing, clients of Johnston Services, Inc. are defined to include those for whom services have been performed by Johnston Services, Inc. within the twelve month period immediately preceding the date on which your employment terminated.

Payment of any sums due, shall be made in four (4) quarterly installments, the first payment being due on the day that the initial service is rendered to the client, with a quarterly installment due on the corresponding day of every third (3rd) month thereafter until the sum is paid in full.

Very truly yours,

Robert Jones
Vice President Human Resources

Acknowledged and agreed to in full:

_____        _____
Signature                                Date

## Letter Regarding Rehire and Reinstatement of Benefits

Date

Ms. Kathleen Kane
1918 North Parkway
Colorado Springs, CO 80906

Dear Kathleen:

We appreciate your responding to our recent advertisement for an insurance administrator and letting us know that you would like to come back to work for American Insurance Company.

We have discussed your return with Jane Ackerman, Human Resources Director, and she agrees that according to our personnel policies you can be reinstated to your old position. Because your lapse in employment was less than one year, we have agreed to treat it as a leave of absence and not as a termination and rehire for the purpose of computing your future vacation and retirement benefits.

Our rehire policy states that employee benefits can be reinstated if the time an employee is gone from the Company is less one year. It is our policy, however, to require a signed agreement before you can be reinstated. This agreement is attached to this letter. Please sign the agreement and bring it to work when you return December 9.

We are pleased that you are coming back to work for American Insurance Company.

Sincerely,

John L. Macon
Vice-President, Administration

Encl. Agreement

## JOB SHARING PROPOSAL

                                                                                                    Date

Mr. L. M. Yates
Vice-President
Harding-Snelling, Inc.
399 Sherman Avenue
Palo Alto, CA 94306

Dear Larry:

Some companies have started using a concept of job design that takes advantage of complementary skills of more than one employee to carry out a specific job function. We have implemented this job- sharing concept for various reasons. Through job sharing we can accommodate the needs of a valued employee or employees, as well as provide added know-how for selected high-demand jobs as in the data processing field.

It is recommended that two candidates fill the position of Data Technician in the Evaluation Department. These two candidates are Debra Johnson and Gloria Mooton. They have expressed their desire to move from the full-time to regular part-time status. Both people have the technical expertise the company needs.

Should the position of Data Technician be shared by these two individuals on a part-time basis, each would work twenty-four hours per week. It is expected that both the quality and quantity of work output will be met, if not improved.

The position involves the collation of large amounts of data into a sensible, workable system. It is, at times, a tedious function that calls for the transferring of data collected in the field onto the computer, and then updating and correcting the computer files on a continuing basis. Over the past two years, the tasks of the technician have grown tremendously. The additional eight hours of work per week, along with the reduced hours per day per individual (six) should increase productivity and improve work flow efficiency.

The scheduling of overlapping hours and the fact that Gloria and Debbie both have good communication skills will assist them in attaining the needed additional coordination that will be required to effectively do the job. There is an anticipated increase in employee benefit costs, because the company will have to furnish benefits for two people instead of one person, but I feel the benefits outweigh the added costs.

We will monitor the effectiveness of this new job-sharing arrangement and keep you apprised.

Sincerely,


Linda M. Lancer
Personnel Manager

## Confirmation of Transfer Decision

Date

Mr. John L. Duncan
10120 West 20th Avenue
Chicago, IL 60602

Dear John:

This letter will confirm our offer to you of a transfer to our California facility at Santa Clara.

The transfer will include the following benefits:

Salary increase from $4,200 per month to $4,900 per month.

Company car—your choice of any mid-size model to be picked up on your arrival at our facility on November 28.

A relocation bonus of $3,000 to cover any out-of-pocket expenses.

Full relocation benefits, including buy-out of your current home through Trans America Relocation Services and assistance in buying a new home of similar cost. You will receive a mortgage interest rate differential payment if there is an increase in the interest rate between your old loan and the new loan.

Ralph Loomis will be your transfer and relocation contact in our personnel department. Please let him know what make of car you decide on, and give him an idea of your timing on all relocation matters. You can reach him at (312) 679-4462. You can count on him to handle all matters relative to your transfer.

I know you will enjoy your new job and the location. Santa Clara is a beautiful area. If you should have any problems at all, please give me a call; we want this transfer to be a positive experience for you and your family.

Sincerely,

Ned F. Gilbert
General Manager

## TO EMPLOYEE REGARDING REQUEST FOR A LEAVE OF ABSENCE

Date

Mr. John Elwood
31406 26th Street
Sunnyside, NY 11104

Dear John:

This letter is in response to your request for a six-month unpaid leave of absence for personal reasons.

I have discussed the leave with your Vice-President, Bob Lawson, and he agrees that you should be given the leave at this time in order to get your personal problems resolved. Bob is very supportive of you and your past performance in the job and wants to assist you in any way he can.

Your leave of absence will commence August 2 and end on February 1. During that time the company will hire a temporary employee to fill in for you on the job and will guarantee you the same position when you return to work.

Your benefits will continue while you are on leave, but you must send us a check each month to cover your medical plan. The check should be made out to the company in the amount of $75.35 and must be received by the tenth day of the month.

Your service date will remain the same. However, you will not earn vacation time or receive holiday pay during your absence.

If we can be of assistance to you in planning your leave or if you have any questions regarding your benefits, please call.

Sincerely,


Karen Kaiser
Personnel Manager

# LETTER TO BRANCH MANAGER ON USE OF INDEPENDENT CONTRACTORS

Date

Mr. Lyle Cappers
Branch Manager
Adamson Manufacturing, Inc.
418 S. Dearborn Street
Chicago, IL 60605

Dear Lyle:

We have had problems recently with some of our outlying plant operations when they use independent contractors. As you know, the IRS takes a strict view of independent contractor arrangements.

Generally the relationship of employer and employee exists when the employer has the right to control and direct the individual who performs the services, not only as to the results but also as to the details and means by which that result is accomplished. Following is a list of factors the IRS would use to determine whether an employer/employee relationship exists, rather than an independent contractor relationship:

- Work performed on the employer's premises, which might indicate control, especially when the work could be done elsewhere.
- The establishment of set hours of work by the employer.
- The furnishing of tools or materials by the employer.
- The existence of a continuing relationship.
- Payment by the employer of the worker's business and travel expenses.

Independent contractors should meet the following criteria:

- They ordinarily use their own methods and receive no training from the purchaser of services.
- They have made a significant investment in facilities and perform services for another.
- They are in a position to realize a profit or suffer a loss as a result of their services.
- Their services are available to the general public.
- They are usually responsible to complete a specific job or are legally obligated to make good for failure to complete the job.

Lyle, please be sure that a true independent relationship exists before you contract for work at the Chicago plant. If there is any question in your mind about the contracting relationship, it is better to put the worker on our payroll and pay social security (FICA) taxes.

Please make all of your supervisors and managers aware of our concern regarding using independent contractors.

Best regards,


John L. Luger
Vice President Human Resources

## TO EMPLOYEES INFORMING OF AN IMPENDING LAYOFF

**DATE:** _____

**TO:**     All Employees

**FROM:**   Bill T. Williams, President

**SUBJ:**   IMPENDING LAYOFF

It is with great regret that I must tell you that International Computer Systems Company must lay off approximately 300 employees by the end of the year in order to avoid closing down our operation altogether. This is not a step we take lightly or without a great deal of soul searching and personal reluctance on the part of our management team.

Some of our branch offices will be closed, others will be reducing staff. The criteria for reducing staff will be performance and seniority, and no bumping of employees with less seniority will be allowed.

We hope that you understand our situation and will assist us in making these moves as fair and compassionate as possible. Detailed layoff procedures including a review of the benefits you will receive will be published at the end of the week by the Human Resource Department. We will provide assistance to employees in getting resumes updated and launching a job search. Severance pay will be one week of severance for each year of employment up to a ceiling of 26 weeks.

Out placement assistance will be provided by the Human Resource Department and will commence the week of July 15.

## NOTIFICATION OF LAYOFF

Date

Ms. Cynthia Green
723 Jones Street
Cambridge, MA 02138

Dear Cynthia:

Current economic conditions and our inability to complete several projects on a timely basis have made it necessary to undergo a reduction in force. Therefore, we are terminating your employment effective Monday, January 6th. The Company agrees to pay you, however, for an additional 30 days through August 31, plus all unused accrued vacation. We will also pay severance pay at the rate of two weeks for each year of service up to a maximum of 12 weeks.

You understand and agree that this severance payment is in lieu of all other payment and benefits due you as a result of your employment by the Cambridge Company and its affiliate companies, except those payments and benefits specifically identified in this letter.

In addition to termination pay, severance pay, and vacation pay, the Company will pay your medical insurance coverage for the months of August and September. All other benefits will cease as of July 30.

The Company is also prepared to provide outplacement assistance to those individuals who request it. Please contact John Lane, ext. 415, by July 6 to participate in our out placement service.

For more specific details on your benefit coverage, refer to the attached summary. If you have any questions, please contact me.

Sincerely,


Toni Law
Vice-President, Human Resources

Attachments

Agreed and accepted:


_____          _____
Signature                                 Date

## LETTER TO EMPLOYEES REGARDING NOTICE OF PLANT CLOSING

Date

Mr. Scott Stevens
8911 E. Bellevue Street
Bangor, ME 04652

Dear Scott:

Effective March 1, the Bangor, Maine facility will be closed. The economic downturn in our business has necessitated the plant closing at this time. This was not an easy decision to make and we are saddened at the thought of shutting down our business in Maine, thus eliminating so many jobs.

It is our desire to compensate our many loyal employees in some manner, and therefore, we have approved a severance pay package that we think will help employees through this difficult transition. The severance pay will be two weeks for each year of service up to a ceiling of 26 weeks.

We are giving you 60 days' advance notice to provide an opportunity to start looking for other employment. We are contacting other companies in the area to let them know that we are closing and asking them to consider hiring our ex-employees when they have openings. Assistance will be provided in updating resumes, and workshops will be held to help employees brush up on interviewing skills.

The Company will extend paid medical benefits to all employees for 30 days after the plant closing. Further, we will make the group medical plan available to employees who want to pay for it, for another 18 months, in accordance with federal law. You will be receiving further information and correspondence regarding your employee benefits in a few weeks.

The Personnel Department has been staffed with extra people to answer questions and assist in any way they can to ease you through this difficult transition.

Sincerely,

Robert W. Wilson
Director, Human Resources

## To All Employees Regarding Company Relocation

**DATE:** _____

**TO:** ALL EMPLOYEES OF THE BISHOP-FOWLER CORPORATION

**FROM:** Lloyd T. Campbell, President

**SUBJ:** COMPANY RELOCATION

---

It is the intent of the Bishop-Fowler Corporation to relocate our main facility from Tenafly, New Jersey to Denver, Colorado on March 1 of next year, and we feel it is important to give employees advance notice of this move.

It is also our intent to provide most employees the opportunity to relocate with us, and those employees who make the choice to move will receive paid relocation benefits. Those employees who will not be offered the opportunity to move will have 60 days' notice before termination. Employees who choose not to move with the company and those who will not be offered that opportunity will receive a severance package which will include all accrued vacation pay earned through March 1, and thirty days of severance pay.

Employees will also have the opportunity to continue their medical coverage for a period of eighteen months after the company closes in New Jersey, providing they pay the monthly premiums.

The decision to move the company was not an easy one, but the savings in facilities costs and ongoing personnel and administrative costs plus other incentives the company will receive from the move make our management believe this is a positive step for us at this time.

We wanted to give you all plenty of advance notice and the opportunity to think about your future. Further information will be forthcoming on a weekly basis commencing next week via a special relocation bulletin to be published by the Personnel Department.

## LETTER INFORMING EMPLOYEE OF BEING PLACED ON
## 60-DAY PERFORMANCE IMPROVEMENT PLAN

Date

Ms. Linda M. Smith
1732 Simms Street
Cambridge, MA 02138

As a result of your unsatisfactory attendance during the past six months and your failure to correct your attendance problem after oral discussions and a written warning, you are now being placed on a 30-day formal evaluation, effective July 9 through August 8.

As we discussed earlier, the reason for this evaluation period is your chronic absenteeism and continual lack of punctuality. Over the past four months, you have been absent 30 days and late 12 times, ranging between 15 minutes and one hour.

The targets we agreed upon for your period of evaluation are:

1.   You will not be absent during the entire period of probation. Should absolute necessity, however, require absence, you will inform me prior to the absence, or, if an unexpected emergency arises, you will phone immediately in the morning and later give written justification of the absolute necessity for the absence; and

2.   You will not be late more than twice during the valuation period, and at no time will you be more than five minutes late.

I have scheduled a counseling session on July 20 to meet with you and to evaluate your progress during this period. Additionally, I would like to assure you that I will be available for discussions and counseling at any other time during this evaluation. I sincerely hope that this action will result in correction of this problem. Failure to correct this situation, however, will result in termination of your employment, either at the end of the evaluation period, or before that time if no positive improvement is evident during the early stages of the evaluation.

_____
Supervisor                                          Date

_____
Supervisor's Manager                          Date

_____          _____
Employee's Acknowledgment          Date          Personnel Manager          Date

## UNACCEPTABLE WORK PERFORMANCE—MUST IMPROVE

Date

L. W. Winthrop
1317 Cole Blvd.
Norman, OK 73019

Dear Len:

This letter is to confirm our discussion about your unacceptable work performance. After our discussion in October, you made substantial improvement and were rated as "adequate" in January. We hoped you would continue to improve. However, your performance over the last several months has again slipped into "unacceptable."

1. Your ability to analyze a business situation and design the appropriate system continues to be a problem. You still have difficulty maintaining enough flexibility to meet the goal that has been identified. The tape review for the Olsen conversion was one example we discussed during our meeting.

   To successfully perform at the programmer/analyst level, you must produce basic detail design work and be prepared to meet your project dates in a timely fashion, without constant review by your project leader.

2. Your ability to function as an effective member of a project team is still not at an acceptable level. You seem to function best when detailed specifications are provided to you and you can work on the specifications, regardless of other activities around you, and then provide results for review. The team concept is critical to successful system development in our Company. This requires that each member of the team not only work on his or her assigned area, but also contribute to the team with suggestions and support as needed.

3. Your overall cooperation and attitude are unacceptable. You exhibit an adversary relationship with management personnel and project leaders with whom you work. The ability to communicate effectively is imperative in your continued role as a programmer/analyst.

Because of the problems mentioned above, work tasks assigned to you have been substandard for the programmer/analyst position. In many cases, the tasks that have been assigned could have been handled by a junior programmer. We hope you realize that we cannot afford to classify you as a programmer/analyst and not assign the full responsibilities associated with that position with confidence that the appropriate communication, analysis, and team effort will be provided.

Over the next three months I will closely track your performance and provide you with written performance appraisals. Clearly, it is up to you to bring your performance up to an acceptable level. Continued and sustained performance is expected, or you could be terminated.

Very truly yours,

R. A. Meade
Director, Human Resources

## LETTER INFORMING EMPLOYEE OF DISCIPLINARY ACTION

Date

Dale L. Bradley
879 6 Dawn Drive
Brooklyn, NY 11210

Dear Dale:

The purpose of this letter is to describe the events that have occurred over the past several weeks and which have resulted in the need for disciplinary action, and to inform you of the conduct required on your part for continued employment with ROC.

On Thursday, January 19, you left your work assignment in Washington, D.C., without the permission of your supervisor, and traveled to Miami, Florida for personal reasons. On Friday, January 20, George Long attempted to reach you at your hotel in Washington, D.C., and was told by the desk clerk that you were no longer registered. Unaware that George had tried to reach you, you subsequently called him from Miami and told him you were still on the job in Washington. Your phone call from Miami was placed a few minutes after George had called for you in Washington. On February 1, you submitted your expense report to your supervisor and falsified the dates that you were on the job in Washington, D.C.

Inconsistencies between your expense report and the hotel receipt were noticed by your supervisor. During a review of this matter, you admitted that (a) you had left Washington, D.C., on January 19; (b) you had called George Long from Miami on January 20 and told him you were on the job in Washington; and (c) you falsified your expense statement to reflect that you were in Washington, D.C., on January 20.

These recent events have resulted in the culmination of a growing concern that I have been experiencing over the past several months relative to increasingly frequent confrontations you have had with both your fellow employees and outside business contacts.

As I have discussed with you, the acts of deception attendant to the above matter, together with the incidents of confrontation, are unacceptable and will not be permitted by either myself or the executive management of ROC. Accordingly, I am placing you on disciplinary probation for a period of six months from the date of this letter. During this period, I will carefully monitor your work activities, placing particular emphasis on your interpersonal relationships with your fellow employees and outside individuals.

Any further incidents observed during this period that are contrary to acceptable standards of behavior will result in your immediate dismissal.

Dale, we want you to succeed, and we hope that your acknowledgment of the seriousness of this situation will have a positive result on your future at Rankin Oil Company.

Sincerely,

Stanley Bishop
Personnel Director

## Letter to Employee Regarding Suspension Without Pay

Date

Mr Kenneth Bronson
60311 Monticello Street
Montgomery, AL 36130

Dear Kenneth,

This letter is to inform you that you are hereby suspended from your job for three working days commencing December 15. This disciplinary action is being taken based on the following facts:

- You fell asleep on your job on December 3 and left safety equipment in the plant unattended for over two hours.
- This is the second such incident in 30 days.

Your conduct as described above constitutes sufficient cause for disciplinary action. In addition, you have been disciplined in the past for the same problem.

Your formal disciplinary action is:

- Suspension without pay for three consecutive working days beginning December 15.

A copy of this letter will be placed in your personnel file. You have the right to respond in writing to present information or arguments rebutting this suspension. If you choose to respond, you have until 5:00 P.M. on December 14 to do so. Your response, if any, will be considered prior to the imposition of the proposed suspension. It will be assumed that you have waived the right to respond if you do not take advantage of the above alternative.

The purpose of this suspension is to impress upon you the seriousness with which we regard the above violation of employment conditions and to give you the opportunity to reflect upon your future compliance with our employment standards. Should you continue to violate the conditions of your employment, you will be subject to termination.

Sincerely,


Linda Trice
Director, Human Resources

## WRITTEN WARNING FOR EXCESSIVE ABSENTEEISM

Date

June Greet
4231 Grant Street
Omaha, NE 68131

Dear June:

This memorandum is a written warning because of your excessive absences. You must immediately improve your attendance record to acceptable standards or further discipline will result.

On several occasions I have spoken to you about your poor attendance record, and improvement was noticed for a time. However, your excessive absences always resumed. For the period covering June 2 through December 31, you were absent 36 days, excluding vacations and normal holidays. These absences are detailed below:

| Days | Reason |
|---|---|
| 18 | Called in sick |
| 7 | Doctor's appointment |
| 11 | Personal business |
| 36 days | Total |

This is more than twice the number of absences accrued by any other Company employee during this same time period.

In our discussion on July 7, you agreed to consult with the Company nurse concerning your health and to enroll in the new Company Employee Assistance Program (EAP). Failure to enroll in the EAP or any unauthorized absences from this date on could be grounds for dismissal.

If you have problems that need discussion, please do not hesitate to talk them over with me, your supervisor or our EAP representative. We will support you in your efforts to remedy this situation, but will not tolerate further absences. If you would like to discuss this further, please call me at x370.

Sincerely,


Bill Smith
Director Human Resources

## LETTER TO EMPLOYEE ON TERMINATION FOR EXCESSIVE ABSENTEEISM

Date

John W. Lawson
Route 1, Box 300
Atlanta, GA 30345

Dear John,

As stated in my letter of August 10 to you, your record of absence from work has kept you from performing the full schedule of assignments for your position. I further indicated that a continuation of that pattern of absence could lead to my recommendation for your termination.

A current review of your attendance indicates that you have been absent from work for 20 out of the last 60 days since my letter of September 12.

In view of your poor attendance record, I am recommending to the Personnel Director, Jan Smith, by copy of this letter, that your employment with the company be terminated effective October 1.

Should you desire to meet with either myself or Jan Smith for the purpose of discussing this intended action, please notify us within ten working days after receipt of this letter.

Sincerely,

Fred Preston
Plant Manager

## Termination for Theft of Company Property

Date

Mr. Larry Moody
10723 Reardon Street
Glendale, CA 91201

Dear Larry:

This letter is to inform you of my recommendation that you be terminated from your position as Purchasing Manager effective November 10.

You are hereby notified of your rights to a pre-termination meeting with the Human Resource Director prior to the effective date and your subsequent right to appeal this action.

This termination action is based upon the following facts:

- You were caught on October 10th stealing a large amount of copper tubing and trying to take the tubing from Company property in your car.

Your actions in this matter constitute a violation of Company policy, and we feel that your conduct constitutes sufficient cause for termination.

All written documents upon which this action is based are attached for your review.

You have the right to respond either orally or in writing or both in order to present information or arguments rebutting this disciplinary action and termination. If you choose to respond, you have until 5:00 P.M. on November 3 to do so. Your response, if any, will be considered prior to termination. It will be assumed that you have waived the right to respond if you do not do so by the above deadline.

Sincerely,


Lane Smith
Director Human Resources

Attachment

## TO EMPLOYEE WITH A SUBSTANCE ABUSE PROBLEM

Date

Mr. Steve Yates
295 Jones Avenue
Cleveland, OH 44105

Dear Steve:

I am writing to confirm our discussion yesterday and to further explain how the Employee Assistance Program (EAP) can be of benefit to you.

The EAP has proven very successful for many of our employees who at one time or another have been troubled by personal problems. Some of these problems are so serious that they affect their jobs and even their lives. I am referring to problems resulting from marital stress, financial difficulties, extreme emotional problems, as well as alcohol or drug abuse.

The objective of the EAP is to offer a method by which the Company can take *constructive* action in dealing with employees who have personal problems that make life difficult and impair their job performance. The goal is to help employees find professional assistance when it is needed because many employees are unable to cope with their problems alone.

The Company will not change job performance standards if you participate in the program. Work performed up to standard is still the basis for continued employment. And it should be understood that the EAP does not constitute any waiver of management's right to use disciplinary measures in situations where they are deemed appropriate.

Everything about this program is confidential. No records will be open to management. No records of the problems you and I have discussed will appear in your personnel file.

Steve, it is my sincere hope that you will avail yourself of this employee assistance program to its fullest extent. As we discussed, your job productivity and attendance record have been poor in the past several months. It will be your ongoing responsibility to work at resolving your problems so that they do not interfere with your job performance.

I am ready to assist you in any way I can. Please call me at (303) 872-6669.

Sincerely,


John Liggett
Director Human Resources

## LETTER TO EMPLOYEE ON TERMINATION FOR INTOXICATION ON THE JOB

Date

Mr. Thomas Jones
1916 Race Street
Philadelphia, PA 19103

Dear Thomas:

This is to advise you that we are terminating your employment effective July 15. This decision is based on the incident report of June 26 submitted to me by your supervisor, John Wills, and his recommendation to terminate your employment due to your intoxication during duty hours.

As you know, the first reported occurrence of your intoxication on duty was May 10. That report was placed in your personnel file, and you were advised at that time that reoccurrence would result in a disciplinary action or possibly dismissal.

This second incident of intoxication threatened the safety of other employees and adversely affected the operational efficiency and effectiveness in your work unit.

Your final paycheck, including all forms of compensation due you, is being placed in the mail today to your home address. You may continue your medical coverage for a period of 18 months if you notify us within the next 60 days of your intent to do so and send us your check for $74.05 each month to cover your medical premiums.

Sincerely,


Larry Plummer
Vice-President, Human Resources

## MEMORANDUM TO ALL EMPLOYEES REGARDING DRUG TESTING

**DATE:** _____

**TO:**   All Employees

**FROM:**  Bob Matthews
         Vice-President, Personnel

**SUBJ:**  DRUG TESTING

---

As you know, our company has a comprehensive policy against the use, sale, or possession of drugs on company property. We intend to enforce this policy as strictly as possible. We have reason to believe that some employees are using drugs at work. We hope this is not the case, but we want to inform employees that when we have reason to believe an employee is taking drugs or selling drugs on our property, we plan to carry out a thorough investigation. Our investigation may include drug testing through urinalysis and may also include the use of undercover detectives from time to time. We certainly don't like the idea of resorting to such drastic measures, but if we find reasonable evidence of drug activity we will have no choice.

It is our desire to provide other avenues for employees to use in getting off drugs, rather than resorting to such serious measures as investigation and prosecution. In keeping with this desire, we have contracted with an outside Employee Assistance Program (EAP) organization. If you need help, you can call this organization and the company will pay for treatment if you stay with the program and get off drugs. This program is strictly confidential. No one in the company will know you are getting help. Getting into the program may save your job and your life. Call 555-9987.

## DEPARTMENT MANAGERS ON TURNOVER ANALYSIS

**DATE:** _____

**TO:**     Department Managers

**FROM:**  Paul M. Mattrill, Personnel Manager

**SUBJ:**  TURNOVER ANALYSIS

---

Attached as a matter of interest is an analysis of turnover for the first four months of this year. The 192 new hires include 61 independent contractors in the Residential Sales Division. Of the 106 terminations, 34 were independent contractors, and 76 of the people had been with the company less than two years. Although a complete turnover report is not available at this time, it appears that with the inclusion of ICs to compare with last year's figures, the rate is running near 14 percent for this period. Excluding ICs, the rate is over 17 percent.

Some points to keep in mind are:

- Some turnover is expected and is healthy.
- A conservative average training cost is $3,000 per person.
- It takes twelve to eighteen months to reach full performance on the average job.
- The company is losing more than 70 percent of its people by the time they reach two years of service.
- $3,000 × 192 = $576,000 training cost, January through April
  70 percent loss by two years = $403,200.

Proper screening and interviewing of applicants and sufficient training by knowledgeable, experienced supervisors will greatly reduce costs in this area and will make it easier to justify those costs that are necessary. The Personnel Department is here to assist you in any way we can.

## REQUEST FOR ADDITIONAL SALARY BUDGET

Date

Mr. William M. Haland
Vice-President, Employee Relations
Wymore Corporation
345 Park Avenue
New York, NY 10022

Dear Bill:

As we discussed on the phone, following is an update of our request for funds to supplement our salary program in order to curtail turnover in our upper- and middle-level management staff.

Since our initial proposal on June 30, our turnover situation has continued to deteriorate. Four more managers have terminated this month, bringing the total to fifteen managers so far this year. The lack of any current major projects and the general slowdown of our business is most frequently given as a major consideration of those leaving. Of course, in almost every case, the managers leaving have accepted more responsible positions at higher salaries. Our turnover continues at one of the highest levels in our history.

To date, with few exceptions, we have been able to fill the manager vacancies internally. Our concern is that we will start losing professionals in the middle management ranks. We know that this group is also in the job market. They are also frustrated by the slowdown of activities and have been encouraged by the apparent success of the key executives who have terminated. As we noted in our initial request for supplemental funds, the actual salaries for this group have fallen behind the industry, and we do expect that we'll need a substantially larger salary budget in the coming year.

Attached is an updated list of terminations. The annualized turnover is now 18.75 percent compared to 12.5 percent for last year.

Thank you for your consideration. Please call if you need additional information.

Sincerely,

Dale L. Myers
Director, Employee Relations
Denver Division

## REVIEWING COMPANY POLICY ON SALARY INCREASES
## WHEN EMPLOYEE IS ON LEAVE OF ABSENCE

Date

Mr. Robert van Dorn
14310 Ralston Road
Arvada, CO 80006

Dear Bob:

In response to our phone conversation yesterday, I am setting out the company policy regarding salary increases effective while an employee is on leave of absence.

The disability policy defines earnings as "your regular rate of monthly compensation, excluding bonuses and overtime, in effect immediately before your disability begins." If a salary increase is processed to become effective during a period of paid disability, your salary continuation of LTD benefits will not be affected.

Benefit levels for life insurance, vacations, and pension will be increased on the effective date of the salary change. Thrift Plan is not affected since it is a function of pay actually received by an employee.

Please advise me if you have questions about the policy. I hope you are on the road to recovery and will be able to return to work soon.

Sincerely,


Joseph A. Gardino
Corporate Benefits Director

# TO EMPLOYEE REGARDING COMPANY PRIVACY POLICY

Date

Ms. Louise W. Griego
444 Cedar Lane,
Tenneck, NJ 07666

Dear Louise:

We have had several inquiries recently regarding employee privacy—privacy of personnel files, medical records, and general employee information—so we thought it would be a good idea to let you know what our current policy is.

It is the feeling of Bob Wilson, our President, and his executive staff that all employees are entitled to know what our organizational privacy boundaries are. Following are statements that relate to our company philosophy:

We will:

- Collect information relevant solely to employment purposes and reveal how that information will be used when an employee makes a request for information.
- Explain the types of records maintained and adhere to a policy of limited internal use and external disclosure.
- Assure accuracy, relevancy, and completeness of information maintained in personnel records and provide reasonable procedures to review, clarify or amend records.
- Regularly review employment privacy practices to ensure compliance with fair information policies and legal requirements.

*Personnel File Guidelines*

GenCorp Industries agrees to:

- Collect and retain personal information needed only for business or legal reasons.
- Limit access to those with a "need to know."
- Limit retention to legal or useful business reasons, and conform to regulatory retention requirements.
- Provide employees who ask with the opportunity to review their personnel file.
- Limit release of information on present or former employs to dates of employment, and current or past position, or that information required by legitimate investigatory or legal need.

- Information about an employee's pay will only be released on the specific written authorization of the individual, and then only furnished in writing.
- Will maintain sensitive information such as medical files in a separate secure location and allow access only to company medical personnel.

We hope that these guidelines on the privacy of personnel records will provide our employees with a measure of comfort regarding the collection and retention of personal information.

If you have any questions regarding this policy, please give me a call or stop by my office.

Very truly yours,


John Byers
Director Human Resources

## To Human Resources Manager Regarding Employee Privacy

Date

Mr. Harvey Long
Manager, Human Resources, Eastern Division
Johnson Computer Group
10445 Newport Harbor Center
365 Thames Street
Newport, RI 02840

Dear Harvey:

I think we will go a long way toward fostering improved employee relations if the company establishes guidelines regarding employee privacy.

As the local manager of human resources, you should be the one to articulate those guidelines, but I would like to provide you with a list of items that I think should be covered.

I would like you to periodically review the following:

- The number and types of records we maintain on employees, former employees, and applicants
- The items maintained on each record
- The uses made of information in each type of record
- Any disclosures made to parties outside of the organization
- The extent to which employees are aware and informed of the uses and disclosures of information in the records maintained on them

The policies that I would like you to set up should do the following:

- Limit the collection of information about employees to that which is relevant to specific decisions
- Inform employees of the uses to be made of any such information
- Inform employees as to the type of information being maintained on them
- Adopt procedures to ensure accuracy, timeliness, and completeness of information
- Permit employees to see, copy, correct, and amend records being maintained on them
- Limit both the internal and external use and disclosure of information

After you have written the policy and procedures on employee privacy, please review them with other executives and with supervisors and managers to get their input. Then, let's get together and review the policy on employee privacy before it is implemented.

Sincerely,

Robert T. Wilson
Vice-President Corporate Human Resources

## LETTER TO PERSONNEL MANAGER REGARDING CORPORATE PROCEDURES FOR EMPLOYEES WISHING TO FILE A COMPLAINT

Date

Mr. James L. Salinger
Personnel Manager
Cunningham Tool and Die Company
P.O. Box 966
Flushing, NY 11371

Dear Jim:

Due to the continuing labor activities at our Flushing facility, we feel it is necessary to institute a procedure to ensure that employee complaints are handled in a fair and timely fashion. Following is that new policy and procedure.

*Policy*

Good employee/employer relationships can exist only if employees believe they are being treated equitably and fairly within the management policies, procedures, and actions that influence this relationship. It is recognized that there are occasions when honest differences of opinion occur regarding the interpretation and application of policies and management actions.

The following procedure is established to provide an effective way for employees to bring problems and complaints to the attention of management, without fear of losing their jobs.

*Procedure*

Step 1—Employee discusses the complaint or problem with immediate supervisor. It is expected that every effort will be made to resolve the complaint in a fair and amicable manner at this level.

Step 2—If the employee is not satisfied with the first attempt to resolve the complaint and a response is not received within ten working days, the employee may discuss the matter with the department manager.

Step 3—If the problem still has not been resolved to the employee's satisfaction after the second step, a formal complaint may be directed to the director of human resources. A final determination is not made at this level. Within ten working days, the employee may take the complaint to the president of the company.

Step 4—The final decision on all employee complaints rests with the president.

*Documentation and Procedure Control*

A.   It is understood that any employee who makes use of the employee complaint procedure will be treated courteously and that the case will be handled confidentially at all times. An employee will not be subjected to discourteous treatment or reproach due to utilization of the complaint procedure.

B.   Under no circumstances will a documentation file become part of an employee's permanent personnel file. However, complaint procedure documentation will be maintained separately by the human resource department.

C.   Only those members of management with a need to know and who are in the employee's chain of command may have access to complaint procedure documentation.

The purpose of this policy is to encourage dialogue between employees and management, in order to resolve differences that might arise between two parties in an amicable, fair, and positive manner.

If you see any problems with this new procedure please contact me immediately. Your input is important to its implementation and success. Please make the procedure effective November 1, and let me know after the first thirty to sixty days how it is working.

Sincerely,


Leslie W. Masters
Personnel Director

## MEMORANDUM TO DIVISION MANAGER REGARDING SEXUAL HARASSMENT

**DATE:**

**TO:**      Peter V. Young
             Division Manager, Atlanta

**FROM:**    Jean M. Lipton
             Director, Human Resources

**SUBJ:**    COMPANY POLICY REGARDING SEXUAL HARASSMENT

---

We recently received a telephone call from Jan Browne regarding an allegation of sexual harassment in the Atlanta division offices.

Peter, please look into this possibility immediately, talking to all of your supervisors and managers and restating our policy on this issue to everyone in management. We will not tolerate sexual harassment.

I know that you understand the seriousness of this issue. Please be sure that our written policy is redistributed to all employees and that everyone in the Atlanta office knows the procedures for filing a complaint.

Following are my recommendations for conducting your investigation and handling the formal complaint if you do get one:

- Carefully interview employees. Obtain written statements if possible.
- Please contact our Atlanta attorneys and review the complete situation with them and get their guidance as you proceed with your investigation.
- Schedule a meeting with the alleged harasser. Interview this person and discuss the evidence obtained. Again, it is highly desirable to obtain a written statement.
- Look at the personnel records of the alleged harasser and the complainant to determine if there are any incidents that will assist in an investigation of the current complaint.
- If you find there has been harassment, consider a possible suspension pending further investigation depending on the seriousness of the situation. The terms of the suspension should require the alleged harasser to stay away from the complainant and refrain from interfering with the investigation.
- Take extreme care to preserve the confidentiality of the investigation and statements obtained. Document every step taken in this investigation.
- After consultation with our attorneys, if a final decision has been made concerning the complaint, inform those involved of your decision. Please call and bring me up to date also. You may prefer to have another management representative present during these meetings.

If you do get a formal complaint, please give me a call and provide me as well as our Atlanta attorneys with the particulars of the case. If you feel that you cannot handle the situation satisfactorily, please let me know immediately.

Please call me within the next few days to bring me up to date on your investigation.

## TO MANAGER REGARDING SEXUAL HARASSMENT COMPLAINT

Date

Gary Ryan
Accounting Manager
7341 Coyne Street
Dayton, OH 45427

Dear Gary:

We have received a complaint of sexual harassment on the part of one of your supervisors. I don't have to tell you how seriously we take any complaint of harassment. I have asked John Gray, Vice President of Human Resources, to start an immediate investigation of this complaint and provide me with the details.

The employee who has been charged with harassment is Larry Brown, a supervisor in your accounting department. Beth Jones has formally complained to us about the harassment. Please proceed with caution. We don't want to falsely accuse anyone of harassment, but at the same time we must move quickly to get to the facts of this unfortunate situation.

Please cooperate fully in this investigation and proceed quickly to learn if this allegation is true. If you find there was sexual harassment, please act immediately to terminate Larry Brown. However, if you have any doubt about the allegation, please contact me. I want to stay personally involved in the resolution of this problem.

Sincerely,


Les Johnson
President

## To Employee Regarding Her Sexual Harassment Complaint

Date

Beth Jones
1246 Timber Lane Avenue
Dayton, OH 45427

Dear Beth:

We have received your complaint of sexual harassment on the part of your supervisor Larry Brown and want you to know that we take any complaint of harassment very seriously.

I have talked to our Accounting Manager, Gary Ryan, and our Vice President of Human Resources, Jean Smith, and followed my telephone discussion with a letter to both executives asking them to launch an immediate investigation into this matter. Please be assured that if we do find harassment has taken place we will not allow it to continue. It is our intent to provide all employees with a positive work environment.

If you wish to discuss this matter further while the investigation is taking place, please feel free to call either Jean Smith or me.

Sincerely,

Les Johnson
President

## To EEOC Regarding Allegation of Age Discrimination Charge

Date

Ms. Mary Beekman
U.S. EEOC
St. Louis District Office
84 N. Hampden
St. Louis, MO 63137
RE: Case No. 111-11-111

Dear Ms. Beckman:

In response to your letter of October 2, 19XX, Manfield Corporation presents the following information for your review in the age discrimination charge filed by Sam Jones:

| *Allegation* | *Response* |
|---|---|
| 1. I was the only plant maintenance engineer over 50 years old who was terminated. | Mr. Jones chose to retire; he was not terminated. Four other engineers over age 50 are still working for the Company. |
| 2. My retirement pay is $40 a month less than the estimates I received four months ago. | The benefits calculation made in January included a tentative percent salary increase for all employees that management subsequently did not grant. The figures given Mr. Jones were preliminary estimates subject to final verification on the date he actually retired. |
| 3. My performance was acceptable, but I was not offered another job. | Since Mr. Jones voluntarily elected retirement, this allegation is not relevant. |

The Company denies that any act of discrimination occurred in Mr. Jones's decision to retire. If you need further information you may call me at (303) 592-4004.

Cordially,

Donna Patrick
Manager, Employee Relations

## TO EMPLOYEES COVERING ANNUAL REPORT OF EMPLOYEE BENEFIT PLANS

Date

Dear Fellow Employees:

As a Crossland Electronics employee, you participate in many excellent benefit plans. If you or a member of your family incurred medical expenses this past year, you are certainly aware of the value of the Medical Insurance Plan. If you have started to plan for your future financial security, you know the importance of the Pension and Savings Plans.

Chances are you are not aware of the extent of the company's cost for providing these benefits. For this reason, we are mailing under separate cover a Summary Annual Report of Employee Benefit Plans. The report is an annual statement on the financial management of certain benefits—those that are insured or have assets in the Trust Fund. In it you will find facts and figures on the following plans:

- Pension
- Life Insurance
- Medical
- Business Travel
  Accident Insurance

- Employee Stock Ownership
- Savings
- Dental
- Accidental Death and
  Dismemberment Insurance

When you consider the vital protection these plans provide, it is easy to see the importance of maintaining them on a financially sound basis. As the report shows, we can be confident that our benefits will be there when we need them. The company pays the entire cost for all these plans, except for any contributions you may make to the Savings Plan and Employee Stock Ownership Plan.

Important as these plans are, they form only part of the total benefit package. For example, you are also eligible for sick pay, long-term disability, and educational assistance. Another benefit—your yearly vacation entitlement—grows automatically with your career at Crossland.

If you have any questions on this report or any other aspect of your employee benefit program, please contact Lane K. Blake, Manager, Compensation and Benefits.

Sincerely,

Larry W. Wisner
Vice President
Human Resources

## LETTER QUESTIONING CLAIMS PROCESSING TIME

Date

Mr. Mark J. Torres
Assistant Benefits Manager
The General Life Assurance Company
    of America
136 Jones Street
Kansas City, KS 66205

Dear Mr. Torres:

I am enclosing a letter and claims log from Mrs. Jean Thompson at Electronic Data Services Corporation concerning General's claims turnaround time and unresolved claims.

We have selected a small sample of claims on the log for you to measure actual turnaround time. Please prepare a report showing date received, date paid, and number of work days required for processing.

As of May 19 we have resolved our problems with turnaround time since your last five weekly claim reports indicate that 80 percent of the claims are processed within another one to five days. Mrs. Thompson indicates a nine-work-day average for April, with a six-and-one-half-work-day average at month's end. These figures are consistent with the significant improvement in turnaround time we experienced during April.

Additionally, Mrs. Thompson indicates on the log that there are a number of claims for which no response has been received from General. Please review these claims and indicate their status to me.

In the future, we will follow up with General on any "no response" claims within twelve work days from date mailed. If this is acceptable to you, please advise me accordingly.

If you require any further information, please let me know.

Sincerely,

Harold T. Bradford
Manager, Employee Benefits

## LETTER TO EMPLOYEE REQUESTING 401(K) HARDSHIP WITHDRAWAL

Date

Ms. Julie K. Hewitt
431 Prince Street
Rochester, NY 14607

Dear Julie:

This letter is in response to your request for a hardship withdrawal from your 401(k) plan with GMI Engineering, Inc. As I mentioned to you on the telephone, GMI is covered, as are all companies who have 401(k) plans, by Internal Revenue Service regulations.

On December 9, 1988, the IRS issued Notice 88-127 which clarifies certain provisions of the 401(k) regulations including those on hardship withdrawals. Under the regulations a 401(k) plan may not make a hardship distribution unless the plan established that (a) an employee has an immediate and heavy financial need, and (b) such need cannot be satisfied from other resources reasonably available to the participant. Other resources might include selling other assets, or borrowing form a bank.

Our benefits committee does not believe that obtaining a hardship withdrawal to consolidate bills would be considered a serious hardship by the IRS, and therefore, we must deny your request for the withdrawal at this time.

Sincerely,


Martha M. Frey
Benefits Manager

## MEMORANDUM TO EMPLOYEES ANNOUNCING A NEW COMPANY BENEFIT

**DATE:** _____

**TO:**   All Employees

**FROM:**  Vern T. Watson
          Personnel Director

**DATE:**  January 1

**REF:**   NEW COMPANY BENEFIT

---

As you know, we are in the process of automating more and more of our administrative, technical, and engineering functions at Matheson Nugent.

In order to provide the necessary computer hardware and to encourage employees to learn how to use personal computers, we have designed the following computer purchase program:

- All employees who can show that a computer will increase productivity in their jobs may participate.

- The computers will be used mainly for work-related purposes, but will become the property of the employee after a two-year period.

- The company will approve an employee's proposal to buy a computer when it appears that the machine will pay for itself within 18 months through improved productivity.

- If the employee uses personal funds to purchase the computer, the company will lease the computer by paying a maximum of $1,000 over a 24-month period.

- Employees who don't have the entire up-front costs can borrow up to $1,000 to purchase the computer and pay the loan back over two years through payroll deduction.

- At the end of either arrangement the computer will belong to the employee. Employees may use the computers for personal business and take them home if they wish.

We hope that this program will enhance productivity and computer literacy and will be viewed as an enhancement to our company benefit program.

## CONFIRMING COMPANY PARTICIPATION
## IN SUPPORT OF EMPLOYEE BOWLING LEAGUE

Date

Mr. Bill Shumane
Brown Engineering Company
Box 200
Orlando, FL 32802

Dear Bill:

I'm following up on your memo and our telephone conversation with regard to the Orlando Bowling League. I have reviewed your request with management and am pleased to confirm the following support for your league:

- The company will pay the cost of shirts, with logos, and any sponsor's fees.
- It will be up to each employee to pay bowling costs and association fees.
- It is our understanding that you will have both a men's and a women's league, and that the leagues are open to all employees.

Please send a Request for Disbursement form to me for approval when you're ready. If you have any questions, don't hesitate to give me a call.

Best wishes for a winning season!

Sincerely,



David Gifford
Employee Relations Director

# To Employees Regarding United Way Drive

**DATE:** _____

**TO:**      All Employees

**FROM:**    Kathy Langston, Personnel Manager

**SUBJ:**    UNITED WAY CAMPAIGN

---

Recently Mr. Jefferson wrote to you about our annual United Way campaign goal of $25,000 in employee pledges. To kick off the campaign, we are holding a series of meetings on Thursday and Friday, October 1 and 2. So that we can avoid having entire departments at one meeting at one time, we have divided the company alphabetically into four groups. Please try to attend at the time indicated for the first letter of your last name. Of course, if you can't attend at that time, you are welcome to attend another session.

| | |
|---|---|
| A–D | 9:00 A.M., Thursday, October 1 |
| E–K | 10:00 A.M., Thursday, October 1 |
| L–R | 9:00 A.M., Friday, October 2 |
| S–Z | 10:00 A.M., Friday, October 2 |

All sessions will be held in Conference Room "A."

The meeting will consist of introductory remarks, a presentation by Norm Compton (a loaned executive from Conoco), details of the campaign, and a film about the work of the United Way.

Last year, our employees contributed $17,000, and the Company contributed $5,000 to the United Way. Attached is a breakdown of how that $22,000 may have been put to use by United Way agencies. It is a graphic illustration of how much good our dollars really can do when united with the dollars of others.

With a fair share contribution from everyone, we will surpass our $25,000 goal easily. Scoreboards will be placed at various locations in the building so that we can see how we stand.

Help us help others—so that when the campaign is over, we can say to each of you, "Thanks to YOU, it really works for all of US."

SAMPLE COBRA LETTER TO EMPLOYEES:
SUMMARY OF RIGHTS AND OBLIGATIONS REGARDING
CONTINUATION OF GROUP HEALTH PLAN COVERAGE

**TO:**          Employees of XYZ Company

**FROM:**       Director Human Resources

**DATE:**       xx/xx/xx

**SUBJECT:**    Continuation of coverage under the group health plan
                maintained by the Employer (the Plan)

---

**IT IS IMPORTANT THAT ALL COVERED INDIVIDUALS TAKE THE TIME TO READ THIS NOTICE CAREFULLY AND BE FAMILIAR WITH ITS CONTENTS.**

The Consolidated Omnibus Budget Reconciliation Act (COBRA) requires that the employer offer to employees, their spouses and dependents the opportunity for temporary extension of health (medical and dental) coverage called "continuation coverage" where coverage under the Plan would otherwise end due to certain specific events (listed below).

**To Whom Does This Continuation Apply?**

Continuation of coverage under a group health plan may be elected for the following Qualifying Events:

*Qualifying Events for Covered Employee*—If you are an employee of the XYZ Company and covered by the Company's medical and/or dental coverage, you may have the right to elect continuation coverage if you lose your group health coverage because of a termination of your employment or a reduction in your hours of employment.

*Qualifying Events for Covered Spouse*—If you are the spouse of an employee of XYZ Company and covered by the Company's medical and/or dental coverage, you may have the right to elect continuation coverage for yourself if you lose group health coverage under the Plan for any of the following reasons:

1. A termination of your spouse's employment or reduction in your spouse's hours of employment with XYZ Company;

2. The death of your spouse;

3. Divorce or legal separation from your spouse; or

4. Your spouse becomes entitled to Medicare.

*Qualifying Events for Covered Dependent Children*—If you are the covered dependent child of an employee covered by the Company's medical and/or dental coverage, you may have the right to elect continuation coverage for yourself if you lose group health coverage for any of the following reasons:

1. A termination of a parent's employment or reduction in the employee's hours of employment with XYZ Company;
2. The death of a parent employed by XYZ Company;
3. Parent's divorce or legal separation;
4. The parent employed by XYZ Company becomes entitled to Medicare;
5. You cease to be a "dependent child" under the XYZ Company Plan (for example, you are between the ages of 19 and 25 and are no longer a full-time student, or you are over the age of 25 irrespective of whether or not you are a full-time student).

Rights similar to those described above may apply to retirees, spouses, and dependents if the employer commences a bankruptcy proceeding and these individuals lose coverage within one year of one or one year after the bankruptcy filing.

The taking of leave under the Family & Medical Leave Act does not constitute a qualifying event under COBRA.

## What Is the Election Period and Coverage?

The employee or a family member has the responsibility to inform the Company/Plan administrator via enrollment/change form of a divorce, legal separation, or a child losing dependent status under the company's medical and/or dental coverage within 60 days of the date of the event or the date on which coverage would end under the Plan because of the event, whichever is later.

When the employer is notified that one of these events has happened, you will be notified that you have the right to choose continuation coverage. You have at least 60 days from the date you would lose coverage because of one of the events described above to inform the employer that you want continuation coverage.

If you do not choose continuation coverage within the 60 day election period, your opportunity to elect group health insurance coverage will end.

If a qualified beneficiary elects continuation coverage and pays the applicable premium, the employer will provide the qualified beneficiary with coverage that is identical to the coverage provided under the Plan to similarly situated employees and/or covered dependents.

## For What Period of Time May the Coverages be Continued?

1. *18 Months of Continued Coverage*

    If the event causing the loss of coverage is a termination of employment or a reduction in work hours, each qualified beneficiary will have the opportunity to continue coverage for 18 months from the date of the qualifying event.

2. *29 Months of Continued Coverage*

Continuation of coverage can be extended to 29 months if a qualified beneficiary is disabled in accordance with the provisions of the Social Security Act at the time of the covered employee's termination of employment or reduction of hours. The extension to 29 months is available only if the qualified beneficiary provides notice of the determination of his or her disability under the Social Security Act within the 18-month period after the qualified event. The notice must be given within 60 days after the date of the disability determination to the employer. The employer must also be notified of any final determination that the qualified beneficiary is no longer disabled.

3. *36 Months of Continued Coverage*

If the event causing the loss of coverage was the death of the employee, divorce, legal separation, or a dependent child ceasing to be a dependent child under the XYZ Company's medical and/or dental plan, each qualified beneficiary will have the opportunity to continue coverage *up to 36 months* from the date of the qualifying event.

*Secondary Events*—An extension of the 18 month continuation period can occur, if *during the 18 months* of continuation coverage, a secondary event takes place (divorce, legal separation, death, Medicare entitlement, or a dependent child ceasing to be a dependent). If a secondary event does take place, then the 18 months of continuation coverage can be extended to 36 months from the original qualifying event.

If a secondary event occurs, it is the responsibility of the qualified beneficiary to notify the employer. In no event, however, will continuation coverage last beyond 36 months from the date of the event that originally made the qualified beneficiary eligible for continuation coverage.

*Medicare Entitlement*—There is a special rule for Medicare entitlement. If a covered employee has an 18-month qualifying event and becomes entitled to Medicare during that period, the continuation coverage period for qualified beneficiaries (for example, spouse less than 65 years old) other than the covered employee will be terminated 36 months from the date the covered employee becomes entitled to Medicare.

**Under what Circumstances May Coverage Under This Continuation Be Terminated?**

The law provides that *if elected and paid for,* continuation coverage may end prior to the maximum continuation period for any of the following reasons:

1. XYZ Company ceases to provide any group health plan to any of its employees;
2. Any required premium for continuation coverage is not paid in a timely manner;
3. A qualified beneficiary becomes covered under another group health plan that does not contain any exclusion or limitation with respect to any preexisting condition of such beneficiary;
4. A qualified beneficiary becomes entitled to Medicare;
5. A qualified beneficiary extended continuation coverage to 29 months due to a Social Security disability and a final determination has been made that the qualified beneficiary is no longer disabled;

6. A qualified beneficiary notifies the employer that they wish to cancel continuation coverage.

### When Must a Decision to Continue Be Made?

A covered employee, spouse, or dependent has 60 days from the date coverage would otherwise terminate or the date the election notice is sent to you, whichever date is later.

### How and to Whom Are Premium Payments Made?

For the first premium payment, you have 45 days from the date you elect to continue coverage to pay the retroactive premium. Thereafter, your premiums are payable on the first of each month. There is a grace period of 30 days for the regularly scheduled monthly premiums. If your payment is not received within this time basis, your insurance will be canceled. No statements will be sent.

### Important Notifications Required by an Employee, Spouse, and Dependent

The employee, spouse, or other family member has the responsibility to inform the employer of a divorce, legal separation, or a child losing dependent status under the XYZ Company's medical and/or dental coverage. This notification must be made within 60 days from whichever date is later, the date of the event or the date on which coverage would be lost because of the event. Please check with the human resource department for procedures to follow in making this notification. *If this notification is not completed in a timely manner. then rights to continuation coverage may be forfeited.*

### Notification of Address Change

To ensure that all covered individuals receive information properly and efficiently, it is important that you notify the employer of any address change as soon as possible. Failure on your part to do so may result in delayed notifications or a loss of continuation coverage options.

### Eligibility, Premiums, and Potential Conversion Rights

A qualified beneficiary does not have to show that they are insurable to elect continuation coverage. The XYZ Company however, reserves the right to verify eligibility status and terminate continuation coverage retroactively if you are determined to be ineligible or if there has been a material misrepresentation of the facts. A qualified beneficiary may have to pay all of the applicable premium plus a 2% administration charge for continuation coverage. These premiums may be adjusted in the future if the applicable premium amount changes. In addition, if continuation coverage is extended from 18 months to 29 months due to a Social Security disability, the XYZ Company can charge up to 150% of the applicable premium during the extended coverage period. There is a grace period of 30 days for the regularly scheduled monthly premiums.

### Any Questions?

If any covered individual does not understand any part of this summary notice or has questions regarding the information or your obligations, please contact the Director of Human Resources at (303) 919-9990.

## SAMPLE COBRA LETTER TO TERMINATING EMPLOYEE OR DEPENDENT

Date

Mr. Eldon Johns
32981 Harbor Street
Boston, MA 02215

Dear Eldon:

You are eligible to receive healthcare coverage from Putman Power Products Corporation as a result of the Consolidated Omnibus Budget Reconciliation Act (COBRA).

The regulation affects former employees, including retirees and dependents of employees whose coverage under our healthcare program has stopped.

Under this law, you may purchase the same medical, dental, and prescription drug coverage provided to current employees for up to 18 months. The attached sheet summarizes the items covered by the medical plan.

Your monthly cost is $175.00 for individual coverage and $300.00 for family coverage. This is equal to the company's cost of providing the same coverage to each of our current employees. You are not required to furnish proof of insurability to receive this coverage.

If you accept the coverage, you must complete, sign, and mail the enclosed application form to our Human Resources Department within 60 days of receipt of this letter. The premium is due within 45 days of your application for coverage and may be paid monthly or in a single payment. Your payments should also be mailed to the Human Resources Department.

Healthcare benefits under this program will stop automatically at the end of the 18-month period, or sooner if you stop making the payments, become covered under another employer's healthcare plan, or become eligible for Medicare. It could also stop if for some reason our company discontinued the employee healthcare plan.

Your dependent children automatically receive the same medical coverage as you if you choose to participate. They will have an opportunity to apply for the individual coverage for themselves when they no longer qualify as your dependents. This happens when they reach age 19, when they are no longer full-time students, or sooner if they get married.

If you fail to apply for coverage within 60 days of receiving this letter, or fail to send your first premium payment within 45 days of enrolling, you will forfeit your right to coverage under the healthcare plan.

If you have any questions about the program or the provision of the law, please write or call me at (212) 555-8931.

Sincerely,


Fred J. Corbin
Human Resources Manager

## SAMPLE ALTERNATIVE COBRA LETTER TO EMPLOYEES

Date

Dear Employee:

You and your eligible dependents may continue participation in the firm's group medical and dental plans even though certain events occur which would otherwise cause loss of coverage. This continued coverage is provided by the Consolidated Omnibus Budget Reconciliation Act (COBRA), a federal law enacted on April 7, 1986. This notice is intended to inform you of your rights and obligations under the continuation coverage provisions of the new law.

### How the Law Will Apply:

1. Your coverage can be extended up to 18 months if one of the following "qualifying events" occurs:
   - Your employment with the firm terminates for any reason (including voluntary resignation or retirement) other than gross misconduct.
   - Your working hours are reduced to a level at which you would no longer be eligible for coverage.

2. Coverage for your eligible dependents can be extended up to 36 months if one of the following "qualifying events" occurs:
   - They are covered under the plans and you die while still employed.
   - You or your spouse become legally separated or divorced.
   - A dependent child reaches maximum age for coverage.
   - Your spouse or dependents are under age 65 when you become eligible for Medicare and are no longer an active employee.

### The Full 18- or 36-Month Extension Will Not Apply If:

- All employer-provided medical or dental plans are terminated.
- You do not pay your required premium in a timely manner.
- You or your dependents become (an employee) covered by any other group medical and/or dental plan.
- Your former spouse remarries and becomes covered under another group medical and/or dental plan.
- A dependent becomes eligible for Medicare (Medicare eligibility terminates coverage only for the Medicare-eligible individual).

### How to Obtain This Continuation Coverage

You or a family member must notify the plan administrator in the event of a divorce or legal separation, or if a child loses dependent status under the Plan. You must notify the plan administrator of the employee's death, termination of employment, reduction of hours, or Medicare eligibility. The plan administrator will, within fourteen days of receiving notification, inform you or the dependent of the right to choose continuation coverage. You do not have to show that you are insurable to choose continuation coverage. Please note that prompt notification is extremely important. You will have at least sixty days from the date you would otherwise lose coverage to inform the plan administrator is you want continuation coverage. If you do not elect continuation coverage, your group health plan coverage will end.

### *Your Cost for Continuation Coverage*

You will be charged the full cost of coverage under the group plan in which you are enrolled. We will no longer pay a portion of it. You will also pay a 2 percent administrative charge. (*Note:* This may still be less expensive and provide better coverage than an individual health policy.)

You may pay for the continuation coverage on a monthly basis. You must make your first payment within forty-five days after the date you elect the continuation of this coverage. Subsequent payments must be made to the Human Resources Manager by _____ _____.

### *This Does Not Affect Your Normal Conversion Privilege*

You will still have the option to convert your group coverage to individual coverage. If you first elect continuation coverage under our group plan(s), your election period to convert to an individual policy will be the last 180 days of your continuation coverage. If you do *not wish* to continue coverage under the group plan(s), you must make your conversion election for individual coverage within thirty days of the date your regular group health coverage ends. The new continuation coverage option under our plan does *not* apply to life insurance. If you wish to convert your group life insurance to individual life insurance, you must elect to do so within thirty days of the date your regular group life insurance coverage ends.

If you have any questions about either the conversion option or the continuation coverage option, please call or write:

*(Insert name of your carrier)*

Also, if you have changed marital status, or you or your spouse have changed addresses, please notify the plan administrator at the above addresses.

Sincerely,

Scott Macon
Human Resources Director

## CONDOLENCES ON DEATH OF EMPLOYEE'S SPOUSE

Date

Mr. John K. Kennedy
1632 Sunset Boulevard
Los Angeles, CA 91607

Dear John:

Please accept our sincere condolences on the death of your wife. Words cannot express the sorrow we feel. We want you to know that our thoughts and prayers are with you.

If there is anything we can do to help you during this time of sorrow, please call on us.

Sincerely,


Harold M. Morrow
Personnel Manager
The Samson Company

# 11

# PERSONNEL CHECKLISTS

- 50 Ways to Save Money in the Human Resources Area
- Employee Planning Checklist
- Checklist of Eight Uses for Temporary Help to Lower Payroll Costs
- Checklist to Use When Writing Recruiting Ads
- Applicant Interview Checklist
- Checklist of Questions You May Not Ask in an Interview
- Checklist for Use in Evaluating Interview or Appraisal Data
- New Employee Orientation Checklist
- Affirmative Action Planning Checklist
- Checklist for Investigating Sexual Harassment Complaints
- Yearly Salary Program Checklist
- Checklist for Meeting Your Training Needs While Saving Your Company Money
- Checklist for Developing New Communications Programs
- Checklist and Guidelines for Using an Outside Consultant
- Human Resource Management (HRM) Merger Checklist
- Checklist and Manager's Guidelines for Handling Drug or Alcohol Problems on the Job
- Checklist for Avoiding Litigation When Terminating an Employee
- Checklist for Use in Preparing for a Layoff
- Checklist of Security Activities
- Checklist for Maintaining a Safe Workplace
- Checklist for Establishing a Complaint or Grievance Procedure
- An ADA Checklist for Employers

# PERSONNEL CHECKLISTS

This chapter includes over twenty personnel checklists and a list of 50 Ways to Save Money in the Human Resource Area. Using checklists can save a lot of time. If you find yourself suddenly faced with the need to lay off employees without much advance warning and time to get ready, turn to the layoff checklist and it will help you get started in the right direction. If you are writing recruiting ads and need some help in getting started, turn to the checklist on writing classified ads. Because most businesspeople face time restraints, these checklists can be a valuable tool.

## 50 WAYS TO SAVE MONEY IN THE HUMAN RESOURCES AREA

Business people are always looking for ways to retain profits. Here are 50 ways to save the valuable dollars in the Human Resources area.

1. Lease workers from an employee leasing company. It covers payroll costs and provides benefits that a small business might not be able to afford. It also handles the unemployment and workers' compensation costs and claims.
2. Use temporary help for short-term assignments. Contract with a temporary help agency and eliminate payroll and benefits costs. Try people on a temporary to permanent basis and ask the temp agency to waive their fee if you try the person and pay a fee for 90 days.
3. Try job-sharing. In an area where it is hard to find good people, you may be able to attract two experienced employees to fill one job. If you provide benefits, however, it could cost you money because you have two people on the payroll instead of one. If you consider them both part-time employees, you may not need to provide any benefits.
4. Post open jobs and recruit inside the company to avoid outside recruiting costs.
5. Ask current employees to help you recruit outside the company to fill jobs. This could also cut recruiting costs.
6. Let people work at home. This saves them transportation expenses and saves you in outlays for utilities, equipment, office furniture and so on. You may need some specific personnel policies to cover home workers.
7. If you have jobs you can't fill, you are losing money while they sit vacant. Try odd-hour scheduling. You may pick up some good, experienced people who need a second job.

8. Use retired workers on a project or part-time basis. They don't expect benefits because most people already have them, and most retired people have an income so they don't demand high wages.

9. If you spend the money to run a help wanted ad, set up an after-hours hotline and recorder to take calls when people are off work and can apply. This saves your staff some time.

10. Train people you already have on staff to take on one or two extra assignments. Most employees are not so busy that they can't do one or two extra things. This also can provide some added incentive to learn something new. Add to an employee's skill bank. If you have job descriptions, add a phrase at the bottom that says, "and may be expected to perform other tasks that may be assigned from time to time."

11. Consider changing the way your company is structured. Perhaps reorganizing a department can eliminate the need to add a new person.

12. Use a new employee orientation program that includes training in the new job and gets a new employee "up to speed" quickly. Many small companies put employees to work in a new job without proper indoctrination or training. Lost production costs directly affect your bottom line.

13. Review recruiting and selection costs on a regular basis to identify unnecessary expenses.

14. Be thorough in pre-employment reference checking to eliminate the possibility of hiring people who are "lob hoppers," or who chronically file for workers' compensation. The costs of replacing people are much higher than you think.

15. If you are a federal contractor, periodically analyze your "impact ratio of hires to applicants by EEO category" in order to avoid litigation costs if there is an adverse impact.

16. When you set up a formal wage and salary program, eliminate as many jobs and layers of supervision as you can and still run a cost-efficient operation. Let attrition eliminate unnecessary jobs.

17. Establish a variable merit pay plan based on performance. Pay your top performers more than the people who simply show up and fill a desk.

18. Use a performance-based (as objective as you can make it) appraisal system. Weed out poor performers; they cost big dollars in lost productivity.

19. Hire a compensation consultant to help you install an income deferral program. This cuts costs of payroll and benefits.

20. If you pay your top executives a bonus, tie the bonus to company profits or sales increases.

21. Pay key executives more in the way of non-cash perks and deferred compensation.

22. To avoid costly litigation, monitor your pay practices. Be sure you don't pay men more than women in the same jobs, and that promotional increases for males and females are equitable and nondiscriminatory.

23. You can save the company money by performing a benefits needs analysis of your workforce. Don't spend money on benefits that are not needed or wanted.

24. Use a health maintenance or a preferred provider organization to cut the costs of medical benefits. Also, require a second opinion before any major surgery.

25. Ask employees to pay a portion of their medical benefits to cut costs.

26. Use careful claims administration of medical, dental, and other insurance claims, including selective audit controls of hospital bills.

27. Monitor coordination of benefits provisions to exclude double payment of the same expense.

28. Perform a training needs analysis to ensure your training dollars are spent where they are most needed, and will provide the best return on dollars spent.

29. If you do a lot of training, perform a training audit once or twice a year to see which departments and managers spend the most money . . . decide if the budget is being spent wisely.

30. If you spend a lot of money on outside training programs, bring the training in-house and use your own trainers. Once you develop your own programs, they can be used over and over again.

31. Use local colleges and universities to train in areas where the college is already teaching the programs you need.

32. Trade training programs and services with trainers in other companies. Ask the other trainers to put on the programs. Be prepared to respond when you are asked to do outside programs for other companies. Barter training to cut costs.

33. Utilize your information services people to teach classes on the PC.

34. Review governmental policies as they apply to your particular industry and your company. Be sure you have the policies you need to avoid future litigation.

35. Policies should provide control without strangling a company. They should set the conditions of employment; when they do, they save the organization money in the areas of unemployment compensation and workers compensation.

36. Have a policy that says employees must take or lose vacation pay. Vacation or sick pay that accumulates does so at an increasingly higher rate of pay as the employee receives raises.

37. Have workable discipline and discharge policies and have people who are terminating voluntarily sign a separation form. A great deal of money can be lost in unemployment compensation claims if terminations are not handled properly.

38. If some of your employees have an alcohol or drug problem, install an employee assistance program, or save money by using an outside consultant.

39. Use a lump-sum salary increase from time to time. You may not want to do this every year, but the lump-sum salary increase can be a one-time pay increase based on performance, and does not increase base pay.

40. Perform a quarterly audit/report on where human resource costs are. If you can identify where the costs are, you can usually install a program to control them.

41. Install safety rules that cut workers' compensation and high medical costs.

42. Make a concerted effort to retain a union-free status. A union costs both the employee and the employer money.

43. If you are a manufacturer, consider installing a quality control program to increase quality and productivity.

44. Institute a suggestion program that pays for suggestions that improve the way things are done in your company. Many companies have experienced substantial cost savings through suggestion systems.

45. You can save the company a great deal of money in salaries if, when you reorganize, you eliminate one or more levels of management. Most companies don't need all the levels of management they have.

46. Gain control of human resource forms. Most departments have more forms than they need. Forms do save an organization money in the long run, but too many forms are just an added cost.

47. Train people who screen and interview applicants to cut down on the time they spend by setting specific interviewing hours, and by being as specific as possible in recruiting ads so the number of people who apply will be smaller but will be better qualified.

48. Audit and review your computer costs. Do a periodic review of the number of computer reports you receive and the need for these reports. Check your computer security on a regular basis.

49. Many businesses with low skill service jobs can successfully employ disabled workers. It saves your tax dollars for support of government social programs in the long run if you employ the disabled.

50. If you add a late shift, you can hire workers who need a second income.

## EMPLOYEE PLANNING CHECKLIST

The following items will assist with preparation of a comprehensive human resources plan:

❏ Prepare a current database for your human resources plan. The database is your current workforce analysis. Prepare a human resource inventory for each department that is to be included in the forecast and the plan for that particular area. Include a measure of productivity (number of projects, amount of sales, etc.). Identify the types and numbers of people to be included in the forecast.

❏ Analyze the data you have compiled. Then, review past economic objectives, productivity, and actual staffing. Review current trends and projected future demands and prepare a preliminary human resource forecast.

❏ Working with each department, review external concerns such as new technology or social and environmental issues. Make assumptions regarding the future and the impact of these changes on the forecast.

❏ Prepare the forecast for review and approval.

❏ Translate forecast numbers into position specifications Write job descriptions. Evaluate jobs. Set salary ranges.

❏ Prepare cost estimates that include numbers of people, recruitment costs, relocation costs, and the costs of salaries, benefits, space, equipment, training, and other miscellaneous items.

❏ Review current employees against projected positions. Employees who do not meet job specifications on forecast positions are screened out.

❏ Prepare a labor market assessment.

After these eight steps have been completed, management will have the opportunity to:

1. Accept the forecast and proceed with implementation of the plan.

2. Modify the forecast as needed to meet the organization's objectives, then authorize the next step in the process.

3. Reject the forecast and repeat the process.

# CHECKLIST OF EIGHT USES FOR TEMPORARY HELP TO LOWER PAYROLL COSTS

❏ Placing employees on the payroll of a temporary help service during their probationary period can minimize a company's unemployment compensation rates.

❏ Temporary help teams are a new service offered by some agencies. Teams of word processors, data processors, salespeople, and so on, can staff a whole department until permanent staffing is arranged.

❏ Mandatory retirement policies can cause an organization to lose valuable employees at a time when a particular project is crucial to the business plan. A temporary help service can assist by transferring the person to its payroll, thus easing the pressures on both the company and the employee.

❏ Before a company recruits a permanent employee for a new position, a temporary worker can be used to determine whether a valid position really exists.

❏ Consider using temporary help for one-time demands involving a special project such as product sampling, assembling an annual report, taking or doing the extensions on inventory, or a data processing conversion program, where a team of persons can go in for a short term and complete the project.

❏ Smoother transitions can be delivered when temporary workers are used during office or plant relocation as job vacancies occur.

❏ Temporaries can fill crucial spots until a hiring freeze is lifted.

❏ Sometimes exactly the right applicant comes along, but it takes a week or more to process the paperwork for authorization to hire the person. During this delay, the prospect may consider another attractive offer. If a manager can place the applicant on the job immediately, but on a temporary service firm's payroll, the problem of losing the applicant may be averted.

# CHECKLIST TO USE WHEN WRITING RECRUITING ADS

A certain percentage of jobs will be filled by help-wanted ads and recruiting literature, but so many ads are sterile and boring. There is no way to know exactly how effective advertising is, even if you keep records of applicants who respond to your ads. Keep these ideas in mind when preparing an ad:

- ❏ People are attracted by class. If you can afford it, use display ads. Be sure the ads reflect the company personality.
- ❏ Use a clean-cut type style and graphics.
- ❏ The first few words need pizzazz to hook the reader and appeal to the people you want to attract. They should be printed in large type.
- ❏ Make sure your ad is placed under the appropriate job classification.
- ❏ Use your company logo if you have one.

When writing your ad, make sure you:

- ❏ List specific skills.
- ❏ List work experience required.
- ❏ State whether relocation is necessary.
- ❏ State educational requirements.
- ❏ Indicate whether the job requires regular travel.
- ❏ State whether you will train.
- ❏ Provide a good review of your overall benefit program and any other items such as "mountain location" or "mild year round climate" that you consider a benefit.

Do not include:

- ❏ References to age or sex or use any other discriminatory language.

# APPLICANT INTERVIEW CHECKLIST

You have to make critical decisions based on the information you get during an interview. Because smart applicants are usually well-prepared, the information they give you may be shaded or even false. You should plan your interview strategy ahead of time. The following checklist will help:

- ❏ Be sure you know the job before you start the interview.
- ❏ Learn about the applicant in advance.
- ❏ Plan the interview in order to come away with the information you need.
- ❏ Establish a comfortable conversational style to build rapport.
- ❏ Use plain language and reveal aspects of yourself in order to give as well as get information.
- ❏ Maintain objectivity about the applicant as the interview progresses.

- ❏ Remain flexible and guide the conversation from general to specific and from harmless to sensitive areas.

- ❏ Listen. Concentrate on what the applicant is saying. Show empathy and respond appropriately.

- ❏ Structure the interview so that you use a variety of questioning techniques. Use more open-ended questions rather than questions that can be answered "yes" or "no."

- ❏ Don't ask questions that could be considered discriminatory.

- ❏ Give information during the interview. There should be a true one-to-one exchange.

- ❏ Use silence to obtain more information. If the applicant seems to run out of things to say, let the silence build up for a few seconds. The applicant probably will offer more information.

- ❏ If there are statements you'd like the applicant to expand on, repeat them in another way. This is called *echoing* and is an effective information-gathering technique.

- ❏ Watch for the "halo effect," where an interviewer permits one or two favorable traits, such as good appearance or speaking ability, to bias judgment favorably on other entirely unrelated traits. The halo effect can work in reverse, biasing the interviewer unfavorably because of one or two bad impressions.

- ❏ Don't talk too much. Respect the applicant's need. Exchange information.

- ❏ Show energy and enthusiasm. A stiff, formal interviewer will turn off most applicants.

- ❏ Don't try to give advice or counsel in a selection interview.

- ❏ Follow up hunches and unusual statements. If the applicant says, "I don't get along with certain kinds of people," you want to find out who those kinds of people are.

- ❏ Maintain control of the interview.

- ❏ Close the interview in a reasonable period of time. Close on a positive note, but don't lead an applicant on or promise anything you can't deliver.

- ❏ As soon as the interview is over, write down the facts and your impressions of the interview.

## Sample Questions

- ❏ I'd like to discuss your technical experience. Tell me about your experience in the technical area.

- ❏ What were your major responsibilities in your last job?

- ❏ In your last job, what duties did you spend most of your time on?

- ❏ How did you feel about the progress you made with your last company?

- ❏ In what ways do you feel your past job developed you to take on greater responsibility?

❏ What are some of the reasons you had for leaving your last job?

❏ What were some of the things you particularly liked about your last job?

❏ Most jobs have pluses and minuses. What are some of the minuses in your last job?

❏ Did you consider your progress on the job representative of your ability? Why?

❏ What are some of the things your boss did that you particularly liked or disliked?

❏ How did your manager rate your job performance?

❏ What did your manager feel you did particularly well? What were major criticisms of your work?

❏ How do you feel about these criticisms?

❏ What kind of people do you like working with? What kind of people do you find most difficult to work with?

❏ What are some of the things in a job that are important to you? Why?

❏ What are some of the things you would like to avoid in a job? Why?

❏ How do you feel your last company treated its employees?

## Unstructured (Open-Ended) Questions

❏ Tell me about . . .

❏ Would you tell me about . . . ?

❏ I'd be interested in knowing . . .

❏ How did you feel about . . . ?

❏ Would you explain how . . . ?

❏ I'm not certain I understand . . .

❏ Would you explain that in more detail?

❏ What do you mean by that?

❏ Tell me more about . . .

❏ Perhaps you could clarify . . .

❏ What was there about . . . that appealed to you?

❏ Did you have an opportunity to . . . ?

## CHECKLIST OF QUESTIONS YOU MAY NOT ASK IN AN INTERVIEW

Questions seeking the following information are illegal and may not be asked of an applicant before he or she is hired:

❏ Date of birth

❏ Maiden name

❏ Previous married name

- ❏ Marital status
- ❏ Name of spouse
- ❏ Spouse's occupation and length of time on the job
- ❏ Spouse's place of employment
- ❏ Number of children and their ages
- ❏ Arrest record
- ❏ Convictions may be asked about, but you may not refuse employment because of a conviction, unless it is a bona fide job qualification
- ❏ Child care arrangements
- ❏ Reasons that would prevent an applicant from maintaining employment Ancestry
- ❏ National origin/race
- ❏ Age
- ❏ Sex
- ❏ Religion
- ❏ Affiliations with a union
- ❏ Garnishment of wages

It should be kept in mind that much of the above is the type of information necessary for personnel records and employee benefit programs. However, the information is obtained only after employment and therefore can have no bearing on the employment decision.

# CHECKLIST FOR USE IN EVALUATING INTERVIEW OR APPRAISAL DATA

Consider the following personality traits of each applicant or employee being appraised. Items preceded by a minus sign are examples of unfavorable findings with respect to a given trait; those preceded by a plus sign are examples of favorable traits. The column on the right is provided for your use in rating applicants or employees.

| PERSONAL FLEXIBILITY | + | − |
|---|---|---|
| + Has shown an ability to handle a number of job assignments simultaneously. | ☐ | ☐ |
| − Personal approach reflects a tendency to be structured; tends to be a perfectionist. | ☐ | ☐ |
| + Seems to like jobs involving contact with many types of people and diverse job situations. | ☐ | ☐ |
| + Is flexible in personal approach. | ☐ | ☐ |
| − Not willing to compromise. | ☐ | ☐ |

## PERSONAL MATURITY                                                              +    −

− Tends to rationalize failures.                                                 ☐    ☐

+ Has learned to accept limitations.                                             ☐    ☐

− Displays chronic dissatisfaction with jobs, working conditions, peers,         ☐    ☐
  and superiors.

+ Has career goals and is optimistic about them.                                 ☐    ☐

+ Has mature outlook on life and work in general.                                ☐    ☐

+ Understands things are not always black or white; can handle ambiguity.        ☐    ☐


## EMOTIONAL STABILITY                                                           +    −

+ Shows an ability to maintain composure in face of adversity or frustration.    ☐    ☐

+ Maintains emotional balance under trying personal circumstances.               ☐    ☐

− Has had problems with supervisors and/or peers on more than one occasion.      ☐    ☐

− Is unable to deal with others' shortcomings.                                   ☐    ☐

− Allows emotions to rule business decisions.                                    ☐    ☐

− Is abrupt with subordinates or staff employees.                               ☐    ☐


## ABILITY TO BE TACTFUL                                                         +    −

+ The manner in which person phrases remarks reflects tact and consideration.    ☐    ☐

− In discussing relationships with subordinates, the person shows lack of        ☐    ☐
  sensitivity.

+ The person is a good listener.                                                 ☐    ☐

− "Bad mouths" previous/current employer.                                        ☐    ☐

− Tells jokes at the expense of others.                                          ☐    ☐

+ Is sensitive to communication needs of others.                                ☐    ☐

+ Is knowledgeable and tactful in business and social situations.


## IS A TEAM PLAYER                                                              +    −

+ The person operates successfully as a team player.                             ☐    ☐

− Is strongly motivated to be the "star."                                        ☐    ☐

+ Seems to place the accomplishments of the group ahead of personal ego.         ☐    ☐

− Displays poor interpersonal skills and tends to be intolerant of others.       ☐    ☐


## DISPLAYS FOLLOW-THROUGH                                                       +    −

+ Once the person starts a job, seems to hang in there.                          ☐    ☐

− There is indication the person starts more things than can be completed.       ☐    ☐

+ Has achieved one or more career goals.                                         ☐    ☐

+ Appears to follow through.                                                     ☐    ☐

− Does not follow through.                                                       ☐    ☐

## SHOWS INITIATIVE                                                         +    −

+ Has demonstrated ability to operate successfully without close supervision.    ☐ ☐
+ Reaches out for increasing responsibility.    ☐ ☐
+ Evidence indicates the person is a self-starter.    ☐ ☐
− Seems to dislike unstructured situations.    ☐ ☐

## SHOWS ASSERTIVENESS                                                      +    −

+ Seems willing to take a stand on what is right.    ☐ ☐
− Not sufficiently demanding of subordinates when the situation calls for it.    ☐ ☐
− Seems overly concerned with the feelings of others.    ☐ ☐
+ Has a positive assertive nature.    ☐ ☐
− Has a negative assertive nature.    ☐ ☐

## PERSONALITY TRAITS                                                       +    −

+ Personality has considerable positive impact.    ☐ ☐
− Tends to be introverted.    ☐ ☐
+ Has an outgoing, personable style.    ☐ ☐
− Is ego-oriented and at times rude.    ☐ ☐
+ Displays empathy and sensitivity.    ☐ ☐
+ Understands and conforms to social graces.    ☐ ☐

## IS CONSCIENTIOUS AND LOYAL                                               +    −

+ Works overtime when necessary.    ☐ ☐
+ Shows a conscientious nature.    ☐ ☐
+ Shows a loyal nature.    ☐ ☐
− Appears aloof and uncaring about management or the organization.    ☐ ☐

## SELF-CONFIDENCE                                                          +    −

+ Appraises own abilities realistically.    ☐ ☐
+ General manner and style show poise.    ☐ ☐
− Does not have sufficient confidence to discuss shortcomings.    ☐ ☐
− Appears overconfident.    ☐ ☐
− Lacks a sense of self-confidence in business dealings.    ☐ ☐

## HONESTY AND OPENNESS                                                     +    −

+ Is willing to give credit when credit is due.    ☐ ☐
− Tends to exaggerate own accomplishments.    ☐ ☐
− Stories seem to be inconsistent in terms of other statements or findings.    ☐ ☐
− Brags about "pulling a fast one" or about accomplishments.    ☐ ☐

+ Is willing to discuss unfavorable aspects of personal business experience. ☐ ☐

+ Is comfortable when discussing own shortcomings. ☐ ☐

TOTAL + s ___

− s ___

These categories can be used effectively to assist in evaluating an applicant or employee. Not all of them pertain to everyone, but they will get you thinking about specific qualities needed for a particular job. You may come up with other questions that better fit your own situation. Are there more pluses or minuses?

It is helpful to write a summary of your feelings immediately after the interview or performance appraisal has taken place. Concern yourself with the most important findings in terms of the person's overall qualifications.

# NEW EMPLOYEE ORIENTATION CHECKLIST

Employees look to supervisors as a prime source of information about the company and working conditions. Here is a list of fifty questions which your supervisors should be able to answer for new employees.

## *Job/Working Conditions*

❏ How long is a new employee on a Temporary evaluation period?

❏ When and how should an employee report an absence from work? How long can the employee remain absent without notice before becoming subject to discharge?

❏ Is promotion determined by merit, by seniority, or by both? How can an employee find out about jobs that may be open?

❏ How is an employee's performance appraised? How frequent are performance evaluations?

❏ How does the grievance procedure work? Exactly what should an employee do when he has a grievance?

❏ What is the policy on layoffs? How long can a layoff last? What are the recall rights of the employee? Does the recalled employee retain seniority?

❏ What about physical examinations? Is an employee's health checked periodically or after an illness?

❏ Can you answer employees' questions about the company medical program? How long are lunch periods and is the employee paid for them?

❏ What eating facilities are available? When are they open? What kind of food is available?

❏ When and how long are rest periods?

❏ How does the seniority system work? Is it plant-wide, departmental, or a combination?

❏ When, where, and under what conditions can an employee smoke?

❏ On what basis is an employee penalized for being late?

❏ What is the company's system of warnings and penalties when rules are broken?

❏ How can an employee make a personal telephone call or receive an incoming call?

❏ Is an employee obliged to join the union as a condition of employment? If so, when? Does the company check off dues?

❏ How much cleanup time is permitted for workers on machines or on a production line?

## Pay

❏ What are the company's overtime policies? What does it pay for work over eight hours in a day? On holidays? On Saturdays? On Sundays? Is there a meal allowance when overtime goes into the evening?

❏ Does an employee get premium pay for working afternoon and night shifts? How much?

❏ When, where, and how is an employee paid?

❏ If there's an incentive system, how does it work?

❏ If an employee reports for work and none is available, is he entitled to call-in pay? How much?

❏ If an employee is injured on the job and sent home, is he paid for a full day, a half day, or just the time he's in the plant? Will he be given other work during convalescence, or won't he be permitted to resume his job until he's completely recovered?

❏ What is the policy on severance pay?

❏ Is an employee given time off to vote?

❏ Does the company pay employees who are on jury duty?

❏ What is the policy on military leave when the employee is drafted? When she enlists? If she's in the National Guard, does the company pay for time spent in encampment?

❏ How is vacation pay computed?

❏ What is company policy on pay increases?

❏ Does the company give periodic bonuses?

## Benefits

❏ Can you explain your company's sick leave program? Is there a paid sick leave besides sickness and accident insurance? If so, how long does it last?

❏ What is the company's leave-of-absence policy?

❏ When does an employee become eligible for pension benefits? Insurance? Hospitalization benefits?

❏ What about vacations? When does a new employee become eligible for a vacation? How long is it? Are longer vacations granted as length of service increases? Can you carry over vacation time from one year to another?

❏ Does the company make loans to employees? Is there a credit union? How does it operate?

❏ Is there a company training program? Does the company sponsor any educational courses? If an employee wants to take an outside course at a college or technical school, will the company pay part or all the cost?

❏ What holidays are given during the year?

❏ Is there an employee stock-purchase plan? If so, how does it work?

❏ If there's a contributory insurance program, how much does the employee pay? The company?

❏ What's provided in the company pension plan? What are the eligibility requirements?

❏ When can an employee retire?

❏ Can you tell an employee what his pension income will be, based on his present earnings?

## *Miscellaneous*

❏ Can you tell an employee how she can get news into company publications? How she can use the bulletin boards?

❏ Is there an employee counseling service?

❏ Do you know what employee organizations there are?

❏ How does the suggestion system operate? To whom should an employee submit an idea? Who decides if it's acceptable? How are awards calculated?

❏ Do you know how big your company is? What it makes? What the product is used for? Its annual sales? Can you give a brief outline of its history?

❏ What is your organizational culture? Your company's management style?

❏ What is your company's reputation in the community and as a corporate citizen?

## AFFIRMATIVE ACTION PLANNING CHECKLIST

Affirmative action plan forms and positions statements are fairly standard today in most organizations. Title VII of the Civil Rights Act of 1964, Executive Order 11246 which applies to federal contractors and subcontractors and Revised Order No. 4 (41CFR Part 60-2) specify requirements of written programs. This checklist will help you get started with your program.

### KEY ELEMENTS OF AN AFFIRMATIVE ACTION PLAN:

- ❏ Corporate policy statement
- ❏ Policy dissemination/communication
- ❏ Assignment of an EEO coordinator
- ❏ Workforce analysis
- ❏ Goals and timetables
- ❏ Development and execution of the program
- ❏ Support of community and outreach programs
- ❏ Effective auditing and reporting systems

In addition to these key elements of the plan you should:

- ❏ Develop and update the affirmative action plan annually.
- ❏ Implement affirmative action plans to include internal and external communications.
- ❏ Design and implement audit and reporting systems that will measure the effectiveness of the AAP, indicate the need for remedial action, and determine the degree to which the company's goals and objectives are being achieved.
- ❏ Identify potential and actual problems within particular departments.
- ❏ Assist management in the resolution of problems related to EEO/AAP.
- ❏ Inform management of the latest developments in the area of equal employment opportunity and on legal issues.
- ❏ Serve as liaison among the company's minority, female, and handicapped organizations and governmental compliance agencies.
- ❏ Participate in the development of goals and timetables and assist department managers with efforts to achieve the established goals.

# CHECKLIST FOR INVESTIGATING
# SEXUAL HARASSMENT COMPLAINTS

You should take every complaint of sexual harassment seriously and investigate it thoroughly using the following step-by-step procedure:

Step 1—Notify the Human Resource Manager immediately when there is a charge.

Step 2—Interview the complainant. What does he/she say happened? Who is named as harasser? Where and when did the incident take place? Were there witnesses? Was it an isolated incident or part of a series? has he/she spoken to anyone else about the incident?

Step 3—Interview the accused harasser. Stay objective. Assume nothing. Put every statement in writing. Remember your notes may end up in court.

Step 4—Interview the witnesses. Phrase the questions so you don't give any information or influence the comments.

Step 5—Weigh all the evidence. Consider the credibility of each party based on the reputations of the employee and the alleged harasser. Is there any possibility that the employee is trying to make trouble for a supervisor? Are there previous complaints against the accused harasser? Have you investigated the charge as thoroughly as you can?

Step 6—Discuss what action to take with the Human Resource Manager or with legal counsel. Once you have all the facts, ask yourself if sexual harassment did occur. If you decide the accusation is without merit, write a detailed report explaining why and have the evidence to back it up. If harassment did occur, there are several options based on the severity of the case. The Human Resource Manager or your legal counsel will help you decide on the ultimate course of action.

Here are some options:

Option 1—First offense, written warning. It should include a statement that sexual harassment is against company policy, and that any additional complaints will result in disciplinary action, up to discharge. The complainant should be aware of any action taken against the harasser. Follow-up is absolutely essential to make sure the harassment stops.

Option 2—Consider transferring the accused or offering a transfer to the complainant. Make sure transfer of complainant is not retaliation and that the complainant accepts the transfer as a positive resolution to the problem.

Option 3—Suspension or discharge is usually reserved for repeated offenses or a sever first offense. You must be consistent in the penalties you impose. You can't fire one manager for sexual harassment and suspend another for identical offense.

## YEARLY SALARY PROGRAM CHECKLIST

As you start the preparation of your next yearly salary program use this checklist to ensure review of all compensation areas.

- ❏ Identify each unit of the organization that will require a separate salary program and merit budget. For example, you may have the corporate headquarters people, salaried and hourly employees at outlying locations, and scientific or special technical people at a research facility. Each of these groups requires a separate survey and separate salary program, and the specific jobs must be correlated with the jobs in the survey in order to ensure that you are comparing apples with apples.
- ❏ Look at the company's competitive position for each group by reviewing appropriate compensation surveys.
- ❏ Review the Bureau of Labor Statistics cost-of-living changes for the past year.

- ❏ Review the organizational changes that have taken place during the past year to see what jobs have changed, what relationships between jobs have been altered, and how the wage structure should change as a result.
- ❏ Look at your local industry practice, especially if the wage surveys you use are national.
- ❏ Review grade, step, or career ladder adjustments.
- ❏ Set merit adjustments based on performance levels and monitor where employees are in their salary range.

In order to motivate and retain employees at all levels of the organization, the salary program and merit budget must be competitive, must reward performance, and must be perceived by all employees as competitive and equitable. In addition, the salary program must be flexible enough to fulfill the needs of each individual in the company.

# CHECKLIST FOR MEETING YOUR TRAINING NEEDS WHILE SAVING YOUR COMPANY MONEY

Organizations are always on the lookout for ways to maximize revenues by more effectively using their employees throughout the organization. It is especially important to look for creative ways to save money and still do a good job of training and development. The following ideas will help you maximize training dollars:

- ❏ Conduct training programs in-house, using current staff. For example, an accounting manager can teach a course on budgeting, an employment manager or interviewer can teach a course for managers on interviewing. By allowing your staff to participate in training and development activities, you give them a growth opportunity and save training dollars.
- ❏ Trade services with training professionals in other companies. For example, if your trainer has expertise in communication skills, and a trainer in another company you know has expertise in time management, it's cost-effective to trade out the training time on an hour-for-hour basis rather than teaching each trainer to present a new program. Maintaining contacts with other companies in order to facilitate trades in expertise makes economic sense.
- ❏ Cut human resources training costs by charging outside seminars and conferences back to the department. When department managers know that outside seminar costs will show up in their budgets, they are more selective when sending employees to outside programs.
- ❏ Develop formal cross-training programs in-house in order to double your on-staff expertise. Include formal shadowing and mentor programs to use the expertise you already have.
- ❏ Use local community colleges to provide training programs. They are usually less expensive then large commercial companies.

❑ Use more video and audio cassette programs. They cost less and can be used over and over to offset initial development costs. A tape course can be taken while on the job or driving to and from work.

❑ Set up a system of formal written critiques of all courses or seminars that the company sponsors for any employee. The critique files will tell you which programs are worthwhile and which are not. This file will help you maximize the return on your investment.

❑ Check with department managers before you schedule training programs to make sure your programs will be held when the largest number of employees are available, to make the best use of the trainer's time. Classes that are not full are not cost-effective.

❑ There are thousands of films, filmstrips, and slide programs that can be borrowed free of charge from companies, associations, governmental agencies, and other sources. *The Educator's Guide to Free Films,* found in most libraries, lists many resources.

# CHECKLIST FOR DEVELOPING NEW COMMUNICATIONS PROGRAMS

❑ Use video newscasts to let employees know what is going on in the company. Send them to all locations on a regular basis.

❑ Implement a program of early evening meetings once a month for discussion of specific topics or current business books. Ask the CEO or other top executive to lead the discussion groups.

❑ Try the new action-oriented bulletin boards that provide cartoons and messages on pertinent subjects.

❑ Start a newsletter or overhaul your current one. Put in more information on what the company is doing and what you expect to occur in the future.

❑ Start lunch-hour programs, brown bag lunches, etc. Have speakers on current topics. You can usually get speakers free or for small cost.

❑ Start inexpensive training programs on skills or subjects that need attention. Trade instructor skills with other companies. If you have someone who can teach stress management, trade time with an instructor in another company who can teach Spanish as a second language.

❑ Appoint committees of employees to look into new ideas, production techniques, customer service approaches, etc., used by other organizations. Have the committee report back at a brown bag lunch on their findings.

❑ Install a company hotline for one or two months. Tell employees in the newsletter you've done this and that if they have any problems or questions they can call in 24 hours a day and let the company know. If they leave their name they will receive a direct answer within a set time limit. If they don't want to leave their name you will still provide an answer in the newsletter.

❏ Have regular employee meetings where executives talk on various topics. Open the meetings to questions from employees.

❏ Provide an annual report to employees on the state of the company. Provide information on personnel and benefit programs.

❏ Have issues-management brainstorming sessions. What issues do employees think will impact the company in the next five years?

❏ Form an in-house speakers bureau. Help employees gain the skills they need to participate. Provide speakers for local community groups.

❏ Provide the mechanism for employees to volunteer to work together in the community to help those less fortunate.

❏ Hold lectures for employees on topics of current interest. Invite political candidates, interesting business people, etc., to speak to employees.

❏ Start an in-house library that includes magazines, books, and tapes on current topics and allow employees to use the materials.

❏ Start health and fitness programs and sponsor athletic events. This can be done for very little cost.

All of these ideas will foster improved communications throughout the organization by bringing employees at all levels together.

# CHECKLIST AND GUIDELINES FOR USING AN OUTSIDE CONSULTANT

Ask yourself and any potential consultants the following questions:

❏ Why should I go outside the organization for assistance? Is their expertise available in-house?

❏ What about the time issue—How immediate is the need? What are the time limits of your staff or yourself?

❏ Budget considerations? Consultants may be less expensive than internal staff. They will concentrate on a specific issue or a specific problem, and some will guarantee results.

❏ Sales calls from consultants should not justify hiring someone or altering your priorities. Be careful of salespersons selling the answer to all your needs.

Assuming that you have decided to look outside the organization for expertise, here are some specific criteria for selection:

❏ Prior track record—what organizations were previously served? What topics or services were rendered? When were the services rendered? Whom can you contact at those organizations to verify results? If they can't supply these kinds of specific data, continue your search.

❑ Can you see or hear the consultant by previewing a demonstration tape? Would they consider a briefing session for a select group of managers or employees at minimal or no cost? What about an executive briefing? What would they charge for a pilot program?

❑ For persons who will be conducting programs, are they adult-centered in their teaching or seminar leading? How would they describe their presentation style? Do they encourage participation? Do they use audiovisuals? If they don't answer these questions to your satisfaction, continue looking.

❑ Are your candidates generalists or specialists? Do they have a list of topics they can consult and conduct programs on? Be wary of "can do all" types. They are probably not the people for your program.

❑ Ask for a written proposal based on what you see as your needs. Look for training objectives and outcomes in such proposals. If they can't write down what the expected outcomes are, it is doubtful that any will be realized.

## HUMAN RESOURCE MANAGEMENT (HRM) MERGER CHECKLIST

❑ How many companies will be involved in the merger?

❑ Are they all in the same business? If not what other business are they in?

❑ What are the key human resource issues that must be resolved?

❑ Does each company have a separate handbook and personnel policy manual? If so, these manuals must be revised into one manual that will cover all the personnel issues that the one merged company will have. Meet with CEO and other key executives to resolve personnel policy issues before revising the manual.

❑ Review compensation plans for each company. What is the best way to bring all employees under one umbrella? Does one pay plan fit the entire group? Should it be a grade plan, or a point evaluation plan? Are there both exempt salaried employees and non-exempt hourly employees? Are there pieceworkers or incentive workers? Do any of the companies have shifts or alternative work schedules? How does management see the compensation program?

❑ Review benefits for the new company and the old companies. Can one new plan be designed that will fit everyone's needs and have a reasonable cost to the organization? Who is handling benefits? Are they planning to review all the benefit programs? Do they have the needed expertise? Should the surviving company "shop" their benefits?

❑ How are the companies handling benefits regulatory issues like COBRA and IRS or other regulatory concerns?

❑ Does the merged company have an adequate affirmative action program? Does the company have government contracts? Have any of the companies ever had a desk audit? Do the companies keep good records? Does the new company need an EEO/AAP internal audit?

❏ Do the companies being merged have training or development programs? Is there one program that is better than the others? How does management feel about training? Is specific training needed because of the merger? If so, what?

❏ Does one company need specific training the other companies don't need? If so, how will that be handled?

❏ How is recruiting and employment handled? Will all merged companies send open requisitions to one personnel person who will handle the recruiting, advertising and so forth?

❏ Does the merged company have a good personnel records or administration function? If not, what is needed?

❏ How about other regulatory concerns? Does the company comply with the Civil Rights Act, ERISA, OSHA, Immigration Law, and so forth? What specific regulatory concerns do you have?

❏ Does the company have good discipline and discharge procedures? Are the procedures being followed?

❏ Have proper safety and health policies and procedures been established? What are the key policies? Review accident reports and OSHA Form 200s records.

❏ Does the organization have security procedures for personal property, commercial property, computers, and so forth. If not, these should be drafted immediately.

❏ Does the main company now do any type of employee planning, including HR staffing reports?

❏ What types of reports are now being done in the HR area? Are they all needed? If not, what reports are needed?

❏ Does the company have a computer/HRIS system? Is it working effectively? Do the other companies have systems that will need to be merged? What will it take to merge computer systems? Is anyone in charge of HRIS? What actions must be taken?

❏ What are the other significant areas of HRM concern and activity needed to effectively complete the merger?

❏ List people/resources in the company who can assist with the merger.

## CHECKLIST AND MANAGER'S GUIDELINES FOR HANDLING DRUG OR ALCOHOL PROBLEMS ON THE JOB

Even when a company has good policies and procedures and an employee assistance program (EAP) benefit, supervisors must be trained to spot problems and must know what to do when faced with an alcohol or drug problem. Following are guidelines for supervisors for discussions with employees.

❏ Make it clear that you are concerned for job performance, productivity, and attendance, and that you want to help the employee improve job performance.

❏ Remember that documented evidence of a downward trend in performance or attendance is the best tool to help a valued employee recognize a possible illness or addiction and to motivate the person to seek assistance.

❏ Behavioral problems that cause declining job performance, which the employee has been unable or unwilling to correct, will only get worse.

❏ Make it clear to the employee that the employee assistance program, if you have one, is a benefit and that assistance is available and recommended.

❏ Explain that employees must decide for themselves whether to seek assistance through the EAP. Either way, unless job performance improves, the employee's job is in jeopardy.

❏ Emphasize that all employee problems are kept completely confidential.

Don't try to diagnose the problem:

❏ Listen, but don't offer advice for solving personal problems. An employee's responsibility includes handling these situations so they do not continue to interfere with job performance. The supervisor's responsibility is to see that the employee gets professional help.

❏ Don't be misled by sympathy-evoking tactics or other seemingly acceptable excuses when they are used excessively. Insist that the employee get help.

❏ Don't moralize—right or wrong, good or bad—concerning personal behavior. It isn't your responsibility to judge. Restrict criticism to your responsibility for subordinate on-the-job performance and attendance.

❏ Don't cover up for friends. Your well-meaning but misguided kindness can lead to delay in the employee receiving needed help, and the situation, without effective intervention, will become more serious.

The key is to take action, to get help for the employee as soon as possible. There are consultants who can help companies set up employee assistance programs.

## CHECKLIST FOR AVOIDING LITIGATION WHEN TERMINATING AN EMPLOYEE

❏ Be sure you use progressive and positive discipline when discipline is necessary.

❏ First give a verbal warning and then a written warning before terminating an employee.

❏ Be sure all employees understand your work rules.

❏ Have specific disciplinary procedures and make sure everyone follows them.

❏ Avoid emotional incidents where a supervisor may fire someone on the spot in a fit of anger.

❏ Don't block a terminated employee's chances to get another job—don't give negative references on a former employee.

❏ Be sure you document any actions taken against an employee in the employee's personnel file.

❏ Be sure that all discipline is handled in an evenhanded manner and is not discriminatory.

❏ Make sure employees have everything they need to do their job well.

❏ Use a termination checklist to make sure you have covered all bases before you complete a termination.

❏ If you have special concerns about a termination consult a labor relations expert or an attorney.

## CHECKLIST FOR USE IN PREPARING FOR A LAYOFF

No one likes the idea of a layoff, but when faced with that possibility it helps to have a well-defined plan. An organized program also gives employees a feeling that they will be treated fairly by the company. Use the following layoff checklist:

❏ How many people will be involved?

❏ What departments are involved?

❏ What will be the layoff criteria? Performance, seniority, job elimination? If it's a job elimination, it may be a reduction in force, rather than a layoff, which means there may be no recall rights involved.

❏ Prepare a layoff policy, stating criteria decided upon and what regular pay, severance, and vacation will be paid. You should pay all unused vacation.

❏ Determine how much advance notice will be given.

❏ Before a layoff or reduction in force, some companies poll employees to determine whether anyone wishes to quit voluntarily. If employees do volunteer to quit, the company should give them the same severance pay other employees will receive.

❏ Ask employees who are old enough to retire if they wish to take early retirement.

❏ When the layoff notice is given, will employees be allowed time to look for a job before the layoff date?

❏ Develop a seniority list.

❏ Review the layoff list to see how your affirmative action plan will be affected. What percentages of minorities, women, handicapped, and people over forty are there?

❏ Review lists of company property held by employees who will be laid off and make provisions to get it back.

❏ Draft letters from management to employees regarding the layoff.

❏ Prepare a press release. Send it to the newspapers after employees have been notified.

❏ Notify corporate people if you have a corporate relationship.

❏ Have appropriate benefits people make arrangements regarding medical and life insurance coverage. Review pension and thrift plans if you have such benefits. Provide insurance conversion forms. Install a procedure for complying to COBRA regulations.

❏ Prepare an information sheet to hand out to employees regarding the benefits they will have and for how long.

❏ Decide on the amount of severance that will be paid to each employee. If you want employees to stay beyond a certain date, state that the severance will be paid only if employees stay through that date.

❏ Prepare an outplacement program that includes workshops résumé writing and interviewing.

❏ Provide employees with information on how to collect unemployment insurance.

❏ Provide a counseling service for employees with special problems.

❏ Contact employers in the area to find out if there are any employment opportunities, and make terminating employees aware of job openings in other companies.

A layoff or reduction in force is never pleasant, but if you have a game plan it makes the whole outplacement effort much easier.

## CHECKLIST OF SECURITY ACTIVITIES

Not many companies have a formal security plan, but a good plan can save a company thousands of dollars. The following checklist will help you establish a security plan.

❏ Screen applicants for potential security risks.

❏ Provide policies and procedures for terminating any employee caught stealing company property.

❏ Employ security guards on staff or on a contract basis if your organization is of a size where the need for guards is indicated.

❏ Install an alarm system to protect facilities.

❏ Mark company equipment for theft prevention and recovery purposes.

❏ Keep an up-to-date inventory of company equipment.

❏ Depending on company size, value of equipment, and building access, require employee identification badges.

❏ Provide procedures for monitoring visitors to facilities. Require visitors to sign in and out, and require that they wear identification badges while on the premises.

❏ Establish a formal evacuation plan for fire, bomb threats, and so on.

❏ Develop written security guidelines for bomb threats.

- ❏ Develop a community relations program. Work with local community leaders and create a "good citizen" public image in the immediate area of the facility.
- ❏ Provide emergency first aid equipment in several locations, and post first aid in- formation in accessible areas. Include fire, police, and ambulance numbers.
- ❏ Communicate company security policies and procedures to employees.
- ❏ If there is a high incidence of theft, some companies employ an undercover detective service.
- ❏ Analyze computer security, and establish firm guidelines for access to your computer system.
- ❏ Audit cash flow and other monetary procedures.
- ❏ If there is an area of significant loss, form a risk management committee to review the problem.

## CHECKLIST FOR MAINTAINING A SAFE WORKPLACE

Your first line of defense against accidents at work is an accident prevention plan. Accident prevention occurs through proper engineering controls, preventive maintenance, safety training, and training on the proper use of equipment. Use the following checklist to help prepare an accident prevention program:

- ❏ Encourage employees to report hazards.
- ❏ Be sure offices and plants are clean, well designed, and controlled for noise, heat, dust, and fumes.
- ❏ Maintain good preventive maintenance programs for production equipment and facilities.
- ❏ Have supervisors inspect work areas informally every day.
- ❏ Worker-management teams using checklists should inspect monthly or quarterly.
- ❏ Annual plant and office safety audits should be completed annually.
- ❏ Base safety training programs and safety checklists on specific hazard information.
- ❏ Make refresher safety training available on a continuing basis for all employees including supervisors.
- ❏ Post all required OSHA notices and any other pertinent safety bulletins and posters.
- ❏ Be sure all electrical equipment is grounded.
- ❏ Inspect to make sure that all machinery guards are in place at the point of operation.
- ❏ Inspect guards for pulleys.
- ❏ Make sure there are guards for live parts of electrical equipment.
- ❏ Be sure there are proper enclosures for blades of fans within 7 feet of working floor level.

❑ Inspect guards for belt, rope, or chain drives.

❑ Eliminate disorderliness in aisles and passageways.

❑ Hold safety meetings on a regular basis.

❑ Maintain a log on all job injuries and illnesses.

❑ Don't let employees work around dangerous machines when they are ill.

### Watch for

❑ Slippery floors and walkways

❑ Tripping hazards such as piping and hoses

❑ Missing entrance and exit signs

❑ Poorly lighted stairs

❑ Loose handrails or guard rails

❑ Broken windows

❑ Dangerously piled supplies or equipment

❑ Open doors on electrical panels

❑ Leaks of steam, water, or oil

❑ Blocked aisles

❑ Blocked fire extinguishers or sprinkler heads

❑ Blocked fire doors

❑ Oily rags

❑ Evidence of smoking in nonsmoking areas

❑ Roof leaks

## CHECKLIST FOR ESTABLISHING A COMPLAINT OR GRIEVANCE PROCEDURE

It is important for management of any company to resolve employee complaints quickly and effectively. Here is a checklist of questions to ask yourself before you establish an employee complaint procedure:

❑ What can be brought to management, what can be grieved?

❑ Who is ineligible to file complaints (management)? Who is eligible (management, employees, terminated employees)?

❑ What are the steps that must be followed?

❑ What are time limits on each step and who has the responsibility to take the next action?

❑ Are extension of time limits permitted?

- ❏ What are the consequences of failing to meet time limitations?
- ❏ Does grievant have the right to representation by another employee, legal counsel, or a union representative?
- ❏ Who has the final step in procedure?
- ❏ Do management representatives in the grievance process have the right to designate a substitute?
- ❏ What is the standard used to review the grievance (good cause, fairness, accuracy)?
- ❏ What is the effect of the final decision on all the parties?

# AN ADA CHECKLIST FOR EMPLOYERS

The company has long supported equal opportunities for people with disabilities. We support the goals of the Americans with Disabilities Act of 1990 (ADA) because we believe it reflects sound human resource and business practices.

Although this checklist is not intended to be a definitive document on ADA compliance, a "No" answer indicates an area you may need to examine for improvement.

| HUMAN RESOURCE POLICIES: | YES | NO |
|---|---|---|
| 1. Have you communicated to all employees your company's policy and commitment to employment and reasonable accommodation for qualified applicants and employees with disabilities? | ❏ | ❏ |
| 2. Have training sessions and/or information been made available to current supervisors and managers regarding their ADA responsibilities? | ❏ | ❏ |
| 3. Is there a process in place to identify the need for reasonable accommodations and other ADA requirements when employees become disabled? | ❏ | ❏ |
| 4. Is a system in place to maintain confidential medical and health information separately from personnel files? | ❏ | ❏ |
| 5. Do you provide the same opportunities of employment to all employees in the same job classification (for example, compensation, benefits, promotion, training, and so on?) | ❏ | ❏ |
| 6. Have you posted notices regarding the individual rights of employees under the ADA? | ❏ | ❏ |

| INTERVIEWING AND HIRING | YES | NO |
|---|---|---|
| 7. Is your application/interviewing process fully accessible to all job applicants? | ❏ | ❏ |
| 8. Have job applications been checked for prohibited questions related to health, disability or workers' comp history, and have interviewers been advised not to ask questions of this nature? | ❏ | ❏ |

9.  Do job descriptions within your company identify the essential
    functions necessary to perform the job?                                    ❏  ❏

10. Do employment tests and procedures for taking the tests accurately
    assess only the necessary skills and aptitudes required to perform
    the essential job functions?                                               ❏  ❏

11. Are all employer-requested physicals conducted only after a
    conditional job offer tendered, and are they required of **all** applicants
    in that job category?                                                      ❏  ❏

12. Do your post-offer physicals assess only the candidate's ability to
    perform the essential functions of the offered position? The results
    of post-offer physicals cannot be used to discriminate against a
    qualified individual on the basis of disability.                           ❏  ❏

13. Are requirements for "reasonable accommodations" understood to
    be a necessary part of the process when considering an applicant?          ❏  ❏

14. Are managers most likely to be involved with reasonable
    accommodations aware of the best approach with a disabled person?
    Have-competent external resources been identified that can be used
    when needed?                                                               ❏  ❏

## OTHER POLICIES                                                          Yes No

15. Have you notified all professional search organizations with whom
    you have contracts of your intention to fully comply with the ADA?         ❏  ❏

16. Do employees with disabilities have equal access to break rooms,
    cafeterias, and other facilities (on-site/off-site) provided by you?       ❏  ❏

17. Have you ensured that your company meets its obligations under the
    Public Accommodations title of the ADA?                                    ❏  ❏

# 12

# SAMPLE PERSONNEL FORMS

- Personnel Requisition
- Application for Employment
- Applicant Appraisal Form
- Telephone Reference Check
- Approval of Estimated Relocation Expenses and Allowances
- Personnel Action Notice
- Payroll Time Report
- Overtime Hours Worked Report
- Employee Attendance Record
- Sample Employee Benefit Program— Plan Highlights
- Job Description Outline
- New Employee Orientation
- Employee Agreement
- Education Verification Reference
- Employee Transfer Request
- Vacation Request Form
- Employee Absence Report Form

- Leave Request/Return from Leave Form
- Application for Funeral Leave
- Mileage Reimbursement Report
- Travel and Expense Reimbursement Request
- Performance Appraisal Worksheet
- Employee Counseling Activity Sheet
- Supervisor's Checklist and Report for Effective Discipline
- Disciplinary Warning Notice
- Employee Warning Notice
- Exit Interview
- Accident/Injury Report
- Supervisor's Report of Accident Investigation
- Attending Physician's Return to Work Recommendations Record
- First Aid Report Log
- Quarterly Safety Performance Record

# SAMPLE PERSONNEL FORMS

This last chapter provides a great many personnel forms. Some of these forms appeared earlier in the text of the book and some of them appear here for the first time. Remember, you should modify any form to fit your organization's specific needs.

Having these forms in one place will provide a handy resource when time is short. Just copy the form, make needed changes, and you're ready to go.

# PERSONNEL REQUISITION

| Job title | | Department | |
|---|---|---|---|
| Salary Grade | Salary Range | Starting Salary | Date Needed by |

**Job Duties:**

_____
_____
_____
_____
_____
_____
_____

**Job Requirements:**

_____
_____
_____
_____
_____
_____

**Working Conditions**

_____
_____
_____
_____
_____
_____
_____

**Job Status**

❑  Existing Position        Replacement for _____
❑  New Position             Reason Needed_____
                            _____

❑  Full Time      ❑  Part Time      ❑  Temporary
Schedule _____

Requested by_____   Date _____

Approved by _____   Date _____

Approved by _____   Date _____

# APPLICATION FOR EMPLOYMENT

## An Equal Opportunity Employer

We do not discriminate on the basis of race, color, religion, national origin, sex, age, or disability. It is our intention that all qualified applicants be given equal opportunity and that selection decisions be based on job-related factors.

Each question should be fully and accurately answered. No action can be taken on this application until all questions have been answered. Use blank paper if you do not have enough room on this application. PLEASE PRINT, except for signature on back of application. In reading and answering the following questions, be aware that none of the questions are intended to imply illegal preferences or discrimination based upon non-job-related information.

Job Applied for_____  Today's Date _____

Are you seeking:  Full-time ❑  Part-time ❑  Temporary ❑  employment?  When could you start work? _____

| Last Name | First Name | Middle Name | Telephone Number |
|---|---|---|---|

| Present Street Address | City | State | Zip Code |
|---|---|---|---|

Are you 18 years of age or older? . . . . . . . . . . . . . . . . . . . . . . . . . . . . . . . . . . . . . . . . . . . . . . . . . . . . . . . . . .  Yes ❑    No ❑
(If you are hired you may be required to submit proof of age.)

Social Security Number _____  If hired, can you furnish proof you are eligible to work in the U.S.?  Yes ❑    No ❑

---

Have you ever applied here before? . . . . . . . . . . . . Yes ❑      No ❑      If yes, when? _____

Were you ever employed here? . . . . . . . . . . . . . . . . Yes ❑      No ❑      If yes, when? _____

Have you ever been convicted of any law violation (except a minor traffic violation)? . . . . . . . . . . . . . . . . . . . . . . . . Yes ❑    No ❑

   If yes, give details_____
   (A "Yes" answer does not automatically disqualify you from employment, since the nature of the offense, date, and the job for which you are applying will also be considered.)

Are you now or do you expect to be engaged in any other business or employment? . . . . . . . . . . . . . . . . . . . . . . . . Yes ❑    No ❑

   If yes, please explain  _____

For Driving Jobs *Only:* Do you have a valid driver's license? . . . . . . . . . . . . . . . . . . . . . . . . . . . . . . . . . . . . . . . . . Yes ❑    No ❑

   Driver's License Number _____ Class of License _____
   Have you had your driver's license suspended or revoked in the last 3 years? . . . . . . . . . . . . . . . . . . . . . . . . Yes ❑    No ❑

   If yes, give details:  _____

List professional, trade, business or civic activities and offices held. (Exclude labor organizations and memberships which reveal race, color, religion, national origin, sex, age, disability or other protected status.) _____

_____

_____

---

| | Number of Years Completed | Diploma Degree Certificate | Subjects Studied |
|---|---|---|---|
| **LIST NAME AND ADDRESS OF SCHOOLS** | | | |

High School or GED: _____

College or University: _____

Vocational or Technical: _____

What skills or additional training do you have that are related to the job for which you are applying? _____

_____

What machines or equipment can you operate that are related to the job for which you are applying? _____

_____

List names of employers in consecutive order with present or last employer listed first. Account for all periods of time including military service and any periods of unemployment. If self-employed, give firm name and supply business references.

**PLEASE GIVE MONTH AND YEAR.**

| NAME OF EMPLOYER | | JOB TITLE AND DUTIES |
|---|---|---|
| ADDRESS | | |
| CITY, STATE, ZIP CODE | | DATE OF EMPLOYMENT: FROM     TO |
| | | PAY: START $     FINAL $ |
| SUPERVISOR | TELEPHONE | REASON FOR LEAVING |
| NAME OF EMPLOYER | | JOB TITLE AND DUTIES |
| ADDRESS | | |
| CITY, STATE, ZIP CODE | | DATE OF EMPLOYMENT: FROM     TO |
| | | PAY: START $     FINAL $ |
| SUPERVISOR | TELEPHONE | REASON FOR LEAVING |
| NAME OF EMPLOYER | | JOB TITLE AND DUTIES |
| ADDRESS | | |
| CITY, STATE, ZIP CODE | | DATE OF EMPLOYMENT: FROM     TO |
| | | PAY: START $     FINAL $ |
| SUPERVISOR | TELEPHONE | REASON FOR LEAVING |
| NAME OF EMPLOYER | | JOB TITLE AND DUTIES |
| ADDRESS | | |
| CITY, STATE, ZIP CODE | | DATE OF EMPLOYMENT: FROM     TO |
| | | PAY: START $     FINAL $ |
| SUPERVISOR | TELEPHONE | REASON FOR LEAVING |

Have you worked under any other name? ............................................................................................... Yes ☐    No ☐

If yes, give names: _____

Are you presently employed? ............................................................................................... Yes ☐    No ☐

If yes, may we contact your present employer? ............................................................................................... Yes ☐    No ☐

Have you ever been fired from a job or asked to resign? ............................................................................................... Yes ☐    No ☐

If yes, please explain: _____

Give three references, not relatives or former employers.

| Name | Address | Phone |
|---|---|---|
| | | |
| | | |
| | | |

**PLEASE READ EACH STATEMENT CAREFULLY BEFORE SIGNING**

I certify that all information provided in this employment application is true and complete. I understand that any false information or omission may disqualify me from further consideration for employment and may result in my dismissal if discovered at a later date.

I authorize and agree to cooperate in a thorough investigation of all statements made herein and other matters relating to my background and qualifications. I understand that any investigation conducted may include a request for employment and educational history, credit reports, consumer reports, investigative consumer reports, driving record, and criminal history. I authorize any person, school, current and former employer, consumer reporting agency, and any other organization or agency to provide information relevant to such investigation and I hereby release all persons and corporations requesting or supplying information pursuant to such investigation from all liability or responsibility to me for doing so. I understand that I have the right to make a written request within a reasonable period of time for complete disclosure of the nature and scope of any investigation. I further authorize any physician or hospital to release any information which may be necessary to determine my ability to perform the job for which I am being considered or any future job in the event that I am hired.

I understand that compliance with the Company's Corporate Code of Conduct is a condition of my employment.

I understand I may be required to successfully pass a drug-screening examination. I hereby consent to a pre- and/or post-employment drug screen as a condition of my employment, if required.

**I UNDERSTAND THAT THIS APPLICATION OR SUBSEQUENT EMPLOYMENT DOES NOT CREATE A CONTRACT OF EMPLOYMENT NOR GUARANTEE EMPLOYMENT FOR ANY DEFINITE PERIOD OF TIME. IF EMPLOYED, I UNDERSTAND THAT I HAVE BEEN HIRED AT THE WILL OF THE EMPLOYER AND MY EMPLOYMENT MAY BE TERMINATED AT ANY TIME, WITH OR WITHOUT CAUSE AND WITH OR WITHOUT NOTICE.**

I have read, understand, and by my signature consent to these statements.

Signature: _____ Date: _____

This application for employment will remain active for a limited time. Ask the organization representative for details.

# APPLICANT APPRAISAL FORM

Interview Date _____

Name of Applicant _____ Position_____

This rating form will become a part of the applicant's personnel record which may be made available to governmental compliance agencies upon request.

| DO NOT FILL OUT IN THE PRESENCE OF APPLICANT<br>Review the current job description and rate the candidate in all categories below. Comment in each section. | Outstanding | Above Average | Average | Below Average |
|---|---|---|---|---|
| 1. *ESSENTIAL JOB FUNCTIONS*—Can the applicant perform the essential functions of this job? | | | | |
| 2. *EXPERIENCE*—How does previous experience relate to current opening? Consider communications and other skills such as knowledge and information and technical competence based on previous training. Review in light of the essential functions of the job. | | | | |
| 3. *MENTAL CAPABILITY*—Verbal ability, judgment, analytical skills, logic, decisiveness, and so on. | | | | |
| 4. *PHYSICAL CAPABILITY*—Can the applicant perform the physical requirements of the job? | | | | |
| 5. *EDUCATION/SKILLS*—Degree(s), professional licenses, registration, certifications, languages. equipment, computer skills. | | | | |
| 6. *GOALS AND AMBITION*—Initiative, persistence, drive, goals are well defined (as they relate to predicting success on this job). | | | | |

General comments: _____
_____

For additional comments use back of form.

Overall Appraisal:

Outstanding _____ Above Average _____ Average _____ Below Average _____

Recommend employment for current opening: Yes _____ No _____

Future consideration: Yes _____ No _____ If yes. for _____ position

Recommendation based upon: Application Review _____ Interview _____ Telephone Contact _____ References _____

| Signature of Interviewer: | Date Completed: |
|---|---|
| | |

# TELEPHONE REFERENCE CHECK

Applicant's Name _____

Company Contacted _____ Phone No._____

1.  When did the applicant work for your company? From _____ To _____

2.  What was the applicant's position/title? _____

3.  What information can you give concerning
    Quality of work?

    _____

    _____

    _____

    Quantity of work?

    _____

    _____

    _____

    Attendance?

    _____

    _____

    _____

4.  Did this person get along well with others? Yes _____ No _____

5.  Why did he/she leave your company?

    _____

    _____

    _____

6.  Is he/she eligible for rehire with your company? Yes _____ No _____
    If not, why? _____

    _____

    _____

Additional Comments: _____

_____

_____

Information From_____ Title _____

Reference Check Made By _____ Date _____

## Approval of Estimated Relocation Expenses and Allowances

Name _____ Social Security Number _____

Account to be Charged _____ Position Title _____

Old Location _____ New Location _____

Effective Date of Hire _____ Present Residence: Own ____ Rent ____

Married_____Single_____Head of Household_____Number of Dependents_____

| | Estimated Cost | Actual Cost |
|---|---|---|
| Cost of moving household goods | _____ | _____ |
| Employee travel and lodging to new location | _____ | _____ |
| Family travel and lodging to new location | _____ | _____ |
| Househunting travel and lodging for employee and/or spouse | _____ | _____ |
| Incidental expenses | _____ | _____ |
| Federal income tax: allowance | _____ | _____ |
| Any other special items to be allowed | _____ | _____ |

Employee's signature _____ Date _____

APPROVALS:

Department Manager _____ Date _____

Vice President _____ Date _____

Chief Financial Officer_____ Date _____

President _____ Date _____

Board (if required) _____ Date _____

# Personnel Action Notice

Employee ID # _____     Team #: _____     Date _____/_____/_____

Employee Name _____     SS #: _____/_____/_____

REASON FOR SUBMITTAL: __ New Hire __ Change __ Termination   Eff. Date: _____/_____/_____
_____ Completion of Evaluation Period     _____ Performance Appraisal Attached

Birth Date: ____/____/____     Sex: __M __F                    __Handicap
__Caucasian     __Black   __Am. Indian                        __Vietnam Era Veteran
__Hispanic      __Asian   __Other_____            __Disabled Veteran

**COMPLETE ITEMS _ONLY IF CHANGED:_**
Address:_____

City: _____     State ____   ZIP: _____   Telephone: _____

Job Title: _____     Grade: _____

1st Division: _____     1st Location:_____     Hrs/Wk: _____

2nd Division: _____     2nd Location:_____     Hrs/Wk: _____

3rd Division: _____     3rd Location:_____     Hrs/Wk: _____
**Check All That Apply:**
_____Full Time          _____Exempt               _____Contract
_____Part Time I        _____Non-Exempt           _____Volunteer
_____Part Time II       _____Supervisory          _____Student
_____Temporary          _____Non-Supervisory      **If not Full Time:**
       Benefits:  __Y __N                            Hours Per Week: _____

**Salary Change**          **Reason for Salary Change (Check One):**
____ Annual _____% ____Merit ____Promotion ____Reclassified ____Other_____
Salary Change: From:                To:
Hourly:      $_____.__            $_____.__
Biweekly:    $_____.__            $_____.__          _____
Annually:    $_____.__            $_____.__          Salary Authorization Signature

Signatures:
Employee: _____     Supervisor: _____

| For Accounting Use Only | TERMINATION |
|---|---|
| G/L Accounts: | _____ **Voluntary**     _____ **Involuntary** |
| G/L _____ ____% | Last Date Worked: _____/_____/_____ |
| G/L _____ ____% | Check-Off List:   __ Completed |
|  |                    __ Attached |
| Date Processed _____/_____/_____ | _____  _____ |
|  | Supervisor's Signature           Date |
| _____  _____ | _____  _____ |
| Payroll Department Signature    Date | Human Resources Director         Date |

**_PLEASE RETURN ENTIRE FORM TO HUMAN RESOURCES FOR DISTRIBUTION_**

# PAYROLL TIME REPORT

Work Unit: _____

Date Completed: _____

Complete by: _____

Title: _____

Pay Period of _____ to: _____, 19 ___

Approved by: _____

Title: _____

Date: _____

| EMPLOYEE NAME | POSITION TITLE | SOCIAL SECURITY NO./ EMPLOYEE NUMBER | DATES AND CODE* | | | | | | | | | | | | |
|---|---|---|---|---|---|---|---|---|---|---|---|---|---|---|---|
| 1. | | | | | | | | | | | | | | | |
| 2. | | | | | | | | | | | | | | | |
| 3. | | | | | | | | | | | | | | | |
| 4. | | | | | | | | | | | | | | | |
| 5. | | | | | | | | | | | | | | | |
| 6. | | | | | | | | | | | | | | | |
| 7. | | | | | | | | | | | | | | | |

Examples of coded entries:
8R - 8 hours regular
4V/4R- 4 hours vacation, 4 hours regular
4.5 SL- 4 ½ hours sick leave

8 WC - workers' comp. time
3 CTO- 3 hours comp. time
8 PD - personal disability

H - holiday
FH- floating holiday

NOTE:
Overtime is calculated on the basis of HOURS WORKED.

# OVERTIME HOURS WORKED REPORT

### Read instruction on reverse side before completing.

**EMPLOYEE REQUEST (Employee complete, print or type)**

| 1. Employee's name | 2. Department/Division |
|---|---|

**3. Overtime Worked**

| Date | Day | 4. Name of supervisor who gave prior approval |
|---|---|---|
| | | |

TIME  From _____ AM / PM   To _____ AM / PM

**Total Hours Worked**

_____ Hrs. _____ Mins.

**5. Purpose for overtime (Explain)**

_____

_____

_____

_____

| 6. Employee's Signature | Date Submitted |
|---|---|

## 7. SUPERVISORY ACTION

**A.** Supervisor receiving report from employee credit overtime to:

( ) **COMPENSATORY TIME OFF (CTO)**          ( ) **TIME AND ONE-HALF PAY**

| | Approve | Disapprove | SIGNATURE | DATE |
|---|---|---|---|---|
| | | | | |
| **B.** | | | | |
| | | | | |

## 8. CLERICAL EMPLOYEE COMPLETE | (√) Completed

| | | (√) Completed |
|---|---|---|
| A. | Verify figures. Calculate for proper overtime credit: round actual to nearest half hour, then multiply at rate specified by supervisor (ITEM 7-A). | |
| B. | Enter hours as calculated here:   AMOUNT: _____ | |
| C. | Enter hours (ITEM 8-B) to "Payroll Form" with "Overtime Worked" key letter "W" | |
| D. | File report in department file | |

# INSTRUCTIONS
# OVERTIME HOURS WORKED REPORT

Each eligible employee must receive prior supervisory approval before overtime can be worked. This report must be submitted to the supervisor within twenty-four (24) hours after completion of the overtime. Actual overtime worked as reported by an employee will be rounded to the nearest half-hour interval by the designated clerical employee, then multiplied at the rate (straight-time or time and one-half) specified by the supervisor.

## Employee Completes Items 1–6

1. & 2.  Self explanatory.

3. Show date and day that overtime was worked in excess of normal workday or shift. Show time period (from/to) and the total hours worked.

4. Show name of supervisor who gave prior approval for this overtime.

5. Describe in detail the purpose for the overtime. Show case or project number, type of overtime (training, court, call-back), and any other appropriate information.

6. Certify this report is correct by signing and dating. Submit to supervisor for action.

## Department Completed Items 7 and 8

7. As designated by department head: First supervisor to receive report shall check appropriate box that overtime is to be credited (either compensatory time off or time and one-half), sign, date, and forward to other supervisors to review as specified, and forward to clerical employee.

8. Clerical employee shall process, make appropriate calculations, and file.

# EMPLOYEE ATTENDANCE RECORD

### For 19 ____

Name ____ Last ____ First ____ Middle ____

Service Date ____

____ Short Term Disability Schedule
(-) ____ Prior Year Usage
(-) ____ Previous Year Usage
____ Short Term Disability Allowance

*(See Reverse Side for Coding Information and Instructions)*

| | | 1 | 2 | 3 | 4 | 5 | 6 | 7 | 8 | 9 | 10 | 11 | 12 | 13 | 14 | 15 | 16 | 17 | 18 | 19 | 20 | 21 | 22 | 23 | 24 | 25 | 26 | 27 | 28 | 29 | 30 | 31 | IA | STD | VAC |
|---|---|---|---|---|---|---|---|---|---|---|---|---|---|---|---|---|---|---|---|---|---|---|---|---|---|---|---|---|---|---|---|---|---|---|---|
| JANUARY | Hrs | | | | | | | | | | | | | | | | | | | | | | | | | | | | | | | | | | |
| | Cd. | | | | | | | | | | | | | | | | | | | | | | | | | | | | | | | | | | |
| FEBRUARY | Hrs | | | | | | | | | | | | | | | | | | | | | | | | | | | | | | | | | | |
| | Cd. | | | | | | | | | | | | | | | | | | | | | | | | | | | | | | | | | | |
| MARCH | Hrs | | | | | | | | | | | | | | | | | | | | | | | | | | | | | | | | | | |
| | Cd. | | | | | | | | | | | | | | | | | | | | | | | | | | | | | | | | | | |
| APRIL | Hrs | | | | | | | | | | | | | | | | | | | | | | | | | | | | | | | | | | |
| | Cd. | | | | | | | | | | | | | | | | | | | | | | | | | | | | | | | | | | |
| MAY | Hrs | | | | | | | | | | | | | | | | | | | | | | | | | | | | | | | | | | |
| | Cd. | | | | | | | | | | | | | | | | | | | | | | | | | | | | | | | | | | |
| JUNE | Hrs | | | | | | | | | | | | | | | | | | | | | | | | | | | | | | | | | | |
| | Cd. | | | | | | | | | | | | | | | | | | | | | | | | | | | | | | | | | | |
| JULY | Hrs | | | | | | | | | | | | | | | | | | | | | | | | | | | | | | | | | | |
| | Cd. | | | | | | | | | | | | | | | | | | | | | | | | | | | | | | | | | | |
| AUGUST | Hrs | | | | | | | | | | | | | | | | | | | | | | | | | | | | | | | | | | |
| | Cd. | | | | | | | | | | | | | | | | | | | | | | | | | | | | | | | | | | |
| SEPTEMBER | Hrs | | | | | | | | | | | | | | | | | | | | | | | | | | | | | | | | | | |
| | Cd. | | | | | | | | | | | | | | | | | | | | | | | | | | | | | | | | | | |
| OCTOBER | Hrs | | | | | | | | | | | | | | | | | | | | | | | | | | | | | | | | | | |
| | Cd. | | | | | | | | | | | | | | | | | | | | | | | | | | | | | | | | | | |
| NOVEMBER | Hrs | | | | | | | | | | | | | | | | | | | | | | | | | | | | | | | | | | |
| | Cd. | | | | | | | | | | | | | | | | | | | | | | | | | | | | | | | | | | |
| DECEMBER | Hrs | | | | | | | | | | | | | | | | | | | | | | | | | | | | | | | | | | |
| | Cd. | | | | | | | | | | | | | | | | | | | | | | | | | | | | | | | | | | |

Lost Time Summary

## SAMPLE EMPLOYEE BENEFIT PROGRAM

### Plan Highlights

| PLAN | BENEFIT | ELIGIBILITY PERIOD | EMPLOYEE CONTRIBUTION |
|---|---|---|---|
| Basic Medical Insurance | • Full cost of semi-private room for 365 days<br>• Full cost of in-hospital service<br>• Prevailing fee surgical payments<br>• Outpatient expenses per schedule | None | None |
| Major Medical Plan | • $100 calendar year deductible<br>• 80% of covered expenses<br>• $250,000 lifetime maximum benefits | None | None |
| Thrift Plan | • Employee contribution 2% minimum—6% maximum of base salary<br>• Company matches ½ of employee contribution | 1 year | Maximum of 6% of base salary |
| Short-Term Disability Income Plan | • Based on years of service 100% of base pay followed by 75% up to 26 weeks | 6 months | None |
| Long-Term Disability | • 60% of base pay | 2 years | None |
| Dental Plan | • 80% of basic services<br>• 50% of prosthetic services<br>• 50% of orthodontic services—$500 lifetime maximum | 1st of the month following 1 year of service | None |
| Pension Plan | • 1½% of "final average earnings" for each year of service up to 30<br>• 1% of "final averge earnings" for each year of service 30 to 40<br>• Less 55% of primary social security | None | None |
| Life Insurance | • Noncontributory—1 × annual base pay<br>• Contributory (optional)—1 × annual base pay | None | None<br>40¢ to 75¢/$1000 based on age |
| Educational Assistance Plan | • 100% reimbursement for approved work related courses | 6 months | None |
| Vacation Plan | • 1 yr.—2 wks; 5 yr.—3 wks; 10 yr.—4 wks; 20 yr.—5 wks. | Per schedule | None |
| Holidays | • 10 per year | None | None |

This sheet describes only the highlights of our benefit program for non-agreement employees. In all instances, the official plan texts, trust agreements and/or master contracts with insurance companies, as appropriate, are the governing documents.

# JOB DESCRIPTION OUTLINE

JOB TITLE:                                    STATUS:

JOB CODE:                                     DATE:

DIVISION:                                     REVISION NO.:

REPORTS TO:                                   REVISION DATE:

---

POSITION SUMMARY:

*Please provide a brief summary of the position. This information will be used for position announcements and advertisements.*

PRINCIPAL ACCOUNTABILITIES:

*Please make a list of job tasks stating what is done and how it's done. Begin each sentence with a verb using present tense singular. For example: <u>ANALYZE</u> financial data using spreadsheet software. <u>PREPARE</u> reports using WordPerfect 5.1 software.*

THIS JOB DESCRIPTION DOES NOT CONSTITUTE A CONTRACT FOR EMPLOYMENT

JOB TITLE:
DATE:
PAGE ____ OF ____

## JOB REQUIREMENTS:

### EDUCATION:

*List minimum acceptable educational requirements to do this job.*

### EXPERIENCE:

*List number of years of experience in the job and specific knowledge requirements.*

### SKILLS:

*List analytical, organizational, interpersonal, technical, managerial skills and so on.*

## SUPERVISORY RESPONSIBILITIES:

*Please list the number of people supervised and their job titles. If you do not supervise put "none."*

## EQUIPMENT TO BE USED:

*Please list computers, fax machines, telephones, calculators, floor waxers, power tools, fork lifts, and so on.*

## TYPICAL PHYSICAL DEMANDS:

*Please list job requirements such as lifting, standing, sitting and so on. Try to be specific. Example: "must be able to lift 50 pounds," "must sit 7 hours a day," "must be able to drive a car."*

## TYPICAL MENTAL DEMANDS:

*List the mental requirements of the job. Example: "must be able to do simple math calculations" or must be able to analyze complex information."*

## WORKING CONDITIONS:

*Please list examples such as "must work evenings and/or weekends, job requires driving _____% of the time" "works in a typical office setting" "works outside 90% of the time" and so on.*

THIS JOB DESCRIPTION DOES NOT CONSTITUTE A CONTRACT FOR EMPLOYMENT

# NEW EMPLOYEE ORIENTATION

NOTE: All employees must attend an orientation session.

---

Employee's Name: _____     SSN: _____

Job Title: _____   Dept. _____   Date: _____

---

HUMAN RESOURCES DEPARTMENT: The information checked below has been given or explained to the employee.

---

*Compensation and Benefits*

- Time sheet/card ( )
- Payroll procedures ( )
- Insurance Program Booklet ( )
- Voice Booklet ( )
- Educational Assistance ( )
- Credit Union ( )
- Stock Purchase Plan ( )
- Savings Bond Plan ( )
- Sick Benefits—A&S—Limitations, and so on ( )

*Leaves, Promotions, and Transfers*

- Performance Evaluations ( )
- Promotions ( )
- Transfers ( )
- Vacations ( )
- Holidays ( )
- Absences—Tardiness ( )
- Jury Duty ( )
- Leaves of Absence— Maternity—Medical & Family, and so on ( )

*General*

- Code of Conduct ( )
- Employee Handbook ( )
- Complaints and Grievance Procedures ( )
- I.D. or Entrance Card ( )
- Introduction to the Department ( )
- Parking Facilities ( )
- Safety Guidelines ( )
- First Aid and Requirements for Reporting Injury ( )
- Bulletin Boards/Company Events ( )
- Voluntary Resignation Notice ( )
- Termination Procedures ( )

**SUPERVISOR:** The following is a checklist of information necessary to orient the new employee to the job in your department. Please check off each point as you discuss it with the employee and return to the Human Resources Department to be placed in the employee's personnel file.

*Welcome the New Employee*

- Review copy of employee's application. Be familiar with employee's experience, training, and education. ( )

- Review job description with employee, including the duties, responsibilities, and working relationships. ( )

- Discuss with the employee the unit organization and the department division organization. Explain the function of your department/division as related to the total organization and how the employee fits in. ( )

- Confirm that employee has a copy of employee handbook, and has read and understands it. ( )

*Introduce Employee to Co-Workers*

- Indicate to each co-worker the new employee's position. ( )

- Explain the functions of each person as you introduce the new employee. ( )

*Show New Employee Around the Facility*

- Tour the department, plant, or company. ( )

- Explain where lavatories, coffee areas, and parking facilities are located. ( )

- Explain the various departments within the organization. ( )

*Introduce the New Employee to Job*

- Insure that new employee's working area, equipment, tools and      (   )
  supplies are prepared and available.

- Explain the levels of supervision within the department.            (   )

- Provide new employee with necessary or required training.           (   )

- Explain use of:     Telephone (personal/company calls)              (   )
                      Copy machines                                   (   )
                      Company vehicles                                (   )
                      Mail procedures                                 (   )
                      Supply procedures                               (   )
                      Personal expense reimbursement                  (   )

- Explain hours of work—overtime—call-in procedures.                  (   )

- Give new employee department telephone number.                      (   )

- Review location of department's first aid equipment.                (   )

- Explain housekeeping responsibilities.                              (   )

*Future Follow-Up*

- Set date and time within one week to cover any questions or         (   )
  concerns of the new Employee.

_____

_____          _____
Supervisor's Signature               Employee's Signature


_____          _____
Supervisor's Title                   Date


_____
Department


_____
Date


*Note:*  Return this form to the Human Resources Department.

## Employee Agreement

This employee handbook and the personnel policy manual describe only the highlights of the company policies, procedures, and benefits. In all instances the official benefit plan texts, trust agreements, and master contracts as appropriate are the governing documents. Your employee handbook is not to be interpreted as a legal document or an employment contract. Employment with the company is at the sole discretion of the company and may be terminated with or without cause at any time for any reason. Nothing in this handbook or in the personnel policy manual constitutes an express or implied contract or assurance of continued employment, or that just cause is required for termination.

Understood and agreed:

_____
(Employee's Signature)

_____
Date

## EDUCATION VERIFICATION REFERENCE

### Employer's Request for Information

The EMPLOYER will fill in the appropriate areas and send this form to the college, together with a stamped, self-addressed return envelope.

Date _____

| NAME AND ADDRESS OF SCHOOL | TO BE RETURNED BY THE SCHOOL TO |
|---|---|
| | EMPLOYER _____ |
| | EMPLOYER REPRESENTATIVE _____ |
| **ATTN: OFFICE OF THE DEAN** | ADDRESS _____ _____ |

REQUEST TO SCHOOL: The individual named below is being considered for employment as _____ .
(Type of position)

Applicant indicates attendance at above school. Your cooperation in furnishing the following information will expedite consideration of the applicant.

| APPLICANT'S NAME AND ADDRESS | Class Number (1) | ON REGISTER OF THIS SCHOOL | | | |
|---|---|---|---|---|---|
| | | MONTH | YEAR | MONTH | YEAR |
| LAST (fill in)      FIRST (fill in) | | FROM | | TO | |
| APPLICANT INDICATES ATTENDANCE AT THIS COLLEGE | | DATE OF BIRTH AS GIVEN BY APPLICANT (FOR SCHOOL RECORD IDENTIFICATION AND VERIFICATION) | | | |
| FROM                    TO | | MONTH | DAY | | YEAR |
| GRADUATION DATE | TYPE OF DIPLOMA | GRADE POINT AVERAGE | | | |
| HAS APPLICATION BEEN MADE FOR ADMISSION TO GRADUATE SCHOOL OR OTHER SPECIAL SCHOOL?  NO ☐      YES ☐ | | | | | |

This information supplied below will be treated as confidential by the employer.

**REMARKS:** (AWARDS, HONORS, CLASS OFFICES HELD, ACTIVITIES)

_____

_____

_____

_____

SIGNED _____      TITLE _____      DATE _____

# EMPLOYEE TRANSFER REQUEST

Date: _____

Employee's Name: _____

SSN or Employee
Position Title: _____          Payroll Number: _____

Hire Date: _____          Current Pay Rate: _____

The following transfer is requested:

|  | FROM (current job) | TO |
|---|---|---|
| Position | | |
| Location | | |
| Department | | |
| Hourly Status | Full Time _____ or<br><br>Part Time _____ | Full Time _____ or<br><br>Part Time _____ (hrs. per week) |

NOTE: Separate forms must be filed for each transfer request

Employee qualifications: _____

_____

_____

_____

_____

Reasons for request: _____

_____

_____

_____

Employee Signature: _____

## VACATION REQUEST FORM

<u>Instructions for Completion:</u> Please print when filling out this Request. All sections must be completed. Be sure to indicate the exact number of days you will be away from the office. This will enable the Human Resources Department to calculate your paycheck and attendance schedule correctly. Obtain your supervisor's approval and forward the completed Request to the Payroll Department <u>prior to the beginning of the vacation.</u>

Employee _____          Date of Hire _____

Department _____          SSN _____ - _____ - _____

      Amount Vacation due _____          Number of Days Requested _____

      FIRST CHOICE:    From _____ To _____

      SECOND CHOICE:  From _____ To _____

Copy to Payroll _____

_____          _____

Employee Signature                                          Date

_____          _____

Supervisor Signature                                         Date

<u>Please Note:</u> Give as much advance notice as possible. In cases of conflict, the employee with the earliest request will be given priority. In cases of duplicate or similar request dates, the employee with the earliest starting date will prevail. We will try to accommodate everyone.

**EMPLOYEE ABSENCE REPORT FORM**

Please <u>print</u> when filling out this form. All sections must be completed. Forward to the Payroll Department immediately upon Supervisor's approval.

Employee's Name _____     Date _____

Social Security Number _____

Company/Department _____

Supervisor's Name _____

Dates of Absence: _____  Through _____

Reason for Absence (check one):

_____ Sick (if available)

_____ Jury Duty (attach copy of jury summons)

_____ Bereavement Leave; Relationship _____

_____ Personal Leave

_____ Other _____

_____

_____     _____
Employee's Signature                           Date

_____     _____
Supervisor's Approval                           Date

**Return this completed form to your supervisor.**

# LEAVE REQUEST/RETURN FROM LEAVE FORM

Employee's
Name _____

Date _____

Social Security
Number _____

Job Title _____

Date Hired _____

LEAVE REQUEST

**REASON FOR LEAVE:**

   ( ) Personal disability

   ( ) Military

   ( ) Training conference

   ( ) Compensatory time off

   ( ) Jury duty

   ( ) Family illness (name) _____

   ( ) Family death (name) _____

   ( ) Other (explain) _____

   _____

   _____

**LEAVE REQUESTED:**

From: Date _____ Time _____ A.M. P.M.      Total number of hours requested: _____

To:    Date _____ Time _____ A.M. P.M.      Total number of days requested: _____

Regular Work Shift: _____

_____

Employee Signature: _____ Date: _____

- - - - - - - - - - - - - - - - - - - - - - - - - - - - - - - - - - - - - - - - -

I recommend that this
leave be approved:

   ( ) With pay
   ( ) Without pay

Authorized Signature: _____ Date: _____

RETURN FROM LEAVE

**ABSENT:**

From: Date _____ Time _____ A.M. P.M.

To:    Date _____ Time _____ A.M. P.M.      Total number of working days absent: _____

   ( ) Excused/warranted

   ( ) Not excused/not warranted (explain) _____

**EMPLOYEE:**

   ( ) Resumed part-time work

   ( ) Resumed full-time work

   ( ) Resumed modified duty (explain) _____

   ( ) Other (explain) _____

Affirmed by: _____ Date: _____

# APPLICATION FOR FUNERAL LEAVE

DATE _____

EMPLOYEE'S NAME _____ DEPARTMENT _____

DATES OF WORK DAYS LOST _____ HOURLY RATE _____

<u>DECEASED</u>

NAME _____ FUNERAL DATE _____

RESIDENCE (CITY/TOWN) _____ STATE _____

BURIAL PLACE _____

RELATIONSHIP TO EMPLOYEE: (Be specific: Employee's spouse, child (including grandchild), parent (including grandparent), or sibling, and those same relatives of the employee's spouse.)

_____

_____

REMARKS _____

_____

_____

EMPLOYEE'S SIGNATURE _____

APPROVED:

SUPERVISOR _____

DEPARTMENTAL MANAGER _____

Time off without loss of straight time pay will be granted for up to three regularly scheduled working days to arrange for and attend the funeral of a member of the immediate family. Immediate family is defined as employee's spouse, child (including grandchild), parent (including grandparent), and sibling, and those same relatives of the employee's spouse.

cc: PAYROLL
    PERSONNEL

# MILEAGE REIMBURSEMENT REPORT

NAME OF EMPLOYEE _____ DRIVERS LICENSE NO. _____

TYPE OF VEHICLE _____ LICENSE NUMBER _____

DEPARTMENT _____ MONTH _____

| DATE | BEGINNING READING | ENDING READING | TOTAL MILEAGE | REASON FOR TRAVEL (PLACE) |
|------|-------------------|----------------|---------------|---------------------------|
|      |                   |                |               |                           |
|      |                   |                |               |                           |
|      |                   |                |               |                           |
|      |                   |                |               |                           |
|      |                   |                |               |                           |
|      |                   |                |               |                           |
|      |                   |                |               |                           |
|      |                   |                |               |                           |
|      |                   |                |               |                           |
|      |                   |                |               |                           |
|      |                   |                |               |                           |
|      |                   |                |               |                           |
|      |                   |                |               |                           |
|      |                   |                |               |                           |

TOTAL MILEAGE FOR MONTH _____ @ $0. _____ per mile = $_____

Approved by: _____

Title: _____

Date: _____

# TRAVEL AND EXPENSE REIMBURSEMENT REQUEST

NAME _____ DATE _____

POSITION TITLE _____

PURPOSE OF TRAVEL _____

### MEAL AND LODGING EXPENSES (Attach receipts)

| DATE | TYPE OF EXPENSE | LOCATION | AMOUNT |
|------|----------------|----------|--------|
|      |                |          |        |
|      |                |          |        |
|      |                |          |        |
|      |                |          |        |
|      |                |          |        |

Subtotal—Meals and Lodging: $_____

### TRANSPORTATION EXPENSES (Attach receipts)

1. Air fare (If paid by Company, do not claim.)      $_____
2. Rental vehicle      $_____
3. Private vehicle use ($0._____/mile) _____ miles)      $_____
4. Company vehicle (actual expense only)      $_____
5. Taxis and public transit      $_____

Subtotal–Transportation   $_____

### OTHER EXPENSES (Attach Receipts)

1. Registration fees (If paid by company, do not claim.)      $_____
2. Incidentals and phone calls      $_____

Subtotal—Other   $_____

### CLAIM AMOUNT

1. Total of meals, lodging, transportation and other expenses      $_____
2. Less amount advanced      $(_____)
3. Net amount due claimant      $_____
4. Net amount owed by claimant      $_____

I certify this to be a true and correct statement of expenses incurred on official business.

_____
Signature of Employee

APPROVED:

_____
Signature

_____
Title

# PERFORMANCE APPRAISAL WORKSHEET

| STRICTLY CONFIDENTIAL | | DATE OF THIS REPORT | |
|---|---|---|---|
| EMPLOYEE NAME | | REPORT OF PERFORMANCE FROM          TO | |
| DEPARTMENT | POSITION TITLE | TIME IN THIS CLASSIFICATION YRS._____  MOS._____ | EMPLOYMENT DATE |

## INSTRUCTIONS

1. All employees should be appraised at least annually.
2. Use in conjunction with the Merit Review Program.
3. Review employee's work performance for the entire period; refrain from basing judgment on recent events or isolated incidents only.
4. Do not allow personal feelings to govern your rating. Disregard your general impression of the employee.
5. Consider the employee on the basis of the standards you expect to be met for the job. Place a check by the area you feel best describes the employee's performance since the last appraisal.
6. REASON MUST BE GIVEN FOR EACH FACTOR TO SUBSTANTIATE AREA CHECKED

**QUALITY OF WORK**—Consider standard of workmanship, accuracy, neatness, skill, thoroughness, economy of materials, organization of job.

☐ FULLY MEETS JOB REQUIREMENTS     ☐ UNSATISFACTORY DOES NOT MEET MINIMUM REQUIREMENTS     ☐ MEETS MINIMUM REQUIREMENTS     ☐ EXCEEDS JOB REQUIREMENTS     ☐ OTHER (Specify)

Reason: _____

_____

**VOLUME OF WORK**—Consider use of time, the volume of work accomplished and ability ot meet schedules, under normal conditions.

☐ DOES NOT MEET JOB REQUIREMENTS     ☐ EXCEEDS JOB REQUIREMENTS     ☐ MEETS MINIMUM JOB REQUIREMENTS     ☐ FULLY MEETS JOB REQUIREMENTS     ☐ OTHER (Specify)

Reason: _____

_____

**ADAPTABILITY**—Consider ability to meet changing conditions and situations, ease with which the employee learns new duties and assignments.

☐ IMPROVEMENT NEEDED     ☐ SATISFACTORY     ☐ OUTSTANDING     ☐ VERY GOOD

Reason: _____

_____

**JUDGMENT**—Consider ability to evaluate relative merit of ideas or facts and arrive at sound conclusions, ability to decide correct course of action when some choice can be made.

☐ VERY GOOD     ☐ NEEDS MUCH IMPROVEMENT     ☐ SATISFACTORY     ☐ OUTSTANDING

Reason: _____

_____

**JOB KNOWLEDGE AND SKILL**—Consider understanding of job procedures and methods, ability to acquire necessary skills, expertness in doing assigned tasks and utilization of background for job.

☐ FULLY MEETS JOB REQUIREMENTS     ☐ IMPROVEMENT NEEDED     ☐ MEETS MINIMUM JOB REQUIREMENTS     ☐ EXCEEDS JOB REQUIREMENTS

Reason: _____

**ATTITUDE**—Consider coopertion with supervisor and co-workers; receptiveness to suggestions and constructive criticisms; attitude toward Company; enthusiasm in attempts to improve performance.

☐ EXCEEDS JOB REQUIREMENTS  ☐ FULLY MEETS JOB REQUIREMENTS  ☐ MEETS MINIMUM JOB REQUIREMENTS  ☐ IMPROVEMENT NEEDED

Reason: _____

_____

**TEAM EFFORT—LEADERSHIP**—Consider ability to inspire teamwork, enthusiasm to work towards a common objective, desire to assume responsibility, ability to originate or develop ideas and get things started, ability to train others.

☐ DOES NOT MEET JOB REQUIREMENTS  ☐ EXCEEDS JOB REQUIREMENTS  ☐ MEETS MINIMUM JOB REQUIREMENTS  ☐ FULLY MEETS JOB REQUIREMENTS

Reason: _____

_____

**SELF-DEVELOPMENT ACTIVITIES OF THIS EMPLOYEE** (To be completed during interview)

_____

_____

_____

### PRESENT STATUS—NEEDS—PLAN OF ACTION

**OVERALL EFFECTIVENESS**—Considering the amount of experience on present job, check the rating which most nearly describes *total* current performance.

☐ EXCEEDS JOB REQUIREMENTS  ☐ DOES NOT MEET JOB REQUIREMENTS  ☐ FULLY MEETS JOB REQUIREMENTS  ☐ MEETS MINIMUM JOB REQUIREMENTS

**WHAT ASPECTS OF PERFORMANCE, IF NOT IMPROVED, MIGHT HINDER FUTURE DEVELOPMENT OR CAUSE DIFFICULTY IN PRESENT CLASSIFICATION (WEAKNESSES OF EMPLOYEE)?**

_____

_____

**WHAT ARE GREATEST STRENGTHS OF EMPLOYEE?** _____

_____

Forward completed performance appraisal to designated approval authority before reviewing with subject employee. After appraisal is approved, review contents of appraisal with subject employee and complete section concerning specific plans to improve performance. Have employee sign the form and then forward original appraisal to the *Personnel Department* — retain copy for your files.

GIVE SPECIFIC PLANS YOU AND YOUR EMPLOYEE HAVE MADE TO IMPROVE WORK PERFORMANCE

_____

_____

_____

| EVALUATED BY: | TITLE: | DATE: |
|---|---|---|
| APPROVED: | TITLE: | DATE: |
| EMPLOYEE'S SIGNATURE (Does not necessarily indicate concurrence) | TITLE: | DATE: |

# EMPLOYEE COUNSELING ACTIVITY SHEET

EMPLOYEE'S NAME: _____

DATE: _____

EMPLOYEE RELATIONS STAFF MEMBER NAME: _____

| | | |
|---|---|---|
| Career Planning | _____ | Disciplinary Problems _____ |
| Compensation/Benefits | _____ | Other _____ |
| Job Posting | _____ | |
| EEO/AA | _____ | PLEASE CHECK ONE CATEGORY |

TIME IN _____     TIME OUT _____

Briefly state the problem.

Follow-up session(s), if necessary.

Results/solution: Explain the outcome of session(s).

_____

Supervisor Completing Form

(Continue on back if necessary)

# SUPERVISOR'S CHECKLIST AND REPORT
# FOR EFFECTIVE DISCIPLINE

This report should be completed when disciplinary action is needed and after the first verbal warning has been given to an employee. If you have any questions or concerns, telephone discussion with Personnel is encouraged.

| Employee's Name | Hire Date | Cost Center |
|---|---|---|

| Date of Incident | Incident |
|---|---|

Give an accurate account of what happened. Be specific.

_____

_____

_____

_____

Indicate corrective steps needed.

_____

_____

_____

_____

Has employee had a chance to tell his or her side of story?　　　　YES ☐　　NO ☐

If not, why not? _____

_____

Was the employee aware of the rule or procedure?　　　　YES ☐　　NO ☐

Were instructions published in writing in a clear, understandable manner?　　　　YES ☐　　NO ☐

Was the applicable policy properly communicated?　　　　YES ☐　　NO ☐

Have you spoken previously to employee about this matter?　　　　YES ☐　　NO ☐

If so, when? _____

Has the policy been consistently enforced?                          YES ☐   NO ☐

Have there been other violations?                                   YES ☐   NO ☐

If so, describe action(s) taken.

_____

_____

_____

_____

Has any previous corrective action with this employee been necessary?     YES ☐   NO ☐

If so, describe briefly.

_____

_____

_____

Can you back up this record with facts?                             YES ☐   NO ☐

What is appropriate and justifiable discipline for this infraction? (Disciplinary action should fit the situation, discourage recurrence, and encourage better performance by employee.)

☐   Informal Warning          ☐   Formal Warning          ☐   Place on Probation

☐   Demotion                  ☐   Lay-off Without Pay      ☐   Discharge

☐   Other (specify) _____

_____          _____
            Date                                Reporting Supervisor

THIS IS A CONFIDENTIAL RECORD THAT WILL BECOME PART OF THE EMPLOYEE'S PERSONNEL FILE. THE DISCIPLINARY WARNING NOTICE FOR THE INCIDENT WILL BE ATTACHED TO THIS REPORT.

# DISCIPLINARY WARNING NOTICE

(This notice is to be completed for any disciplinary action
after the first verbal warning to employee.)

EMPLOYEE'S NAME _____ COST CENTER _____
                        Last            First           Init.

POSITION TITLE _____

DATE OF INCIDENT _____ INCIDENT _____

REASON FOR NOTICE:



ACTION TAKEN ON THIS NOTICE:

☐   First warning—verbal (This notice is optional.)

☐   Second warning—written                  ☐   Suspension for _____ days

☐   Other (specify) _____

    _____

    _____

NEXT STEP IF INFRACTION IS REPEATED:

☐   Second warning—written                  ☐   Suspension for _____ days

☐   Other (specify) _____

    _____

    _____

SUPERVISOR COMMENTS:



EMPLOYEE COMMENTS:



Signed _____         Signed _____
                Supervisor                               Employee

Date _____         Date _____

ORIGINAL TO BE FORWARDED TO PERSONNEL
FOR EMPLOYEE'S FILE.

# EMPLOYEE WARNING NOTICE

EMPLOYEE NAME: _____

Social Security
Number: _____

POSITION TITLE: _____

Date of
Warning: _____

| **TYPE OF VIOLATION** | ( ) Tardiness | ( ) Quality of Work | ( ) Carelessness |
|---|---|---|---|
| | ( ) Absenteeism | ( ) Quantity of Work | ( ) Safety |
| | ( ) Insubordination | ( ) Neatness | ( ) Intoxicaiton or Drinking |
| | ( ) Other: _____ | | |

Was there a witness
to the violation? _____ Witness Name: _____

**VIOLATION:** Date _____

**WARNING NOTICE:** ( ) First Date: _____

**VIOLATION:** Time        A.M.        P.M.

( ) Second Date: _____

( ) Final

**PLACE VIOLATION OCCURRED:** _____
_____

| **COMPANY STATEMENT** | **WARNING DECISION** |
|---|---|
| 1. Describe in detail what the employee has done. | 1. Explain in detail what employee must do to improve performance or change behavior. |
| 2. Cite how this interferes with work environment, employee performance, business operations, or the well being of other employees. | 2. Cite date by which improvements must be in place. |
| 3. Cite verbatim the rule, policy, law, standard, or regulation that was violated. | 3. Cite consequences if improvements are not achieved by date specified. |

APPROVED BY: _____        TITLE: _____

DATE: _____

## ATTACH SEPARATE PAGE IF NEEDED FOR DETAILED EXPLANATIONS

EMPLOYEE COMMENTS: _____
_____
_____
_____
_____

_____
Employee's Signature                                        Date

_____
Supervisor's Signature                                      Date

## EXIT INTERVIEW

Employee Name: _____  Date:_____

1.  What is your reason for leaving?

2.  Why did you decide to seek employment elsewhere?

3.  Are there any other reasons why you are leaving?

4.  Was your job here the way you thought it would be after hearing it described in your hiring or promotional interview?

5.  As an employee, were you given all of the information you needed to perform your job?

6.  How did you feel about the quality of training you received for your job?

7.  How did you feel about the supervision in your unit?

8.  How did you feel about your job? Were you accomplishing something worthwhile through your job?

9.  How did you feel about your rate of pay in relation to the type of work you did?

10. How did you feel about opportunities for advancement within the company?

11. What do you think of company benefits?

12. What was the most common complaint of fellow employees?

13. What were the things you liked most about working here?

14. What were the things you like least about working here?

15. What changes would you make to make this a better place to work?

16. Would you refer friends to the company?

17. Is there anything you would like to add about your reasons for leaving?

*NOTE:* Use only with voluntary terminations.

_____      _____
Employee Signature                     Interviewer Signature

# ACCIDENT/INJURY REPORT

**Supervisor must complete report and return to the Human Resources Department within 24 hours.**

Name: _____     SSN: _____ - _____ - _____

Date of Accident: Day _____ Mo. _____ Yr. _____

Time of Accident: _____ AM/PM

Place Of Accident: _____

Witnesses: (if any)                                    First Aid Given? _____ Yes _____ No

Name: _____     By Whom? _____

Address: _____     Hospitalized? _____ Yes _____ No

_____     Physician: _____

Phone #: _____

Nature and extent of injuries: _____

_____

How did accident/injury occur? (Be specific; use extra sheet if necessary): _____

_____

_____

Job or activity engaged in at time of injury (Be specific): _____

_____

_____

Describe any unsafe conditions, methods or practices related to the accident: _____

_____

_____

_____          _____
Employee's Signature                                     Date


_____          _____
Supervisor's Signature                                   Date


_____          _____
Department/Company                                       Location

# SUPERVISOR'S REPORT OF ACCIDENT INVESTIGATION
CONFIDENTIAL REPORT - FOR CORPORATE USE ONLY

Injured Employee _____ Date of This Report _____

Occupation _____ Dept. _____ Age ____ Sex ____ Length of Employment _____

Date And Time Of Accident _____ Exact Location _____

Description Of Accident (Detail what employee was doing and what tools, equipment, structures, or fixtures were involved)

_____

_____

_____

_____

_____

_____

_____

Nature of Injuries _____

_____

Report To Supervisor or First Aid Delayed? _____ Why? _____

_____

_____

Check Accident Causes On Reverse Side Of This Report And Comment Fully Here _____

_____

_____

_____

_____

_____

What Should Be Done, And By Whom To Prevent Recurrence Of This Type Accident In The Future?

_____

_____

_____

What Action Are You Taking To See That This Is Done? _____

_____

_____

Supervisor's Signature _____

Comments By Department Head Or Manager _____

_____

_____

_____

ATTENDING PHYSICIAN'S
RETURN TO WORK RECOMMENDATIONS RECORD

COMPANY NAME

| PATIENT'S NAME (First) | (Middle Initial) | (Last) | DATE OF INJURY/ILLNESS |
|---|---|---|---|

DIAGNOSIS

### TO BE COMPLETED BY ATTENDING PHYSICIAN – PLEASE CHECK

I saw and treated this patient on _____ and:
                                   Date

1. ☐ Recommend his/her return to work with no limitations on _____ .
                                                              Date

2. ☐ He/She may return to work capable of performing the degree of work checked below with the following limitations:

| DEGREE | LIMITATIONS |
|---|---|
| ☐ **Sedentary Work.** Lifting 10 pounds maximum and occasionally lifting and/or carrying such articles as dockets, ledgers, and small tools. Although a sedentary job is defined as one which involves sitting, a certain amount of walking and standing is often necessary in carrying out job duties. Jobs are sedentary if walking and standing are required only occasionally and other sedentary criteria are met. | 1. In an 8-hour work day patient may:<br>a. Stand/Walk<br>  ☐ None          ☐ 4-6 Hours<br>  ☐ 1-4 Hours     ☐ 6-8 Hours<br>b. Sit<br>  ☐ 1-3 Hours   ☐ 3-5 Hours   ☐ 5-8 Hours<br>c. Drive<br>  ☐ 1-3 Hours   ☐ 3-5 Hours   ☐ 5-8 Hours |
| ☐ **Light Work.** Lifting 20 pounds maximum with frequent lifting and/or carrying of objects weighing up to 10 pounds. Even though the weight lifted may be only a negligible amount, a job is in this category when it requires walking or standing to a significant degree or when it involves sitting most of the time with a degree of pushing and pulling of arm and/or leg controls. | 2. Patient may use hands for repetitive:<br>  ☐ Single Grasping     ☐ Pushing & Pulling<br>  ☐ Fine Manipulation |
| ☐ **Medium Work.** Lifting 50 pounds maximum with frequent lifting and/or carrying of objects weighing up to 25 pounds. | 3. Patient may use feet for repetitive movement as in operating foot controls:     ☐ Yes     ☐ No |
| ☐ **Heavy Work.** Lifting 100 pounds maximum with frequent lifting and/or carrying of objects weighing up to 50 pounds. | 4. Patient is able to:<br>                    Frequently  Occasionally  Not at all<br>a. Bend . . . .      ☐            ☐            ☐<br>b. Squat . . . .     ☐            ☐            ☐<br>c. Climb . . . .     ☐            ☐            ☐ |
| ☐ **Very Heavy Work.** Lifting objects in excess of 100 pounds with frequent lifting and/or carrying of objects weighing 50 pounds or more. | |

OTHER INSTRUCTIONS AND/OR LIMITATIONS:

3. ☐ These restrictions are in effect until _____ or until patient is reevaluated on _____ .
                                            Date                                                    Date

4. ☐ He/She is totally incapacitated at this time. Patient will be reevaluated on _____ .
                                                                                Date

| PHYSICIAN'S SIGNATURE | DATE |
|---|---|

### AUTHORIZATION TO RELEASE INFORMATION

I hereby authorize my attending physician and/or hospital to release any information or copies thereof acquired in the course of my examination or treatment for the injury identified above to my employer or his representative.

| PATIENT'S SIGNATURE | DATE |
|---|---|

# FIRST AID REPORT LOG*

This form is for the purpose of profiling routine occurrence of minor injuries such as small cuts and bruises which do not require medical treatment or lost work hours.

| Date of Injury | Time of Injury | Name of Employee | Description of Injury or Illness (Specify part of body affected) | Injury/Illness | | Treatment Administered | Administered by Whom | Injury Report Filed | |
|---|---|---|---|---|---|---|---|---|---|
| | | | | New | Recurring | | | YES | NO |
| | | | | | | | | | |
| | | | | | | | | | |
| | | | | | | | | | |
| | | | | | | | | | |
| | | | | | | | | | |
| | | | | | | | | | |
| | | | | | | | | | |
| | | | | | | | | | |
| | | | | | | | | | |
| | | | | | | | | | |

*Minor injuries should be recorded on the Supervisor's Report of Work Injury.

## QUARTERLY SAFETY PERFORMANCE RECORD

For the Period: _____

| LOCATION | CURRENT QUARTER | | | YEAR-TO-DATE | | | LATEST NATIONAL RATES |
| --- | --- | --- | --- | --- | --- | --- | --- |
| | HOURS WORKED | LOST WORK DAY INJURIES | INCIDENCE RATE | HOURS WORKED | LOST WORK DAY INJURIES | INCIDENCE RATE | |
| | | | | | | | |
| | | | | | | | |
| | | | | | | | |
| | | | | | | | |
| | | | | | | | |
| | | | | | | | |
| | | | | | | | |
| | | | | | | | |
| | | | | | | | |
| | | | | | | | |
| TOTALS | | | | | | | |
| REMARKS | $$\text{INCIDENCE RATE} \atop \text{LOST WORK DAY INJ}} = \frac{\text{No. OF CASES} \times 200{,}000}{\text{HRS. WORKED}}$$ | | | | | | |

# INDEX